WORD AND IMAGE IN RUSSIAN HISTORY

ESSAYS IN HONOR OF GARY MARKER

Photo courtesy of Media Services, Stony Brook University

WORD AND IMAGE IN RUSSIAN HISTORY

ESSAYS IN HONOR OF GARY MARKER

EDITED BY

MARIA DI SALVO,

DANIEL H. KAISER,

AND

VALERIE A. KIVELSON

Boston
2015

Library of Congress Cataloging-in-Publication Data:
A catalog record for this book is available from the Library of Congress.

ISBN 978-1-61811-832-5
ISBN 978-1-61811-460-0 (electronic)

Cover design by Ivan Grave

Published by Academic Studies Press in 2015
28 Montfern Avenue
Brighton, MA 02135, USA
press@academicstudiespress.com
www. academicstudiespress.com

Contents

Religion

Forms of Literacy

Civil Society and Politics

Acknowledgements

Publication of this book was made possible by gifts from the College of Arts and Sciences at Stony Brook University with the generous support of former Dean Nancy Squires, and from the Stony Brook University Department of History—thankfully without the knowledge of the present chair, Gary Marker. Special thanks to Margarita Zhivova for her guidance in navigating fonts, and to Joseph Bradley, Olga Greco, and Maria Ispolnova for translation assistance; thanks, too, to the University of Michigan for additional support. We also owe thanks to Media Services, Stony Brook University; Elena Smilianskaia; the Vologda State Historico-Architectural and Art Museum; Dumbarton Oaks Research Library and Collection; the Russian State Archive of Ancient Acts, and New York Public Library for images reproduced here. Special thanks to Ann Brody who supplied a number of photographs we could not otherwise have obtained. Finally, many thanks to De Dudley who formatted and prepared the final manuscript.

List of Illustrations

Introduction

For the past several years, we have collaborated with friends and colleagues of Gary Marker to prepare a volume that celebrates and honors him. As the *Tabula gratulatoria* indicates, Gary has many friends all around the globe—so it was an easy job to find contributors, even if several who wished to participate could not because of other commitments. We sought essays that considered themes similar to those Gary has pursued, even if they did not share his focus on the eighteenth century. *Word and Image in Russian History*, therefore, aims to highlight and build upon Gary Marker's own scholarship.

Beginning with his dissertation on eighteenth-century publications and continuing with his more recent study of Ukrainian intellectuals, Gary has probed the ways in which the printed word has affected Russian society. Several essays here celebrate this theme, stretching the analysis from Kyivan Rus' into the twentieth century. Viktor Zhivov, Gary's long-time friend and colleague, was one of this volume's earliest and most enthusiastic contributors. Sadly, Viktor passed away before the book came together, but we are pleased that he had already contributed an essay to the project. Zhivov's article examines the connections between Byzantine and Kyivan law, and carefully considers the words used and how they reveal—and sometimes obscure—reality.

Maria Di Salvo's essay carries the subject forward to study Peter the Great's ship *Predestinatsiia.* Heavily freighted with semiotic meaning and decorated to that end, Peter's ship, Di Salvo shows, points to the sovereign's confidence in divine "prescience" and the tsar's own heroic role in Russia's future. Christine Ruane's essay turns attention to eighteenth-century Russian flora and the ways in which these botanical manuals brought scientific knowledge to the Russian reading public. Elena Smilianskaia focuses upon the divide between official discourse and reality during Catherine the Great's war with the Turks. Talk about "freedom" for the Greeks increasingly gave way to discussion of "protection" and possession, indicative of Russian paternalism instead of liberation.

Tracing eighteenth-century genres into the modern era, Daniela Steila writes about the Marxist interest at the turn of the twentieth century in reproducing the Enlightenment encyclopedia, but written from the proletarian viewpoint. At a time when many encyclopedias were coming into print, the Russian Marxists found themselves divided over exactly what kind of project would be appropriate and how it might be funded. The 1917 Revolution overtook these discussions, with the result that an idea originally conceived to be revolutionary ended up being realized by the State Publishing House, inevitably dooming the utopian fantasies of the project's first proponents.

Gary Marker's intensive study of iconographic representations of St. Catherine showed the importance of carefully reading images no less than written texts, and several essays in the present collection follow this lead. Daniel Kaiser examines a late-Muscovite portrait of the Vologda merchant Gavrila Fetiev to see how much meaning can be extracted from such a spare painting. Nancy Kollmann takes a different tack, following the publishing history of Adam Olearius's *Travels* to discover how later publishers of the work adapted it to a variety of formats and sizes, freely adding and subtracting images and thereby reconstituting it in novel ways. Cynthia Whittaker's essay looks at how Catherine the Great collected images, including many works of the most famous western European artists. An early practitioner of

blockbuster purchases, Catherine understood, Whittaker tells us, how possession of great art could also express political power.

Simon Dixon examines a different sort of image, the historical image of Peter the Great that Vasilii Rozanov absorbed and propagandized in the turbulent years around the dawn of the twentieth century. Although Rozanov's reception of Peter suffered some variation over time, what never escaped the writer's admiration was Peter's energy and activity. This Peter, arrayed against the apparent stillness and monastic calm of Muscovy (as Rozanov understood it), prospered in "the heroic stream of history" and became "the founder of everything in Russia."

Gary Marker's study of Catherine I was important not only for its use of images, but also for its contribution to the study of female rule, and Evgenii Anisimov devotes his essay to this important issue. In his view, the eighteenth-century female sovereigns contributed to a desacralization of power, a function of the enduring misogyny that imperial Russia inherited from Muscovy. Only a thin layer of Russian society seems to have embraced the change in gender relations that Peter's reign encouraged. Alexander Kamenskii, however, discovers in registers of promissory notes evidence that in provincial Bezhetsk, at least, women—married and unmarried, noble and non-noble—were active in business as lenders and borrowers.

Religion, especially Russian Orthodoxy, depends upon both word and image. In recent years Gary has increasingly directed his attention to Petrine-era religious activists and their writings, focusing special attention upon those Ukrainians who played an important part in developing the official discourse of Petrine rule. Giovanna Brogi Bercoff pursues this avenue of study in her essay. Examining a seemingly-small event in the seventeenth-century Ostroh principality—a dispute between Orthodox Christians in an Easter procession and the retinue of the local Catholic princess over who should cross a bridge first—Brogi Bercoff discovers the gulf between Orthodox and Uniate Catholics as recounted in various narratives of the event. The seventeenth-century "Liament," employing language that might be applied equally well today to religious and ethnic conflict, urged the application of reason and a mutual respect for difference.

Robert Weinberg treats a more modern version of religious conflict—the 1913 Mendel Beilis trial and the bizarre evidence deployed by prosecutors. Not only did the state argue that fanatic Jewish ritual had motivated murder, prosecutors also claimed that the pattern of wounds on the dead teenager, when decoded, signified the ritual crime that the victim had supposedly suffered. Despite the acquittal of Beilis, the case reveals a fascinating juxtaposition of pre-modern and modern forms of anti-Semitism gathering around this unusual image—a pattern of wounds.

Three papers follow Marker's own studies of literacy in late Muscovy and eighteenth-century Russia. Ol'ga Kosheleva investigates seventeenth-century manuscript miscellanies composed with the aim of providing instruction, in this way complementing Gary's study of printed primers and psalters. If in many respects the manuscripts embraced traditional educational subjects, they nevertheless innovated by introducing secular rules of behavior and fostering communication across social ranks. Maksym Iaremenko excavated data on clerical education in the Kyiv eparchy in the 1770s and finds that, despite efforts of the church hierarchy to improve and formalize education of the clergy, many priests could boast no more than an elementary education, and the much-vaunted "Latin learning" was unevenly distributed across the district. Janet Hartley's essay moves the discussion into the nineteenth century, providing a detailed examination of the Omsk Asiatic School. Founded late in the eighteenth century, the Omsk school provided a vital service to the multi-ethnic Russian Empire by teaching Tatar, Mongolian, Arabic, and other languages to a small-but-steady stream of students. Graduates became translators for diplomatic and trade missions, but were also posted in the empire's forts far from the capital, becoming implements of the state.

The final group of essays looks more broadly at imperial Russian society. Patrick O'Meara provides an intimate look at Vasilii Nazarevich Karazin, an early nineteenth-century enthusiast of constitutional reform who thought that Alexander I shared his sentiments. When he learned that the sovereign's views had changed, Karazin plowed stubbornly

forward, to his obvious detriment. Roger Bartlett uses his essay to pursue Marker's study of Westernization in eighteenth-century Russia. However, instead of studying how Russians went west, Bartlett examines an immigrant Baltic German family: Johann Georg Eisen immigrated to Estland in the 1740s, bringing with him the values of Enlightenment Germany. His descendants prospered in the Russian Empire, fully assimilating the conservative values of the elite and making themselves useful tools of the state. Joseph Bradley contributes an essay that reveals how vigorously the Russian Technical Society pursued an agenda of increased civic involvement. Here, in early twentieth-century Russia, then, one discovers the long-term consequences of Petrine-era literacy and schooling that Gary Marker has studied so well.

The essays published here highlight and honor the scholarship of our colleague and friend, Gary Marker, who has pointed the way to numerous productive lines of investigation. Always situating his findings in a comparative context, he has also dealt with a series of questions whose importance continues to resonate well beyond the frontiers of Russia and the eighteenth century. We celebrate with this volume our colleague's scholarship, and look forward to learning from him still more productive questions to ask of Russia's past.

Tabula Gratulatoria

Jennifer Anderson, Stony Brook University
Judith Lefkowitz Anderson, Securities and Exchange Commission
Juan Pablo Artinian, University of Buenos Aires
John Frederick Bailyn, Stony Brook University
Michael Barnhart, Stony Brook University
Norberto Barreto, Universidad del Pacifico, Lima, Peru
Laurie Bernstein, Rutgers University-Camden
Christina Y. Bethin, Stony Brook University
Eric Beverly, Stony Brook University
Maria Cristina Bragone, University of Pavia
Jane Burbank, New York University
Paul Bushkovitch, Yale University
Robert Chase, Stony Brook University
Robert Collis, Helsinki Collegium for Advanced Studies, University of Helsinki
Alix Cooper, Stony Brook University
Tony Cross, University of Cambridge
Katia Dianina, University of Virginia
Lisa Diedrich, Stony Brook University
James and Susan Dooley

Sara Duke, Library of Congress
Paul Dukes, University of Aberdeen
Michael Edwards
Rebecca Edwards, University of Sydney
Rosemary Effiom, Bowdoin College
Froylan Encisco, Stony Brook University
Alexei Evstratov, Wissenschaftskolleg zu Berlin
Amanda Ewington, Davidson College
Jared Farmer, Stony Brook University
Lee A. Farrow, Auburn University
Lori Flores, Stony Brook University
Stephen P. Frank, UCLA
Gregory Freeze, Brandeis University
Lawrence Frohman, Stony Brook University
David Gasperetti, University of Notre Dame
Richard Gatteau, Stony Brook University
Olga E. Glagoleva, University of Toronto
William Glenn, University of Texas at San Antonio
Harold Goldberg, University of the South
Paul Gootenberg, Stony Brook University
Bonnie Gordon, University of Virginia
Paul Grannis, Stony Brook University
Barbara Grannis
Gitta Hammarberg, Macalester College
Magally Alegre Henderson, Pontificia Universidad Católica del Peru
Victoria Hesford, Stony Brook University
Susan Hinely, Stony Brook University
Heather Hogan, Oberlin College
Young-Sun Hong, Stony Brook University
Hilde Hoogenboom, Arizona State University
Leonie Huddie, Stony Brook University
Andrey V. Ivanov, University of Wisconsin-Platteville
Gareth Jones, Bangor University
Paul Keenan, London School of Economics
Susan Kippax, University of New South Wales

A. M. Kleimola, University of Nebraska-Lincoln
Joachim Klein, University of Leiden
Natal'ia Kochetkova, Institut russkoi literatury (Pushkinskii Dom)
Galina Kosmolinskaia, Institut mirovoi istorii RAN
Ned Landsman, Stony Brook University
Brooke Larson, Stony Brook University
Herman (Gene) Lebovics, Stony Brook University
Manuel T. Lerdau, University of Virginia
Marcus C. Levitt, University of Southern California
Shirley Lim, Stony Brook University
Sara Lipton, Stony Brook University
Benjamin and Martha Luft
Iona Man-Cheong, Stony Brook University
Elena Marasinova, Institut Rossiiskoi istorii RAN
Jason Marcus
Celia Marshik, Stony Brook University
Alexander Martin, University of Notre Dame
April Masten, Stony Brook University
Erin McBurdon, London School of Economics
Kevin J. McKenna, University of Vermont
Wilbur Miller, Stony Brook University
Janis Mimura, Stony Brook University
Martin Monsalve, Universidad del Pacifico, Lima, Peru
Giovanna Moraci, Università di Chieti-Pescara
George Munro, Virginia Commonwealth University
Joan Neuberger, University of Texas at Austin
Elizabeth Newman, Stony Brook University
Tom Newlin, Oberlin College
Max Okenfuss, Washington University
Deborah Pearl, Cleveland State University
Serhii Plokhii, Harvard University
Marshall Poe, New Books Network
John Randolph, University of Illinois at Urbana-Champaign
David Ransel, Indiana University
Irina Reyfman, Columbia University

Alfred E. Rieber, Central European University,
Budapest; University of Pennsylvania
Donna Rilling, Stony Brook University
Vladislav Rjeoutski, Deutsches Historisches Institut Moskau
Gowen Roper
Joel Rosenthal, Stony Brook University
Naomi Rosenthal, Stony Brook University and SUNY-Old Westbury
Laura Rossi, University of Milan
Ian Roxborough, Stony Brook University
Blair A. Ruble, Woodrow Wilson Center
Sally S. Ruble, U.S. Treasury Department
Susan Rupp, Wake Forest University
Will Ryan, Warburg Institute
David Saunders, Newcastle University
Matthew Schneer, U.S. Department of Education
Chris Sellers, Stony Brook University
Shobana Shankar, Stony Brook University
Barbara Skinner, Indiana State University
Sarkis Shmovonian, Armenian Linguistics
Douglas Smith, Seattle, Washington
Tatiana Smoliarova, Columbia University
Susan Squier, Penn State University
Nancy Squires, Stony Brook University
Mark D. Steinberg, University of Illinois, Urbana-Champaign
Joshua Teplitsky, Stony Brook University
Nancy Tomes, Stony Brook University
Olga Tsapina, The Huntington Library
Steven A. Usitalo, Northern State University
Angelina Vacheva, Sofia University "St. Kliment Ohridski"
Olufemi Vaughan, Bowdoin College
Ronald Vroon, University of California, Los Angeles
Frank Wcislo, Vanderbilt University
Barbara Weinstein, New York University
Faith Wigzell, University College London
Kathleen Wilson, Stony Brook University

Elise Wirtschafter, California State Polytechnic University at Pomona
Richard Wortman, Columbia University
Robert Zebroski, St. Louis College of Pharmacy
Lee S. Zhu, Loras College
Ernest A. Zitser, Duke University

A Biographical Essay: The Making of the Historian

Daniel H. Kaiser
(Grinnell College)[1]

Russian studies in the United States owes a great deal to the periodic cataclysms that drove emigration from the Russian Empire and its Soviet successor states. Among the most obvious cases are men like Michael Karpovich,[2] George Vernadsky,[3] and Marc Raeff,[4] all of whom left behind the cyclones that buffeted their homeland and settled in the United States where they left a deep imprint upon Russian studies. Less obviously part of this legacy is the great wave of emigration from the Russian Empire in the late nineteenth and early twentieth centuries.[5] Unlike Karpovich, Vernadsky, and Raeff, these immigrants themselves—most of whom sprang from rural or urban working classes—did not usually acquire college or university teaching positions in America. Rather, it was their descendants who, though born and raised in the United States, found themselves drawn to the study of the lands from which their ancestors had fled. Gary Marker is part of that larger, less well-known story.

Both his paternal and maternal grandparents were born in nineteenth-century Russia and, in the wake of the anti-Semitic violence that shook the last years of the empire, immigrated to the United

States.[6] Samuel Marker emigrated from Vilno, evidently traveling the difficult overland route to Belgium, where he boarded the *Antwerp* on August 1, 1890, and arrived in Philadelphia two weeks later.[7] He was working as an insurance agent in 1908 when he declared his intention of becoming a US citizen; in 1910 he married,[8] and soon thereafter petitioned for US citizenship. Then a salesman of Ladies and Gents Furnishings, Samuel settled with his bride on Fairmount Avenue.[9] By the time of the 1920 census, he and his wife, Bertha, were living in Lancaster, Pennsylvania, where Samuel was a supervisor in a cigar factory; the couple had two children—Helen, eight, and Victor, who was a little older than three.[10] Before the next census the family had moved again, taking up residence in North Philadelphia. Samuel returned to the sale of men's clothing, and by this time there were three children: Helen, eighteen; Victor, thirteen; and Leon, eight.[11] When the census-takers next found the Marker household, the family had moved again, settling on North Gratz Avenue.[12] According to the census report, by 1940 Helen had moved out, and only the two boys remained. Victor was then twenty-two and would soon marry.

Bertha Robinson Marker was also born in Vilno (1885), and came to the United States and Philadelphia at about the same time as her future husband. The 1910 census found her mother (Naiona, the census taker called her), then fifty-two years old and widowed, as head of household on North Seventh Street in what is now called Templetown, near Temple University. The census reported Bertha, age twenty-five, working as a bookkeeper; her twenty-two-year-old sister Reba worked as a sales lady in a department store, and their youngest brother, Simon (seventeen), was still in school. An older sister, Lena (twenty-seven), and her husband, Charles Nowick, lived with the family, as did a nephew, Daniel Menkin, and a lodger.[13] Not long after the census official left, Bertha married Samuel Marker.

Harry Weissman, Gary's maternal grandfather, was born in 1883 in Odessa.[14] Family lore reports that Harry and his two brothers had received different surnames in hopes that they could thereby escape conscription into the Russian army (each might be counted as eldest son). However, Harry did not escape, ended up in uniform, and soon thereafter became entangled in some illicit scheme of his commanding officer. Given a pass to escape, Harry fled west and made his way to Le Havre, where in late October, 1906, he boarded the SS *Sardinian*, bound for Montreal via London.[15] In early 1907 he entered the United States and soon arrived in Philadelphia, finding there a cousin in the three hundred block of South Street in Philadelphia's Jewish Quarter.[16] At the time of the 1910 census, Harry was working as a peddler, and boarded with Isaac Jacob and his family at 136 Pemberton, a two-story brick home close to the docks.[17] He married in 1913,[18] and he and his wife settled at 611 Passyunk Avenue, a few blocks from Weissman's cousin on South Street.[19]

His bride, Gussie Usivitch, was also born in Russia, and, according to US census reports, arrived in the United States in 1906 or 1907. Tracking her family is difficult, however, as the family name seems to have changed or been badly copied by officials. In any case, Gussie and Harry married in Philadelphia in 1913,[20] and in 1917 welcomed their only child, a daughter, Beatrice.[21] At the time of the 1920 census, the threesome was still living on Passyunk Avenue,[22] but by 1930 they had moved out to Susquehanna Avenue;[23] the 1940 census found them at Gainor Avenue.[24]

It was Beatrice Weissman whom Victor Marker married in June 1940.[25] Since both Victor and Beatrice were born and raised in Philadelphia and had married in Philadelphia, it was natural for them to make

Gary Marker at home, ca. 1954. Photo courtesy of Ann Brody

Philadelphia their home. So the young Markers settled in central Philadelphia—for a time at 2114 Pine Street,[26] then later a few blocks away at 2138 Delancey—and here the Markers raised two sons: Richard was born in 1945 and brother Gary arrived October 1, 1948. The family attended the nearby Temple Beth Zion on Eighteenth Street where Gary had his Bar Mitzvah in 1961.[27]

Young Gary attended grade school at City Center Elementary (since replaced by Alfred M. Greenfield Elementary),[28] and junior high at what is today called Julia Masterman Laboratory and Demonstration Middle School at the corner of Seventeenth and Spring Garden Streets in central Philadelphia.[29] From his family home the daily journey to Masterman was about two miles, several blocks beyond Logan Circle. Life included more than school, of course, and at this time Gary found the Philadelphia Phillies, who played baseball in Connie Mack Stadium.[30] Perennial also-rans, the 1950s Phillies included the likes of "Go-Go" Chico Fernandez, Harry "the Horse" Anderson, Willie "Puddin' Head" Jones, and Granny Hamner. Gary became a faithful fan of the Phillies, fixing his attention on high achievers like

CLASS OF 1965

GARY MARKER
2131 Delancey Place
Philadelphia, Pennsylvania
October 1, 1948

Entered Eleventh Grade

Gary . . . class treasurer . . . no one younger . . . Magic Marker . . . serious . . . member of the basketball and soccer teams . . . brother at Penn . . . has his own fan club . . . Math IV and Physics . . . "Dues, please, And pay for the whole week - - don't come up with a nickel!" . . . "What is this?" . . . observant.

1965 Friends Select High School Yearbook, p. 83; courtesy of Ann Brody

Richie Ashburn, Robin Roberts, and Curt Simmons, as well as on the numerous journeymen who wore the Phillies uniform in these years.[31] Long after leaving Philadelphia, Gary could easily recall the names of these would-be stars and their memorable underachievement.

When Gary began Central High School at Seventeenth and Olney, he had even further to travel from home. Still all-boys then (despite several lawsuits, the school only became coeducational in 1983), Central had a strong academic reputation.[32] But it was also a big school. Consequently, in 1963, Gary transferred to the smaller Friends Select High School at Seventeenth and Benjamin Franklin Parkway for eleventh grade, graduating in 1965.[33] As the school yearbook confirms, Gary was very active at Friends Select: he played both varsity soccer and varsity basketball, was news editor of the school paper, and in his senior year was elected class treasurer.[34] "Magic Marker," as friends called him, was a very popular student.

With his older brother already enrolled at Penn, Gary matriculated at the University of Pennsylvania in September 1965. Penn was just across the Schuylkill River from his family's home, and so the university might have been the closest school Gary had attended since grade school. However, just at this time his parents moved to Pottstown in connection with his father's work at Mayer Pollock Steel.[35] Having declared a major in political science, Gary soon found himself attracted to Russian history, the consequence of having taken the Russian history survey course from Alexander Riasanovsky and then, later, upper-division courses from Alfred Rieber, both of whom were known at the university as stimulating, demanding teachers and recognized scholars.[36]

Even more important than discovering Russian history was discovering Ann Brody, whom he met his senior year at Penn. As the photo from the 1969 Penn Yearbook proves, the undergraduate Gary Marker was a very handsome fellow and, if the sense of humor he commanded in adulthood was at all evident in college, he must have swept Ann off her feet. The two quickly connected, and so began a lasting relationship of love and mutual support.

After receiving his BA in 1969, Gary enrolled in graduate school at the University of Illinois, continuing his study of Russian history in

1969 Record, University of Pennsylvania Yearbook; courtesy of Ann Brody

**August 23, 1970: Wedding of Gary and Ann Brody;
photo courtesy of Ann Brody**

Champaign-Urbana with Ralph Fisher, David Ransel, and Benjamin Uroff. Ransel, who then taught a graduate course on Russia from Peter the Great to 1855, helped introduce Gary to eighteenth-century Russia, and Benjamin Uroff, who taught intellectual history at Illinois, must have begun Gary's education in things cultural. However, the plains of Illinois could not keep him anchored there, and in 1970 he and Ann decided to move to California. Before moving, they married—August 23, 1970, in Washington, DC, Ann's hometown; a wedding photograph reveals a very happy historian and his lovely bride.

Moving to the University of California, Berkeley brought Gary under the wing of Nicholas Riasanovsky, whose younger brother had taught Gary at Penn.[37] Riasanovsky became Gary's adviser and deepened Gary's interest in imperial Russian cultural history. Part of that education came while Gary worked as a research assistant for Riasanovsky's intellectual history of early nineteenth-century Russia, *A Parting of the Ways*.[38] Reggie Zelnik, who in those years had gathered around him a group of students who concentrated on labor history, was another major influence.[39] Martin Malia and others then active on the Berkeley faculty also taught and mentored Gary,[40] as he and a large cadre of fellow students shared the excitement of those years, initiated life-long friendships, and helped stimulate one another's education.

Part-way through graduate school, Gary accepted an IREX fellowship to the Soviet Union, spending most of the academic year 1974-75 in Moscow. Along with some twenty-five other Americans, the Markers took up residence in *zona V* of Moscow State University atop Moscow's Sparrow Hills. It was here that I met Gary, who would occasionally pop into our *blok* as a preliminary to heading off to the metro and the Lenin Library. Most of the exchangees felt enormous excitement in this adventure, but there was also plenty to complain about—difficulties in accessing archives, transportation issues, scarcity of food, and much more. As was typical, however, Gary found humor in most of these hardships—his recounting of the multiple uses to which the Lenin Library's call slips were put could bring laughter hard enough to generate tears.

Midway through the year, he arranged a *kommandirovka* to Leningrad, but it was granted only on condition that the Markers trade their *blok* in Moscow with an American exchangee couple living in the university dormitory in Leningrad. Consequently, the Markers traded rooms with Blair and Sally Ruble, which meant that Gary and Ann moved into room 72, one of the tiniest rooms in the infamous Shevchenko Street dormitory. The dormitory itself was a microcosm of Soviet afflictions: it was inconveniently located near the western edge of Vasil'evskii Island and poorly served by public transit; in addition, there were few shops or conveniences within reach, which meant that finding food, not to mention entertainment, required an adventure. Cooking facilities were spartan, and the communal toilets demanded from users an efficient bravery. Heat and hot water appeared irregularly and the whole building periodically went dark. To cap it all off, the dormitory was overseen by Nikolai Timofeich, a Ukrainian commandant stationed near the entrance; regularly under the influence of alcohol, Timofeich often launched into diatribes aimed at dormitory residents as they came and went. Gary became expert at imitating the imbibing *kommendant,* so much so that even the mention of Nikolai

IREX exchangees at Medeo Skating Rink near Alma Ata, 1974; photo courtesy of Ann Brody

Timofeich generated laughter in the dormitory. Soon Gary and Ann's room became a haven for all the foreign scholars headquartered there, and many holidays and birthday parties were convened within the narrow confines of room 72.

One of the high points of the annual IREX exchange was the group excursion to distant parts of the Soviet Union, and Gary coordinated planning for the journey through the Caucasus and Central Asia. Most of the American exchangees, as well as a handful of other "capitalist" scholars then studying in Moscow, joined the group, which visited Erevan, Baku, Samarkand, Bukhara, and Alma Ata. The inevitable complications of Soviet life presented themselves, of course, but Gary's sense of humor conquered the occasional frustration, and the multinational group of *kapstran* travelers was unanimous in praise of their leader.

On his return to Berkeley in 1975, Gary began writing up his research, dividing time between this work and his duties as a teaching assistant. In 1977 he successfully defended his dissertation, "Publishing and the Formation of a Reading Public in Eighteenth Century Russia," and received his PhD. That year Gary took his first academic post at Oberlin College, a one-year temporary appointment. The demands of teaching full-time at a place like Oberlin were considerable, especially with a one-year sunset visible from the first day, but the experience proved valuable.

The following year Gary returned to Berkeley where a lectureship provided more teaching experience as he resumed the search for a regular, tenure-track position. These were not good years for academic job-seekers, and Gary can tell hilarious tales about some of the interviews, including one for which we both had received invitations. Gary came to stay with us at our Oak Park apartment; my interview was scheduled for mid-afternoon in a motel room near the airport, and Gary's for later over dinner. We agreed that I would drive to my interview, return home and hand the car over to him. My interview was brief (with the negative result that a brief interview implied), and I returned home promptly, transferring the car keys to Gary. He set off optimistically, our good wishes ringing in his ears. Hours later, however, we had not heard from him, so we worried. Did he get lost in greater

Chicago? Had he been mugged? Should we call the police? If so, what would we say to them? Where would they look for him? Indecision kept us from doing anything, which was just as well: sometime after midnight, Gary came dragging into our apartment. It seems that his host had encouraged a drive through the neighborhoods of western Chicago in search of authentic eastern European cuisine, converting the job interview into a multi-hour extravaganza along unfamiliar city streets, followed by a leisurely late evening dinner at a Bohemian restaurant! Gary's narration of this experience was almost good enough to make the miserable job market worth the pain!

Happily, however, a very good position soon came Gary's way. In 1979 he accepted appointment at State University of New York at Stony Brook (now Stony Brook University), and that year he and Ann moved to Long Island. The relationship with Stony Brook proved a happy and long-lasting one, and Gary made his way through the ranks, gaining promotion and tenure in 1985, and promotion to full professor in 1996. In addition to regularly teaching the undergraduate two-semester Russian history survey, Gary has also taught a series of upper-division undergraduate courses on Russian intellectual history, social history, and autobiography. Graduate courses included "Gender, Religion and Modernity," "Popular High Culture and the State," and "Empire and Multi-Confessionalism in Early Modern Europe," among others. Gary has especially enjoyed teaching the thesis prospectus course as well as collaborating with a colleague to teach the Core Seminar, a year-long introduction to historical theory and research required for all graduate students.[41]

His research prospered, resulting in a long string of fellowships. In 1984 another IREX fellowship took Gary back to the Soviet Union, after which he and Ann went to Oxford with the support of a Fulbright-Hays Faculty fellowship. A few years later, Gary was back in Leningrad, thanks to fellowships from the American Council of Learned Societies and the Soviet Academy of Sciences. In the 1990s a series of grants sent Gary to Moscow and Leningrad, now known again as Saint Petersburg; in between, Gary spent 1993-94 at Harvard University's Russian Research Center. Additional fellowships from the American Philosophical Society, the Bibliographic Society of America, the American Council of Learned Societies, National Council for Eurasian and East European Research, and the Guggenheim Foundation supported Gary's research during the first decade of the new century, and took him to London (2001-2) and to Kiev several times to pursue a new project.

Through all these years of teaching and research Gary also served his department and university well, including three terms as department chair. During his first and second terms (1995-2001), he helped reorganize the departmental curriculum away from the traditional geographical fields towards a more synthetic, topical organization. This reform accorded well with Gary's own comparative approach to Russian history, but also strengthened a good undergraduate program and helped a small graduate program remain attractive and effective in placing its students. Beyond the campus Gary was active in numerous academic enterprises, including membership on the editorial boards of *Vek prosveshcheniia*, *Symposion*, *Russian Studies in History*, *Kyivska Akademiya*, and *Solanus*. He is co-founder and co-editor of *Vivliofika*, an online refereed journal, and, in addition to membership in various academic associations, was elected President of the Southern Conference of Slavic Studies (2004-5).

All these experiences helped define Gary Marker the historian, but beyond the library and classroom, he was also son, brother, husband, and later father and grandfather. After his father's death and until his mother's in 2009,[42] Gary and his brother had much to do to see that their mother was cared for in her Philadelphia home. At home in Port Jefferson, Gary and Ann balanced home duties with some wonderful travel experiences, visiting Australia, Patagonia, and Alaska, among other places. When Joshua was born in October 1978, Gary became a father and found in this new relationship especially rich returns. Joshua's 2011 marriage brought Gary and Ann a daughter-in-law, Katherine Watts Marker. Soon granddaughter Madelyn Louise followed (January, 2013), a whole new source of joy and a representative of yet another generation of Markers.

That the historian himself is at least in part a result of processes and people who preceded him is no surprise. Nevertheless, Gary's grandparents in Vilno and Odessa could have had no idea that one of their grandsons would one day be writing the history of the country in which they were born. Likewise, Victor Marker and Beatrice Weissman, both of whom were born in Philadelphia and came to maturity there, could not have fully understood how the mix of life experiences there might affect their son's life and occupation. These various threads, some stretching back to imperial Russia, came together in their son—who also became a husband and a father, a Phillies fan as well as a historian of Russia, and, of course, much more.

This unique combination of history and experience helped form the person whom Gary's colleagues and friends value so highly. From elementary school onward, his education benefitted from skilled teachers in strong schools, a foreshadowing of his own impressive professional accomplishments. More than that, however, the person who has taught generations of students, who has written books about

Marker Family after Joshua's 1991 Bar Mitzvah: (left to right) Ann, Joshua, Gary, Richard, Beatrice, and Victor Marker; photo courtesy of Ann Brody

imperial Russia, and who has endured the occasional travails of research in Russia is also a most humorous, thoughtful, supportive, and stimulating friend and colleague. All of us who collaborated in producing this volume in Gary's honor and all whose names appear on the *Tabula gratulatoria* wish him not only more academic success, but also much happiness and satisfaction in all his endeavors in the years ahead.

NOTES

1 In addition to printed material and various online data sets available to me, I took advantage of many of Gary's friends and colleagues to collect information for this essay, and I appreciate their help. Ann Brody was singularly helpful, and I could not have written the essay without her. She provided many family particulars, gave me ideas about whom I might contact to learn more, corrected errors, and provided scans of the photos that accompany this essay—I am very grateful.

2 For more on Karpovich's life and career, see Philip E. Mosely, Martin E. Malia, William Henry Chamberlain, and Dimitri von Mohrenshildt, "Michael Karpovich, 1888-1959," *Russian Review* 19 (1960): 56-76.

3 Alan D. Ferguson, "George Vernadsky, 1887-1973," *Russian Review* 32 (1973): 456-58.

4 Alain Besançon and Paul Bushkovitch, "Marc Raeff (1923-2008)," *Cahiers du Monde russe* 49 (2008): 5-15.

5 See N. L. Tudoreanu, *Ocherki rossiiskoi trudovoi emigratsii perioda imperializma* (Kishinev: Shtiintsa, 1986); V. V. Obolenskii (Osinskii), *Mezhdunarodnye i mezhkontinental'nye migratsii v dovoennoi Rossii i SSSR* (Moscow: TsSU SSSR, 1928); and V. M. Kabuzan, *Emigratsiia i reemigratsiia v Rossii v XVIII-nachale XX veka* (Moscow: Nauka, 1998), 173-95.

6 For a survey of the numbers involved, the chronology of migration, as well as the origins and destinations of the immigrants, see Simon Kuznets, "Immigration of Russian Jews to the United States: Background and Structure," *Perspectives in American History* 9 (1975): 35-124. Arguing against the view that Russian pogroms explained massive Jewish emigration from the Russian Empire, John Klier thought demographic and economic factors more powerful vectors. See John D. Klier, "Emigration Mania in Late-Imperial Russia: Legend and Reality," in *Patterns of Migration, 1850-1914,* ed. Aubrey Newman and Stephen W. Massil (London: Jewish Historical Society of London and Institute of Jewish Studies, University College London, 1996), 21-29.

7 Antwerp was said to have been one of the worst departure ports, prospective passengers being forced to pay high prices for miserable accommodations prior to boarding ship (Tudoreanu, *Ocherki,* 141). I did not succeed in locating any records for the SS *Antwerp*, on which, according to Samuel Marker's naturalization petition, he traveled to Philadelphia (see note 9). Most immigrants to Philadelphia came on ships of the Red Star Line, operating between Antwerp and Philadelphia. The great majority of these passengers traveled at the cheapest fare—steerage; by

one account, as much as 40% of the entire Jewish emigration may have arrived on Red Star ships (http://www.archives.gov/philadelphia/public/red-star-line/ [accessed August 25, 2014]).

8 Ancestry.com, *Philadelphia, Pennsylvania, Marriage Index, 1885-1951* [database on-line], Provo, UT, 2011.

9 National Archives and Records Administration, Washington, DC, *Naturalization Petitions for the Eastern District of Pennsylvania, 1795-1930*, NARA series M1522, Roll 107, Petition Nos. 14101-14460.

10 Bureau of the Census, *Fourteenth Census of the United States, 1920* (Washington, DC: National Archives, [1920]), T625: Lancaster, Pennsylvania, T625__1584, Page 7A, Enumeration District 68.

11 Bureau of the Census, *Fifteenth Census of the United States, 1930* (Washington, DC: National Archives and Records Administration, 1930), T626: Philadelphia, Pennsylvania, roll 2134, Page 21A, Enumeration District 1055.

12 Bureau of the Census, *Sixteenth Census of the United States, 1940* (Washington, DC: National Archives and Records Administration, 1940), T627: Philadelphia, Pennsylvania, roll T627__3755, Page 8A, Enumeration District 51-2191.

13 Bureau of the Census, *Thirteenth Census of the United States, 1910* (Washington, DC: National Archives, [1910]), Record Group 29: Philadelphia, Pennsylvania, roll T624__1394, Page 7A, Enumeration District 0372.

14 As commonly happened among the immigrant population in these years, Weissman provided different dates-of-birth to various inquirers: when he registered for the US draft in 1918, he claimed to have been born August 10, 1883; when in 1942 he again registered for the draft, officials recorded his date-of-birth as August 10, 1889. The Social Security Death Index confirms the date of August 10, but lists the year of birth as 1884.

15 Passenger Lists of the *Sardinian* Arriving in Quebec, Que. and Montreal Que. on 1906-11-08 (http://www.bac-lac.gc.ca/eng/discover/immigration/immigration-records/passenger-lists/passenger-lists-1865-1922/Pages/item.aspx?Id Number=4656& [accessed September 2, 2014]). How Harry (or "Ajser," as the ship's manifest identifies him) reached Le Havre is unknown. However, the great majority of emigrants from central and southern Russia had to make their way through Germany, either to embark at German ports (Hamburg or Bremen) or to pass through to other European ports. Either case might oblige passengers to disembark at an English port, perhaps travel overland to another port, and re-board ships there to cross the Atlantic. To learn more about this process, see Zosa Szajkowski, "Sufferings of Jewish Emigrants to America in Transit Through Germany," *Jewish Social Studies* 39 (1977): 105-16; Harry D. Boonin, "Coming to America Through Hamburg and Liverpool," *Avotaynu* 22, no. 4 (Winter 2006): 15-22; Boonin, "Coming to America Through Hamburg and Liverpool. Part II: Crossing the Atlantic," ibid., 24, no. 1 (Spring 2008): 28-30; and Gordon Read, "Indirect Passage—Jewish Emigrant Experience on the East Coast-Liverpool route," *Patterns of Migration, 1850-1914*, 267-82.

16 Weissman declared his contact to be Max Kataroff, a cousin who resided at 308 South Street, Philadelphia. See National Archives and Records Administration, Washington, DC, *Manifests of Passengers Arriving at St. Albans, VT District through Canadian Pacific and Atlantic Ports, 1895-1954*, National Archives Microfilm Publication M1464, Record Group "Records of the Immigration and Naturalization

Service" (January, 1907). According to Harry D. Boonin, in 1910, shortly after Weissman's 1907 arrival, "all but two of the seventy-one adult residents [in the three hundred block of South Street] identified Yiddish as the native language of their parents. . . . Almost every parent of the adult residents listed was born in Russia." *The Jewish Quarter of Philadelphia: A History and Guide 1881-1930* (Philadelphia: Jewish Walking Tours of Philadelphia, 1999), 93. For a survey of Jewish settlements in Philadelphia, see Maxwell Whiteman, "Philadelphia's Jewish Neighborhoods," in *The Peoples of Philadelphia: A History of Ethnic Groups and Lower-Class Life, 1790-1940,* ed. Allen F. Davis and Mark H. Haller (Philadelphia: Temple University Press, 1973), 231-54.

17 *Thirteenth Census of the United States: 1910*, Philadelphia, Pennsylvania, roll T624_1388, page 15B, Enumeration District 0056.

18 Ancestry.com, *Philadelphia, Pennsylvania, Marriage Index, 1885-1952* [database online], Provo, UT, 2011.

19 A photograph of the intersection of Passyunk, Fifth, and Bainbridge streets, only a block from Weissman's home, can be seen at Boonin, *The Jewish Quarter of Philadelphia,* 139.

20 Ancestry.com, *Philadelphia, Pennsylvania, Marriage Index, 1885-1951* [database online], Provo, UT.

21 Ancestry.com, *US, Social Security Death Index, 1935-2014* [database online], Provo, UT. Apparently Beatrice often identified 1918 as her birth year, and a 1980 replacement of her birth certificate cites 1918 for date of birth. However, the 1920 census (dated January 3, 1920) lists her age as "2 10/12"—about two months shy of three years old, meaning that she probably was born in late February/early March, 1917. The 1930 and 1940 census age data are consistent with this date, confirming the Social Security Death Index date.

22 *Fourteenth Census of the United States, 1920*, Philadelphia, Pennsylvania, roll T625_1616. Page 3B, Enumeration District 107.

23 *Fifteenth Census of the United States, 1930*, Philadelphia, Pennsylvania, roll 2119, page 7A, Enumeration District 0429.

24 *Sixteenth Census of the United States, 1940,* Philadelphia, Pennsylvania, roll T627_3724, Page 6B, Enumeration District 51-1159.

25 Ancestry.com, *Philadelphia, Pennsylvania, Marriage Index, 1885-1951* [database online], Provo, UT, 2011.

26 Ancestry.com, *US City Directories, 1821-1989* [database online], Provo, UT.

27 Subsequently renamed Temple Beth Zion-Beth Israel after merging with a nearby congregation in 1964. See http://www.bzbi.org/home/About/History.aspx (accessed August 29, 2014).

28 http://www.kidsincentercity.com/schools/go/albert-m-greenfield-school (accessed August 23, 2014). Greenfield was born in south-central Ukraine in 1887, and emigrated from Russia about the same time as Samuel Marker, arriving in Philadelphia in 1896 (http://en.wikipedia.org/wiki/Albert_M._Greenfield#Early_life_and_business_activities [accessed September 11, 2014]). For more, see Dan M. Rottenberg, *The Outsider: Albert M. Greenfield and the Fall of the Protestant Establishment* (Philadelphia: Temple University Press, 2014).

29 http://www.mastermanschool.org/pages/Masterman_Julia (accessed August 23, 2014).

30 Formerly Shibe Park where the Philadelphia Athletics also played before their 1954 move to Kansas City, the stadium at Twenty-First and Lehigh was renamed after Connie Mack in 1953. The building was demolished in 1976, and a church has since been erected on the site. See http://www.conniemackstadium.com/index.htm (accessed August 26, 2014).

31 For more on the Phillies of these years, including the famous 1964 end-of-season swoon, see Tyler Kepner, *The Phillies Experience: A Year-By-Year Chronicle of the Philadelphia Phillies* (Minneapolis: MVP Books, 2013), 102-19.

32 http://www.centralhigh.net/pages/CentralHigh (accessed August 23, 2014). On the decision to open enrollment to women, see Patricia Ford, "Philadelphia Court's Ruling Admits Girls to Single-Sex High School," *Education Week*, September 7, 1983 (http://www.edweek.org/ew/articles/1983/09/07/04010015.h03.html [accessed September 9, 2014]).

33 http://www.friends-select.org/ (accessed August 23, 2014).

34 1965 Friends Select High School Yearbook (Philadelphia: Friends Select High School, 1965), 36, 41, 54-55, 75, 83.

35 Ancestry.com, *US Phone and Address Directories, 1993-2002* [database online], Provo, UT. The Markers were living at 340 Grandview Rd., Pottstown.

36 A brief biography of Rieber accompanies the guide to his papers deposited at the University of Pennsylvania Archives; see "Alfred Joseph Rieber Papers," UPT 50 R548: http://www.archives.upenn.edu/faids/upt/upt50/rieber__aj.html (accessed August 24, 2014).

37 See Gary Marker, "Nicholas V. Riasanovsky, 1923-2011," *Slavic Review* 70 (2011): 981-82; and Paul Vitello, "Nicholas V. Riasanovsky Dies at 87; Set Standard for Russian History," *New York Times*, May 28, 2011 (http://www.nytimes.com/2011/05/29/world/europe/29riasanovsky.html?__r=0 [accessed August 30, 2014]).

38 Nicholas V. Riasanovsky, *A Parting of the Ways: Government and the Educated Public in Russia, 1801-1855* (Oxford: Oxford University Press, 1976).

39 Daniel Orlovsky, "Obituary: Reginald E. Zelnik, 1936-2004," *Slavic Review* 63 (2004): 703-704; Laura Engelstein, "Reginald E. Zelnik (1936-2004)," *Perspectives on History* (November 2004) (http://www.historians.org/publications-and-directories/perspectives-on-history/november-2004/in-memoriam-reginald-e-zelnik [accessed August 30, 2014]).

40 Stephen Kotkin, "On Martin Malia (1924-2004)," *New York Review of Books*, January 13, 2005, 39; Michael T. Kaufman, "Martin Malia, 80, Soviet-Era Skeptic, Dies," *New York Times*, November 24, 2004 (http://www.nytimes.com/2004/11/24/obituaries/24malia.html [accessed August 30, 2014]).

41 To see a complete listing of the departmental undergraduate curriculum, see http://sb.cc.stonybrook.edu/bulletin/current/academicprograms/his/courses.php; for the Stony Brook graduate curriculum, see http://history.sunysb.edu/graduate/courses/ (both accessed September 9, 2014).

42 Ancestry.com, *US, Social Security Death Index, 1935-2014* [database online], Provo, UT, 2011. Gary's father, Victor E. Marker, died in 2001.

From Publishing to Prokopovich: Gary Marker's Scholarly Contributions

Valerie A. Kivelson
(University of Michigan)

Gary Marker's ironic wit, combined with his warmth and enthusiasm, make him a beloved friend to all of us contributing to this volume and to countless others as well. Had he had the opportunity to meet Anna Labzina, the eighteenth-century noblewoman whose life-writings he has brought to English-speaking audiences, she would have filled her diary with reports of tearful prayers of gratitude for having found such a friend. In an essay such as this, however, and in our less sentimental age, rather than indulging in the rhetoric of emotion or trading anecdotes about brilliant retorts and inimitable quips, we should more appropriately confine ourselves to discussion of his contributions to the field of early modern Russian history.

Marker's work has placed him at the forefront of scholarship on eighteenth-century Russia since his first book, *Publishing, Printing, and the Origins of Intellectual Life in Russia, 1700-1800*, appeared with Princeton University Press in 1985. Since that time, his topics have ranged far and wide and his studies have drawn inspiration from a shifting palate of theories and methodologies. Stepping back and considering his work as a whole, one finds several signature features coming into focus: his imagination in posing novel questions, shifting the frame, and defining new areas of research; his fearlessness in tackling daunting sets of sources; and his resourcefulness in finding practical ways to illuminate dark, usually inaccessible reaches of the past. His combined rigor and creativity allow him to erase commonly accepted categorical boundaries and to play with the entrenched binaries that have defined historical vision.

Each of these characteristics was already evident in his first book, which addressed the great, irresolvable problem of assessing Russian culture in the eighteenth century. Did Russia enjoy the kind of sophisticated, educated exchange that would qualify it for membership in the European "Republic of Letters"? And did the banter encouraged by Catherine the Great form the basis of a true civil society, or was it merely the yapping of a lapdog performing for a hypocritical and controlling autocrat? Marker ingeniously turned these stock questions around, looking not so much at the isolated peaks and troughs of political discourse but rather at the nuts and bolts of the publishing trade. Willing to put in grueling hours tracking the print-runs and sales records of particular works, he was able to document the finances of the publishers and the nature of the books that enjoyed wide circulation. Mass readership, such as there was, did not coalesce around the rarefied philosophical or literary works that have since entered the Russian canon. Instead, Marker infers,

> readers had extensive practical concerns about the laws but quite limited interest in the principles or philosophy of law. They were more likely to be drawn to literature of general-interest nonfiction that presented easy and concrete examples or guides to personal behavior and fulfillment. . . . They were eager to read descriptions of other times and other places, whether real or imaginary. . . . All of this points to a reading public with an overriding concern for aspects of everyday life, the ways in which other cultures lived and behaved, how they themselves should behave, and above all, how they should raise their children.[1]

Turning to the charged issue of freedom of the press, *Publishing, Printing, and the Origins of Intellectual Life* examines the rise and fall of the newly authorized private presses that appeared under Catherine, and from financial records demonstrates that their rapid closures were due not to the pressures of oppressive censorship but rather to weaknesses of the bottom line. Making a profit in publishing was not an easy business, either then or now. Marker's nuanced findings temper extravagant claims about the breadth and depth of Russian participation in Enlightenment discourse, while at the same time demonstrating the vitality of readers and publishers in creating a reading culture within the framework of a market-driven system, rather than one created, shaped, and fueled from above by the state. The book documents the creation of a small, fragile public sphere on the basis of real evidence about publication and readership, instead of relying on vague impressions and unsupported assertions.

Literacy and reading practices anchor much of Marker's subsequent work as well, both as topics in and of themselves and as tools for digging below surface representations to understand the ways that Russians in the seventeenth and eighteenth centuries actually lived their lives. In a pair of articles devoted to literacy and "literacy texts" in Muscovy, he weighed into an ongoing and highly polarized debate concerning the level of literacy in seventeenth-century Russia.[2] As he himself observed,

> The problem is well known: The array of sources upon which historians of other cultures typically rely to estimate levels of literacy—parish records, wills, service records, and tax lists—either do not exist for pre-Petrine Russia or do not provide the volume of data necessary for computing literacy in a statistically meaningful way.[3]

In typically ingenious fashion, he finds a work-around solution that allows him to assess literacy rates using the sources that do exist—"literacy texts," that is, primers and abecedaria (used to teach reading), and breviaries and teaching psalters (used for students moving beyond reading to writing). In particular, he puts to good use an inventory of publications of the Moscow printing office compiled by the Holy Synod in 1777. He uses this list to track formats and press runs of various texts between 1621 and 1707, and then situates the data on printing and text survival in the context of what he can find about teaching practices. Where the more advanced teaching texts survive in good numbers the primers have all but vanished, suggesting that they were used intensively, probably by a single student, and were literally "read to pieces."[4] From these careful reconstructions of numbers of copies printed, patterns of usage, and "brief life spans for individual copies," Marker is able to extrapolate what penetration these literacy tools would have enjoyed within a Muscovite population of close to ten and a half million in the late 1670s, concluding that it was dismally low. Muscovites had access to "one primer printed per annum for every 1,700 people as compared to one teaching psalter for every 6,600 people," yielding a rudimentary literacy rate of 3-5 percent and intermediate literacy of 1 to 2 percent. He concludes that "In the last analysis, late Muscovy, even with its apparently sharp improvement in literacy, would seem by any comparative measure to have been a profoundly illiterate society in which reading was the privilege of a few and writing the domain of a tiny minority."[5]

Looking forward again from the Muscovite era, Marker returns to the eighteenth century in another set of articles in which he applies similar techniques to chip away at master narratives about literacy, culture, and change. The age of Peter the Great is normally credited with an expansion of literacy and a dramatic shift in the kind of literacy on offer. With Peter's introduction of a simplified civilian script in 1707, form as well as content was changed. Having dispensed with any inflated claims about Muscovite literacy, Marker turned his critical gaze to the generally held notion that this civilian script rapidly replaced the antiquated Slavonic alphabet with its elaborate shapes and superfluous letters. Again following the trail of literacy texts, Marker finds that contrary to the accepted idea that the civilian script elbowed out the old church script, students continued to learn from the tried and true primers, which schooled them in Slavonic script. Only students at more advanced stages of learning encountered the civilian script, and, by definition, that was a far smaller number than would master the traditional forms. Even among the secular elite, he finds, mastery of the civilian script came slowly. In the short twenty-five pages of an article entitled "The Consequences of Diglossia," he manages, gloriously, delightfully, to puncture a bubble of Petrine hype.[6]

This counterintuitive picture of the persistence of religion in the famously secular eighteenth century finds reinforcement in subsequent studies. For example, in an article assessing the degree to which early modern Russians might have recognized the biblical allusions that adorned the newly developing genre of the sermon, Marker documents a sharp increase in the number of bibles published as time went by. "From all this one may venture the hypothesis that knowledge of Scriptural texts widened as never before during the mid-eighteenth century, yet one more curious paradox of the Russian Enlightenment."[7] Actually, however, the cumulative force of Marker's work hammers in a more radical revision. The intensification of biblical knowledge and of religiosity in general in the Age of Reason was no mere curiosity; rather, it defined Russia's Enlightenment.

In his extended investigation of literacy and its uses, Marker put the social historians' tools of quantitative analysis and aggregate sources to work in solving tough cultural questions. His next steps took him in quite different directions. Through the memoir and diary of Anna Labzina, an eighteenth-century noble woman, he was able to reach important insights into recalcitrant questions of spirituality and affect, and to explore issues of gendered writing practices and modes of self-representation.[8]

This cluster of work—two articles and an annotated translation (with Rachel May) of Labzina's autobiographical texts—explores the ways in which Enlightenment rationalism and humanism intersected with and reinforced Labzina's Orthodox commitments. The pieces also tell a riveting story. In her memories of her life, set to paper many years later, Anna describes her childhood and young adulthood in dramatic fashion. Raised in uncompromising austerity by a righteous, sometimes delusional mother, married off at the age of thirteen to a rising star of the scientific flowering of the Enlightenment, outraged by her new husband's godless philosophy, she ultimately found some respite in her second marriage. Her second husband, Labzin, opened the world of

Masonry to her, inculcating in her the Masonic philosophy of civic virtue. Remarkably, Labzina was welcomed as an honorary member of her husband's Lodge, an extraordinary distinction for a woman.

Labzina's complicated subject position allows Marker once again to upend the binary divisions that have so deeply colored interpretations of the eighteenth century: Enlightenment rationalism versus traditional religious piety; male versus female; public versus private. "She simultaneously observed and subverted this relationship between privacy and authority by making the personal public, the feminine powerful, and the sacred social."[9]

With his close study of this rare and rich source, Marker advances our understanding of countless otherwise unreachable issues in the inner life and practices of the time, most pointedly the interactions of religion and Enlightenment thinking and the effects on women of the new cultural practices of the day. Labzina's over-the-top sentimentality, demonstrated by the seemingly constant tears of joy and sorrow, at first seems to sit uncomfortably with the clear-headed rationality that we associate with her era. Marker builds on the important work of other scholars, particularly Marc Raeff, who note that enlightenments came in various flavors, including the German-inspired "enlightenment of the heart" that was favored in Russia.[10] Adding a note of caution, however, Marker insists that the quest for a single, homogeneous explanatory model will never suffice. Individuals and societies manage to maintain multiple, simultaneous currents—sometimes contradictory, sometimes compatible—and they can combine in curious ways. Commitment to interior virtue, to public service and sacrifice, and to an expressive emotionality could have derived from Labzina's Orthodox childhood as readily as from her exposure to the swirl of Saint Petersburg society, despite their apparent diametrical opposition.

Affect served Labzina as a useful tool in a world in which she had few defenses. Her constant invocation of "friendship" as an all-encompassing mode of interaction allowed her to navigate a wide range of social interactions. She casts her mother, her mother-in-law, her male mentors, and even Count Potemkin as dear friends. Even her first husband, Karamyshev, who carries on with his own niece, sexually abuses servant girls, and exhorts his wife to take lovers, becomes her "friend" at moments of reconciliation. On the other end of the social spectrum, she sees her enserfed nanny as her "dear friend," who nearly dies from the rude trauma of separation. Kind tradesmen forgive debts and other "friends" provide her with a lavish new home, complete with flowering gardens and songbirds. Friendship proves to be a useful and flexible commodity! Under its loving guise, brutal social hierarchies are rendered invisible and crass or coercive relationships are elided through the force of this one word. Labzina's vivid, emotive palette proves a vital key to understanding the world she inhabited.

Moving from one rich vein of analysis to another, Marker reveals the surprising ways that Labzina's piety and acceptance of patriarchal subjugation allowed her to participate in precisely those spheres that traditionalism should ostensibly have precluded. Piety offered her ammunition to justify participation in a public world of service and sociability; insistence on her right to defend the purity of her soul supported defiance of her husband's hedonism and abuse; and literacy gave lasting voice to the outrage that she repeatedly insists she never expressed. Findings of this kind support Marker's sense that seemingly opposing cultural forces could simultaneously clash, coexist, combine, and reinforce each other. In Labzina's case these various strands came together in an idiosyncratic set of gendered expectations that shaped and constrained her horizons.

A delightfully satisfying part of Marker's work on Labzina is his skewering of previous scholars, who either sanctified her as a long-suffering martyr or else labeled her hysterical, delusional, or simply misguided in her charges against her husband. How could a shining figure of science, a beacon of rationality such as Karamyshev, possibly have been such a brute? Marker wins a chuckle with his paraphrase of Lotman, who supposed that Karamyshev was actually working late at the lab, leading his love-starved wife to manufacture her dark, suspicious fantasies.[11]

Similar themes—gender, faith, power, and politics, and the public/private divide—emerge in Marker's book and in several articles on Catherine I, the second wife and successor of Peter the Great.[12] The first woman to reign as empress of Russia, and the first of a century-long sequence of female rulers that ended with Catherine the Great, Catherine I might seems an obvious subject for historians interested in the origins and significance of female rule. Yet, prior to Marker's investigation, she remained in the shadows, a figure entirely overlooked in the literature except for brief descriptions of her as Peter the Great's widow, a former courtesan or camp-follower who inherited the throne with no preparation or ability for the part and served out her short reign as a pawn of the ruling clique: "a coarse, illiterate and licentious woman with neither ability nor desire to conduct affairs of state."[13] In a grand tradition of history as the story of Great Men, Catherine I appears only as the first of a line-up of foolish women who turned the Russian court into a site of intrigue despoiled by handsome, self-serving favorites. Marker ingeniously places this unlikely figure, or at least the image of her that her husband and his publicists crafted, at the heart of a major new interpretation.

Although Peter himself never expressly endorsed his wife, or indeed anyone else, as his chosen heir, and several of his favorite publicists expressed deep reservations about female rule, he did oversee an energetic campaign to embellish her image and to polish her credentials. He elevated her from mistress to bride (though belatedly, after the birth of their two daughters) and eventually crowned her empress. Alongside these ceremonial steps, he conducted an active public relations campaign that celebrated his consort as the living embodiment of her namesake saint, Catherine of Alexandria. Marker disentangles the threads of this unlikely parallel between wise, learned, virginal martyr-saint and illiterate former camp-follower, wife, and mother, and finds the inner logic that made the connection plausible.

In this work Marker's primary goal is not to write a biography of Catherine, but to uncover the potential bases for legitimate female rule that were available to Peter's spokesmen. The idea of a female ruling in her own right had to be constructed more or less de novo at the same time that it had to be ostentatiously clothed in the sanctity of ancient tradition and precedent. The project was not without its detractors. Reading between the lines of Prokopovich's panegyrical sermons, which ostensibly celebrated and justified Catherine's accession to the throne, Marker finds a persistent reluctance, a resistance to female rule, in spite of Prokopovich's dutiful fulfillment of the job entrusted to him.

Catherine lived and ruled for less than three years after Peter's death, but she opened the floodgates to a series of women, children, and foreigners who succeeded her on the throne. Catherine's successors, and particularly her daughter, who reigned as Empress Elizabeth, were cognizant of her pivotal role in redefining political practice. Elizabeth, known in historical retrospect for flaunting her descent from her illustrious father, actually boasted of the heritage from both her parents—"a fact," Marker dryly observes, "that would have been obvious long ago had the practice of cutting off the quotes just before her mother was named not been adopted."[14]

The Russian Empire shifted with remarkable ease from exclusively male rule to a succession of females on the throne. Marker pushes his analysis of that process of accommodation further, beyond the particulars of the uses of the image of Saint Catherine to gild the reputation of an empress, and offers an important reflection on the perennial debate over continuity and change under Peter the Great:

> The Petrine use and invention of precedence were themselves based on precedents deeply embedded in Russian culture, rhetorical strategies for making troublesome decisions seem normal, jarring discontinuities seem primordial and divinely sanctioned. Peter and his inner circle saw fit to deploy precedence, what might be termed a discourse of continuity, alongside their more celebrated displays of innovation, renewal, modernity, and anti-tradition from the 1690s until Peter drew his final breath. Ultimately, therefore, the political culture of the Petrine era, for all its breathtaking transformations, cannot be completely grasped without recognizing this dynamic.[15]

Consistent with his earlier work on the ongoing importance of traditional Orthodox spirituality and forms of literacy, Marker here makes a strong case for the persistence of religious framing of politics and culture in an era better known as a time of Enlightenment and militant secularization.[16]

In the course of his work on the first reigning empress, Marker expanded his terrain along multiple axes. Methodologically, he began to draw on visual analysis and enriched his study of the image of Catherine to include visual as well as verbal representations.[17] Textually, he moved from primers and secular writings to the baroque language of ecclesiastical texts. Chronologically, he shifted his primary research back to the early eighteenth century and even further, into the Muscovite period. Geographically, he began a widening of his scope to include the Ukrainian lands, a region that has taken center stage in his current work on the relationship and interactions between Russia and the scholar-clerics of Kyiv and Ukraine.

Spatial analysis has given sharp analytical edge to his ongoing research on the Ukrainian clerics' sermons and religious rhetoric.[18] If following the money and counting press runs took patience and tenacity, then wading through the complex language and thoughts of men like Dmitrii Rostovskii, Feofan Prokopovich, Ioasaf Krokovs'kyi, and Pylyp Orlyk—thickets that would make others quail—may arguably qualify Marker for sainthood himself. A more timorous scholar would steer clear of the baroque acrostics, visual emblems and elaborate iconography, and the mixes of languages and religious cultures that characterize these men's works. Marker advances undeterred. This alone is a feat worth applauding. That he is able to draw revelations both original and surprising from these abstruse homiletics is profoundly impressive.

Marker is never content with simply offering a close, careful reading of a given author or particular document, although he provides those unfailingly. He also builds toward important analytical arguments. Looking at Pylyp Orlyk's Constitution of 1710, he eschews the common set of questions about the text as a political blueprint for separation of powers and instead poses an original and productive set of questions about "the probable resonance of the text among his [Orlyk's] contemporaries, what these phrases might have signified *at that time and in that context*, and why, consequently, Orlyk chose [to write in] Latin."[19] This extraordinary piece encapsulates much of the heated debate about the meanings of "nation" and "people" in medieval and early modern times. Marker parses Orlyk's use of these terms and their meanings at the time, and successfully destabilizes any effort to read the 1710 document as a precocious expression of modern nationalism. Orlyk's constitution, it turns out, was a defense of the privileges of a particular group (Cossacks) on the basis of ancient, even primordial, constitutional rights. Far from reformist, inclusive, and egalitarian, Orlyk's ideas followed the general pattern of European thought of his time in claiming particularist rights on the basis of purportedly ancient constitutional protections. "If none of that sounds particularly modern," Marker concludes, "it nevertheless was quintessentially European."[20]

The writings of Dmitrii Tuptalo, Metropolitan of Rostov (Saint Dmitrii Rostovskii) spark further important revisions. In his article on Dmitrii's "Questions and Answers," Marker detects a remarkable innovation in pastoral teaching. Not only does the catechism encourage readers to view their faith as personal, internal, and individual, something that other scholars have already noted taking shape in late seventeenth-century sermons, but also, and more unexpectedly, Tuptalo carves out faith as a distinctive realm, apart from the secular or political:

> The catechism was the vehicle through which [Tuptalo] hoped to convey the autonomy of faith to his diocese. In this setting Mary and not the Tsar became the pathway to God, one that was directly accessible and comprehensible to every believer once he or she had come to know the tenets of faith with proper guidance. . . . Seemingly in response to heretics and the authorities alike he was drawing a picture of faith utterly independent of Peter, salvation independent of social discipline, in which Mary's human life, earthly example, and intercession stood not between God and the Tsar (to use Isolde Thyret's apt term) but directly between God and humanity.[21]

Marker's 2007 article "Love One's Enemies: Ioasaf Krokovs'kyi's Advice to Peter in 1702" begins with a characteristically wry assessment of previous scholarly coverage of Krokovs'kyi, an obscure literary figure, archimandrite of the Kyivan Caves Monastery at the very beginning of the eighteenth century. By and large, scholars have ignored Krokovs'kyi, either overlooking him completely or granting him a passing reference. His one claim to fame was his entanglement with the Tsarevich Aleksei Affair; in fact, he died en route to being questioned in connection with that matter. A few scholars have dedicated slightly more extensive passages to him, such as Georges Florovsky, who dismissed his thinking as entirely derivative, and V. Askochenskii, a mid-nineteenth century historian who inexplicably and without foundation described him as a "bold genius" on par with the greatest of European thinkers. In Marker's colorful phrase: "Precisely what he said or wrote to merit such gaudy praise is never explained. . . . Thus, even when showered with praise, the man remains obscure."[22]

In an entertaining article, "Love One's Enemy," Marker uncovers a coded message that Krokovs'kyi embedded in a special edition of the *Paterik* presented to Peter the Great. The article exposes the way the edition was constructed as a physical artifact so that the various parts directed the reader and viewer to notice Krokovs'kyi's inserted messages. "The archimandrite knew that the reader of record was the tsar, and one must assume that he assembled the ornamentation, introduction, and verses—that taken together formed a discrete unit separate from the *Paterik* itself—so as to capture the sovereign's eyes, to direct what he saw first and what he read."[23] The archimandrite directed a repetitive, didactic lesson to the tsar: "Love one's enemies." The text and the illustration in conjunction placed peace and love as the highest virtues, a lesson not necessarily welcome or expected in the opening phase of the Northern War. In such a martial moment, Marker asks, what did the preacher mean when he spoke of peace and loving one's enemies? Visually and textually, Krokovs'kyi presents the monks of the Caves Monastery as "the sovereign's prayer givers of choice," direct and effective intercessors with the Queen of Heaven. This spatial framing draws attention to the specific, strategic importance of the monastery itself. Beyond the *lavra*, though, further geographical and military-political particulars are emphasized in the frontispiece to the work, which includes small depictions of the fortresses of Azov and Kazikermen at the bottom. These images "very likely constitute an additional layer of local meaning, one with a decidedly secular content."[24] With his inclusion of references to recent bloody battles, victories earned with the participation and sacrifice of Peter's people and especially of the Zaporozhian Cossacks, the archimandrite made a pitch for the vital contributions of his Ukrainian region not only to the heavenly but also to the earthly success and prosperity of Peter's Russia. Watching the storms of war gathering, Krokovs'kyi composed his preface to the tsar, expounding on the importance of love and peace. "Support us, he is saying: we are the ones who will pray for you. But bring us peace."[25]

As one might expect given Marker's track record, his exploration goes far beyond recovering and decoding Krokovs'ky's work. Even more importantly, the article identifies an important and hitherto unnoticed site of relatively free and open expression within the otherwise closely monitored and harshly policed world of Petrine political culture:

> Krokovs'kyi's text demonstrates with unusual clarity the intellectual plasticity of the nominally rigid scholastic homiletic format, even in the hands of a less than elegant writer. Its availability for putting into print ideas and arguments directly to the sovereign made it a venue for relatively free expression that would have been all but inadmissible in any other type of publication of the time. . . . This comparative openness gave clerical writing a decided advantage over other modes of original expression in the Petrine era, a privileged discursive space to which Peter's clerical intellectuals, virtually alone, had entrée.[26]

In other words, in this sphere of clerical writing, where Kyivan-trained churchmen predominated, Marker has found an early form of the public sphere that he has focused on from the beginning.[27]

Armed with this understanding, Marker has proceeded to study the writings and visual images of the Kyivan clergy, situating them in the context of geopolitical, religious, and cultural currents of their time. These studies further demonstrate the significance of Ukrainian churchmen as incubators of the idea of Russia. This important finding, undoubtedly controversial at the present moment, when completing claims have fractured the Ukrainian lands and precipitated outright warfare in the region, forms the centerpiece of his book-in-progress,

"Mazepa and the Preachers: Ukrainian Clerics and the Making of the Russian Idea." Mazepa, the arch-traitor figure of Russian history and sometime hero of (some) Ukrainian narratives, has been much studied—but mainly in the context of military and diplomatic history, and of course in the time-honored tradition of name-calling and labeling. Marker shifts his lens to look at the effects of Mazepa's betrayal on the development of a sense of distinctive Russian national culture and identity, a process that was only in its very first stages in that significant year, 1708. Looking at the disruptive events of 1708 in the context of the century-long intimacy between the court of the Muscovite tsardom and the highly educated Ukrainian clergy, Marker has set out an entirely original framework for examining the rise of a Russian national idea as articulated not by the Russian *narod*, and not by their political leaders, but rather by the pens of Ukrainian churchmen. This congenital connection between a nationalist idea and religion evokes eerie echoes in today's world, and his exciting project promises to explore the origins of that complex bond. Familiarity with the earlier discourses of Ukrainian clerics allows Marker to interpret the notorious defection not only as a calculated response to particular ins and outs of diplomacy, but within the longer and deeper context of Ukrainian-Russian intellectual life and relations. This is one of those unique projects that leap off the page as immediately exciting, obviously important, and totally and absolutely new. With shots being fired in Ukraine today, it is also the rare historical project with real present-day relevance. This latest direction showcases his gift for defining topics and posing questions that move far beyond any traditional historiographic approaches or frameworks.

In an ongoing intellectual journey, Gary Marker has excavated deeply, mining analytical gold out of unpropitious soil. Working in material ranging from tattered breviaries to subscription lists, from baroque sermons to Enlightenment treatises to politicized icons and ornamental frontispieces, and using an impressive array of languages, he has illuminated aspects of late seventeenth- and eighteenth-century history that would have otherwise remained untouched and unconsidered. With his gift for raising new questions, considering unexplored possibilities, and looking at matters in new ways, he has changed the way we look at this period and the problems we try to explain. With a quick, incisive mind and productive irreverence, he continues to enlighten and entertain all who encounter him and his work.

NOTES

1 Gary Marker, *Publishing, Printing, and the Origins of Intellectual Life in Russia, 1700-1800* (Princeton: Princeton University Press, 1985), 210.

2 Gary Marker, "Primers and Literacy in Muscovy: A Taxonomic Investigation," *Russian Review* 48 (1990): 1-19; Marker, "Literacy and Literacy Texts in Muscovy: A Reconsideration," *Slavic Review* 49 (1990): 74-89.

3 Marker, "Literacy and Literacy Texts in Muscovy," 74.

4 Ibid., 81.

5 Ibid., 88-89.

6 Gary Marker, "Faith and Secularity in Eighteenth-Century Russian Literacy, 1700-1775," in *Christianity and the Eastern Slavs*, vol. 2, Russian Culture in Modern Times, ed. by Robert P. Hughes and Irina Paperno (California Slavic Studies XVII) (Berkeley: UC Press, 1994), 3-24. Also see Marker, "Books and Print in the Reign of Peter the Great," in *Russia in the Reign of Peter the Great: Old and New Perspectives*, ed. A. G. Cross (Cambridge: Study Group on Eighteenth Century Russia, 1998), 119-32.

7 Gary Marker, "Scriptural Pieces: A Muscovite Publishing History of Books of the Bible," *Russian History* 35, no. 3-4 (2008): 335-56 (quote on 356).

8 Anna Evdokimovna Labzina, *Days of a Russian Noblewoman: The Memories of Anna Labzina*, trans. and ed. Gary Marker and Rachel May (DeKalb: Northern Illinois University Press, 2001); Marker, "The Enlightenment of Anna Labzina: Gender, Faith, and Public Life in Catherinian and Alexandrian Russia," *Slavic Review* 59 (2000): 369-90; Marker, "God of Our Mothers: Popular Orthodoxy and Spirituality in Russian Women's Autobiographical Writings in the Late Eighteenth and Early Nineteenth Centuries," in *Orthodox Russia: Beliefs and Practice Under the Tsars*, ed. Valerie Kivelson and Robert H. Greene (University Park: Pennsylvania State University Press, 2003), 193-211.

9 Labzina, *Days of a Russian Noblewoman*, 372.

10 Ibid., 371.

11 Ibid., 377.

12 Gary Marker, *An Imperial Saint: The Cult of Saint Catherine and the Dawn of Female Rule in Russia* (DeKalb: Northern Illinois University Press, 2007).

13 Michael T. Florinsky, *Russia: A History and an Interpretation*, 2 vols. (New York: Macmillan, 1953), 1:436.

14 Marker, *Imperial Saint*, 218.

15 Ibid., 227.

16 Some of this assessment is taken from Valerie Kivelson, review of *Imperial Saint: The Cult of Saint Catherine and the Dawn of Female Rule in Russia*, by Gary Marker, *Cahiers du Monde russe* 48 (2007): 679-82.

17 Marker, *Imperial Saint*, passim; Marker, "Iconography and the Power of Women: The Alexander Nevskii Icon of St. Catherine of 1721," in *Picturing Russia: Explorations in Visual Culture*, ed. Valerie Kivelson and Joan Neuberger (New Haven: Yale University Press, 2008), 63-67.

18 Gary Marker, "Crafting Mazepa's Legacy: Feofan Prokopovich and Pylyp Orlyk," *Slavonic and East European Review* 88 (2010): 110-33. Also published in *Personality and Place in Russian Culture: Essays in Memory of Lindsey Hughes*, ed. Simon Dixon (London: Modern Humanities Research Association for the University College, London, School of Slavonic and East European Studies, 2010); Marker, "Staffing Peter's Church: The Transmigration of Kyivan Clergy in the Early Eighteenth Century," *Kyivs'ka Akademiya*, no. 8 (2010), 79-91; Marker, "Imperial Retrospect: Peter the Great's Ideologists Look Back on Kyiv," *Universals and Contrasts: Journal of the New York-St. Petersburg Institute of Linguistics, Cognition and Culture* 1 (2012): 113-26; and his unpublished piece, Marker, "Marian Miracle Tales and The Geopolitics of Bogomater Between Warsaw and Moscow in the Late Seventeenth Century," (Microsoft Word file). Several of the articles discussed here herald another book, tentatively titled "The Boundaries of Language: The Practices of Literacy in Russia, 1649-1801," that Marker has well underway.

19 Gary Marker, "*Constitutio Medievalis*: The Language of Politics and the Politics of Language in Pylyp Orlyk's Constitution of 1710," in *Pylyp Orlyk: Zhittya, politika, teksty*, ed. Maksym Yaremenko et al. (Kyiv: Mohylyans'ka Akademiya, 2011), 248-66 (quote on 250; italics in the original).

20 Ibid., 265.

21 Gary Marker, "Catechizing in the Diocese: The Place of Mary in Dimitrij Rostovskij's Questions and Answers," *Russian Literature* 75 (2014): 391-413.

22 Gary Marker, "Love One's Enemies: Ioasaf Krokovs'kyi's Advice to Peter I in 1702," *Harvard Ukrainian Studies* 29 (2007): 193-223 (quote on 200).

23 Ibid., 206.

24 Ibid., 212.

25 Ibid., 217.

26 Ibid., 218.

27 He reaches a similar finding about conceptually distinct spiritual and temporal spheres in a sensitive reading of Dmitrii Rostovskii's *Diariusz*: "A Saint's Intimate Life: The *Diariusz* of Dimitrii Rostovskii," in *Everyday Life in Russian History: Quotidian Studies in Honor of Daniel Kaiser*, ed. Gary Marker et al. (Bloomington: Slavica, 2010), 127-44.

Once Again on Whether Byzantine Law Was Applied to the Administration of the Law in Medieval Rus'

Viktor Zhivov
(University of California, Berkeley and Moscow State University)

In my article written in the beginning of the 1980s and published in 1988, I argued that in medieval Rus' Byzantine law, or at least a substantial part of the Byzantine legal regulations, was never applied in the administration of the law.[1] Only local customary law, codified initially in the Russkaia Pravda, played any practical role. My main argument was simple. Byzantine law existed in Rus' in a Slavonic translation. The translation was not particularly good, so that it was impossible to understand a number of its provisions. One cannot apply a norm that one is unable to understand. As an example I cited an article from the Ecloga (XIV, 11):[2]

Послѹси клицѣм же числомь сѹть. до ·д҃· точью. бѡ нинѹда привѡдать ꙗ. кѡегѡждо привидѣнига. кдинъ д(е)нь прикмлюще. ли преже д҃.го привидениꙗ ѿреч(е)тьсꙗ приводали. и послѹшьствованиꙗ ѿдавна бѹд(е)ть. посемь не привѡдить емѹ иногѡ послѹха. но пребывати сдѣꙗныхъ гласѣхъ (MP. fol. 187v).

I would not try to translate this text, but its Greek original could be rendered:

> Whatever the number of witnesses, they have to be called in not more than four groups; the testimony of each group should not take more than one day. If before the testimony of the fourth group the usher transgresses his office and discloses [to the fourth group] the testimony of the preceding [groups], it is forbidden to call another witness but one has to confine oneself to the collected testimonies.[3]

It is impossible to extract this meaning from the Slavonic text; the text is syntactically deficient (for instance, it is impossible to determine to which antecedent the pronoun **ѥмꙋ** refers) and semantically incoherent. In my opinion, such texts could not have had any practical function. It is not the only example of incomprehensible provisions; hence my general conclusion that such juridical norms were never applied in practice.

Though my general conception gave rise to heated polemics, no objections have ever been made to this simple philological argument. Ludwig Burgmann refers to a Slavic compilation of the Ecloga articles, "On the witnesses and their number," as a proof that these articles were operative.[4] It is clear, however, that such articles could be copied by East Slavic scribes without the scribes necessarily comprehending their original meaning; consequently, their inclusion in compilations cannot be regarded as a proof of their application.

The process of transmission of Slavonic translations of Byzantine legal codes could be seen as evidence of just the opposite claim. For instance, in the translation of the Procheiron (XXXIX, 63) in the copy of the fourteenth century we read: "**Иже свою кꙋмꙋ именемь брат(а) своѥго пойметь... кꙋпно и ѡбѣма носа оурѣжють.**"[5] Literally this means: "A man who takes [in marriage] his relative through baptism in the name of [his] brother . . . the noses of both of them must be cut;" in the Greek original it is said: "Ὁ τῇ ἰδίᾳ συντέκνῳ ἢ ὀνόματι γάμου ἀγαγόμενος... ἅμα αὐτῇ ῥινοκοπείσθω".[6] It is clear from the comparison that there was a scribal error: **именемь брата**, "in the name of [his] brother," appeared instead of **именемь брака**, "under the pretense of marriage." Such errors are usual in bookish texts, but it is difficult to imagine that it could happen with an operative legal regulation. Translated Byzantine laws, which presented cultural models, were viewed in opposition to local customary law, which offered effective practical regulations.

I believe that this opposition is reflected in the contrasting terminological systems. Translations of Greek legal codes use legal terms different from those that are deployed by the Russkaia Pravda and other legal documents based on customary law. This opposition is underlined by the fact that the same Slavic words could have different meanings in these two systems (in these two types of texts). Thus, *rukopisanie* meant "promissory note" in the translated Greek legal codes (as a calque from Greek χειρόγραφον), but it acquired the meaning of "testament" in local East Slavic legal documents.[7] In the same way, *zadnitsa* meant "inheritance" in local East Slavic legal documents; the term was borrowed in Slavonic translations of Greek juridical texts but was used there in the special meaning of *legatum* (bequest, legacy), corresponding to Greek λεγάτον.[8] Two legal systems with homonymous terms could hardly function simultaneously.

Simon Franklin raises an objection to this claim. He writes:

> On what basis does Zhivov continue to insist, as if on a fundamental axiom, that "legal systems in which the same words have different meanings cannot be simultaneously in use"? Why not? Surely the crucial criterion is that a given word should be functionally comprehensible in a given context, not that all terminology must be consistent in all contexts.[9]

No doubt, legal texts could accommodate polysemous words, but no legal code can permit polysemous terminology. Terminology in a certain field of knowledge or skill forms a system, in which different terms interact with each other; terms of the same system are usually monosemantic. The best way to explain the existence of two systems of terminology is to posit a legal dualism, a dualism embracing Byzantine law on one hand and indigenous customary law on the other.

My critics dismiss the idea of legal dualism; it seems to be too structuralist for them. The first version of my work on the history of Russian law was written thirty years ago when structuralism was still alive and I was imbued with its approaches. I have repented of my structuralist inclinations since that time. I became disillusioned with the idea of Russian and Church Slavonic diglossia. Answering the critique of Ludwig Burgmann, I abandoned the scheme I had used earlier, in which the dualism of the "Byzantine" and "Russian" law was tied to the Russian and Church Slavonic diglossia. In this scheme the two were treated as strictly parallel phenomena, a stark division that I no longer fully maintain.[10] I am not attracted in any way by the mechanics of binary oppositions. Nevertheless, some binary oppositions still exist—even after the demise of structuralism (right and left, male and female, and so on). I am not sure that the advantages of getting rid of all binary oppositions greatly outweigh the benefits of preserving a modicum of structuralist discourse.

My main claim is that the Byzantine codes were never (with extremely rare exceptions[11]) applied in practice either as the norms of direct operation or as a *jus subsidiarium*. To be sure, this claim could be true only if monastic rules and penitentials are not treated as "law."[12] This situation (unusual from the perspective of Western legal history) leads to the question: for what reason were these codes copied and referred to? In my opinion, it was done because they were conceptualized (sometimes in contradiction with their content) as describing the Christian order of things, the model by which a Christian society should live: their value was religious, and not practical.

This does not mean that Byzantine law had no influence on Russian legal culture. We should posit this influence, however, with rational reservations, not treating every similarity as an instance of influence. Until the reign of Aleksei Mikhailovich (and the *Ulozhenie* of 1649), we find practically no direct borrowings from Byzantine legal texts in Russian law codes. Iaroslav Shchapov in his introduction to the new edition of the Slavonic Ecloga astutely remarked: "A direct borrowing of Byzantine norms in ancient Russian law is extremely rare; in the passages in which it can be discovered, there is no textual match between Slavonic translations of the Greek originals and the Russian texts."[13] This observation applies not only to the Ecloga but also to other Byzantine legal codes.[14]

The Byzantine influence was selective because, from the beginning, the spheres of legal regulation in Roman law and in East Slavic legal practices were different: a much wider area of social relations was covered by the Byzantine codes than by the Russkaia Pravda or the early *sudebniki*. The sphere of legal regulation in Russian legal documents gradually became larger and larger. This is the process that Daniel Kaiser aptly called "the growth of law."[15] Russian law codes covered such areas as Christian marriage, inheritance laws (which depend on conjugal rights), blasphemy and other religious crimes, moral (sexual) transgressions and so on. Presumably these new regulations were based on notions that accompanied Christianity and civilization from Byzantium. But notions are not laws; Russian rules used many notions borrowed from the Greeks, but they did not reproduce Byzantine norms. For example: the specific kinds of moral transgressions listed in the Statute of Iaroslav fall under the competence of the ecclesiastical court and their content reflects Byzantine notions of Christian social order; however, the penalties given consist of fines, as was characteristic of the Russian legal system, and not the corporeal punishments prescribed by the Byzantine law codes.[16]

Not all resemblance between sets of norms necessarily results from borrowing. For instance, Shchapov discusses the fact that in the fourteenth and fifteenth centuries, testaments in northeastern Rus' began to be witnessed by three, five, or seven witnesses. He regards this innovation as a "reception" of the norms of the Ecloga. He indicates, nevertheless, that the number of witnesses in the northeastern testaments is often different, and "can be designated as 'plus one,' that is four or six persons."[17] It is easy to see that any number of witnesses from three to seven is possible, so that the norms of the Ecloga are not reproduced intact and may well have nothing to do with the innovation under discussion. The increase in the number of witnesses could be a natural result of the growing use of written documentation: if a written document is the main basis for a legal action, then the greater number of witnesses gives it a greater evidential effect; a Byzantine source is hardly necessary for this legal improvement.[18]

George Weickhardt believes that all features that characterize the growth of law in Russia were the product of Byzantine influence (or, in his terms, the influence "of the canon law system"), including "the use of rational modes of proof, such as eyewitness testimony and documentary evidence, and the use of written legal records."[19] But he does not explain why, for instance, the use of eyewitness testimony should have a Byzantine source; we read in the Kratkaia Pravda:

> If someone be beaten so that he bears bruises and is bloody, then he need seek no eyewitness [*vidok*] [to confirm his complaint]; if he bears no sign [of the fight], then [let] an eyewitness come forward; if the [complainant] is unable [to produce a witness], then that is the end of the matter; if [the victim] is unable to avenge himself, then he is to take for the offense three grivnas, and also payment for the physician.[20]

There is no need whatsoever to seek a Byzantine source for this ancient norm; it demonstrates that eyewitness testimony came into existence in East Slavic legal practice quite independently of any Byzantine influence.

Weickhardt claims further: "Thus, the Byzantine-inspired church and canon law of Rus' and Byzantine practices as to deeds, wills, judgments and royal grants of law unquestionably played a key role in both the transition to a triadic system and the transition to a written legal system in the secular world."[21] The transition from a dyadic to a triadic system (or from a horizontal to a vertical system) inevitably accompanies the growth of "a hierarchy of institutions which may compel obedience to their command."[22] Franklin treats the same process as "the gradual intrusion of the regulatory authority of the polity . . . into the regulatory authority of the community."[23] In the framework of this process, "officials in vertical systems, specifically designated for conducting investigations and adjudication, take steps decreed by existing state order, and ultimately fix the state's penalties upon those judged to have violated behavioral norms."[24] The growth of law is connected with the growth of state power. The role of Byzantine practices in the latter process was secondary (if any existed at all), limited probably to the very general functioning of a civilization model—to the extent that state building can be regarded as part of the civilization process.

Lust for power is a very widespread phenomenon; it exists in various forms and does not need specific models for imitation. Moscow princes did not live or govern their subjects exactly in the same way as Byzantine emperors or as khans of the Golden Horde did. They issued the *sudebniki* not to imitate foreign monarchs but to strengthen their authority and control over their subjects. Aleksei Mikhailovich was the first Muscovite ruler who aspired to a position similar to that of the Byzantine emperor, and his legislative activity was connected with this high ambition. His laws, starting with the *Ulozhenie* of 1649, became cultural statements; what these laws gained in cultural status they lost in operative force. This theme is beyond the scope of the present essay, but I, in an old-fashioned penchant for far-reaching generalizations, connect these imperial ambitions of the lawgiver with the alienation of Russian from the legal system enforced by the state, and its ambivalent approach to law, as both effective controlling force and abstract symbol of imperial might. Effective laws develop organically out of necessity and practice, whereas cultivated laws, developed out of pure principle or imported for show, remain distinct from social realities, and therefore non-operative. This may sound like the positing of a structuralist constant for Russian cultural history, but I hope that the dualist nature of this statement can be amended by presenting this history as an age-old dynamic through which a simple opposition acquires ever new meanings. My highly esteemed friend Gary Marker is a great master of following these changes of meaning through historical contexts and individual agendas, and I hope that he would not look censoriously on the efforts of his colleague.

NOTES

1 V. M. Zhivov, "Istoriia russkogo prava kak lingvo-semioticheskaia problema," in *Semiotics and the History of Culture* : *in Honor of Jurij Lotman*, UCLA Slavic Studies 17 (Columbus, Ohio: Slavica, 1988), 46-128.

2 *Merilo Pravednoe po rukopisi XIV veka*, ed. M. N. Tikhomirov (Moscow: Izd-vo AN SSSR, 1961), fol. 187v.

3 *Ecloga. Das Gesetzbuch Leons III. und Konstantinos' V*, ed. Ludwig Burgmann, Forschungen zur byzantinischen Rechtsgeschichte 10 (Frankfurt: Löwenklau-Gesellschaft E.V., 1983), 216.

4 Ludwig Burgmann, "Zwei Sprachen—zwei Rechte. Zu einem Versuch einer linguo-semiotischen Beschreibung der Geschichte des russischen Rechts," *Rechtshistorisches Journal* 11 (1992): 119. This compilation has been studied by L. V. Milov in his "Drevnerusskii perevod Eklogi v kodifikatsionnoi obrabotke kontsa XIII v.," *Vestnik Moskovskogo universiteta*, Seriia *Istoriia* (1984): no. 3, 56-65. Burgmann cities this study and bases his arguments on Milov's interpretation. His approach clearly illustrates the dangers of ignoring philological evidence and analyzing ancient texts without proper philological instruments. Milov wrongly believed that the compiler must have had the exceptionally high qualifications in order to achieve such "preciseness and clarity of translation" (Milov 1984, 63); to prove this assertion he quotes a scarcely understandable passage (Ecloga V, 8) in which an anaphoric pronoun has no proper antecedent and a literate person (who is able to write a testament) is designated by the words "книгъ имѣя" (literally "having books") instead of the original "свѣдыи книгъ" which meant "literate," but which the compiler could not understand because книги was not used in Russian Church Slavonic with the meaning "letters." The original translation of this article was also full of errors that rendered the prescribed norm meaningless (see Shchapov's commentary in *Die slavische Ecloga*, eds. Jaroslav Nikolaevič Ščapov and Ludwig Burgmann, Forschungen zur byzantinischen Rechtsgeschichte 23 [Frankfurt: Löwenklau-Gesellschaft E.V., 2011], 127-28. For unknown reasons Shchapov quotes Milov's observations, but abstains from commenting on them). It seems that Burgmann is unable to evaluate the quality of Milov's arguments and repeats them uncritically. Generally speaking, Milov's theories proceed from the supposition that the Ecloga was translated into "Old Russian" in the time of Vladimir I and was used as a model for the codification of local East Slavic customary law. This hypothesis is unverifiable (see V. M. Zhivov, *Razyskaniia v oblasti istorii i predystorii russkoi kul'tury* [Moscow: Iazyki slavianskoi kul'tury, 2002], 300-303); there is no need to return again to the discussion of its fallacy. I'll mention in passing that I do not see any fundamental disagreements between Milov's and my representations of Russian legal history. I believe that our views are quite similar and largely traditional, going back to Nevolin, Goetz, and Vladmirskii-Budanov. I disagree with Milov not on fundamental issues but on his reconstruction of the early reception of Byzantine law (the so-called legal reforms of Saint Vladimir).

5 *Merilo Pravednoe po rukopisi*, fol. 328.

6 Zachariae, Karl Eduard von Lingenthal, *Imperatorum Basilii, Constantini et Leonis Prochiron* (Heidelberg: J. C. B. Mohr, 1837), 250.

7 Zhivov, *Razyskaniia,* 202-203.

8 Ibid., 203-204.

9 Simon Franklin, "On Meanings, Functions and Paradigms of Law in Early Rus'," *Russian History* 34 (2007): 69.

10 Zhivov, *Razyskaniia*, 291-93.

11 Ibid., 222-23.

12 Simon Franklin defines monastic rules and penitentials as laws and "para-legal" texts respectively (Franklin, "On Meanings, Functions and Paradigms," 63-81, esp. 67, 73-74). It is unnecessary to deal here with the problem of the extent to which various penitential regulations were applied in Russian pastoral practice, in other words, to what extent penitentials were operative. In some cases they share

the non-functional nature of Byzantine laws in their East Slavic reception; on this topic, see V. M. Zhivov, "Zametki o epitimiinikakh kak istochnike po istorii russkoi pokaiannoi distisipliny," in *Medieval Russian Culture to Modernism: Studies in Honor of Ronald Vroon*, ed. Lazar Fleishman et al., Russian Culture in Europe 8 (Frankfurt: Peter Lang, 2012), 15-22. Franklin justly remarks that a priest "had no economic or coercive power of enforcement, and could only impose such penalties as his flock were willing to accept. The frustration is almost tangible in the sources" (Franklin 2007, 75). Priests did not have coercive power precisely because penitentials were not "laws"; I am not sure that the sources demonstrate any serious frustration on their part; evidently they were reconciled to the lack of penitential discipline and worried about quite different things.

13 Ščapov and Burgmann, *Die slavische Ecloga*, 43.

14 A sober survey of literature on the problem of the influence of Roman and Byzantine law on Russian legal norms can be found in Ferdinand Feldbrugge, *Law in Medieval Russia* (Leiden: Martinus Nijhoff, 2009), 59-69, 94-128. Feldbrugge points out that "the claims for direct Roman law influence on early Russian law cannot in any individual case be corroborated. . . . In the purely secular law of early Russia, especially the *RP* [Russkaia Pravda] in its two versions, not only the Roman, but also the Byzantine element is absent" (ibid., 125-26). Unfortunately, the author does not know a considerable part of the relevant literature, such as the work of Leonid Milov, Ludwig Burgmann (on Russian law), Kirill Maksimovich, Simon Franklin, George Weickhardt, and others. The bulk of his critique is directed against a prerevolutionary monograph by Nikolai A. Maksimeiko (*Opyt kriticheskogo issledovaniia Russkoi Pravdy*, vol. 1 [Kharkov: Tip. i lit. M. Zil'berberg i s-v'ia, 1914]), and a more recent article by E. V. Salogubova ("Vliianie rimskogo prava na rossiiskoe grazhdanskoe zakonodatel'stvo," *Vestnik Moskovskogo universiteta*, seriia *Pravo* [1997]: no. 2, 29-37), which make for easy targets. Nevertheless, some of Feldbrugge's comparisons of Byzantine and Russian provisions, demonstrating the lack of any real connection, are very shrewd and useful. A good example is the analysis of the norms of inheritance by widows in the Ecloga; Feldbrugge convincingly shows that these norms are only superficially similar to those of the Prostrannaia Pravda (Feldbrugge 2009, 115-16) and that V. I. Sergeevich's speculations on the influence of the Byzantine norm are unsupported (V. I. Sergeevich, *Lektsii i issledovaniia po drevnei istorii russkogo prava* [Saint Petersburg: Tipografiia M. M. Stasiulevicha, 1910], 554); Feldbrugge's critique can be applied with the same effect to later works by George Weickhardt (cf. George G. Weickhardt, "Legal Rights of Women in Russia, 1100-1750," *Slavic Review* 55 [1996]:1-23.).

15 Daniel H. Kaiser, *The Growth of the Law in Medieval Russia* (Princeton: Princeton University Press, 1980).

16 Ardalion Popov, *Sud i nakazaniia za prestupleniia protiv very i nravstvnnosti po russkomu pravu* (Kazan': Tipo-litografiia Imp. Universiteta, 1904), 58-64; Ia. N. Shchapov, *Kniazheskie ustavy i tserkov' v drevnei Rusi XI-XIV vv.* (Moscow: Nauka, 1972), 296-306; Shchapov, *Vizantiiskoe i iuzhnoslavianskoe pravovoe nasledie na Rusi v XI-XIII vv.* (Moscow: Nauka, 1978), 237.

17 Ščapov and Burgmann, *Die slavische Ecloga*, 44-45. Shchapov refers to an article by G. Semenchenko, in which these testaments are analyzed; Semenchenko correctly regarded the presence of the spiritual father as in

keeping with "the ancient Russian tradition of testifying," but less convincingly argues that the number of witnesses made an even number only with the addition of the spiritual father (G. V. Semenchenko, "Vizantiiskoe pravo i oformlenie russkikh zaveshchanii XIV-XV vv.," *Vizantiiskii vremennik* 46 [1986]: 166). However, of the testaments with an uneven number of witnesses, one can find some that include among the witnesses a spiritual father; they should probably be treated as two or four plus one, and by this token as contrary to the Byzantine model. See, for instance, document no. 168 in *Akty sotsial'no-ekonomicheskoi istorii Severo-vostochnoi Rusi kontsa XIV-nachala XVI v.* (ASEI), 3 vols. (Moscow: AN SSSR, 1952-1964), 2:103-105. Witnesses to this testament made by Nason Zakhar'in in the second half of the fifteenth century include the testator's spiritual father, Abbot Aleksei, and four other persons; this fact evidently destroys Semenchenko's argument and Shchapov's reasoning.

18 Simon Franklin, *Writing, Society and Culture in Early Rus, c. 950-1300* (Cambridge: Cambridge University Press, 2002), 160-86.

19 George G. Weickhardt, "Early Russian Law and Byzantine Law," *Russian History* 32 (2005): 10.

20 *Pravda Russkaia*, ed. B. D. Grekov, 3 vols. (Moscow-Leningrad: Izd-vo AN SSSR, 1940-1963), 1:70; Daniel Kaiser's translation: *The Laws of Rus'—Tenth to Fifteenth Centuries*, ed. and trans. Daniel H. Kaiser (Salt Lake City: Charles Schlacks, 1992), 15.

21 Weickhardt, "Early Russian Law and Byzantine Law," 14.

22 Kaiser, *Growth of the Law*, 7.

23 Franklin, "On Meanings, Functions and Paradigms," 71.

24 Kaiser, *Growth of the Law*, 7.

About Peter the Great's Ship *Predestinatsiia*

Maria Di Salvo
(University of Milan)

In the summer of 1695 the young Tsar Peter I launched his first military campaign against the Turkish fortress of Azov, which managed to withstand the siege thanks to regular provisions of food and weapons supplied by the Turkish fleet. The failure of this undertaking convinced Peter that Russia had to intensify efforts already begun by his predecessor Aleksei Mikhailovich and Peter himself to acquire a strong fleet fit for the high seas. To this end, the tsar set up naval shipyards in Voronezh and other locations and hired thousands of men from all over the country to work in them. By the following year, a number of galleys and ships of various kinds had already been built. These made an effective contribution to the second, more successful attack on Azov, which surrendered to the Russian army on July 18, 1696.

As is well known, shipbuilding became one of Peter's consuming interests. To achieve his aim he hired experts and technical consultants from Europe's greatest maritime powers—England, Holland, and the Republic of Venice. He devoted most of his Grand Embassy in the countries of Western Europe (1697-1698) to visiting the Dutch and

English naval shipyards in person and learning the skills of a shipwright: the image of the tsar busily sailing up the Thames or laboring, axe in hand, became a common feature in history books and even in popular literature.

Forced by reports of the *strel'tsy* uprising to return to Russia, Peter had to forego the final stage of his diplomatic-educational tour, scheduled to take place in Venice. He reached Moscow on August 25, 1698 and dealt personally with the inquiry into the revolt and with suppressing the rebels in order to restore power to his own hands. He even found time to divorce his wife, Evdokiia Lopukhina, who was locked away in a convent in Suzdal'. As soon as these most important issues had been addressed, the tsar was off to the Voronezh shipyards, where on November 19 he officially announced the start of work on a ship that was to occupy his thoughts for over a year. After a few months of intense work in the capital, in mid-February, 1699, he began another long stay in Voronezh to keep an eye on the work in progress on the fleet and on his ship. In the meantime, Peter took care of important affairs of state, such as the secret agreement signed in April with the Danish ambassador in preparation for a confrontation with Sweden, and the negotiations underway between the European powers and Turkey, which led to the Treaty of Karlowitz. The following February Peter returned to inspect the shipyards, and at last on April 27, 1700,[1] his ship, the *Predestinatsiia* (*Predestination*), was launched in a solemn ceremony, amidst cannon shots and drum rolls, in the presence of the Tsarevich Aleksei, the tsar's favorite sister Natal'ia, numerous boyars with their families, diplomats, and residents of Moscow's Foreign Quarter, all specially invited to join him in Voronezh.

In the tsar's absence, shipbuilding in Voronezh was supervised by Fedosei Skliaev and Luk'ian Vereshchagin. These two trusted Russian shipwrights, like the tsar himself, had honed their skills abroad, completing their training in Venice; the project may have been based on a design brought from England, but in a note about the ships of the Voronezh fleet written at the time of the launch, the tsar, with some degree of modesty, claimed responsibility for the work, adding among other things: "As regards the ship, named *Bozhie Predvedenie* [see below for the meaning of this name], we cannot discuss its proportions, ruggedness, or seaworthiness, since it is a project for which we provided the measurements and actually worked on ourselves."[2] The foreign diplomats present at the launch reported back to their own governments, praising the beauty and originality of the ship; engravings depicting it were prepared by Adrian Schoonebeck, a Dutch artist in the service of the tsar, to be sent to foreign courts. The wealth of decorative features, not only on the outside, but including oak paneling in the captain's cabin, was described in detail by the painter Cornelius de Bruyn, who saw it in 1703 in Voronezh. The following year Claesz Pool, the Dutch master with whom the tsar had learned shipbuilding in the East India Docks, wrote to him to express his approval.[3]

The technical details of the ship that Peter built have been the subject of numerous studies. These give varying assessments of its originality (compared to the English and Dutch models) and of the possibility of Venetian origin for certain embellishments. But they also underline the ingenuity of the solutions found to specific problems, such as the considerable distance of the Voronezh shipyards from the sea and the lack of water in the rivers that the fleet would have to sail down to reach the mouth of the Don.[4] Having no experience of these issues myself, I leave them to naval historians or to equally knowledgeable modeling enthusiasts. I would, however, like to add a couple of considerations about the scanty information afforded by the few documents concerned with the ship, which those scholars, as is natural, interpret in the light of their own research and interests.

First, the name of the ship. Both before and for a time after his return from the Grand Embassy, Peter did not align himself with the European custom of naming ships after members of their royal families: looking through the lists connected with the Azov fleet (1699-1700) published in an appendix to Sergei I. Elagin's book, *Istoriia russkogo flota* (History of the Russian navy),[5] we can only find one such case, a yacht named *Natali'ia* in memory of the tsar's mother, Natal'ia Naryshkina. Later, however, we can see that the finest ships of the fleet were the *Printsessa Anna*, *Printsessa Elizaveta*, or even *Petr I and II*. These names point to the growing association of the tsar's public image with the dynastic principle, a development also revealed by the numerous painted portraits of family members or by their marriages to scions of other European dynasties, candidates to future succession.

In his most recent research, Gary Marker has made frequent reference to that link between word and image, typical of the Ukrainian-Polish (and, via this, European) baroque tradition, which was part and parcel of the political-cultural discourse of Peter's age; Gary's skillful analysis of baroque language has shown the implications of various documents written in this period in Ukraine and Russia, and highlighted the interaction between words, images, and ideology.[6] The form in which such elements are combined most neatly is that of emblems, figures, or scenes of a symbolic nature, often along with a phrase explaining their meaning. Like many European monarchs before him, Peter made liberal use of this device when celebrating his own victories in public ceremonies, in the books he had printed, and also in the names he chose for the ships that were to make up his beloved fleet. The tsar's papers include a list of these last, dating to about 1700, "with figures and captions written on them" (*s figurami na nikh i podpisiami*),[7] which testifies to the close attention he paid to this aspect of his shipbuilding. It was not yet customary to display names on a ship's stern, so the emblem and its explanatory motto were key to identifying a ship; in addition, and more importantly, these emblems and mottos provided a more intuitive and effective way of conveying the symbolic and educational meaning that the autocrat wished to impress not only on his subjects, but also on his enemies. To achieve this, Peter used his own direct knowledge of the collections of emblems published in Europe and amply represented in his personal library.[8] The experience of the engraver Adrian Schoonebeck, hired by the sovereign in Amsterdam and brought to Moscow, was also fundamental: Schoonebeck helped prepare illustrations documenting the taking of Azov and executed numerous commemorative engravings.

Choosing emblematic names was very popular at the time the Azov fleet was being built, as shown by the list of names published by Elagin; but earlier, at the time of the tsar's journeys to Archangel (1693-94) and of his first direct contact with the sea, another model (with its own tradition) seemed to predominate: the vessel was entrusted to divine protection or to the intercession of a saint. At that time the *Sviatoi Petr* and *Sviatoi Pavel* (*Saint Peter* and *Saint Paul*) were launched, and the following years saw the *Apostol Petr* and *Apostol Pavel* (*Apostle Peter* and *Apostle Paul*). In the meantime, the burgomaster of Amsterdam, Nicolas Witsen, was commissioned to supply the tsar with an impatiently awaited frigate, the *Santa Profeetie* or *Sviatoe prorochestvo* (*Holy Prophecy*),[9] which thus inaugurated the tradition of dual Russian and Dutch names. Likewise, the Azov fleet included the *Mirotvorets/Vredemake* (*Peacemaker*) and *Agnets/Lamgotes* (*Lamb of God*). Dutch came naturally to Peter because of his familiarity with the Foreign Quarter in Moscow, and increasingly so as he later spent more time in the Dutch shipyards. But the existence of variants of the same name in several languages can also be explained by the diverse origins of the men who worked in them. It is also worth noting that the meaning of the name, often symbolic, had to be comprehensible to foreign observers, whether friends or foes.

There was a clear link between the choice of the patron saints and the figure of the sovereign: "Peter" and "Paul" were not just the names of two revered apostles, but were also the saints commemorated on June 29, the tsar's own name day. Similarly, it was no coincidence that the subsequent *Sviatoi Andrei* was named for the apostle Saint Andrew, for whom Peter expressed special devotion, increasingly advancing him as a national saint even in preference to Saint Peter. In fact, the tsar chose the Saint Andrew's cross as the emblem of the Russian navy and, following his return from the Grand Embassy, created the Order of Saint Apostle Andrew the First Called.[10] It is not clear from the sources whether the name "Santa Profeetie" had been chosen by the tsar, but, like others that were to follow, it contains a clear reference to and harbinger of his future efforts at expansion. So too did the galley *Principium*, from the deck of which he followed the victorious Azov campaign, and the similarly named *Blagoslovennoe nachalo* (*Blessed Beginning*).

Neither could the new ship designed and built by Peter fail to have a highly symbolic name. In fact, in the log for the year 1699

(*Iurnal 207 godu*) one reads: "On November 19, the day on which we commemorate the martyred saint Abdias [Obadiah],[11] the foundations were laid for a ship to be named *Bozhie Predvedenie*, with a keel 130 feet long and 33 feet wide."[12] According to Afanasii F. Bychkov, editor of the tsar's letters, the full name in Russian was *Bozhie semu est' predvedenie*,[13] which could be translated as "Of this there is divine prescience." Elsewhere, as for example in a list of ships drawn up in Peter's own hand in 1701,[14] we read [*Goto*] *Predestinatsiia*, a name that commentators invariably deem macaronic due to the mixture of Dutch and Latin, similar to what we already noted in "Santa Profeetie." As is well known, the concept of predestination is foreign to the Slavic Orthodox tradition, which refused it as a contradiction with the principle of free will. In this, it sided with Saint John of Damascus (seventh—eighth century), who in his *An Exact Exposition of the Orthodox Faith* (Book 2, chapter XXX) distinguished prescience, as a manifestation of the omnipotence of God, from predestination, which, from his point of view, would imply predetermination of human actions. Leaving aside disquisitions of a theological nature, suffice it to point out that the Orthodox Church has always kept its distance from the thinking of Saint Augustine and, even more so, from that of John Calvin, with which the doctrine of predestination is generally associated. In the middle of the seventeenth century, when the echoes of the Protestant Reformation began to reach Eastern Europe, a council of Constantinople (1638) reasserted loyalty to the teaching of John of Damascus.

Peter the Great may have picked up the word *predestinatsiia* in Holland or even from his Genevan Calvinist friend Franz Lefort, but it is hard to believe that the choice of this word (which, moreover, was not a correct equivalent of the Russian *predvedenie*) would have had any clear theological implications for him. It is much more likely to have had the approximate meaning attributed to it in colloquial language, of "presage" or "foreshadowing." In any case, the original Russian name of the ship refers to divine "prescience," i.e., to God's foreknowledge of human affairs and their meaning and significance in the universal design or plan—a name conceptually close, therefore, to the "holy prophecy" we started with,[15] by which Peter stressed how his beginning (*principium*) was in harmony with God's true will (but not necessarily predetermined by it).

As mentioned above, the ship was elaborately decorated and adorned with gilt sculptures, identifiable thanks to the contemporary engravings and drawings done by Adrian Schoonebeck,[16] his step-son Peter Picart, and by a less famous Swedish soldier and cartographer, Pieter Bergman.[17] As well as figures of cupids, nymphs, tritons, and masks (perhaps of Venetian inspiration), the side galleries at the bow featured two of the labors of Hercules: the hero's struggle with the Nemean lion and the theft of apples from the garden of the Hesperides. In this respect, one should keep in mind that the decoration was carried out in the context of the imminent war against Sweden (which began in August, 1700), a country conventionally symbolized by a lion. By this time it had already become customary to draw parallels between Hercules and Peter: huge statues of Hercules and Mars supported the vaulted triumphal arch erected on September 30, 1696 to celebrate the victory of Azov, signifying "the irresistible, superhuman force that Peter attached to a modern army."[18] This device was repeated in the panegyrics of the students of the Slavo-Greek-Latin Academy, featured in the choreography of the coronation of Ekaterina Alekseevna (1723), and reiterated in the decoration of the sovereign's funeral bier. In 1715 the tsar himself tried his hand at a drawing that portrayed Hercules slaying the Hydra (here representing Islam).[19] If the link between Peter and Hercules proved extremely stable and based on the theme of physical prowess, in the *Predestinatsiia* carvings, one element enriches the other, as often happens with symbols. The two labors of Hercules, in fact, underline the hero's two different talents: the body to body struggle with the lion reveals his strength, but in the other episode the hero not only kills the serpent guarding the garden, but also demonstrates his cunning in cheating Atlas, the other guardian. In this way the sculpture conveys two messages, first by linking the character of Hercules with the tsar and then, for those familiar with the myth, it adds a further layer of meaning. To the identification of these episodes, shared by all scholars, Valerii I. Rastorguev has recently added another:

the release of Prometheus from his chains by Hercules.[20] It is not easy to verify this reading in reproductions of the Schoonebeck etchings, but if it were correct, the image of Hercules-Peter would be enriched with yet another feature, i.e., the merit of having restored freedom to the hero who had brought fire to man, teaching him the art of building. Peter would have been familiar with this legend, as he was with those about the labors of Hercules, via the pseudo-Apollodorus' *Library*, and it was no coincidence that this was among the books that he had translated and published in 1725.

The decoration in the middle of the stern was even more complex: a sort of large medallion contains the image of Saint Peter kneeling against a background of the sea on which a small boat is sailing. That this was the focal point of the entire ornamentation is demonstrated by the fact that, lacking any wording that might identify the name of the ship, the onlooker's attention turned to this scene, as if to an emblem. The result was a series of confusing reports, in which the *Predestinatsiia* is referred to as *Moliashchiisia Apostol Petr* (*Apostle Peter at Prayer*) or simply as *Apostol Petr*, or, as in the report of the resident Dutchman, Hendrick van der Hulst, to the General States of his country, *Petrus Verschynningh* (*Apparition to Peter*).[21]

In the image, the apostle kneels in prayer while Jesus hands over to him the keys to the kingdom of Heaven, a dove descends from above with a twig (of myrtle, according to descriptions) in its beak, and a scroll on high bears the words "On this rock I shall build my church" (*Na sem kamne ia sozdam tserkov' moiu*). This gospel quotation (Matthew 16:18) introduces further motifs, such as the Peter-foundation stone equivalence, which was soon to become a very widely used topos in panegyric literature (beginning with the sermons of Feofan Prokopovich) and the identification of the tsar with the apostle, another cornerstone of tsarist propaganda for the man who was soon to inaugurate his new capital, his "paradise," as he liked to call it, with the name of Saint Petersburg.

Mariia A. Alekseeva has identified yet another emblem, created by the tsar himself, on the small boat in the background of the main scene: on it a winged figure (Time) hands a naked man the helm so that he can take charge of the boat. This image also enjoyed considerable popularity, and it was no coincidence that in his sermon devoted to the peace treaty with Sweden in 1721 Feofan Prokopovich mentioned it, explaining that the image was "meant to express Russia's military condition at the beginning of the war. Indeed was then Russia naked and defenseless."[22] The two emblems (the apostle in prayer and the boat) coexist and illuminate each other, and the delivery of new tools (the fleet) and the ability to use them form the backdrop for the promise of paradise that Jesus made directly to the apostle/tsar.

A further point of interest lies in the words written on the scroll, those which in the Gospel according to Matthew assign Peter a sort of primacy among the apostles. The relevant interpretation, as is well known, is a source of disagreement between the Orthodox and the Roman Catholic churches, based on the latter's claim to the superiority of the pope. I believe that the reference to the foundation of the church is significantly linked to a complex set of ideas that the tsar was working on at that time, when he increasingly oriented his own political-institutional discourse toward the model of imperial Rome, to the extent that he took on the titles "father of the country" and "emperor." Numerous aspects of Peter's ideology have been highlighted by Iurii Lotman and Boris Uspenskii, Richard Wortman and Viktor Zhivov, and there is no need to go over them again here;[23] in this context it is only worth pointing out that claiming Rome's historic legacy implied a competition with papal Rome, as an attentive reading of the symbols implicit in the foundation and development of Petersburg shows. Lotman and Uspenskii recount a significant oral communication on the part of G. V. Vilinbakhov, who maintained that the crossed anchors, which imitate the keys of the papal coat of arms, allude to the implement (the fleet) with which Peter (the tsar, not the apostle) planned to open the gates of his paradise. Here, too, we behold Peter the apostle (and his successor, the pope) being replaced directly by the tsar. It should not be forgotten either that in the carnivalesque ceremonies of the All-Drunken Assembly, to which the tsar attributed a very important public function because they helped discredit old customs and former authorities, a key role was played by the *kniaz'-papa* (Nikita Zotov): pope and patriarch were often united in a single parody, which, as Zhivov explains, "symbolized two forms of 'clericalism,' contrasted with the monocratic power of the tsar."[24] The power of the pope (and of the patriarch) was derided as the deceitful fruit of usurpation, while the true head of the Christian peoples became the monarch.

Nothing satirical, of course, is present in the decoration at the stern of the *Predestinatsiia*, but the superimposition of the tsar over Peter the apostle as founder of a church is evidently linked to that new civil cult of the sovereign, which precisely in this period was being strenuously promoted by Peter's propaganda, along with the idea of a radical, new beginning. And it is entirely understandable why this message was so clearly impressed in the wood of the ship to which Peter had devoted such huge personal effort and which he was bringing to the attention of the Russians and of the entire world with such pomp and circumstance.

The destiny of the *Predestinatsiia* did not, however, live up to her enormous symbolic significance: the ship did not play a decisive role in Peter's subsequent campaigns, but stood almost idle for a long time as a "sort of heirloom of the tsar."[25] In 1711, during negotiations that followed war with Turkey, attempts to obtain permission for her to pass through the straits and, via the Mediterranean, on to Petersburg, failed. So she was then sold to the Turks themselves, a sign of the tsar's pragmatism and, probably, of the fact that the pioneering stage of the Azov fleet was by then over.

NOTES

1 Or April 28: two of the main sources differ as regards the date, though April 27, given by Elagin, seems the more likely. S. I. Elagin, *Istoriia russkogo flota. Period Azovskii* (Saint Petersburg: Tipografiia Imperatorskoi Akademii Khudozhestv, 1864), 1:163; N. Ustrialov, *Istoriia tsarstvovaniia Petra Velikogo* (Saint Petersburg: Tipografiia II-go otdeleniia Sobstvennogo Ego Imperatorskogo Velikogo kantseliarii, 1858), 3:363.

2 "Mnenie o nekotorykh sudakh Voronezhskogo flota (1700, posle aprelia 25)," *Pis'ma i bumagi imperatora Petra Velikogo*, 13 vols. to date (Saint Petersburg: Gosudarstvennaia Tipografiia, 1887), 1:356-57.

3 These reactions are reported by Ustrialov, and are taken up by commentators of every era, who invariably underline the successes achieved "with the efforts of the Russian people." Ustrialov, *Istoriia tsarstvovaniia Petra Velikogo*, 3:364.

4 A synthetic account, complete with numerous illustrations, is that of V. G. Krainiukov, "K voprosu: Istoki russkogo korablestroitel'noi shkoly: 'Bozhie Predvidenie'—58-pushechnyi korabl' Azovskogo flota (1700 g.)," *Morskaia istoriia* 1 (1999): 44-62.

5 "Spisok sudov Azovskogo flota 1696-1712," in Elagin, *Istoriia russkogo flota. Period Azovskii*, 1:1-47 (appendix).

6 See, for example, Gary Marker, "Love One's Enemies: Ioasaf Krokovs'kyi's Advice to Peter in 1702," *Harvard Ukrainian Studies* 29 (2007): 193-223, which refers to events chronologically close to those we are dealing with.

7 *Pis'ma i bumagi imperatora Petra Velikogo*, 1:323-24.

8 Among the books he had printed in Amsterdam is *Simvoly i emblemata* (1705), later re-published in Russia. Aleksandr A. Morozov has studied the ships in Peter's fleet and, not having the drawings that distinguished them at his disposal, has analyzed the names and mottos, which fit into an age-old and broad European tradition. A. A. Morozov, "Emblematika barokko v literature i iskusstve petrovskogo vremeni," in *XVIII vek*, sb. 9: *Problemy literaturnogo razvitiia v Rossii pervoi treti XVIII veka* (Leningrad: Nauka, 1974), 184-226, esp. 209-15.

9 M. M. Bogoslovskii discussed them at length. Bogoslovskii, *Petr Pervyi. Materialy dlia biografii. 1672-1697*, 5 vols. (Moscow: Tsentrpoligraf, 2007), 1:189-92.

10 For details of the cult of St. Andrew, see Georgii V. Vilinbakhov, "K voprosu uchrezhdeniia ordena Andreia Pervozvannogo i evoliutsii ego znaka," in *Kul'tura i iskusstvo Petrovskogo vremeni*, ed. G. N. Komelova (Leningrad: Avrora, 1977), 144-58.

11 In fact, it refers to the prophet Abdias; the martyr of this name is commemorated on another day.

12 Ustrialov, *Istoriia tsarstvovaniia Petra Velikogo*, 3:618.

13 *Pis'ma i bumagi imperatora Petra Velikogo*, 1:752.

14 *Pis'ma i bumagi imperatora Petra Velikogo*, 1:433.

15 We should also wonder why *predvedenie* is often replaced with *predvidenie* in modern essays on the *Predestinatsiia*. *Predvidenie* (equivalent to Latin *providentia*, German *Vorsehen*) is certainly less archaic and more familiar to modern readers, but not identical in meaning. In fact, one word contains the root *ved-* (to know), while the other derives from *vid-* (to see).

16 The three engravings by Schoonebeck, the most detailed, have been studied from the historical-artistic point of view by M. A. Alekseeva, *Graviura Petrovskogo vremeni* (Leningrad: Iskusstvo, 1990), 25-34. Valerii I. Rastorguev has recently turned his attention to them several times, in particular in "Ubranstvo pervogo lineinogo korablia Rossii 'Bozhie Predvidenie' ('Goto Predestinatsiia')," *Materialy nauchno-prakticheskoi konferentsii ot 27 noiabria 2011 goda. Voronezhskoe kraevedenie: Traditsii i sovremennost'* (Voronezh, 2012), 89-107. I thank V. I. Rastorguev for having placed this and other publications of his that are quite hard to find at my disposal. The reproductions do not afford easy reading of these pictures; the details are clearer if one enlarges the images on websites, such as: http://www.russianprints.ru/printmakers/sh/schoonebeck__adrian/predestination.shtml (accessed September 9, 2014).

17 On the importance of this watercolor for the reconstruction of the technical details of the *Predestinatsiia*, see A. V. Ivanov, "Unikal'nyi risunok pervogo russkogo lineinogo korablia 'Goto Predestinatsiia,'" *Menshikovskie chteniia 2010.*

Nauchnyi al'manakh (Saint Petersburg: Izdatel'stvo "XVIII vek," 2010), 1(8):55-75.

18 Richard Wortman, *Scenarios of Power: Myth and Ceremony in Russian Monarchy*, 2 vols. (Princeton: Princeton University Press, 1995-2000), 1:43.

19 Morozov, "Emblematika barokko," 199. On the importance of classical mythology as an element of Peter's state policy, see the wealth of documentation reported by Viktor M. Zhivov and Boris A. Uspenskii, "Metamorfozy antichnogo iazychestva v istorii russkoi kul'tury XVII-XVIII veka," *Antichnost' v kul'ture i iskusstve posleduiushchikh vekov* (Moscow: Sovetskii khudozhnik, 1984), 204-85.

20 Rastorguev, "Ubranstvo pervogo lineinogo korablia," 90.

21 Bogoslovskii, *Petr Pervyi,* 4:368. The translation "Apparition of Peter," usually suggested, is at odds with the scene described. It is also worth noting that the Italian singer Filippo Balatri, who was present at the launch, understood that the tsar had given the ship his own name. See his "Vita e viaggi di Filippo Balatri," Manuscript Section, Russian State Library, f. 218, N. 1247, vol. 2, p. 12.

22 M. A. Alekseeva, "Adrian Shkhonebek. Khudozhnik v kontekste barochnoi kul'tury," *Russkoe iskusstvo epokhi barokko: Novye materialy i issledovaniia. Sbornik statei,* ed. A. G. Pobedinskaia (Saint Peterburg: Gosudarstvennyi Ermitazh, 1998), 111. This is the source of the quotation of Prokopovich's sermon, published in 1723 and now reprinted in his *Sochineniia* (Leningrad: Nauka, 1961), 115. Prokopovich, of course, alluded to the emblem as it had been engraved by Peter Picart for the frontispiece of the *Kniga ustav morskoi*, published in Petersburg in 1720.

23 I shall just recall their most enlightened contributions: Iu. M. Lotman and B. A. Uspenskii, "Otzvuki kontseptsii 'Moskva—tretii Rim' v ideologii Petra Pervogo (K probleme srednevekovoi traditsii v kul'ture barokko)," in *Khudozhestvennyi iazyk srednevekoviia*, ed. V. A. Karpushin (Moscow: Nauka, 1982), 236-49; Wortman, *Scenarios of Power*, vol. 1; Zhivov and Uspenskii, "Metamorfozy antichnogo iazychestva," 204-85; V. M. Zhivov, "Kul'turnye reformy v sisteme preobrazovanii Petra I," in *Iz istorii russkoi kul'tury*, ed. A. D. Koshelev, 5 vols. (Moscow: Iazyki russkoi kul'tury, 1996), 3:528-83.

24 V. M. Zhivov, "Kul'turnye reformy v sisteme preobrazovanii Petra I," in V. M. Zhivov, *Razyskaniia v oblasti istorii i predystorii russkoi kul'tury* (Moscow: Iazyki slavianskoi kul'tury, 2002), 413.

25 Krainiukov, "K voprosu," 51-52.

Eighteenth-Century Botanical Literature and the Origins of an Elite Russian Gardening Community[1]

Christine Ruane
(University of Tulsa)

Gary Marker's first monograph, *Publishing, Printing, and the Origins of Intellectual Life in Russia, 1700-1800*, tells the story of the printed word in eighteenth-century Russia. Part business history and part inquiry into intellectual life, Marker's book explores the development and tastes of Russia's reading public as revealed through print runs, publications lists, and networks of book sellers scattered across the empire. He argues that printing played a more circumscribed role in Russia than it did in Western Europe. Most of the initial efforts went toward publishing government documents and Orthodox prayer books, despite Peter the Great's effort to bring Western science and technology to Russia. According to Marker, "Most of the Academy [of Science]'s new books, whether translated or original, had print runs of 1,000 copies or less, and literary, philosophical, and scientific books rarely exceeded print runs of 600."[2] It was only in the second half of the century, with the rise of private publishing houses, that these entrepreneurs began to publish works that were intended to advance Russian cultural development.[3]

While acknowledging the small number of scientific publications in eighteenth-century Russia, this article seeks to understand their role in imperial life and culture by taking a preliminary look at a genre of scientific writing, the flora, which developed in Western Europe in the sixteenth and seventeenth centuries. Brought to Russia by European naturalists, these books served to reorder Russian vegetation according to Western scientific systems of classification. A close reading of these works will suggest the ways in which the Russian flora gave shape to a gardening community among the Russian elite based on Western European science.

WESTERN EUROPEAN FLORAS

The early modern period in European history is rightly called the age of discovery. Adventurers, merchants, and scientists left their native lands to explore and conquer areas outside of Europe. As employees of European colonial powers, scientists mapped these territories and their natural resources so that the home country would have a greater sense of what wonders they now supposedly controlled. Exotic spices and plants were shipped to Europe where they had a powerful impact on European visual and material culture.[4] This flood of the new and the exotic created a countervailing reaction on the part of some Europeans. Historian Alix Cooper argues that, in response to this influx of the exotic and the foreign, scientists began to study in a serious and sustained way the indigenous natural world of Europe. One of the results of this effort was the creation of a new kind of botanical work, the flora.[5]

What then were floras? Intended primarily for medical students, their purpose was to provide a complete botanical description of all the plants in a particular locality. Using a series of symbols as a kind of shorthand, they included information about where particular plants were found and their preferred growing conditions. Small in size, floras were intended for a pocket or bag. That way, physicians and medical students could carry floras with them at all times to help them identify the plants used in medicine. The language of the floras was scientific Latin, but vernacular names of plants were also included. The "author" of a flora was usually an academic physician whose institution sponsored the work, but it is important to stress that floras were always compendia of the work of many scientists and even amateurs. No one person could catalogue all the plants even in a small principality. Because scientists received academic positions outside the areas in which they grew up, physicians and naturalists compiled local floras even though they were foreigners in the locales in which they were writing.[6] By the end of the seventeenth century, European naturalists had come to accept the genre of the flora as the proper way to record botanical information. Furthermore, governments that ultimately had more financial resources than universities began to subsidize scientists to collect and publish floras for entire regions or countries.[7]

THE FLORA IN RUSSIA

In a memorandum submitted in 1716, Gottfried Leibniz, one of Europe's great scientific thinkers at that time, outlined for Peter the Great a series of government-sponsored actions to encourage scientific development, including the establishment of the Academy of Sciences. One of his suggestions was that Peter should authorize "a systematic survey of the plants, animals, and ores of Russia and her southern neighboring areas"[8] so that the tsar would have a better understanding of his empire's potential. Consequently, several such expeditions were organized, but because there were so few Russians trained in Western natural history, foreigners, primarily Germans, were invited to participate. Their job was to map these unknown lands and record the natural resources that they found. Since naturalists were used to recording unfamiliar flora and fauna, this use of foreign scientists presented no particular problem to the Russian government or the men chosen for these expeditions.

Two botanists published their expeditionary findings once they returned to Saint Petersburg. Johann Amman, a Dutch doctor and naturalist, was invited to Russia in 1733 to become professor of botany at the Saint Petersburg Academy of Sciences. He also founded the botanical garden in Saint Petersburg with its herbarium and library of rare books. In 1739, he published *Stirpium rariorum in Imperio Rutheno sponte provenientum icones et descriptiones*, a scientific description of some of the plants found in the Russian Empire. *Stirpium* was a compilation of Amman's botanical discoveries along with the unpublished work of Daniel Messerschmidt, Johann Christian Buxbaum, and Johann Georg Gmelin.[9] The same Gmelin participated in the Second Kamchatka Expedition (1733-1743) and published his botanical findings in the four-volume *Flora sibirica* between 1747 and 1769. The work contained scientific descriptions of over eleven hundred plants, many of which Gmelin was the first western European to identify.[10] While Gmelin did much of the fieldwork for this study himself, he also used the work of other colleagues to provide this portrait of Siberian vegetation.[11]

No longer analyzing the vegetation in a small local area, Amman and Gmelin produced floras about the vast spaces of the Russian Empire. Writing in Latin, Amman and Gmelin intended to describe the plants, their locations, and their origins. Since there were several competing systems of plant classification in the first half of the eighteenth century, the authors employed them equally to establish a scientific name for Russian plants, systematically incorporating them into European science.[12] Both Amman and Gmelin introduced an eighteenth-century innovation into their flora by including precise botanical drawings of many of the plants in their published accounts. As a result, the encyclopedic nature of *Stirpium* and *Flora sibirica* and the large format of these books meant that their intended home was a library or government office, not a physician's rucksack. The use of scientific Latin and European classification systems also suggests that the audience for these publications were individuals such as themselves—Western European scientists—not the Russian reading public.

Boiaryshnik (Russian)/Hawthorn (English). "Crataegus Cerasi foliis, floribus magnico," plate XXXI from Iogann Amman, _Stirpium rariorum in Imperio Rutheno sponte provenientium icones et descriptiones_ (Saint Petersburg: Ex Typografia Academiae Scientarum, 1739), 195-96. Dumbarton Oaks Research Library and Collection, Rare Book Room, Washington, DC.

EIGHTEENTH-CENTURY RUSSIAN GARDENING

Before the arrival of western European naturalists, the inhabitants of the Russian Empire lived in a world of local tradition and culture. A single plant found in many parts of the empire might have multiple names depending upon the languages of the areas in which the plant grew. And these different ethnic groups and tribes would have developed distinctive usages for native plants that could vary greatly from locale to locale. In addition to indigenous plants, vegetation from other parts of the world—Byzantium, Central Asia, and the Far

East—had found a home in medieval and early modern Russian gardens.[13] As was the case in Western Europe, this botanical information was collected and compiled in herbals (*travniki* or *lechebniki* in Russian). The purpose of these collections was to gather together information about plants used in medicine. Because of this, Russian herbals were a mixture of information about native plants and older botanical and medical knowledge. Each author combined local practice with medieval western European and ancient Greek medical texts. Consequently, the Russian herbals sometimes gave information about plants that did not grow in northern Europe or gave contradictory medical advice. Despite these drawbacks, the Russian herbals remained an important native source of botanical information until the end of the eighteenth century.[14]

While Tsar Aleksei Mikhailovich did much to bring new life, including ideas and plants from Western Europe, to the Kremlin and royal estate gardens, it was his son, Peter the Great, who popularized the fashion for Western European gardens in Russia. In his new capital city of Saint Petersburg and its suburban palaces, Peter had constructed first Dutch and later French gardens. To assist with the design and implementation of building these new gardens, foreign gardeners came to Russia, bringing with them new designs and new plants. Because the climate and soil conditions of Western Europe were very different from those of the Russian Empire, gardeners relied heavily upon greenhouses and orangeries to grow non-indigenous plants. Russia's wealthiest aristocrats followed the tsar's lead and built themselves palaces and pleasure gardens based on Western European designs. In this way, Western European pleasure gardens and a penchant for exotic plants became part of the larger Europeanization process that Peter initiated in the Russian Empire.

This process of cultural reform accelerated when, in 1762, Emperor Peter III decreed that the Russian nobility was freed from mandatory state service. While the contours of this emancipation are still being studied, certain aspects are clear. Although some nobles continued to serve the government either in the military or the bureaucracy, others retreated to their rural estates. Their arrival was typically not a happy one, as many estates had been neglected in their owners' absence. For the more industrious of the nobility there was only one thing left to do—transform their estates into economically productive oases of European culture and landscape design.[15]

The introduction of western European plants and gardening information created a situation comparable to that of Western and Central Europe two centuries earlier: the exotic trumped the indigenous. Russian aristocrats fell in love with non-native plants such as the pineapple, and were determined to grow them on their estates. To ensure a ready supply of exotic plants, aristocrats hired foreign gardeners to supervise their serfs in the cultivation of non-native plants in special greenhouses and orangeries. Among the elite, possession of exotic plants became a way to demonstrate European sophistication, but in order to grow these exotic plants accurate information was needed to ensure their survival.

One scientist, Peter Simon Pallas, led the effort to provide the necessary information to the Russian reading public, not just to European scientists. In one of his many publications, Pallas identified his mission as an opportunity to spread an understanding of botany throughout the Russian Empire.[16] A gifted scientist and naturalist, he came to Russia from Berlin in 1767 at the invitation of Catherine the Great to join the Academy of Sciences. In the 1770s Pallas traveled around the Russian Empire, recording his observations of the flora and fauna. These records would serve as the raw data for his scientific publications. One result of his scientific explorations was the publication of *Flora Rossica*, which he dedicated to his royal patron Catherine the Great. The scientist pulled together previous botanical work and combined it with his own to create what he hoped would be a comprehensive scientific analysis of plant life found in the Russian Empire.[17] At first glance, *Flora Rossica* appeared to follow Amman and Gmelin in its presentation. Each plant was described in much detail in Latin, but Pallas added richly colored botanical prints for each plant. This made *Flora Rossica* a much more attractive work that could be admired not just for its scholarly erudition, but also for the beauty of the plants. More importantly, while the text was in Latin, Pallas included the name of each plant according to different systems of plant classification and in multiple languages. These languages included the major Western European and Slavic languages, but also plant names from the non-Russian speaking areas of the empire. The inclusion of indigenous names allowed Russian scientists to recognize familiar plants by their scientific names. At the same time, they could understand indigenous vegetation as part of a much larger family of plants, extending far beyond the borders of the empire.

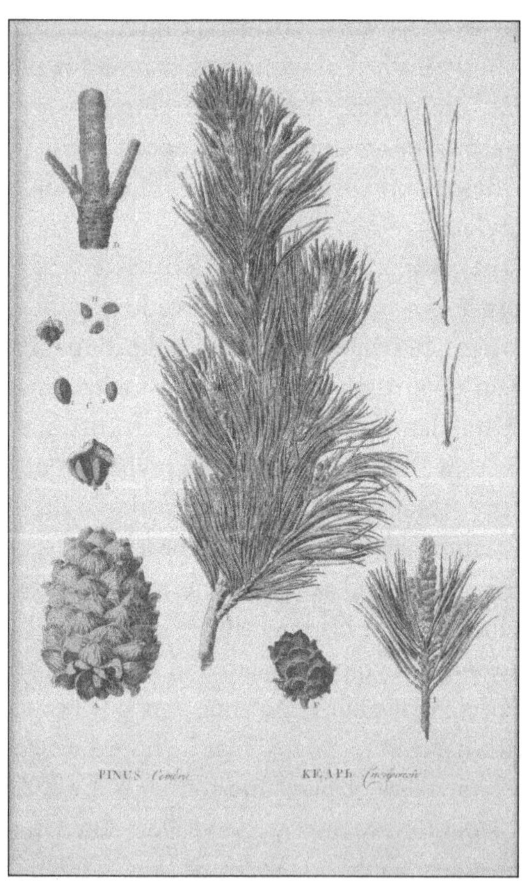

"*Pinus Cembra Kedr sibirskii* (Siberian cedar)," plate ii from P. S. Pallas, *Flora Rossica*, vol. 1 (Saint Petersburg, 1774), Dumbarton Oaks Research Library and Collection, Rare Book Room, Washington, DC. While Amman used only the Latin name for the plants in his flora, Pallas included both the Latin and the Russian name for his prints.

In addition to the scholarly *Flora Rossica*, Pallas also wanted to reach beyond the rather small number of individuals that constituted his reading public of fellow scientists. His first attempt was published in 1779 in an Academy of Sciences' popular science publication, *Akademicheskie izvestiia*.[18] In his essay, "O sibirskikh derev'iakh i kustakh," Pallas introduced his readers to the many varieties of Siberian trees and bushes that he had encountered on his travels throughout the region.[19] Rather than present his findings in scientific Latin, he wrote the article in Russian and used the vernacular names with the scientific names in parentheses. He began his article with a complaint that the English desire for exotic trees had been copied by the French, Dutch, Swedes, and Germans. But, he argued, Russians did not need to ape their European counterparts because they could plant Siberian trees that not only were suited to the climate, but were just as stunning as the cedars of Lebanon, which the English were importing.[20] For every tree and bush, Pallas explained where they originated in Siberia, the conditions under which they grew, recommendations for planting, and their uses as food, medicine, or in industry. In other words, he provided the kind of information that would be useful to a gardener or to a landowner improving his estate. Indeed, Pallas as a learned botanist was speaking directly to his aristocratic readers, trying to encourage them to abandon their desire to replicate Western European fashions. He wanted them to consider Siberian vegetation as just as beautiful as trees from Lebanon or North America, but better adapted to Russian growing conditions. Landscape historian E. P. Shchukina credits Pallas with introducing the Siberian larch (*listvennitsa*), fir tree (*pikhta*), and yellow acacia (*gorokhovnik*) into central Russian estate gardens.[21]

In 1780, Pallas spent a month on the estate of Prokopii A. Demidov, a member of one of Russia's wealthiest and most powerful families. An avid gardener, Demidov had a vast estate on the Moscow River near the Donskoi Monastery. In 1756 he had built a house and created vast gardens with orangeries and greenhouses filled with exotic plants. During his stay at Demidov's, Pallas and his host agreed that the naturalist would publish an inventory of his vast collection. In this work, instead of describing the indigenous plants that grew in the surrounding

КАТАЛОГЪ

РАСТѢНІЯМЪ НАХОДЯЩИМСЯ ВЪ САДУ

Его Превосходительства, Статскаго Дѣйствительнаго Совѣтника,

Прокофья Акинфіевича Демидова

CLASSIS I.	ПЕРВОЙ КЛАСЪ
Monandria.	*Монандрїа.*
1. Canna *indica.* ♃ *vir.*	Канна *Индика* ♃ *ор.*
2. — *anguſtifolia.* ♃ *vir.*	— *ангустифолїя.* ♃ *ор.*
3. Amomum *Zingiber.* ♃ *vap.*	Амомумъ *Цингиберъ.* ♃ *ларн.*
4. Kaempferia *Galanga.* ♃ *vap.*	Кемферіа *Галанга.* ♃ *ларн.*
5. Boerhavia *erecta.* ♃ *vap.*	Бургавїа *еректа.* ♃ *ларн.*
6. — *diffuſa.* ♃ *vap.*	— *дифуза.* ♃ *ларн.*
7. — *hirſuta.* ♃ *vap.*	— *гирзута* ♃ *ларн.*
8 — *ſcandens.* ♃ *vap.*	— *скандексъ.* ♃ *ларн*

A 9.

A page showing the plant names in Demidov's gardens. The elaborate "4" indicates a perennial, the Russian abbreviation, or, indicates that the plant should be placed in an orangery, and the Russian abbreviation, *parn*, means that the plant belongs in a hotbed or forcing frame. From P. S. Pallas, *Katalog rasteniiam nakhodiashchimsia v Moskve v sadu . . . Prokopiia Akinfievicha Demidova* (Saint Petersburg, 1781), 1. Gray Herbarium Library. Harvard University.

countryside, Pallas focused his attention on the plants that Demidov had acquired for his estate. Indeed, in Pallas's *Katalog rasteniiam*, an understanding of botany was more important to him than a strict accounting of local vegetation. Consequently, Pallas included the Latin names (along with Russian transliterations) of the more than two thousand plants found on the Demidov estate. As any flora would do, he also provided simple gardening instructions by using a set of symbols that indicated the type of plant (annual, perennial, etc.) and where to plant it (orangery, greenhouse, etc.).[22] The use of the Russian language and planting instructions in the text meant that landlords now had practical information about the plants that could be cultivated on their estates in a small book that they or their head gardeners could carry in their pocket. Furthermore, this publication would allow them to familiarize themselves with European plant classification systems, without having to learn Latin. Rather than keep botanical knowledge in the hands of foreign scientists such as himself, Pallas hoped to foster an appreciation of exotic and native plants and the scientific knowledge that would allow them to flourish. In so doing, Pallas transformed the genre of the local flora to meet the needs of a growing Russian elite gardening culture.

At the end of the eighteenth century, another German scientist made a further contribution to the botanical literature in Russia, combining the scientific and the medical with the popular. In 1797 Peter Gofman began publishing a multi-volume popular scientific work, *Sobranie liubopytstva dostoinykh predmetov iz tsarstva proizrastenii* (1797-1810).[23] Gofman was a medical doctor who immigrated to Russia in the 1780s and received permission to practice medicine in 1786.[24] In his adopted homeland, he served as medical doctor at Russia's first clinic that dealt with venereal diseases, the Kalinkinskii Institute, and as professor at the Saint Petersburg Medical-Surgical Academy.[25]

As was true of so many European-trained physicians, Gofman also had a clear interest in botany and particularly medicinal plants. Imbued with the spirit of the Enlightenment with its emphasis on classification, improvement, and utility, he began publication of his *Sobranie* in 1797. His purpose was to write about those plants used "in medicine and in the household" and to foster "the distribution of generally useful knowledge: attention, care, and observation."[26] To do this, he produced a series of short pamphlets that, all told, contained stunning illustrations of two hundred plants. Whereas Pallas had included ethnographic descriptions in his writings on botany, Gofman emphasized the medical uses of each plant and where to place it in the garden. He also included the Latin names along with their French and German equivalents. To give some examples, in his entry on *roza tsentifol'naia* (*Rosa centifolia*, sometimes known as the cabbage rose), Gofman recommended planting it in pleasure and kitchen gardens. In the eighteenth century, this particular rose had many home uses: it was an essential ingredient in rose water, rose jam, vinegar, and a number of drinks. Another plant, *maioran* (*Origanum majorana*, i.e. marjoram), he recommended planting in the kitchen garden. Used in medicine, marjoram helped with the treatment of the stomach, menstrual cycle, breathlessness, and colds.[27]

In addition to providing medical information and beautiful botanical prints, Gofman included some of the history of his publication, which allows us a tantalizing glimpse at the growing influence of floras. The Rare Book Room at the Dumbarton Oaks Research Library possesses a partial copy of Gofman's *Sobranie* that came from the

Peter Gofman, "Glorioso superba *Tshcheslavitsa velichavaia* (Flame Lilly)," unpublished print. Dumbarton Oaks Research Library and Collection. Rare Book Room, Washington, DC.

library of Tsar Paul. These large format pamphlets were clearly a presentation copy for the royal family, as they contain individual dedications to Empress Maria Fedorovna, the future Tsar Alexander I, and Grand Duchess Aleksandra Pavlovna, the fiancée of Archduke Joseph of Austria, governor of Hungary. The stunning pamphlets must have appealed to Maria Fedorovna, as she was an accomplished gardener in her own right.[28] This copy demonstrates that royal patronage continued to be important for Gofman's project, just as it had been for Pallas's.

Beginning with the publication of his fifth notebook in 1801, Gofman began to innovate by dedicating certain plates to members of the Russian nobility "out of gratitude." As it turns out, Gofman received financial support from some of Russia's most prominent families—the Sheremetevs, Iusupovs, Lobanov-Rostovskiis, Musin-Pushkins, Razumovskiis, and Golitsyns—to help with publications costs. Over eighty individuals are mentioned by name.[29] Reasons why so many nobles contributed to Gofman's project are not hard to find. Gofman's publication was intended to provide them with a list of plants that were not only beautiful, but also useful. For instance, among his recommendations are *Sarsaparel'* (*Smilax sarsaparilla*, or sarsaparilla), native to Mexico and Brazil, and *Kofeinoe derevo* (*Coffea arabica*), native to Arabia. Despite the rather far-flung origins of these plants, Gofman argued for their place in Russian gardens or greenhouses. As a physician at one of Russia's hospitals dealing with venereal diseases, he claimed that sarsaparilla had much success in curing such illnesses.[30] Not only would such plants save their owners from buying expensive medical concoctions, exotic plants would also enhance the prestige of the families that owned them.

By 1803 Gofman retired from his position at the Medical-Surgical Academy. He had planned to move to Moscow to continue working on *Sobranie*. However, some unexplained misfortune derailed his plans, and he ended up in the village of Noskov in Dmitrevskii district. Thanks to his aristocratic connections in Moscow, Gofman's patrons quickly provided him with a subsidy so that he could continue his work. In his next pamphlet he thanked the "Moscow personages of high rank" for allowing him the opportunity to continue his botanical work. He complimented them on their single-minded love and goodwill toward works of patriotic zeal and diligence.[31]

As a result of his patrons' generosity, Gofman was able to move to Moscow where he had greater access to the plant materials and books that he needed. There he became acquainted with Khariton A. Chebotarev, rector of Moscow University from 1803 to 1805. Chebotarev helped Gofman with "needed sources and information." As rector he could have granted the Saint Petersburg doctor access to the university's botanical garden and apothecary garden as well as introduced him to other botanists and scientists.[32] Thus, Gofman's *Sobranie* provided an important bridge between the scientific community and the Russian landed elite. In their native tongue, Russian landlords could now gain access to important botanical and medical information. Meanwhile, the colorful prints provided them with a greater appreciation of the beauty of the natural world, which they could try to replicate in their gardens.

CONCLUSION

As this brief overview of eighteenth-century Russian flora suggests, these publications may have been small in number, but they played a critical role in disseminating information based on Western European botanical theories and practice. As Russian elites became caught up in the desire to mimic their Western European counterparts in everything from clothing and houses all the way down to the exotic plants they favored, the Russian landed aristocracy needed to procure the correct plants and obtain accurate information about how to grow them. The eighteenth-century floras contained this information. And while the first floras of Amman and Gmelin were not really intended for a Russian reading public, by mid-century naturalists were producing works that the elites would want to purchase for their own use. As the Russian nobility began to build elegant gardens and parks based on the information contained in the flora, the demand for floras and scientific information increased. And while the print runs for the floras may not have been large, those aristocrats who possessed them could share the information with neighboring landowners either through correspondence or in conversation.[33] Thus, from this rather inconspicuous beginning in the early eighteenth century, the floras, a genre that brought together academic and popular science, fostered the development of Russian botanical writing, and helped create and sustain an elite gardening community in imperial Russia for many generations to come.

NOTES

1 A fellowship in the Garden and Landscape Studies program at the Dumbarton Oaks Research Library provided financial and research support for this article. I want to thank Linda Lott, head of the Rare Book Room, for introducing me to the texts described here. I also want to thank Anatole Tchikine, Christine Worobec, and the editors of this volume for their critical reading of an earlier version of this article.

2 Gary Marker, *Publishing, Printing, and the Origins of Intellectual Life in Russia, 1700-1800* (Princeton: Princeton University Press, 1985), 61.

3 Ibid., 230-31.

4 Daniela Bleichmar, *Visible Empire: Botanical Expeditions and Visual Culture in the Hispanic Enlightenment* (Chicago: University of Chicago Press, 2012).

5 Alix Cooper, *Inventing the Indigenous: Local Knowledge and Natural History in Early Modern Europe* (Cambridge: Cambridge University Press, 2007).

6 This summary of the development of the flora is from ibid., 51-86.

7 Ibid., 116-51.

8 Alexander Vucinich, *Science in Russia Culture: A History to 1860* (Stanford: Stanford University Press, 1963), 46-47.

9 Iogann Amman, "Praefatio," *Stirpium rariorum in Imperio Rutheno sponte provenientium icones et descriptiones* (Saint Petersburg: Ex Typographia Academiae Scientarum, 1739), no page numbers; "Amman (Iogann)," *Entsiklopedicheskii slovar'*, 41 vols. in 82 books, ed. I. E. Andreevskii (Saint Petersburg: I. A. Efron, 1890-1907), 1:653-54; and "Buksbaum (Iogann-Khristian Buxbaum)," *Entsiklopedicheskii slovar'*, 4:877.

10 Vucinich, *Science*, 100.

11 W. Watson, "An Account of a Treatise, presented to the Royal Society, intitled, *Flora Sibirica sive historia plantarum Sibiriae*," *Proceedings of the Royal Society* 22 (1753): 144-45.

12 Vucinich, *Science*, 100.

13 For more on this, see V. D. Chernyi, *Russkie srednevekovye sady* (Moscow: Rukopisnye pamiatniki Drevnei Rusi, 2010).

14 European herbals also provided medical information. See Agnes Arber, *Herbals: Their Origin and Evolution, A Chapter in the History of Botany, 1470-1670*, 2nd ed. (Darien: Nafner, 1970). For more on the herbal as the predecessor of the flora, see Cooper, *Inventing the Indigenous*, chapter 1. For an introduction to the literature on Russian herbals, see T. A. Isachenko, ed., *Prokhladnyi vertograd* (Moscow: Arkheograficheskii tsentr, 1997) and A. B. Ippolitova, *Russkie rukopisnye travniki XVII-XVIII vekov: Issledovanie fol'klora i etnobotaniki* (Moscow: Indrik, 2008).

15 The literature on estate gardens and parks is rapidly growing. For an introduction, see the essays found in the journal, *Russkaia usad'ba: sbornik Obshchestva izucheniia russkoi usad'by*, which began publication in 1994.

16 Peter Simon Pallas, *Katalog rasteniiam nakhodiashchimsia v Moskve v sadu ego Prevokhoditel'stva, Deistvitel'nogo Statskogo Sovetnika i Imperatorskogo Vospitatel'nogo Doma Znamenitogo Blagodetelia, Prokopiia Akinfievicha Demidova* (Saint Petersburg: Pri Imperatorskoi Akademii Nauk, 1781), xxix.

17 Peter Simon Pallas, *Flora Rossica* (Saint Petersburg: Ex Typographia Imperiali J. J. Weitbrecht, 1774-1778). Only one volume in two parts was ever published.

18 A. G. Dement'ev, *Russkaia periodicheskaia pechat' (1702-1896 gg.): Spravochnik* (Moscow: Gosudarstvennoe izdatel'stvo politicheskoi literatury, 1959), 59-60.

19 Peter Simon Pallas, "O sibirskikh derev'iakh i kustakh, mogushchikh sluzhit' k ukrashcheniiu i zavedeniiu roshchei v severnykh stranakh," *Akademicheskie izvestiia* 1 (1779): 341-78.

20 Ibid., 341-42.

21 E. P. Shchukina, *Podmoskovnye usadebnye sady i parki kontsa XVIII veka* (Moscow: Rossiiskii nauchno-issledovatel'skii institut kul'turnogo i prirodnogo naslediia imeni D. S. Likhacheva, 2007), 24.

22 Ibid, xxx.

23 Petr Gofman, *Sobranie liubopytsva dostoinykh predmetov iz tsarstva proizrastenii* (Moscow: V Universitetskoi tipografii u Lobiia, 1797-1810). This work is a set of fourteen notebooks, but is considered to be one book. There are no page numbers in the text. There are instead plate numbers for the botanical engravings and their descriptions. In the following footnotes, for the sake of clarity I will give first the notebook and then the plate number.

24 "Gofman, Petr Martynovich," http://dic.academic.ru/dic.nsf/enc__biography/38815/Gofman (accessed April 14, 2014)

25 "Gofman (Petr)," *Entsiklopedicheskii slovar'*, 9:452. For more on the Kalinkinskii Institute, see "Kalinkinskaia bol'nitsa," http://ru.wikipedia.org/wiki (accessed April 14, 2014). See "Akademii Mediko-Khirurgicheskiia," *Entsiklopedicheskii slovar'*, 1:259-60.

26 Gofman, *Sobranie*, 10: no page number.

27 Ibid., 12:148 (marjoram), 12:156 (cabbage rose).

28 Suzanne Massie, *Pavlovsk: The Life of a Russian Palace* (Boston: Little, Brown and Company, 1990), 77-92. The first notebook is missing from both the Dumbarton Oaks and Russian State Library microfilm, so it is not clear whether Gofman also included a dedication to Tsar Paul.

29 Gofman, *Sobranie*, passim.

30 Ibid., 8:63 (sarsaparilla), 8:67 (coffee).

31 Ibid., 9: no page number. Sarsaparilla is still used in the treatment of venereal diseases: http://www.webmd.com/vitamins-supplements/ingredientmono-379-SARSAPARILLA.aspx?activeIngredientId=379&activeIngredientName=SARSAPARILLA (accessed August 1, 2014).

32 Gofman, *Sobranie*, 12: no page number.

33 For more on these information networks among the Russian nobility, see Katherine Pickering Antonova, *An Ordinary Marriage: The World of a Gentry Family in Provincial Russia* (New York: Oxford University Press, 2013).

Catherine's Liberation of the Greeks: High-Minded Discourse and Everyday Realities[1]

Elena Smilianskaia
*(National Research University Higher School of Economics, Moscow)**

In the small village of Kampos on the island of Tinos in the Greek archipelago can be found a remarkable Orthodox church dedicated to Saint Catherine. According to the story preserved on Tinos (no Russian documents confirming the story have yet been discovered), the small Orthodox community of Kampos quarreled unsuccessfully with the Catholic majority on the island about the allotment of land for building an Orthodox church. In 1771, through the auspices of a priest, this community turned to Count Aleksei Orlov, director of a Russian military expedition against the Turks in the Aegean archipelago, with a request for help. They received not only authority to build the church, but also a handsome donation for the project. According to legend, Orlov established only one condition for his gift: that this church be dedicated to the "imperial saint," Saint Catherine.[1] Accordingly, Empress Catherine II sent an icon of Saint

Catherine (now lost) for this church.[2] Physical confirmation of the story of Russian aid in constructing the church comes from a Russian coat of arms mounted on the church's northern portal (Figure 11).

This marble bas-relief, featuring the two-headed eagle with an image of Saint George embedded on a shield on its chest, was probably carved by an eighteenth-century Greek stone-worker. The master might have copied the two-headed eagle and Saint George from any piece of Russian money, but the uniqueness of the piece lies in another aspect of the work: above the heraldic shield the master placed two male figures in pantaloons and pointed caps, one of whom is holding a cross. During the reign of Catherine II, the Russian Empire's coat of arms did not include this upper part. The figures of the two heralds, the archangels Michael and Gabriel, appeared on the Russian coat of arms only much later, in the middle of the nineteenth century. The symbolism of the composition on the Tinos church, created during the struggle of the Russian Empire and the Greeks against the Turks, is remarkable: as

Russian coat of arms mounted above the northern portal, Church of Saint Catherine, Kampos, Greece. Personal collection of the author

the following exposition will demonstrate, it fully reflects the hopes and feelings of the Greeks in the Ottoman Empire (indeed, perhaps it is they who are depicted on the crest) who were prepared to submit to the Russian eagle in the name of emancipation from the heathen Turks. In Russia at this time there appeared more works (two of them now held in the Tret'iakov Gallery) that were no less remarkable: an unknown artist put to canvas a depiction of Aleksei Orlov together with grateful Greeks after the Battle of Chesme in 1770;[3] and in 1771 Stefano Torelli completed his famous painting, *Allegory on the Victory of Russia over the Turks and Tatars*, in which Catherine is depicted in the helmet of Athena, surrounded by the freed peoples of the Balkans.[4] Thus both Greek and Russian depictions communicate that Russia's intervention during the critical early phase of this conflict was welcomed by the Greek population, which heralded the Russians as its liberators in the face of Ottoman oppression. As we shall see, the Russians continued to tell themselves this story even after the immediate political interests of Greeks and Russians began to diverge.

Emancipation of the Greeks became for Catherine an important, although not exclusively so, aspect of her southern policy; other goals along included countering the Turkish threat, conquest of the Crimea, and Russian penetration of the Mediterranean "concert of powers." For appealing to European popular opinion, the idea of Greek emancipation long proved the most successful cover for resolving other, altogether more pragmatic problems of the Russian Empire. However, at least at the beginning, in the early 1770s, Russia's engagement in the region rather idealistically aimed for more than diplomatic self-interest. As the partially-worn crest on the Saint Catherine church at Tinos indicates, the Greeks (at least the Greeks of the Aegean archipelago) understood Catherine's intention, and placed their hopes for winning independence and creating their own state in Russian support. This early confluence of the goals of Russian imperial power and those of their Greek coreligionists has been lost to history because Catherine's Greek idea, and her Mediterranean policy in general, underwent a serious transformation during the first two decades of her reign. Early idealism gave way to more practical international politics. Examining the hopes of the Osman Greeks and the messages of the Tinos crest in the context of Russian military and diplomatic activities allows us to understand how the Russian empress, who between 1762 and the early 1770s promised to aid the Greeks in their quest for an independent state, by the early 1780s would all but ignore the Greeks themselves when she decided to grant them (with Austrian help) their emancipation from the Turks.

"SOME ADVANTAGES" FOR THE GREEKS

The idea of Greek liberation appeared very early in Catherinian discourse—only four months after her accession to the throne in 1762. At that time Grigorii Orlov introduced the empress to Grigorii Papazoli, a Russian officer who was Greek or Macedonian by origin. Soon Papazoli and two other Greeks—Manolis Saro, resident of Saint Petersburg, and Ioannis Palatino, who lived in the Venetian territories—left Trieste for the Peloponnese with a secret paper from the Russian empress.[5] The original text of the empress's letter was lost when the Russian emissaries were captured by pirates, but later copies of the text circulated throughout the Greek colonies even in the nineteenth century.[6] From these later copies we know that the gist of the letter was that Catherine, as a true Orthodox ruler, was seeking a suitable occasion to take up arms against the enemy of the Orthodox faith in order to liberate the Greeks living under the Ottoman yoke ("*opolchitsia protiv vraga very pravoslavnyia i svobodit' narod grecheskii pravoslavnyi, nakhodiashchikhsia v plenenii ottomanskom*"). The Greeks, it seems, understood this to mean that the Russian empress would soon dispatch an army dedicated primarily to their emancipation. These hopes were supported by rumors that circulated for centuries in the Balkans about a "fair-haired race from the North" that would liberate the Greeks, and about "the Marble Emperor who slept below the Golden Gate of Constantinople [and who] would rise and restore the Byzantine Empire."[7]

Like the Greeks, the Russian empress and her circle also mistook their own dreams for reality. Preliminary information received from the

Balkans assured Catherine and the Orlov brothers that the Greeks were ready to take up arms against the Turks, that they were waiting only for the Russians to initiate the uprising that would allow the Greeks to revive their former state and its flourishing culture. Perhaps Catherine imagined the Greeks as modern Spartans, ancient heroes now committed to the Orthodox cross. The empress's papers—especially her correspondence with Voltaire—show that the Enlightened ruler of the Russian Empire was attracted to the Spartan ideal, one that also found considerable resonance in the West at this time.[8] It follows, then, that when the Russo-Turkish War began in 1768, Catherine sent her first squadrons to the Peloponnese, hoping to attract real military support from the Greeks, especially from the Greeks living in formerly Spartan areas (in the Mani region).

It is evident, then, that already at the start of the Russo-Turkish War of 1768-1774 the main problem on both sides of the anti-Turkish coalition—Greek and Russian—was a misunderstanding of the nature of their collaboration.[9] The Greeks expected a mighty invasion by a great power bearing emancipation. But Catherine herself was only prepared to contribute to the independent struggle of the Greeks, and to use their help in her own efforts against the Turks. In other words, both sides exaggerated the potential power and commitment of the other.

At the beginning of the war (November 27, 1768), Grigorii Orlov, Catherine's favorite and an enthusiastic partisan for the idea of supporting Russia's Greek co-religionists in their war against the Turks, first openly raised the Greek question at a session of the recently-created Supreme Council (*Sovet pri Vysochaishem dvore*). For now, Orlov only proposed the creation of a monetary fund to support the liberation of the Orthodox.[10] Orlov probably expected that the money of this institution could help the Greek rebellion, and then gather the Orthodox co-religionists "under the protection of Russia" (*pod protektsiiu Rossii*). Remarkably, however, Grigorii Orlov supposed that the Greeks would select their own rulers and form of governance: "to choose their own lords, leaving them freedom in their choice" (*sdelat' raznykh vladel'tsev, ostavia im v vybore voliu*).[11]

Of course Orlov expressed an opinion shared by the empress, but by 1769 the Russian empress herself was much more prudent in her promises to the Greeks than she had been in 1762. Now she proposed that in the Russo-Turkish War all combatants—Russians as well as the Balkan peoples—use whatever advantages each might obtain: "keeping those advantages that they obtain through their brave feats in this our war with the treacherous enemy" (*sokhranenie tekh vygodnostei kotorye oni svoim khrabrym podvigom v sei nashei voine s verolomnym nepriiatelem oderzhat*).[12] In the future, the empress's play on words—whether the Greeks were worthy or unworthy (*dostoiny* or *nedostoiny*) of the freedom that their "Russian heroes" delivered to them—appears frequently in Catherine's discourse. More and more often the disappointing fact that the Greeks were unworthy became for the empress an excuse for the failure of her ambitious plans.[13]

When the first squadrons under the command of Admiral Grigorii Andreevich Spiridov reached the southern Peloponnese in February, 1770, Greeks of the Mani region met them enthusiastically. But it was difficult to imagine these Russian forces as the army of a great power: no more than sixty Russian soldiers and fourteen hundred Greeks made up the two newly created military units. Consequently, despite some initial victories, defeat seemed inevitable.

In May, 1770, the empress, taking pleasure from the first successful naval actions, already spoke more carefully about the rebirth of an independent Greece, although she expressed satisfaction in recognizing the names of ancient persons and places: "Evidently," she wrote in a letter to Voltaire, "Greece may again be free, but it is now very far from that condition in which it once was; nevertheless, it is pleasing to hear recalled the names of those places that washed over our ears in childhood." Voltaire replied, evidently in all seriousness, that "Your undertaking in Greece is the most praiseworthy event of the last two thousand years."[14]

But defeat in Morea and unsuccessful land operations soon followed, and only with difficulty did the Russian fleet establish contact with the scanty Russian ground detachments and Balkan insurgents. On the other hand, the Russian fleet itself (without Greek help!)

enjoyed several successes, including the great victory at Chesme (June 24-25, 1770). Thereafter the Russian fleet became master of the eastern Mediterranean, blockading the Dardanelles and Constantinople, and inspecting all ships sailing in the region. All told, it appeared that the Russians might receive a great deal from the war.

But what about the Greeks? Might they achieve their freedom? After the battles in Morea the empress had some reason to hope for the resurrection of a glorious, classically inspired Greece. But her discourse increasingly substituted for the word "freedom" (*vol'nost'*) expressions about "possession" (*vladenie*) and "protection" (*pokrovitel'stvo*). In her correspondence with Voltaire, for example, Catherine expressed these wishes in unmistakable terms:

> For Greece to come back to life depends entirely upon the Greeks. I did all that I could to complete the geographical maps with the connection from Corinth to Moscow. I don't know what will be the consequences of that. Your dear Greeks gave many proofs of their ancient bravery, and they have some spirit, but in their minds they leave much to be desired.[15]

Catherine's subjects proved less careful in discussing the Greek theme. After first news about *victories* in Morea they already spoke not about the freedom of the Greeks, but about the subjection or subordination of Greece to the Russian throne. In 1770, in Peterhof, on the feast day of Saints Peter and Paul, Platon (Levshin) delivered a sermon in which he said: "Before spring with its saintly beauty made glad our eyes . . . the Peloponnese and Lacedaemon, much praised in antiquity, were already found under the Russian scepter."[16] Meanwhile, the *Saint Petersburgskiye Vedomosti* concluded that "soon the *sacred cross and Russian eagle* will be raised everywhere on the Morean peninsula."[17]

Only after the Chesme victory did Catherine finally speak openly about acquisitions in Greece. Even then, however, the empress was quite careful when, in notes about a possible peace treaty with the Ottoman Empire, she wrote that, as spoils for the costly but victorious war, she wanted only a small island with a port in which to install a garrison, and that she did not need a large island like Rhodes, Cyprus, or Crete (January 4, 1771).[18] It is indicative that, as in the summer of 1770, so also in January of 1771 the archbishop Platon (Levshin) in a court sermon spoke openly about seizures of Greek land and about Greek possessions. One can only guess with whose secret thoughts he wished to identify:

> The Russian fleet from the remotest north, watching over the shores of Europe, flew to the east and immediately overthrew [Turkish] dominion in the Archipelago. . . . The peoples living there accepted them as their rescuers and saviors. And what do I say? The Russian has never gone anywhere where he was not invited by the inhabitants of that land and was not met with unalloyed joy. Witness to this fact are Moldavia, Wallachia, Morea, the Archipelago, and Georgia. And this very natural order of things makes [Russia] the legal possessor of those places. For who can rule a people legally if he is not loved and does not provide peace and well-being?[19]

No one in Saint Petersburg at that time could have known that at that very moment on the island of Paros in that same archipelago, Admiral Spiridov had begun to bring the inhabitants of the islands into allegiance to Catherine and to create an Aegean principality. By the same token, Spiridov could not have known about speeches like those of Platon!

RUSSIAN PATERNALISM, OR HOW THEY TAUGHT THE GREEKS TO BUILD A STATE

When Catherine and the Orlovs discussed the idea of Greek liberty (*volnost'*) they could hardly have had a detailed plan of state-building for the lands liberated from the Ottoman yoke. Indeed, they left to the Greeks the choice of rule "in their liberty." And the empress, like her favorite, Grigorii Orlov, at that time preferred to think that the Greeks, making use of the Russian presence, would be able to create their own state. In a letter of Count Nikita Panin, chief of the Russian foreign office, one finds a proposal to build in Greece "something like the Dutch states."[20]

By late autumn, 1770, the Russian command (primarily Aleksei Orlov and Grigorii Spiridov in Orlov's absence) decided to create the main base of the Russian Fleet in the Mediterranean on the island of Paros in the Bay of Naousa. And so the Russian idea of a Greek state got its start not in the Peloponnese but in the Bay of Naousa.[21] Reality forced the military to divide the islands of the Greek archipelago into those that were prepared to take an oath of loyalty to Russia and receive its protection, and those that, declining to take the oath, remained as conquered territories during the war. Russia's "own" islands, whose residents took an oath to Catherine and created an "Archipelago principality," had to bear the burden of war (mainly to supply food and pay taxes), but received in return the protection of the Russian army.[22] Others obeyed the Russians "as conquerors," as Aleksei Orlov wrote in 1770.[23] They paid no taxes, but did have to accede to military levies. Meanwhile, the Russian navy created a new administration and capital on Paros, and local administrations on other islands. Consequently, this became the first Russian attempt to create an overseas base, albeit here with a co-religionist population.

So, having been confirmed on the islands of the Aegean, these military men—not policy-makers—saw the need to create some sort of state structure, and they could hardly look to the Dutch example invoked earlier by Panin. Admiral Spiridov by and large acted on his own when he imposed an oath of loyalty to Catherine on the deputies and elders of the islands, creating for them rules and laws. In this he never deceived the islands' residents about the nature of their impending freedoms. These "freedoms," for which Spiridov nobly took full responsibility, did not depend on Admiral Spiridov nor on the "plenipotentiary general of Her Majesty Catherine the Second of All Russia," Aleksei Orlov. The Russian admiral could promise the islands' inhabitants only that, after a period of submission to the Russian command, they would gain their freedom and possible independence if the Russian military discerned in the inhabitants "a proper diligence and a desire to receive freedom, which, by gift of God, would be quickly fulfilled for [the Greeks] by merciful grant of her Most High Mother, Her Imperial Majesty," (*priamoe userdie i zhelanie o poluchenii vol'nosti, chto, darui Bozhe, daby vskorosti ispolnilos' vysokomaternee Eia Imperatorskogo Velichestva ob . . . [Grekakh] miloserdnoe zhelanie*).[24]

One must note that in this period Spiridov believed that the "wish of the Most High Mother" was to give "freedom" (*vol'nosti*) to inhabitants of the Aegean islands, and not their annexation to the Russian Empire. At the same time Spiridov understood that the "wishes of the most High Mother" were constrained to a significant degree by the interference of European rulers: "if these islands should become an archdukedom, as it is said they were long ago, or a free republic [this will be decided] by the kindness of our Most High Mother, our Great Sovereign, and that of other Christian sovereigns. . . ." (*i budut li si ostrova pod arkhidukstvom, kak to skazyvaiut davno napred sego i bylo, ili volnoiu respublikoiu po vysokomaternei velikoi nasheia gosudaryni milosti i drugikh khristianskikh gosudarei. . . .*).[25]

In this context all the activity of the Russian military in constructing an "Archipelago principality" can be seen not so much as an attempt to create a trans-oceanic colony with a Mediterranean Kronstadt on the island of Paros, but as an attempt to convey to the Greeks a Russian understanding of the meaning of liberty and of how their republic or archdukedom could exist. Practically every communication that Spiridov addressed to the Greeks bears the imprint of paternalism, and contains not only requests, but also directives explaining why it was necessary to pay taxes, how important it was for the islands to unite, and on what bases administration and defense could be organized. For example, if they chose the archdukedom, Spiridov asserted, it would be important that a decent monetary grant be provided the archduke so as to satisfy his domestic needs and maintain him without scrimping—and also to increase his honor: "the archduke [should be allotted] an appropriate sum of money for the comfort of his home and his domestic needs, thereby increasing his honor, so he would be able to maintain himself without [living in] squalor" (*arkhigertsogu na udovol'stvie domu i domashnikh evo, chtob po uvelichivaniiu chesti mog sebia soderzhat' bez ubozhestva, poriadochno denezhnaia summa*).[26]

Admiral Spiridov's brother-in-law and aide-de-camp, Pavel Nesterov, addressed the islands' residents in the same spirit. In the spring and summer of 1772, developing Spiridov's ideas, Nesterov worked out a series of determinations ('Uchrezhdeniya') to regulate the activities of the islands' central chancelleries and of their deputies' commissions. He also established a system of taxes and imposts, legal procedure in civil cases, and much more. On June 24, 1772, Nesterov even began a census of the islands of the Aegean "state."[27] Nesterov's records reveal that this state was composed of units (each island constituted a unit) that every year had to elect their "heads" as well as the "main members of the whole island" or "island's deputies" (as there were no precise regulations issued to govern elections, it is quite possible that elections were organized according to the existing traditions of each island).[28]

As had been true before the Russians arrived, deputies exercised functions both administrative and judicial, and they gathered in the chancellery of each island to settle state and public affairs. In their legal practice deputies were ordered to follow mainly their own laws and only in uncertain cases to ask the central chancellery for help. By 1772, it was clear that the Russian authorities did not intend to introduce much change in the practices of the former overlords, the Turks; they only wanted to reform civil administration "properly."[29]

Nevertheless, a pompous and paternalistic lexicon dominated Pavel Nesterov's communications with the islands' inhabitants. For example, one of his determinations ended with these words: "I command every one and all of you together to love each other; forsake hostility and behave according to the expectations of our Greek Orthodox Christian faith . . . and you will [thereby] gain the mercy of our great commanders and my true love and support."[30]

The Greeks were prepared to adopt a similar tone in relations with their liberators. Prospects for the construction of a republic, archduchy, or state seem to have remained foggy to inhabitants of the Aegean islands. In 1773, for example, residents of Samos, who did not have the "Regulation on Self-Administration" of Pavel Nesterov, asked to have a "Russian who knows Russian laws" (*rossiiskii chelovek kotoryi znaet rossiiskie zakony*) sent to them, in order to aid in the administration of the island (even though, as noted above, Nesterov's regulation suggested that all matters should be decided on the basis of the islands' traditions).[31] Samos islanders expressed tearful gratitude when the Russians sent them Naval Lieutenant Nikolai Kumani, "because previously we were like sheep without a shepherd, but as soon as we heard that he, Kumani, had come to our island, we gathered together from all the villages in sincere joy . . . to recognize him as our honorable commander."[32]

No less revealing than the attempts of Spiridov and Nesterov to teach the residents of the islands independence in the administration of their "free state" were the attempts of Aleksei Orlov to create the first civil school for the "new generation" of Greeks. Presumably it was the empress's idea (only realized by Orlov) that orphans and children from families of various backgrounds (only with their parents' permission and "without any coercion") be sent to Naxos, all their expenses being paid by Orlov himself. Giovanni Azzali, a native of Patra, was made director and bursar of the school.[33] As Orlov wrote in 1774 to Admiral Elmanov:

> I provided clothing, food and education to all the Greeks boys in the Naxos school—to the children of primates, as well as to orphans and children of poor islanders—all in accordance with the magnanimity and generosity of our All-Merciful sovereign . . . who, like a Mother, tends to the upbringing of these poor families. . . . Teachers assigned to them . . . [taught] the basics of Christian law and grammar, as well as the Russian language.[34]

These children lived in isolation from their families and were supposed to constitute "a new breed of people," grateful and loyal to the Russian Empire: "the intention of his grace [Orlov] is that the generation of these poor children extol the compassion and generosity of our All-Merciful Sovereign—nurturer of orphans and protector of peoples that share our faith, who took part in this war and grew wretched because they lost their homes and fatherland."[35] The school grew rapidly, populated not only with Aegean children but also with students from the Ionian Islands, possibly refugees from the Peloponnese. On the island of Zante (Zakynthos) there were more than three hundred boys and girls ready to be enrolled in the school![36]

From July, 1773, Orlov, wanting to give his school experiment more resonance, transferred the "Greeklings" to Pisa, where he acquired a house specifically for the school.[37] At this time, Orlov wrote to Spiridov:

> I ask you not to abandon the Greek children, who are already recruited and will be recruited in the future, and who, in groups of

> about fifteen, should be sent to me here [in Pisa] by ships when the opportunity arises. I am establishing a school for them here, and acquired a big house in Pisa for this purpose; I do not know what the Court will order done with them in the future, but I think that there is a house prepared for them there [Saint Petersburg] as well, where they will be admitted for various kinds of learning.[38]

In his study of the Aegean islands, Matvei Kokovtsov summarized the history of the Naxos school in the highest style: "All the islands felt the abundantly flowing generosity of the Great and Most Wise Catherine, Who, wishing to restore lapsed learning, ordered that a school be founded on Naxos. However, as the islands have now been returned to the Ottoman Porte, the students were transported by the Russian fleet to Saint Petersburg, where they marvel at Minerva's Motherly care."[39] In fact in 1775 the returning Russian frigate *Natalia* brought students of the Greek school to Russia; some later continued their educations in the Corps of Foreign Coreligionists and pursued military careers, while others returned to Greece.[40]

The 1774 Treaty of Kuchuk-Kainarji ended the history of the Aegean principality. Russia could not insist on maintaining the Aegean islands' independence from the Turks, and in June, 1775, the last Russian ship left the former capital in Ausa/Naussa. According to the treaty, inhabitants of the islands—former "subjects of Catherine the Great"—were invited to move to the Russian Empire, but not a single word was said about their independence, the republic, or the senate. Only the system of Russian consulates, established by the conditions of the peace treaty and distributed across the islands with the main consulate at Mykonos, reminded the Greeks of the Russian presence in the Aegean. Henceforth, families of Greek immigrants, like the students of Orlov's Greek school, served in the Russian Empire, and only there finally came to understand what could be given to them and what was expected of them in place of Russian sovereignty.[41]

THE GREEK PROJECT, OR FOREIGN GIFTS FOR THE GREEKS

The first Aegean expedition radically changed Catherine and her circle's views about Orthodox unity with the Greeks and about Greek liberation in general. After the events of 1770 in Morea, the Russians began to blame the Greeks for their inability to fight against their enemies in a regular army, and by 1772 even Voltaire, who had long defended the Greeks in letters to the Russian empress, had to admit: "My sorrow is multiplied by the fact that the Greeks are not worthy (*ne dostoiny*) of liberty, which they could reacquire if they only had the courage to contribute to your triumphs. I shall read no more Sophocles, Homer or Demosthenes".[42]

The attempt to create an Aegean principality in 1771-74 also convinced both the Russian naval command and the empress that the Greeks were not ready to live in an independent state, to defend it, to create an administration, or to respect modern laws. Russians, who had come to liberate fellow believers, gradually lost their patience with and trust in the Greeks, and became irritated with and sarcastic toward the Greeks. In January, 1771, for instance, Spiridov, inspired by the idea of building a new Greek state in the Aegean, wrote: "The Greeks, because of their situation, deserve pity rather than criticism from us, because . . . they fear the Turks. . . ."[43] Soon, however, such ideas were replaced by statements about the laziness and cunning of Catherine's subjects on the Aegean islands, as well as remarks about their refusal to work even for substantial pay. Already on February 11, 1771, Spiridov wrote Rear Admiral Andrei Elmanov: "I advise your excellency to trust the Greek witnesses no more than your dreams, and examine their stories very carefully."[44] In 1774, Elmanov complained that he could not find carpenters to repair his ships ("excluding the present Admiralty workers, of which there are few, who are tired and drained by the work and cannot be counted on as workers"). Greeks could not be hired "either by coercion or for money, even if promised a piaster a day . . . on top of that, they cannot work for more than three days, after which, they run away."[45]

Brigadier Kokovtsov expressed an opinion common among members of the expedition about the mores of the islands' inhabitants:

> The Greeks who live in the Archipelago, and who prospered under the rule of Catherine the Great from 1771-1775 . . . [now live] in ignorance and poverty, and barely get enough from their harvests

> to survive. The reason is their laziness, ignorance, and the disorganized Turkish rule . . . they use their wits for trickery, falsehood, and hypocrisy. . . . Greed rules their hearts . . . if they see any occasion to make a profit, they are happy to sacrifice their best friends and relatives for the luster of metal [coins]. Their main pastime is listening to and telling fables. They are superstitious, jealous when it comes to women, and, like Turks, they keep their women locked up.[46]

According to Kokovtsov, only inhabitants of the islands of Tinos, Syros, Mykonos, Naxos, and Patmos, all involved in sea trade with Europeans, could be considered enlightened. Residents of Tinos and Andros, in Kokovstov's opinion, were "relatively enlightened and constantly involved in seafaring, trading in goods from other islands," while Greeks on the island of Skyros, covered in "dense forests," were "badly educated," since "they are engaged only in agriculture."[47]

The change in relations with the Greeks was not only the product of the frustration of possible cooperation, but also of a radical shift in Russian perceptions of the Greeks. From the late 1770s the image of the unenlightened Greeks, in contrast to the earlier image of the noble Spartans, became more significant for the new Greek project of Catherine II. Accordingly, it became difficult to trust the Greeks to choose independently their liberty, their manner of rule, or their ruler. As is well known, soon the court began to prepare the grandson of the empress, Constantine (b. 1779), and a "trusted person" (presumably Catherine's favorite, Grigorii Potemkin) to rule a proposed kingdom of Dacia in European lands, once it had been liberated from Turks.[48] The new project ignored the possibility of Greek insurgents. The plan could be realized only with the cooperation of the European great powers, and Catherine's choice was the Holy Roman Empire and Emperor Joseph II. With him, and not with the "unhappy Greeks," Catherine planned anew to redraw the map of southeastern Europe.[49]

The empress continued to play a serious game, but the mythology of the Marble Emperor, Constantine, "who slept below the Golden Gate of Constantinople," now edged out the earlier fantasies of ancient Sparta. The allure of Constantine as Christian emperor and geo-political symbol was still powerful, so much so that a writer like

Fedor Tumanskii in 1786 could dedicate books to the new Constantine, who would bring liberation "from the banks of the Neva" and restore "the Greek tsardom."[50] It is quite possible that knowledge in Saint Petersburg of the Russian coat of arms on the church in Tinos (the description of which opened this article) could have encouraged a self-serving idea among the Russians that the Greeks could pin their hopes only on the imperial eagle. But by the 1780s the idea of Greek liberation was discussed in Russia almost without mention of the Greeks themselves.

NOTES

* Translated by Elena Smilianskaia and Daniel H. Kaiser. This study was supported by research grant No. 12-01-0011 from the National Research University Higher School of Economics Academic Fund Program.

1 For details of this association, see Gary Marker, *Imperial Saint: The Cult of St. Catherine and the Dawn of Female Rule in Russia* (DeKalb: Northern Illinois University Press, 2007).

2 On the northern wall of the church a marble bas-relief depicting Saint Catherine bears the date 1767, which seems to contradict the legend, according to which Orlov in the 1770s insisted on the dedication of the church to the patron saint of the Russian empress.

3 *Gosudarstvennaia Tret'iakovskaia galereia: Katalog sobrania. Zhivopis' XVIII-XX vekov,* 6 vols. (Moscow: Tret'iakovskaia galereia/Krasnaia ploshchad'/SkanRus, 1997-2009), 2:304.

4 See, for example: http://artclassic.edu.ru/catalog.asp?ob__no=15337&cat__ob__no=15321 (accessed May 7, 2014).

5 This expedition is very well studied. For details, see Irina Smilianskaia, Mikhail Velizhev, and Elena Smilianskaia, *Rossiia v Sredizemnomor'e: Arkhipelagskaia ekspeditsiia Ekateriny Velikoi* (Moscow: Indrik, 2011), 38-54, 483-498; Grigorii Arsh, *Rossiia i bor'ba Gretsii za osvobozhdenie* (Moscow: Indrik, 11-34).

6 A. I. Markevich, "Doklad deistvitelnogo chlena A. I. Markevicha o posylke greka Georgiia Papazogli na Balkanskii poluostrov v 1763–1764 gg.," *Zapiski Odesskogo obshchestva istorii i drevnostei* 19 (1896): 42–46.

7 Philip Mansel, *Levant: Splendor and Catastrophe on the Mediterranean* (New Haven: Yale University Press, 2011), chapter 2, note 129. See also Ariadna Camariano-Cioran, "La Guerre Russo-Turque de 1768–1774 et les Grecs," *Revue des études sud-est européennes* 3 (1965): 513–547; Richard Clogg, "The Byzantine Legacy in the Modern Greek World: the Megali Idea," in *The Byzantine Legacy in Eastern Europe*, ed. Lowell Clucas (Boulder: East European Monographs, 1988), 259–265; N. Ροτζώκος, *Ορλωφικά και ελληνική ιστοριογραφία* (Athens, 2007); Paschalis Kitromilides, *Enlightenment and Revolution: the Making of Modern Greece* (Cambridge: Harvard University Press, 2013).

8 Elizabeth Rawson, *The Spartan Tradition in European Thought* (Oxford: Clarendon Press, 1969), 292; David Roessel, *In Byron's Shadow: Modern Greece in the English and American Imagination* (New York: Oxford University Press, 2002); Vera Proskurina, *Creating the Empress: Politics and Poetry in the Age of Catherine II* (Brighton: Academic Studies Press, 2011).

9 It is notable that this "misunderstanding" is still influential in Western (especially Greek) and Russian historiographies. Compare, for example: Ροτζώκος, *Ορλωφικά και ελληνική ιστοριογραφία* and G. A. Grebenshchikova, *Baltiiskii flot v period pravleniia Ekateriny II* (Saint Petersburg: Nauka, 2007).

10 *Arkhiv Gosudarstvennago Soveta*, 5 vols. (Saint Petersburg, 1869-1904), 1:357.

11 Ibid.

12 Cited from A. N. Petrov, *Voina Rossii s Turtsiei i pol'skimi konfederatami s 1769 po 1774 g.*, 5 vols. (Saint Petersburg: Veimar, 1866-74) 1:106.

13 For example, Catherine to Voltaire, September 28/October 9, 1770: "The Greeks and Spartans are completely transformed, and care more about looting than their freedom. They will perish irretrievably if they don't heed the orders and advice of the hero [Aleksei Orlov] I sent them." *Perepiska rossiiskoi imperatritsy Ekateriny II i gospodina Vol'tera*, trans. Mikhail Antonovskii, 2 vols. [Saint Petersburg, 1802], 1:123; again, Catherine to Voltaire, August 14/25, 1771: "If your beloved Greece, which does nothing more than it wishes, behaved with the same courage as the possessor of the pyramids [Ali-bei, who was conducting a successful rebellion in Egypt against the Turks], then the Athens theater would no longer be a garden, nor the Lycée a stable." Ibid., 2:30.

14 *Perepiska rossiiskoi imperatritsy Ekateriny II*, 1:87, 90.

15 Ibid., 1:97, 98; ibid., 2:31. The letter dates 'July 22, 1770', long before in Saint Petersburg the empress recieved news about the Battle of Chesme.

16 Platon (Levshin), *Slovo v den' pervoverkhovnykh Apostolov Petra i Pavla i tezoimenitstva Ego imperatorskogo Vysochestva* (Saint Petersburg, 1770).

17 *Sankt-Peterburgskie vedomosti*, no. 57, July 16, 1770; emphasis the author's.

18 Rossiiskii gosudarstvennyi arkhiv drevnikh aktov [hereafter RGADA], f. 10, op. 1, d. 79, fols. 5a–6.

19 Platon (Levshin), "Slovo na novyi 1771 god," *Pouchitel'nye slova pri vysochaishem dvore . . . Ekateriny Alekseevny s 1763 goda po 1780 god skazannyia . . . Platonom (Levshin)* (Moscow, 1780), 2:318-19.

20 "Perepiska grafa N. I. Panina s grafom A. G. Orlovym-Chesmenskim, 1770-1773," *Russkii arkhiv*, 18, no. 3, bk. 2 (1880): 230.

21 For more details, see Smilianskaia, Velizhev, and Smilianskaia, *Rossiya v Sredizemnomor'e*, 143-218; Elena B. Smilianskaia, "'Protection' or 'Possession': How Russians Created a Greek Principality in 1770-1775," in *Power and Influence in South-Eastern Europe: 16th-19th century*, ed. Maria Baramova et al. (Berlin-Zurich: Lit Verlag, 2013), 209-217.

22 By late February, 1771, Spiridov had received replies from the elders and clergy of twelve islands, who appealed to the empress "to accept into [her] eternal protection and patronage the unhappy Archipelago" (Rossiiskii gosudarstvennyi arkhiv voenno-morskogo flota [hereafter RGAVMF], f. 190, op. 1, d. 16. fols. 53v., 78-78 v., 84). This led Spiridov to proclaim this group of small islands a "Great Archipelagic Principality." The number of islands that officially accepted Russian protection and were considered to have joined the Russian Empire grew from

fourteen to about thirty between 1771 and 1774. These included the Cyclades islands (Paros, Antiparos, Naxos, Mykonos, Tinos, Andros, Milos, Kimolos, Ios, Kea, Kythnos, Syros, Sifnos, Serifos, Anafi, Folegandros, Thera [Santorini]), the Lesser Cyclades, Thermi, Amorgos, Samos, Skopolos, Alonissos (Northern Sporades), along with Patmos, Hydra, and the fortress of Kastelorizo.

23 RGAVMF, f. 190, op. 1, d. 16. fols. 7-8.

24 RGAVMF, f. 190, op. 1, d. 16, fols. 76-76 a.

25 Smilianskaia, Velizhev, and Smilianskaia, *Rossiia v Sredizemnomor'e,* 507.

26 Ibid., 508.

27 Κ. Στέφανος, *Ανέκδοτα έγγραφα αποσταλέντα προς τους κατοίκους των Κυκλάδων κατα την υπο των Ρώσων κατοχήν.* Σελ. 33.

28 RGAVMF, f. 190, op. 1, d. 121, fols. 99-100a, 67-68, 94-97.

29 RGAVMF, f. 190, op. 1, d. 121, fols. 94-97.

30 Ibid., fol. 100a.

31 Ibid., f. 188, op. 1, d. 91, fols. 78-78a.

32 Ibid., f. 190, op. 1, d. 2, fol. 82. Nikolai Petrovich Kumani (1730-1809) was born on the island of Crete, and entered Russian service in 1769, but hardly knew Russian laws. He remained in service, reaching the rank of rear admiral (1797), but never did learn how to read and knew only how to sign his name. See V. M. Lur'e, *Morskoi biograficheskii slovar': Deiateli Rossiiskogo flota XVIII veka* (Saint Petersburg: Informatsionnyi tsentr "Vybor," 2005), 133.

33 RGAVMF, f. 190, op. 1, d. 119. He was later named Russian consul in Cyprus (V. A. Ulianitskii, *Russkie konsul'stva za granitsei v XVIII veke* [Moscow, 1899]).

34 RGAVMF, f. 188, op. 1, d. 92, fols. 158-159. About education in the Russian language, Elmanov wrote: "so that they will be taught Russian grammar, and become able to read and write".

35 RGADA, f. 21, d. 67, fol. 1.

36 G. A. Spiridov also participated in this educational enterprise, although he was more practical, thinking it necessary to teach boys "navigation," so that "forty-six young Greeks from Naxos" were temporarily sent out "as cabin boys to various ships" (RGAVMF, f. 188, op. 1, d. 92, fols. 158-159; see also Grebenshchikova, *Baltiiskii flot*, 411-413). In a July 2, 1773, letter to Count Mocenigo, who represented Russian interests in the Adriatic, Spiridov wrote that boys between fourteen and twenty years of age should be sent with passing ships to Naxos at the expense of the Russian treasury, but that both boys and girls could also be sent directly to Livorno, so that, after quarantine, they could enroll in the school founded by Count Orlov (RGADA, f. 21, d. 67, fols. 1-1a).

37 On the Russian presence in Tuscany in the 1770s, see Smilianskaia, Velizhev and Smilianskaia, *Rossiia v Sredizemnomor'e*, 283-332 and Cesare Ciano, *Russia e Toscana nei secoli XVII e XVIII. Pagine di storia del commercio e della navigazione* (Pisa: ETS, 1980).

38 RGAVMF, f. 190, op. 1, d. 119, fol. 29 a.

39 Matvei Kokovtsov, *Opisanie Arkhipelaga i Varvariiskago berega* (Saint Petersburg, 1786), 68-72. In January, 1775, a special school for Greeks boys from the Aegean islands was established in Saint Petersburg, and transformed in 1792 into the Corps of Foreign Coreligionists, closed only after Catherine the Great's death in

1796. Grigorii Arsh, *Tainoe obshchestvo "Filiki Eteriia": iz istorii bor'by Gretsii za sverzhenie osmanskogo iga* (Moscow: Nauka, 1965).

40 T. S. Fedorova, "Vypuskniki Grecheskoi gimnazii (korpusa)—vospitanniki Morskogo kadetskogo korpusa," http://rgavmf.ru/lib/fedorova_grecheskaya_gimnaziya.pdf (accessed May 8, 2014); RGADA f. 10, op. 1, d. 645, fol. 205a. Two Greek pupils of the former school on Naxos requested money for their return trip to Greece from Saint Petersburg and received "one hundred rubles on the voyage."

41 See RGADA, f.10, op.1, d. 644, 645 for Greek appeals to Catherine II about rewarding their participation in the Russo-Turkish war.

42 Voltaire, March 6, 1772. *Documents of Catherine the Great: The Correspondence with Voltaire, and the* Instruction *of 1767 in the English Text of 1768,* ed. W. F. Reddaway (Cambridge: Cambridge University Press, 1931), 62.

43 RGAVMF, f. 190, op. 1, d. 44, fol. 19.

44 RGAVMF, f. 190, op. 1, d. 43, fol. 71a.

45 *Materialy dlia istorii russkogo flota*, 17 vols. (Saint Petersburg, 1865-1917), 12:242.

46 Kokovtsov, *Opisanie*, 68-71. For more on Russian attitudes to the Greeks, see Iannitsi Feodora, *Grecheskii mir v kontse XVIII—nachale XX vv. Po rossiiskim istochnikam; k voprosu ob izuchenii samosoznania grekov* (Saint Petersburg: Aleteia, 2005), 51-63.

47 Kokovtsov, *Opisanie,* 23-24, 36, 12.

48 In fact, Constantine learned to speak Greek before he learned Russian, and Catherine commemorated his birth with a medal depicting the Hagia Sophia. One of Catherine's operas, *The Beginning of Oleg's Reign*, is said to have represented the empress's plans to take Constantinople.

49 For new material on this question, see M. A. Petrova, *Ekaterina II i Iosif II: formirovanie rossiisko-avstriiskogo soiuza, 1780-1790* (Moscow: Nauka, 2011); and compare with Hugh Ragsdale, "Evaluating the Traditions of Russian Aggression: Catherine II and the Greek Project," *Slavonic and East European Review* 66 (1988): 92.

50 Fedor Tumanskii, "Posviashchenie," in Kokovtsov, *Opisanie*, 3.

A Proletarian *Encyclopédie*

Daniela Steila
(University of Turin)

"In the second half of the eighteenth century, the progressive bourgeoisie prepared its great revolution by energetically collecting and organizing its own forces. They *conceived* wrongly the meaning of ideas within life, but correctly *felt* their power in organization. That is why a progressive group of ideologues created at that moment the famous *Encyclopedia*."[1] With these words Alexander Bogdanov, leader of the so-called Left Bolsheviks, introduced his proposal for a new proletarian encyclopedia a few years before the October Revolution. At the beginning of the twentieth century, it would play the same role that the bourgeois encyclopedia had played on the eve of the French Revolution. Through that momentous work, Bogdanov continued, "the liberating movement received its solid ideological basis: one who read and understood the *Encyclopedia* could surely say that he knew his own place within nature and society, he knew where he came from and where he was going, what humankind needed and what every rational, active individual needed." In short, "the *Encyclopedia* was the crystallized truth of that time," although it was not the same truth with which one could be satisfied in Bogdanov's time, since "every epoch has its own truth."[2]

In Bogdanov's view the latter statement was not simply the consequence of historical materialism. According to this conception, in any economically determined historical moment there would necessarily be a particular cultural truth, since cultural superstructure depends on the economic structure. In Bogdanov's worldview, however, things were more complicated: culture played an essential creative role and, although depending in the end on the existing economic relations within society, was concretely active in the organization of the human world in general. Far from being the reflex of a given reality, truth became rather an instrument, "a machine by which one cuts, splits, and re-sews reality."[3]

From this perspective, the struggling proletarians had to provide themselves with new cultural means, with a new structure of knowledge. To envisage a new encyclopedia did not mean merely systematizing already-established knowledge by summarizing it and perhaps shaping it to be more accessible for a social class that, on the whole, was still not very educated. Rather, according to Bogdanov, the encyclopedia would be an instrument for the organizing and building of knowledge from the point of view of the new social class.

This idea that economic and political revolution would also lead to a radical change in culture was so wide-spread among Russian revolutionaries that it sometimes provoked sardonic comments. The poet Valerii Briusov in a 1907 letter to Zinaida Gippius reported that a Social Democrat with whom he was talking had maintained that, "were their social system realized, everything would be different," even the multiplication table![4]

In principle almost all the Russian revolutionaries might have agreed, although they would probably have split over the question of whether the radical change concerned only the social sciences or the whole of knowledge—including natural sciences and mathematics—and to what extent. But they were divided on another important point: in order to develop a new proletarian culture, should they wait for the constitution of the new economic-political system, or would the creation of a collectivist worldview and of the corresponding form of knowledge rather be a precondition for the authentic proletarian revolution? Bogdanov and the Left Bolsheviks who sided with him supported the second option. They stated that "the hidden premise of Bolshevism" was "the idea of creating nowadays, within the present society, a great proletarian culture, stronger and more graceful, incomparably freer and more creative, than the culture of the declining bourgeois classes."[5]

According to Bogdanov, Plekhanov and Lenin, who claimed to be ideologues of the working class but denied the possibility of a cultural hegemony of the proletariat, were victims of a "radical psychological contradiction." On the one hand they acknowledged the leading political role of the working class, but, on the other hand, they showed a deep distrust of the proletarian "creative forces."[6] In Bogdanov's opinion, if science and philosophy were to unify and organize human experience, the proletariat, whose experience was very different from the experience of any other social class already existing within the conditions of capitalism, could not wait for the revolution to create a new knowledge.[7] A workers' encyclopedia was to express that new worldview, as an "instrument of organization of human collective activity, created within the historical cooperation of generations."[8] Thus, the encyclopedia would become "the basis and the flag of proletarian ideological identity," as Bogdanov foresaw in the conclusion of his second utopian novel, *Engineer Menni*, published in 1913.[9]

The idea of a new encyclopedia became a basic element in Bogdanov's concept of proletarian culture at the beginning of the twentieth century, and it has been considered as such by most historians.[10] In particular, the workers' encyclopedia represents Bogdanov's ideal of the democratization of knowledge, though this ideal was consciously opposed to any project devoted to the popularization of already-established sciences. Bogdanov wrote,

> The task of the proletarian democratization of knowledge does not equate in any way with a good popular exposition of already-existing scientific data, such as they are, with their division into specializations. One should systematize differently and anew the scientific experience accumulated in the various fields, and overcome not only the sectorial incomprehensibility of the language of special branches, but the specialization itself, as far as it causes the disintegration of the system of knowledge and the limitation of the knower's point of view.[11]

Specialized, erudite knowledge, enclosed within its own jargon and generating mutual incomprehension, would be useless to proletarians. On the contrary,

> The production of socialist knowledge should . . . strive for the simplification and unification of science, for retrieving its own general ways of research, which would give a key for the most different specializations and would allow one to quickly take control of them. . . . Science, the great instrument of work, in this way will be socialized, as socialism requires for all and every instrument of labor.[12]

This new encyclopedia was an ideal that Bogdanov discussed widely and developed from 1910 forward. Before that time, however, the proletarian encyclopedia had been a concrete, though never realized, publishing project. Here I would like to sketch out the story of this failed project of a workers' encyclopedia, and of its path toward its very different ultimate realization—that is, the *Soviet Encyclopedia*. In doing so, I will try to follow two maxims that I learned from Gary Marker's work: first, that in history ideas have to measure themselves against the actual conditions of the book market; and second, that texts that are clearly theoretical programs or manifestos must be considered within the context of direct testimonies and accounts, such as memoirs and letters, in order to understand their specific historical milieu.[13]

In our case, Bogdanov's theory about a workers' encyclopedia appeared some years after Maksim Gorky had developed a more concrete project along similar lines. Being a self-educated man himself, Gorky gave enormous importance to publishing: as is well known, in September, 1900, he had joined the Saint Petersburg publishing house Znanie in order to support talented young authors and to produce low-cost volumes for the general public. Beginning in 1905, Znanie published a series of books called the Economic Library, which made available the works of many important authors (such as Gorky himself, Bunin, Leonid Andreev, et al.), printing up to twenty thousand copies of each volume (in Gorky's case, more than fifty thousand), and selling these high-quality books at very popular prices.[14] An encyclopedia written especially for workers was thus consistent with Gorky's publishing programs at the beginning of the century. He deemed the project a crucial endeavor. While Bogdanov was busy with debates within the Bolshevik faction about the Social Democrats' participation in the Duma, Gorky called him to work for the encyclopedia: "that is really more important than the question of 'boikotizm,' 'otzovizm' or any other word in bad Tatarian language!"[15]

Besides Bogdanov, the first to be involved in the project was probably Vladimir Bazarov, a Bolshevik economist and philosopher. He was also one of Bogdanov's oldest friends, his former schoolmate in Tula, and his colleague as a lecturer within the local workers' circles of self-instruction. When Bogdanov recounted the genesis of the idea of the democratization of knowledge that the encyclopedia was to realize, he pointed out that it had been suggested precisely by their work as young men among the workers. Whereas the lecturers tried to transmit isolated notions, the workers would raise questions on more general matters, which ranged from natural sciences to philosophy, thereby compelling their young teachers (Bogdanov, Bazarov, and I. I. Skvortsov-Stepanov) to strive for the synthesis and reformulation of existing knowledge. Bogdanov wrote that

> The absolute impossibility of communicating to students in a short time the factual material in every field that aroused a lively interest forced lecturers to focus their answers on the methodologies of those sciences, some notion of which ought to be given to the young questioners. The result was that students got even more interested, not in the specialized character of the different methods, but, on the contrary, in their reciprocal connection, in what was common and similar among them. In front of us there were some inborn monists, who expected from us—not always with success, obviously—monistic answers to all possible questions, cursed or not.[16]

Bogdanov's monistic perspective found its first motivation in that encounter. It is reasonable to surmise that his friend Bazarov was also influenced by that experience.

Bazarov was one of the first who enthusiastically responded to Gorky's invitation to take part in the collective enterprise of a workers' encyclopedia.[17] That was one of the main topics discussed during an April, 1908, meeting in Capri. Bogdanov, Bazarov, and Lunacharsky gathered in Gorky's villa together with Lenin, whom Gorky had invited in the hope of overcoming the disagreements that poisoned the atmosphere within their faction. Gorky knew very well that "Ilich [Lenin] puffs like a boiling samovar, he blows his polemic steam in every direction,"[18] but he thought that "a wide and circumstantial conversation with Ilich became more and more necessary."[19] Lenin, however, had no intention of discussing the themes that divided them. Mariia Andreeva, Gorky's partner, reported that Lenin stopped Gorky's diplomatic attempts as soon as he arrived in Capri, on the way to Gorky's villa:

> Aleksei Maksimovich started talking to Vladimir Ilich of Bogdanov's burning commitment to him, to Lenin, and about the way that Lunacharsky and Bogdanov were both extraordinarily talented and smart people . . . Vladimir Ilich gave Aleksei Maksimovich a side-long glance, half-closed his eyes, and very resolutely said: 'Don't try, Aleksei Maksimovich. You won't get anything.'[20]

The week was spent in more or less friendly talks, visits to museums in Naples and Pompeii, a trip to Mount Vesuvius, fishing, and playing chess—as they were recorded in some of the best-known (and, later, most famously doctored) pictures in history.[21] When Lenin arrived at the island, on April 23, the publishing plan of the encyclopedia had already been discussed. The day before, Gorky had outlined it in a letter to Piatnitskii:

> History of Russia – political
> " " " – economic development
> " " " – foreign relations—i.e., history of foreign politics
> " " " – development of political thought
> " " " – development of juridical ideas
> " " " – church
> " " " – literature

To those volumes, all to be published in about two or three years, was added an introductory book by Bogdanov, with the title "Organization of Experience and Types of Class Psychology." The project was estimated to require twelve to fifteen volumes, each using twenty typographic sheets.[22] Some weeks later, Gorky sent G. A. Aleksinskii, former Social Democratic representative in the Second Duma and Bolshevik émigré involved in the workers' encyclopedia and the party school since the very beginning, quite a different plan, which means that discussions among the people at Capri had continued after Lenin's departure. Once he returned to Geneva, Bogdanov told Aleksinskii, who was considered as a possible author, that the project had been started by Gorky. Therefore, Aleksinskii wrote Gorky to learn more about the project. But Gorky made clear that "the initiative has been collective, and so should also be the redaction of the books." In the same letter Gorky announced that he would not personally take part in the realization of the encyclopedia: "neither the extent of my knowledge nor my professional duties allow me that." Nevertheless, Gorky seemed to be very well informed about publication:

> The plan is to publish a series of books that lay out the history of Russian cultural life. The books must be rigorously scholarly, yet completely popular. The first book is a sort of general philosophical introduction to the whole series: Bogdanov must write this book, about the organization of human experience. The second one—"The History of Popular Creative Work"—is built on the contrast between the strength of the collective psyche and the weakness of the individual in the fields of myth, poetry, etc. Then "The History of Russian Literature," "The History of Russian Foreign Policy," "The History of the Russian Church," "The History of Philosophical Thought" (i.e., ideology), "The History of Internal Politics, Industry and Commerce," and "The History of the Peoples that Came to Make Up Rus." Here, in crude terms, is the plan of the work.[23]

In a subsequent version, dated March, 1909, the project was presented to Mikhail Pokrovskii, the well-known historian, with the aim of engaging him in the enterprise. This time the names of the authors expected to write the different sections were included:

1. The Organization of Experience and the Types of Class Psychology—Bogdanov. It seems that he has already started writing this book.

2. The History of Popular Creative Work and Russian Literature—Lunacharsky. He has collected materials, and a part of the work is started.
3. The History of Russia—you.
4. The History of Russian Foreign Policy—you.
5. The History of Philosophical Thought—Bazarov.
6. Churches and Sects—person not appointed.
7. A Course of Political Economics in Relationship to the History of Culture—Bogdanov-Stepanov. The work has been started.
8. The History of the Development of Industry and Commerce—Stepanov.
9. The History of the Peasantry and the Agrarian Question—Lenin.
10. The Contemporary Situation—collectively.[24]

One must observe that for the first time Lenin was mentioned as the author of a volume. Of course, the agrarian question was one of his areas of expertise,[25] but it seems that Lenin was never actually involved in the project. He could hardly have agreed to take part in an enterprise that was so clearly influenced by Bogdanov's and Bazarov's philosophy—at exactly this time Lenin was preparing to attack them with his *Materialism and Empirio-criticism*. Probably by claiming that he would involve Lenin in the project, Gorky wanted to present it as an independent project rather than the work of one faction.

At no time did Gorky ever specify which publishing house would actually publish the encyclopedia. Such haziness was deliberate, since Gorky and his friends would have liked to build up their own publishing house specifically with the aim of publishing the encyclopedia, probably together with I. P. Ladyzhnikov, who was in charge of the German publishing house bearing his name where Gorky regularly published his works in Europe.[26] Between 1908 and 1909 the prospects of collecting the necessary funds were still too uncertain to openly write about this design. As Gorky suggested, "So far it is better . . . to consider this matter [founding their own publishing house] as hardly realizable. We will acknowledge its feasibility not one hour before we shall have the money in our hands!"[27] Among the anticipated sponsors were Fedor Chaliapin, the well-known bass singer, who was one of Gorky's old friends and a generous donor for the writer's enterprises, and Serge Koussevitzky, a musician who in 1908 debuted as orchestra director. However, cultivating financial sponsors proved difficult.

Chaliapin, who had been in Capri between the end of April and the beginning of May, 1908, when the Capri Bolsheviks were actually discussing the project of the encyclopedia,[28] promised twenty-five thousand rubles for the new publishing house.[29] But when Lunacharsky met Chaliapin in Paris a few months later in June to settle the matter, it seemed that at least part of the money (twelve thousand rubles, or francs) would be diverted to the coffers of the Bolshevik faction.[30] Gorky immediately telegraphed Lunacharsky, warning that it was better not to talk with Chaliapin about the promised money, since too direct a request might make him stifle "any desire to deal with Lunacharsky and all the others."[31] Lunacharsky reassured Gorky that there had been no lack of tact with his friend. He had not asked for money, but Chaliapin himself had sent three thousand francs directly to Gorky for his personal projects, since, as he said, "my money won't help the party very much, but Aleksei [Gorky] needs it badly."[32]

Worse problems attached to the contacts with Koussevitzky, who had become very rich after his marriage to one of the granddaughters of the "King of Tea," Alexander Kuznetsov.[33] Chaliapin had promised to engage him in the project of the encyclopedia and the new publishing house. But Chaliapin was unable to raise the subject with Koussevitzky, much less persuade him to join in supporting the project, even though Gorky was ready to go to Paris in order to draw up the agreement.[34] In May, 1909, Ladyzhnikov, at the urging of Gorky, made another attempt. Gorky provided rather specific advice:

> When you speak with Koussevitzky, show him that our encyclopedia will have a rigorously scholarly and widely democratic character. Emphasize its democratic nature, without mentioning the party and the proletariat—this would be premature. Act on the artist: explain that there will be many books about art history, about aesthetics, and individual works about music and theater—these are not just

> words, but something that will be accomplished. Point out that the edition of this encyclopedia will establish as well its publisher's historical renown, and his name may become more respected than Bayle's and the publishers of the French *Encyclopedia*. Moreover, it seems to me that one may remind him that the French *Encyclopedia* publishers, having spent 1,700 livres for their project, received incomes of 2,600—it is a fact![35]

Above all, Gorky emphasized that he wanted to meet Koussevitzky personally: "I might be able to persuade him of the enormous importance of the enterprise, by which he could really build himself the most marvelous monument."[36]

Gorky's arguments deserve some attention. At the turn of the century, such ideas must have been quite common, since many publishing houses leapt at the publication of encyclopedias and multivolume encyclopedic dictionaries. As is well known, the publishing house created by an agreement between the German publisher F. A. Brockhaus and the Saint Petersburg printmaker I. A. Efron published a huge *Encyclopedic Dictionary* between 1890 and 1907. Its success was such that in the following years they published two editions of a *Small Encyclopedic Dictionary*—in three volumes (1899-1902), and later in four volumes (1907-1909)—as well as a *Jewish Encyclopedia* in sixteen volumes (1908-1913). In 1911, a new, shorter version of the *Encyclopedic Dictionary* came out. The first ten volumes were printed in twenty thousand copies, reduced to sixteen thousand in 1913. The war would halt the new Brockhaus *Encyclopedia* at the twenty-ninth volume in 1916.[37]

In addition to the success of a traditional work such as the Brockhaus-Efron *Dictionary*, which had generic educational aims, one must also notice many similar enterprises that were more clearly politically oriented. Between 1898 and 1901 an *Encyclopedic Dictionary* came out in fascicles as appendices to the journal *Nauchnoe obozrenie*. The new dictionary was edited by the review's board and by its chief editor, M. M. Filippov. Eventually it was republished as a free appendix to the journal *Priroda i liudi* in 1901-1902, and again in three volumes at P. P. Soikin's publishing house in Saint Petersburg in 1901. This

Dictionary was aimed at making its readers better able to understand articles in the journal, which combined popular essays in the natural sciences, philosophical articles on epistemology, and rather open political writings. S. G. Strumilin, a well-known statistician, wrote in his memoirs: "*Nauchnoe obozrenie* was a real podium for materialist thought and the struggle against *narodnichestvo*. This journal interested us, young Marxists, not only because it illuminated philosophical questions; in the pages of *Nauchnoe obozrenie* there were always articles and remarks that could be used as weapons in the revolutionary fights."[38] With good reason the chief of the police department, S. E. Zvolianskii, who was closely following Filippov's activities, wrote that Filippov's *Scientific-Encyclopedic Dictionary* should rather be called "socialist," "since in it the items and bibliographical data concerning socialism were developed in a very detailed and thorough way."[39]

F. F. Pavlenkov's *Encyclopedic Dictionary* also came out at the turn of the century. Its first edition was published in Saint Petersburg in 1899, just before the death of its publisher, who also was its main editor and author. Being convinced of the importance of education for the future of Russia, Pavlenkov oriented his dictionary toward school teachers, middle school and high school students, and qualified workers and employers. To this end he decided to publish a one-volume illustrated dictionary at a very low price. Its success was enormous: the dictionary sold more than one hundred thousand copies. In 1905 Pavlenkov's heirs published a second edition, but they regretted the fact that the revolutionary events of that year, which they deemed of the utmost importance to the country, overshadowed this edition. Therefore, in 1907, they hastened to prepare a third edition, identical to the second but for the addition of an appendix with openly political entries such as "Agrarian Movement," "Unemployment," and "Punitive Expeditions." Entries on the main political parties and outstanding figures of the revolutionary movement were also included. Censorship banned the appendix and the publishing house was forced to cut it away from all the already printed copies. But this only increased the renown of Pavlenkov's dictionary, and the second edition sold out.[40] Gorky and his companions appreciated Pavlenkov's dictionary: Gorky himself ordered ten copies to be used in the Capri school,[41] which was the Left Bolsheviks' first experiment with a workers' school offering instruction in agitation and propaganda. As we shall see, it was closely connected, at least in the founders' intentions, to the project of the proletarian encyclopedia.

The *Great Encyclopedia*, edited by S. N. Iuzhakov and published by Prosveshchenie, was closer to the ideas of the Populists (*narodnichestvo*). It came out in twenty-two volumes between 1900 and 1909; though initially printed for a run of twelve thousand copies, this was increased to twenty-seven thousand after the eleventh volume. Its success was so great that before 1910 it went through six reprintings. However this work, too, had troubles with censorship. In 1908, Saint Petersburg censors denounced the authors and editors who had published articles on Russian revolutionaries' biographies and on their parties; these entries applauded the revolutionaries as the best people in Russia, who struggled for "the real interest and the good of their homeland." The court, however, did not find that enough to condemn the encyclopedia, and the work continued to circulate.[42]

At that time, Bogdanov, Gorky, and their friends were not alone in thinking about a new systematization of knowledge that would provide an instrument for the education of the people. Moreover, the success of encyclopedias and dictionaries showed that publishing such works could be good business. Gorky, who was most interested in the publishing aspects of such a business, wrote in one of his letters: "An encyclopedia is the main bait for a publisher, and the soundest deal. The necessity to [publish one] now is understood even by the Cadets."[43] As soon as they had begun working out this project, Gorky had asked his friends to keep it strictly confidential, so that nobody could steal their ideas.[44] In spring, 1909, he wrote of having heard that "in Moscow . . . people from *Kriticheskoe obozrenie*, i.e., Frank, Kistiakovskii, etc., are talking about an 'Encyclopedia for Workers.'"[45] But this project was never realized.

In spite of the financial obstacles to building a new publishing house, and the fact that many of the founders of the *Workers' Encyclopedia*, first of all Bogdanov, were then busy with other activities,[46] the project was still alive in early 1909. Mikhail Vilonov, a worker who came to Capri to cure his tuberculosis and was immediately welcomed by Gorky and the Bolshevik group as a representative of the new Russian workers' intelligentsia,[47] wrote his wife in Russia to say that "G[orky], L[unacharsky] and B[ogdanov] are working on the encyclop[edia], which will include all the necessary information and knowledge for workers. That will be an important thing."[48] But in a few weeks, alarming desertions began to take place. In the second half of March, a very worried Gorky pointed out to Bogdanov: "Bazarov is going to Crimea, instead of coming straight here," "Pokrovskii is already writing his *History*, which must be included in our plan for the encyclopedia." He concluded: "It seems to me that everything begins to unravel and fall into disarray."[49]

As a matter of fact, Pokrovskii did not give up completely. Because he had received only partial information about the project, and that belatedly, he had independently engaged with the publishing house Mir to write a history of Russia.[50] Therefore he responded to Gorky's proposal carefully: "Of course even now I do not refuse to take part in general, but my participation may be limited to writing an essay on Russian foreign policy, since that section, luckily for me, was not included in the program contracted with Mir." As for the internal history of Russia, Pokrovskii suggested that the most recent events should be told by the workers themselves, the main actors in these events. For the earlier history he proposed N. A. Rozhkov, although he was on trial at the time for his revolutionary activity as a Bolshevik. Pokrovskii therefore suggested: "Wait for the end of his trial, in April, and maybe you will gain a new and very valuable participant."[51] In April, however, instead of Rozhkov, Kheraskov, also recommended by Pokrovskii, was invited to take part in the encyclopedia.[52]

One might have expected that the philosophy section, dominated by Bogdanov, would have been the most consistent part of the encyclopedia, but conflicts appeared here too. Stanislav Vol'skii, who was a prominent Otzovist leader, had just published a book entitled *Philosophy of Struggle* in Moscow, but without any mention of the most important philosophers among the Left Bolsheviks in general, and the group organizing the party school in particular.[53] Gorky thought this act a clear violation of the collectivism that was supposed to characterize all the activities of the group. When new sources of funding surfaced, thanks to Bunin,[54] Gorky began to express doubts about the feasibility of the encyclopedia: "as regards publishing houses, personally I find more and more obstacles to decisive negotiations. [The publishers] pose the question: what exactly will your book be? Now I can only describe a series of collections; I do not have the right to make any more promises about the encyclopedia."[55] Bogdanov's reply sounded encouraging: "Take the money for the encyclopedia, don't be shy; we will arrange it."[56] But Gorky was still worried. They had no precise plan for publication of such a huge work, and Gorky feared that the collective character, which should have been the most important and specific trait of their work, had already been lost. Gorky wrote:

> This [work] must be done collectively, as we earlier agreed. Each author, developing his own topic, refers to this or that chapter in his companion's book. For instance, the author of the study on sects refers to the history of the church, while the author of the section on history directs the reader to the history of literature to look for the literature of a certain time, to the other section for information on sects, etc. In this way all the books represent one whole work, and each book will be edited by the collective, which will help us avoid big mistakes and maintain a common point of view.[57]

During those very months the same group of Bolshevik intellectuals responsible for the encyclopedia expended enormous energy over the organization of the so-called Capri school. As a matter of fact, they thought that such a school would be not only the first attempt to educate Russian party workers for the revolution, but also, and mainly, the first attempt to build up a new proletarian culture. The letters that they wrote to each other in the spring and summer of 1909 leave no doubt about that, nor does the program of activities of the school. From its first drafts, the program divided activities into four sections: party organization (that included the most traditional education of agitators and propagandists), political theoretical education (where great attention was paid to political economy and the history of workers and trade-union movements in Europe and Russia, as well as to the history of Russia), general world-view (with lessons on philosophy, aesthetics, literature, and the forthcoming "socialist culture"), and a shorter concluding section devoted to an evaluation of the current state of revolutionary struggle. Some items within the program repeated the subjects of the volumes of the workers' encyclopedia. To Bogdanov and his friends it was clear that working together with the workers would help the authors of the encyclopedia to develop their topics from a proletarian standpoint. At the same time, the hoped-for advance from the publishing house would help the authors devote time to teaching at the school.

Trotsky, who received the program of the school when he was invited to take part in it, radically objected to its organization. In a letter to Gorky, Bogdanov disposed of Trotsky's objections by observing that "it is clear that [Trotsky] views the school as nothing more than a propaganda circle of a slightly higher type; the *creative* aspect of it does not exist for him, the aspect which, according to us, expresses itself in the link between the school and the encyclopedia."[58] In particular, Trotsky protested that it would be better to give the proletarians a method rather than a particular body of knowledge. He remarked, "Within three, four months, how much specific knowledge could be taught or learned? The most dangerous thing in these cases is to contribute to the development of some *self-satisfied semi-educated* person. It is a revolting figure, whoever he is—intellectual or worker!"[59] In order to avoid this outcome, Trotsky suggested that they build on Marx's *Capital*, in which the method had been scientifically applied to the field of political economics. He continued:

> Of course, the problems of literature, arts, and morality are very interesting for the workers. . . . But where is the Marxist ethic or Marxist aesthetic mature enough *to be taught in a school*? I do not know. And nobody knows, since they do not exist, do not exist *so far*. Here, unavoidably, we are condemned to collectivism.[60]

But it was exactly this point that most interested the founders of the Capri school: the collective efforts to create an entirely new culture. The school should not repeat ideas that were already settled, but instead elaborate new ones within a collective of peers that included both teachers and learners. From this last point emerges one of the most original traits of the Left Bolsheviks' school project: to overcome the hierarchical difference between teachers and learners, together with the specialization of the different scientific fields and disciplines. The character of their students dictated new relationships: "being people, who were already able to study and think a lot, and who were generally rather educated, in spite of different gaps in their knowledge and a certain lack of system, they [worker-students] received critically everything proposed to them, and seriously discussed both the contents and the form of lessons."[61] The new proletarian encyclopedia should build upon the same foundation, as Bogdanov declared a little later:

> The new encyclopedia will naturally form itself from the works of the New University, whose different courses, gradually improved in their method by the strength of common labor and verification, will serve as its basis. There [the encyclopedia] will be nourished by the experience and thought of that class, which needs it first of all as the ideological basis for collecting its strength in pursuit of its super-class mission.[62]

The experience of the Capri school, which was considered a sort of model for the future Proletarian University, fell far short of its founders' ideals and aims. During the Soviet years, some of its founders could feel proud that a small number of their students took part in the revolution, and thereby confirmed the success of the school itself. But the small group of proletarians that local Russian committees had sent to Capri split up very soon. When Bogdanov proposed that the students during their free time discuss his replies to the attacks of the Bolshevik newspaper *Proletarii*, five students and Vilonov sided with Lenin and left Capri. Conflicts also emerged about the evaluation of proletarian culture: Lenin and his supporters thought that proletarian culture would be the *result* of the revolution, and therefore impossible to anticipate; Left Bolsheviks, on the contrary, deemed proletarian culture an element essential to the revolution itself.

In addition to the main political conflict, other personal but no less deep-splits afflicted the Capri school. So far, the reasons behind the personal divisions among the founders of the school have not been made completely clear. Certainly Mariia Andreeva played a very important role. She was increasingly worried about Gorky not having enough tranquility and time to devote to literature, and she seemed in some way to boycott the cultural and publishing projects of the group. Already in April, 1909, before the beginning of the school, Lunacharsky wrote a very alarmed letter to Bogdanov:

> in general A[leksei] Maks[imovich]'s attitude towards us all remains unfailingly friendly and even affectionate. But *gutta cavat lapidem*! The facts: M[ariia] F[edorovna] arrives in Naples[63] and says: "The school will not be realized. They [Lunacharsky, Bogdanov, et al.] proposed to A[leksei] M[aksimovich] to launch the idea, the encyclopedia, and the school, but nobody supports him."[64]

According to Mariia Andreeva, it would have been better to convince Gorky to devote himself exclusively to writing, instead of engaging in common projects. Moreover, Andreeva was absolutely opposed to the idea of a new publishing house, which would have meant the breakdown of Znanie and a substantial financial loss for Gorky. Lunacharsky quoted Andreeva's words: "I will not allow that A[leksei] M[aksimovich] be ruined for any project and collective. Nobody worries about him; [instead] everybody just steals from him—really, everybody!" In November, Bogdanov and Lunacharsky had a heated discussion with Gorky, during which they probably tried to estrange him from Andreeva. Gorky concluded that he did not wish to deal with them anymore, once the school was done.[65] Personal relationships grew colder over time, and finally broke down in 1910-1911. When students of the Bologna school, the second party school run by the Left Bolsheviks, invited Gorky to give some lessons, he answered to Kalinin, who had been in Capri as a student and now worked in the organization of the new school, that he would not take part in it, "since I do not want to meet people whom I do not appreciate."[66]

The encyclopedia project, therefore, was doomed by divisions within the Capri school and by worsening personal relationships. Things were no better at the financial level. Also in 1909, Sytin, a well-known Russian publisher, showed an interest in some of Gorky's plans, including the encyclopedia. Gorky believed that, together with Sytin, he could establish a "publishing house of an encyclopedic character for a broad public,"[67] but only in 1911 discussed the topic with Bogdanov.[68] By that time Gorky had already come to consider Sytin a "crocodile,"[69] eager to gain money at the expense of the independence of their publishing enterprise.

No doubt, Sytin was very interested in encyclopedias. Between 1910 and 1915 his publishing house printed three such works: a *Popular Encyclopedia of Applied Knowledge,* aimed at a very wide public; a *Military Encyclopedia*, conceived for officers and soldiers; and a *Children's Encyclopedia*, a work of scientific popularization that had outstanding success and sold out very quickly.[70] At the same time, two other quite important encyclopedias appeared, filling up an already well-supplied market. As soon as Iuzhakov's *Great Encyclopedia* was finished, appearing at the same time as Brockhaus and Efron's *New Encyclopedic Dictionary*, a new *Russian Encyclopedia* was issued. As its very title indicated, *Russian Encyclopedia* emphasized its deep roots in Russian culture, and thereby challenged competitors that had adapted foreign works (like the Brockhaus dictionaries or Meyer's *Lexicon*).[71] Most importantly, in 1910 the *Granat Encyclopedic Dictionary* came out in a completely revised seventh edition.[72] The catalogue of the publishing house connected the enterprise with "the fracture suffered by Russia," and declared the *Granat Encyclopedic Dictionary* "the first Russian formative dictionary of the twentieth century, the first formative encyclopedia of the renewed Russia."[73] By publishing broad essays, the *Granat Dictionary* became "a systematic formative encyclopedia, reflecting the ideas that prevailed in the 1890s and the first decade of the 1900s among progressive circles of the Russian intelligentsia and young professors."[74] Some Bolshevik authors took part in the new work; Lenin, Pokrovskii, Bonch-Bruevich, and Friche all contributed. Thanks to a system of installment payments, qualified workers and democratic readers from the farthest parts of Russia were able to subscribe to the dictionary.[75]

In Russia there was still a strong demand for encyclopedias among general readers. Perhaps for that reason Bogdanov did not completely give up the old project, even when his relationship with Gorky was already strained. In a January 16, 1910, letter to his former friend, Bogdanov told Gorky about his meeting with E. N Skarzhinskaia, a Ukrainian noblewoman who sympathized with Tolstoyanism. She had provided financial support for some publishing enterprises of Russian émigrés in Switzerland. Through N. N. Ge, who was close to Tolstoy and one of Skarzhinskaia's friends as well as an acquaintance of Bogdanov's wife, Bogdanov obtained about one thousand francs to pay off the expenses of the Capri school. Bogdanov intended to turn to Skarzhinskaia again in the near future to help fund the encyclopedia, but in the end nothing was done.[76]

After the revolution, especially during the First All-Russian Congress of Proletkult, the workers' encyclopedia again became a subject of public discussion. At the Proletkult congress, Bogdanov, one of the main leaders of the movement, gave a talk on the topic "Science and the Proletariat," in which he revived the idea that the workers' encyclopedia was at the same time a result of and an essential instrument for the new proletarian culture. Bogdanov restated that it would not be sufficient to spread bourgeois culture among the workers, as if the problem was just to overcome the ignorance of the lower classes. A worker who simply learned bourgeois culture without criticizing and reformulating it anew, he said, "breaks away from the nature of labor that is proper to science and from the relationship with his own working class. Without noticing it, he transforms himself into a spiritual aristocrat with the typical signs of sectorial limitation."[77] On the contrary, Bogdanov continued, science itself should be transformed according to a new, proletarian point of view. Only in this way, by overcoming the linguistic fences put up by specialization, could science become in the consciousness of the masses what it already was in reality—"human practical experience, the instrument of organization of the human praxis."[78] In order to realize a proper "socialization of the sciences," it would be necessary

> to create . . . an organization for the distribution of knowledge and to foster the widest display of the creative forces of the working mass. The distribution of knowledge and scientific work are

> indissolubly linked one to the other; the Workers' University and the workers' encyclopedia must become their lively embodiment.[79]

In particular the Workers' University was supposed to work out the new encyclopedia. By going through the great encyclopedias in history, Bogdanov observed that

> the forms of encyclopedias always depended in themselves on the ways of thinking of the class that created them: sacerdotal ones, such as the Bible, had a moral-historical cast, oriented toward the revelation of an established leadership in different aspects of life; uncoordinated bourgeois thinking found its best expression in a dictionary, where pieces of knowledge simply connect themselves to single words. The proletarian encyclopedia arises as a whole picture of methods and results of both labor and knowledge. As such it will be the best instrument of the victorious class struggle and of its creative construction.

Bogdanov's speech concluded by launching new slogans to great applause: "Our common slogan in the field of thought is the socialization of science. Our organizational slogans are *the Workers' University, the Workers' Encyclopedia.*"[80]

During the intense days of the Proletkult congress, however, participants mostly discussed organization of the university, and the encyclopedia was no longer mentioned. It is true that, at least according to Bogdanov, a new systematization of knowledge aimed to create an entirely new educational system on the basis of anti-authoritarian and anti-hierarchical relationships between learners and teachers, in addition to a complete upheaval of all the distinctions between the different sciences. Therefore, according to Bogdanov, to prepare the new educational system would imply, as a matter of fact, to work at the same time for the new culture. However, the close link between the two elements, upon which Bogdanov always insisted, seemed to disappear from the project that emerged from the Proletkult congress. According to this schema, first comes the reform of the university system, and only then—much later—the encyclopedia. As a result, far from being the fundamental instrument for building a new proletarian culture, the encyclopedia would once again contain its systematization *ex post.*

In very similar terms the project surfaced once more, in its last historical installment: the *Socialist Encyclopedia* that the *Vestnik Sotsialisticheskoi Akademii* announced in its first issue in November 1922. According to Bogdanov's original projects, the Socialist Academy itself would constitute the "academic collective" of the Proletarian University, "a certain part of which had been able to form itself earlier in accordance with certain conditions," but which would soon melt into the new organization.[81] In fact, however, the Socialist Academy was established with very different tasks, and presented itself as the main Marxist ideological center of the new country. As such, it was meant to "assist in the formation of the new socialist system, in order to help the introduction of scientific development into the praxis of socialist building."[82] The project of a *Socialist Encyclopedia*, developed by a special Commission and approved by the Presidium of the Academy on October 21, 1922, met both scientific and educational aims, and had as its self-proclaimed task not the "popularization" but the "democratization" of knowledge. The words were indeed the same that Bogdanov had used a few years before, but the project was quite different. In the announcement published in *Vestnik* one reads: "Its aim is to give to a qualified reader from the working intelligentsia a condensed but complete exposition and explanation, in a comprehensible form and with absolutely scientific contents, of both the theory and history of socialism and of the workers' movement."[83] The project would be clearly oriented towards "intellectual workers," and would not grow from within the working class as a whole; it was much closer to a traditional systematization of already-existing knowledge, rather than meeting Bogdanov's challenge of elaborating a radically new culture. The encyclopedia would contain four main sections: the history of socialist movements; Marxism and political economics; the history of socialist theories (which would include pre-Marxist and non-Marxist theories as well); and the reflections of the socialist movement within the arts.

The project was approved by the General Meeting of the Academy on February 22, 1923. The tasks of preparing a more precise plan and choosing the authors were committed to a troika—F. A. Rotshtein, M. B. Vol'fson, and V. A. Bazarov.[84] A few months later, on October 11, Rotshtein reported to the General Meeting of the Academy that the editorial board had been decided; he himself would be the chief editor, while Vol'fson would be the liaison with the State Publishing House that would print the encyclopedia. S. Krivtsov was appointed scientific secretary of the editorial board, while Bazarov ceased to be named, although he was still a member of the academy. The editorial board worked very hard until May, when Rotshtein had to desert the project, since he was busy with other assignments in foreign policy.[85] But actually the problems were much more significant than the loss of an editor. Some members of the academy openly raised the question of whether a work such as the encyclopedia would exceed the abilities of the academy in that difficult period. In the end, they decided to solicit cooperation from a younger generation of scholars, who at the time were free of the heavy burden of building a new state, and from foreign socialists, on the model of the *Granat Dictionary*, "which at that time was publishing its section on socialism," as one member of the academy observed during the debate.[86]

At the General Meeting on April 17, 1924, when the academy decided to change its name to "the Communist Academy," not a single word was said about the encyclopedia. The theme was discussed again, for the last time, one year later when, at the annual general meeting, O. Iu. Shmidt described the project that was already becoming the *Great Soviet Encyclopedia*. Touching on the earlier discussions about the *Socialist Encyclopedia*, Shmidt acknowledged that the new one would be something different. The *Socialist Encyclopedia* concentrated on the social sciences, and attempts to realize it within the State Publishing House consisted of the effort "to recast the best of the old encyclopedias—the Granat one—in a modern way."[87] However, the State Publishing House soon became convinced that "in no way could one adapt an old encyclopedia to modern requirements, that it was impossible to pour enough new life into an old organism; later the question was really posed, that one needed to provide something similar in its form, i.e., to try to create an encyclopedia with their own forces."[88]

At the beginning of the century, in Gorky's and Bogdanov's plans, the encyclopedia had been the essential project for a new proletarian culture. Now it would become an enterprise of the State Publishing House. Only the consideration that such a work would require a long time and a stable leadership, which the quick changes within the organization of the Publishing House could not provide, argued for entrusting the Communist Academy with supervision of the encyclopedia.

The *Soviet* (changed from *Workers'*) *Encyclopedia* borrowed its form from earlier Russian models. It would be an encyclopedic dictionary, and it would pursue "two tasks—an exact scientific-propagandistic task, i.e., laying out in broad essays a certain systematization and orientation on one or another problem, and an informational task."[89] Its target would not be the masses of workers and peasants (Shmidt remarked, "it is evident that one will need to give the vast masses another dictionary, and that task is much more difficult than to provide a dictionary for the élite"),[90] but the "Soviet functionary." Shmidt explained:

> What is the level of such a functionary? What is his level in education? As regards mere linguistic education, the former dictionaries appealed to people who had finished grammar school, who had studied different languages, especially the so-called dead languages, and were interested in literature and philology. The present dictionary will address itself to a reader who does not know [foreign] languages, but has a wide social experience and wonderfully [*velikolepno*] deals with the problems of society. . . . We will write articles that might be read by informed people with middling education [*srednim obrazovaniem*].[91]

Pokrovskii, who presided at the meeting, stated that there was no need to approve the project, since it was the realization of an idea that the academy had supported for years. But it is really doubtful that it was still the same project.

Unlike all the other projects for the creation of a Bolshevik encyclopedia, the *Soviet Encyclopedia* was actually published, beginning in 1926.[92] Nevertheless, scarcely anything could have been more remote from Bogdanov's dream of building a new, collectivist, proletarian culture, of which the encyclopedia would have been both the instrument and result. Like many other Left Bolshevik collectivist dreams, the workers' encyclopedia and the new proletarian culture that the encyclopedia was intended to express and promote were doomed to the realm of utopian fantasy, in spite of all efforts to realize these ambitions.

NOTES

1 A. A. Bogdanov, *Kul'turnye zadachi nashego vremeni* (Moscow: Izd-vo S. Dorovatovskogo i A. Charushnikova, 1911), 58.
2 Ibid.
3 A. A. Bogdanov, "Kak nado uchit'sia filosofii?," *Zagranichnaia gazeta*, no. 4 (1908), 7.
4 V. Briusov's Letter to Z. Gippius, 18 June 1907, in *Literaturnoe nasledstvo*, vol. 85, *V. Ia. Briusov* (Moscow: Nauka, 1976), 698.
5 A. A. Bogdanov, "Na nado zatemniat'," in *Ko vsem tovarishcham!* (Paris: RSDRP, [1910?]), 4.
6 See Bogdanov, *Kul'turnye zadachi*, 30.
7 See A. A. Bogdanov, "Sotsializm v nastoiashchem (1910 g.)," in A. A. Bogdanov, *Voprosy sotsializma* (Moscow: Izd-vo politicheskoi literatury, 1980), 102.
8 A. A. Bogdanov, *Kul'turnye zadachi,* 60.
9 A. A. Bogdanov, "Inzhener Menni (1913)," in Bogdanov, *Voprosy sotsializma*, 282.
10 The question has been considered both in the context of Bogdanov's thought (see for instance Zenovia A. Sochor, *Revolution and Culture: The Bogdanov-Lenin Controversy* [Ithaca: Cornell University Press, 1988], 126, 144-45; David G. Rowley, "Bogdanov and Lenin: Epistemology and Revolution," *Studies in East European Thought* 48 [1996]: 11; Bernice Glatzer Rosenthal, *New Myth, New World: From Nietzsche to Stalinism* [University Park: Pennsylvania State University Press, 2002], 91-92), and in the context of Proletkult (see Lynn Mally, *Culture of the Future: The Proletkult Movement in Revolutionary Russia* [Berkeley: University of California Press, 1990], 47-48; N. L. Krementsov, *A Martian Stranded on Earth: Alexander Bogdanov, Blood Transfusions, and Proletarian Science* [Chicago: University of Chicago Press, 2011], 53-54). As for the first attempt to consider the "Worker's Encyclopedia" within the correspondence between Gorky and Bogdanov, see Georges Haupt and Jutta Scherrer, "Gor'kii, Bogdanov, Lenin: Neue Quellen zur ideologischen Krise in der bolschewistischen Fraktion (1908-1910)," *Cahiers du Monde russe et soviétique* 19 (1978): 331-33.
11 Bogdanov, *Kul'turnye zadachi*, 57.
12 Bogdanov, "Sotsializm v nastoiashchem," 102.
13 In addition to numerous conversations with Gary Marker over the years, I would like to mention here specifically the momentous contribution of his *Publishing, Printing, and the Origins of Intellectual Life in Russia, 1700-1800* (Princeton:

Princeton University Press, 1985), and, regarding the intersection of public and private themes, the book written with Rachel May, *Days of a Russian Noblewoman: The Memories of Anna Labzina* (DeKalb: Northern Illinois University Press, 2001), and the article "The Enlightenment of Anna Labzina: Gender, Faith, and Public Life in Catherinian and Alexandrian Russia," *Slavic Review* 59 (2000): 369-90.

14 Compare O. D. Golubeva, *Gor'kii—izdatel'* (Moscow: Kniga, 1968), 29.

15 Maksim Gor'kii, *Polnoe sobranie sochinenii. Pis'ma*, 24 vols. (Moscow: Nauka, 1997-), 6:201. Both terms refer to political debates among the Social Democrats about the newly-devised Duma. On theoretical and political debates within Russian Marxism at the beginning of the century, see my *Nauka i revoliutsiia: Retseptsiia empiriokrititsizma v russkoi kul'ture (1877-1910 gg.)* (Moscow: Akademicheskii Proekt, 2013), 272-75.

16 Bogdanov, *Kul'turnye zadachi*, 72. See also A. A. Bogdanov, *O proletarskoi kul'ture. 1904-1924* (Leningrad: Kniga, 1924), 239-41.

17 See *Gor'kii i ego korrespondenty* (Moscow: IMLI RAN, 2005), 131.

18 Maksim Gor'kii, *Neizdannaia perepiska s Bogdanovym, Leninym, Stalinym, Zinovevym, Kamenevym, Korolenko* (Moscow: Nasledie, 1998), 36.

19 Gor'kii, *Neizdannaia perepiska*, 37.

20 M. F. Andreeva, *Perepiska. Vospominaniia. Stat'i. Dokumenty*, 3rd ed. (Moscow: Iskusstvo, 1968), 124.

21 See Alain Jaubert, *Le commissariat aux archives: Les photos qui falsifient l'histoire* (Paris: Barrault, 1986).

22 Gor'kii, *Polnoe sobranie*, 6:221.

23 Ibid., 240-242.

24 Ibid., 7:99.

25 Lenin was invited to give some lectures at the Capri school on this topic as well. For the decision of the School Council to invite Lenin at the beginning of August, 1909, see Columbia University Libraries, Bakhmeteff Archive of Russian and East European Culture, Grigorii Alekseevich Aleksinskii Papers (hereafter Aleksinskii Papers), Box 8, *Otchet n. 1 o dejatel'nosti partiinoj shkoly*, p. 1, and the letter to Lenin sent by some of the Capri students. All the unpublished documents quoted in this article are part of a collection, edited by Jutta Scherrer and myself, an Italian translation of which will be published by Fondazione Basso, Rome.

26 I. Ladyschnikow Verlag, Berlin. See M. F. Andreeva's Letter to I. P. Ladyzhnikov, 8 June/26 May 1908, quoted in Gor'kii, *Polnoe sobranie*, 6:252.

27 Gor'kii, *Neizdannaia perepiska*, 37-38. Gorky delivered the same advice to A.V. Amfiteatrov (Gor'kii, *Polnoe sobranie*, 6:229).

28 See *Letopis' zhizni i tvorchestvo A.M. Gor'kogo*, 4 vols. (Moscow: AN SSSR, 1958-60), 1:280, 2:35.

29 See Gor'kii, *Neizdannaia perepiska*, 37.

30 See Gor'kii, *Polnoe sobranie*, 6:252.

31 M. F. Andreeva's Letter to I.P. Ladyzhnikov, 6 June/24 May 1908, quoted in *Arkhiv A. M. Gor'kogo*, 16 vols. (Moscow: Khudozhestvennaia Literatura, 1939-), 14:41.

32 Ibid., 40. Lunacharsky explained the financial situation within the faction, which was handled by a financial commission made up of Bogdanov, Krasin, and Lenin:

"Since I knew from my conversations with A. A. [Bogdanov] and N. N. [Krasin] that there is no longer any serious need, and that they definitely do not want to take those francs, but they planned to receive more than that from Chaliapin, I approved F. N. [Chaliapin]'s plan to send his money to You. Nik. Nik. [Krasin] wholly approved that too" (ibid.).

33 On Koussevizky's marriage with O. A. Naumova, see Gor'kii, *Polnoe sobranie*, 6:521. On Kuznetsov's most important role within Russian and international tea market, see *Torgovo-promyshlennoe tovarishchestvo "Preemnik Alekseja Gubkina A. Kuznecov i Ko." 1891-1916. Iubilejnyj ocherk* (Moscow, 1917).

34 *Arkhiv A. M. Gor'kogo*, 14:40.

35 Gor'kii, *Polnoe sobranie*, 7:125-26. Some days later he suggested again to Ladyzhnikov that, when talking with Koussevitzky, he emphasize Bunin's presence on the editorial board; "that is important because Bunin is not a party member" (ibid., 7:131).

36 Ibid., 7:131. Koussevitzky, however, decided to concentrate his investments in the musical field and in 1909 founded a publishing house whose proceeds would go to composers. Rakhmaninov, Shkriabin, Prokof'ev, Stravinsky, and others benefitted from this arrangement.

37 See *Kniga v Rossii. 1895-1917*, ed. I. I. Frolova (Saint Petersburg: Rossiiskaia natsional'naia biblioteka, 2008), 125-32; I. M. Kaufman, *Russkie entsiklopedii.* Vyp. I: *Obshchie entsiklopedii: Bibliografiia i kratkie ocherki* (Moscow: Gosudarstvennaia Biblioteka SSSR im. V. I. Lenina, 1960), 69.

38 S. G. Strumilin, "Predislovie k pervomu izdaniiu," in B. M. Filippov, *Ternistyi put' russkogo uchenogo. Zhizn' i deiatel'nost' M. M. Filippova*, 2nd ed. (Moscow: Nauka, 1969), 3.

39 "K istorii zhurnala *Nauchnoe obozrenie*," *Istoricheskii arkhiv*, no. 6, (1958), 107-138, quoted in Kaufman, *Russkie entsiklopedii*, 63.

40 Besides the third edition, mentioned above, a fourth edition appeared in 1910 and a fifth in 1913. See Kaufman, *Russkie entsiklopedii*, 58-62; *Kniga v Rossii, 1895-1917*, 112-18.

41 See Gor'kii, *Polnoe sobranie*, 7:158. A few days later Gorky asked Bogoliubov for ten copies of Pavlenkov's *Dictionary of Foreign Words* (*Slovar' inostrannykh slov, voshedshikh v sostav russkogo iazyka*, ed. F. Pavlenkov [Saint Petersburg, 1900]; a second edition appeared in 1907. See Gor'kii, *Polnoe sobranie*, 7:158).

42 See *Bol'shaia entsiklopediia; Slovar' obshchedostupnykh svedenii po vsem otrasliam znania*, 22 vols. (Saint Petersburg: Prosveshchenie, 1900-1909). Besides Iuzhakov, the first volumes name P. N. Miliukov as responsible co-editor, but the latter did not really take part, and his name disappeared from the title page after the sixth volume. See Kaufman, *Russkie entsiklopedii*, 65-67; *Kniga v Rossii. 1895-1917*, 142-43.

43 *Gor'kii v zerkale epokhi*, eds. P. A. Spiridonova et al. (Moscow: IMLI RAN, 2010), 53.

44 See Gor'kii, *Polnoe sobranie*, 6:221, 240-42.

45 *Gor'kii v zerkale epokhi*, 53. *Kriticheskoe obozrenie* was a critical and bibliographical review published in Moscow between 1907 and 1909 by B. A. Kistiakovskii; S. L. Frank took part in it as well.

46 Gorky often blamed Bogdanov since he "wasted his time" with party controversies, instead of devoting himself wholly to thinking and writing (see, for instance,

Gor'kii, *Neizdannaia perepiska*, 40-41). For his part, Bogdanov justified his lectures and other activities, telling Gorky that they "helped" his work on the encyclopedia (see *Neizvestvnyi Bogdanov*, 3 vols. [Moscow: AIRO-XX, 1995], 1:156-57).

47 See S. Livshits, *Mikhail Zavodskoi (Nikifor Efremovich Vilonov)* (Moscow: Izd-vo vsesoiuznogo obshchestva politkatorzhan i ss. poselentsev, 1929); Jutta Scherrer, "Un 'philosophe-ouvrier' russe: N.E. Vilonov," *Le Mouvement social* 111 (1980): 165-87.

48 Rossiiski gosudarstvennyi arkhiv sotsial'no-politicheskoi istorii, f. 455, op. 1, ed. khr. 7, l. 51 ob. (N.E. Vilonov's Letter to M. M. Vilonova, 5 February 1909).

49 Gor'kii, *Neizdannaia perepiska*, 46.

50 See M. N. Pokrovskii, *Russkaia istoriia s drevneishikh vremen*, 5 vols. (Moscow: Mir, 1910-1913).

51 *Arkhiv A.M. Gor'kogo*, 14:127-28. Rozhkov was actually condemned on May 1, 1909, to be exiled to eastern Siberia. At one point Gorky had the idea of organizing Rozhkov's escape during his transfer to Siberia, but the project was not realized. See Gor'kii, *Polnoe sobranie*, 7:133.

52 See *Gor'kii v zerkale epokhi*, 53-55. Kheraskov remained faithful to the encyclopedia project, even if he abstained from other Left Bolshevik enterprises to avoid conflicts with Lenin (ibid., 68).

53 See S. A. Vol'skii, *Filosofiia bor'by (Opyt postroeniia etiki marksizma)* (Moscow: Slovo, 1909)

54 At the end of March Bogdanov announced that some unnamed sponsors had offered "ten thousand rubles for our encyclopedia (they already have this sum), and then *probably about* ten thousand more, *if* we, on our side, will find twenty to twenty-five thousand, which would guarantee the reliability of the business. What to answer? The deadline for the answer to the second ten thousand is a month; an answer from us is requested before that time." Gorky answered that he had found financial support through Bunin: "Bunin states for sure that he, returning to Russia, will try to find fifty to one hundred thousand for the organization of our publishing house. He named the people who might give money—I know them, and I think that they really will give, since our capital is growing remarkably within the public," (*Gor'kii v zerkale epokhi*, 49-52).

55 Ibid., 52-53.

56 Ibid., 53-55. So, with new enthusiasm, Gorky resumed his contacts with Koussevitzky, about whom he regularly informed Ladyzhnikov (see Gor'kii, *Polnoe sobranie,* 7:125-26,131).

57 *Gor'kii v zerkale epokhi*, 55-56.

58 Ibid., 66-67.

59 Aleksinskii Papers, Box 3 (L. D. Trotskii's letter to M. Gorky, 20/7 June 1909).

60 Ibid.

61 Bogdanov, *Kul'turnye zadachi*, 73.

62 Ibid., 74.

63 At that time Lunacharsky and his wife lived in Naples.

64 Archivio della Fondazione Lelio i Lisli Basso-Issoco (Rome), Fondo A. A. Bogdanov (A. V. Lunacharsky's letter to A. A. Bogdanov, after 22/9 April 1909).

65 Piatnitskii wrote about this fight in his journal, which is kept in IMLI Archive in Moscow. The passage is quoted in Gorkii, *Polnoe sobranie,* 7:512. See also Andreeva, *Perepiska. Vospominaniia. Stat'i. Dokumenty,* 137.

66 Archivio della Fondazione Lelio i Lisli Basso-Issoco (Rome), Fondo A. A. Bogdanov (M. Gorky's letter to F. I. Kalinin).
67 Quoted in Golubeva, *Gor'kii—pisatel'*, 41.
68 See *Gor'kii v zerkale epokhi*, 71-72. For more on Gorky's contacts with Sytin, see Gor'kii, *Polnoe sobranie*, 7:125.
69 See *Gor'kii v zerkale epokhi*, 65-66; *Arkhiv Gor'kogo*, 7:33.
70 See *Narodnaia entsiklopediia nauchnykh i prikladnykh znanii*, 14 vols. (Moscow: Tip. I. D. Sytin, 1910-1912); *Voennaia entsiklopediia*, 18 vols. (Saint Petersburg 1911-1915); *Detskaia entsiklopediia*, 10 vols. (Moscow, 1913-1914). See *Kniga v Rossii, 1895-1917*, 80-82.
71 Compare *Russkaia entsiklopediia*, eds. S. A. Andrianov, E. D. Grimm, A. V. Klossovskii and G. V. Khlopin, 11 vols. (Saint Petersburg/Petrograd: Knigoizd. T-vo Deiatel', 1911-1915); I. M. Kaufman, *Russkie entsiklopedii*, 71.
72 The seventh edition included fifty-eight volumes, and was completed in 1948, after the deaths of both Granat brothers.
73 *Izdanie tovarishchestva "Br. A. i I. Granat." Katalog* (Moscow, 1910), 3-4, cited in *Kniga v Rossii, 1895-1917*, 138.
74 K. P. Simon, "Entsiklopediia v dorevoliutsionnoi Rossii," in *Entsiklopedicheskii slovar' Granat*, 58 vols. (Moscow: Br. A. i I. Granat, 1912-48), 54:332, cited in *Kniga v Rossii, 1895-1917*,138.
75 See *Kniga v Rossii*, 1895-1917, 140; Kaufman, *Russkie entsiklopedii*, 76-77.
76 See *Gor'kii v zerkale epokhi*, 2-74. Traces of the original project for a workers' encyclopedia remained only in the works that revived that atmosphere and those ideas. In his preface to the first volume of *Russkaia istoriia s drevneishikh vremen*, for instance, Pokrovskii emphasized the originality of his materialist method, which forced the author not to be satisfied with previously published conclusions, but instead to do primary research himself. See Pokrovskii, *Russkaia istoriia s drevneishchikh vremen*, 1:5-6.
77 *Protokoly Pervoi Vserossiiskoi Konferentsii Proletarskikh Kul'turno-Prosvetitel'nykh Organizatsii*, ed. P. I. Lebedev-Polianskii (Moscow: Proletarskaia Kul'tura, 1918), 33.
78 Ibid.
79 Ibid, 34.
80 Ibid., 35-36.
81 Bogdanov, *O proletarskoi kul'ture*, 261-62.
82 O. V. Grishaev, "Sozdanie Kommunisticheskoi Akademii i ee rol' v razvitii istoricheskoi nauki v sovetskoi Rossii v 20-e gody XX veka," in *Vestnik Moskovskogo Gosudarstvennogo Universiteta.* Seriia: *Istoriia. Politologiia. Sotsiologiia*, no 2, (2011), 27.
83 *Vestnik Sotsialisticheskoi Akademii*, no. 1, (1922), 207.
84 Ibid., no. 3, (1923), 441.
85 Ibid., no. 6 (1923), 425-26.
86 Ibid., 435 (words of B. I. Gorev).
87 Ibid., no. 12 (1925), 384.
88 Ibid.
89 Ibid., 385-86.
90 Ibid., 386.
91 Ibid.
92 *Bol'shaia Sovetskaia Entsiklopediia*, ed. O. Iu. Shmidt, 65 vols. (Moscow: Sovetskaia Entsiklopediia, 1926-1947).

The *Parsuna* of Gavrila Fetiev: Can a Picture Speak?[1]

Daniel H. Kaiser
(Grinnell College)

> The 1721 icon of St. Catherine from the Alexander Nevsky Monastery in St. Petersburg . . . lends itself to a multidimensional political reading . . . a visual articulation of the commingling of antiquity and modernity, patrimony and empire, faith and state. . . . We can imagine the value of visual representations to this type of hagiography, the interpolation of the tsaritsa into consecrated space under the approving gaze of Christ. Accessible to all, such representations overwhelmed the faithful with God's judgment. How could a sinful mortal, bereft of insight into the holy mysteries, hope to confront the blended image other than through acceptance?[2]

Writing about her second career as an artist, Nell Painter, better known to historians as Nell Irvin Painter,[3] recently observed that "visual meaning and verbal meaning are very different things." "Painting is more like poetry than scholarship," she continued,

> because juxtaposition rather than tight narrative composes meaning, and meanings need not remain stable. The viewer makes meanings . . . I don't mind at all when viewers see things in my work different

> from what I had in mind as I painted. For me, one beauty of the visual is its freedom from having to make sense. It's like creating visual fiction.[4]

If Painter is right, visual evidence presents important challenges to historians in search of the past. Peter Burke seems to agree, asserting that "images are an important form of historical evidence." Nevertheless, because "images are mute witnesses . . . it is difficult to translate their testimony into words."[5] "Difficult" may understate the problem: although most historians might agree that images can provide information unrecorded in traditional written sources, decoding symbolic meanings said to be embedded in images and uncovering "modes of viewing" and "seeing practices" proves more controversial.[6] In a recent interview, Aden Kumler, historian of medieval European art, cast doubt on this sort of retrospective viewing: "I don't believe I will ever see like a medieval person or think like a medieval person or feel like a medieval person."[7] It seems obvious to observe that the viewer—especially (although not only) if removed in time and place—brings to viewing different experiences and a different vocabulary; this is one reason, perhaps, why over time works of art come into and go out of fashion. If, then, as Nell Painter allowed, visual images are not stable, does it matter to historians what the artists intended *then* and *there?* And, if so, is it possible to recover those intentions?

The late seventeenth-century portrait of the wealthy Vologda merchant, Gavrila Fetiev, presents an image of which we might ask these questions. Evidently the first portrait of someone outside the Muscovite ruling family or its immediate elite,[8] the *parsuna*—an early attempt at portrait—is painted on canvas, 93 × 78 cm, an oval within a rectangle.[9] Apparently painted soon after Fetiev's 1684 death, for more than two centuries the picture hung in the sacristy of the Vologda church dedicated to the Vladimir Mother of God, a stone building constructed with funds from Fetiev's last will and testament.[10] In 1927 the picture was moved to the Vologda State Historico-Architectural and Art

Vologda *Gost'* G. M. Fetiev ca. 1684 (VOKM 2797). Published with the permission of the Vologda State Historico-Architectural Art Museum, Vologda, Russian Federation.

Museum, where it remains today, the beneficiary of a single restoration carried out in 1963.[11]

Experts are inclined to liken Fetiev's parsuna to icons, the artist presumably more comfortable with conventional religious painting.[12] The picture presents only the upper torso of the subject: Fetiev, outfitted in a red caftan with gold and silver-filigree buttons and gold embroidery, looks straight at the viewer. Not even hands distract from the subject's face, which, by some accounts, betrays an eastern origin, the dark eyes somewhat elongated and separated by a prominent nose.[13] A black beard and black hair (neither of which show any trace of aging) blend into the picture's dark background, thereby highlighting the face.[14] Nothing betrays location, occupation, or successes of the subject.

Although quite a bit is known about the adult life of Gavrila Fetiev, his origins are obscure.[15] The first mention of him appears in the 1646

Vologda census book (*perepisnaia kniga*), where he is listed with three brothers in the house of his father, Martynko, himself identified as a smith and townsman (*posadskii chelovek*).[16] Beginning in the 1650s, Gavrila appears often in the historical record. He is twice identified as having supported construction of new churches in Vologda, and the customs books (*tamozhennye knigi*) document his increasingly successful trading activities, as a result of which he accumulated considerable property in land as well as movables.[17] Additional evidence of success is his being named *gost'* in 1675, apparently without having first joined the lower merchant ranks. And Fetiev was the first of the Vologda merchants to affix his name to the 1667 New Trade Regulation (*Novotorgovyi ustav*), although the illiterate merchant had to have someone else sign in his stead.[18]

His rank and financial success inevitably brought him into contact with some of Muscovy's leading servitors, including V. V. Golitsyn, I. M. Miloslavskii, and A. S. Matveev. Connections like these were much envied, but they could also prove hazardous, as Fetiev learned to his sorrow. In the wake of Matveev's 1676 fall and arrest, Fetiev also drew the attention of the authorities: one of the men interrogated over the Matveev affair alleged that Fetiev, known to be on close terms with Matveev, practiced *chernoknizhie*, using books of "black magic." The accusation led to Fetiev's imprisonment, confiscation of all his property, and a series of interrogations of the merchant as well as many of his servants and associates.[19] Luckily, Fetiev escaped these charges by being able to demonstrate that he was illiterate, and, hence, could not have made use of the books he was said to have consulted. His property—nicely inventoried, to the advantage of subsequent historians[20]—was returned to him, and Fetiev enjoyed a few more years of activity before his 1684 death in Kholmogory in the presence of Archbishop Afanasii, with whom he seems to have been close.[21]

Sensing his end, in November and December, 1683, Fetiev dictated a most remarkable testament.[22] An enormous document, the testament provided a detailed list of the merchant's substantial property, as well as recitations of those who owed him and those to whom he owed money. As might be expected of a man of means, Fetiev also made numerous bequests to relatives and friends, as well as to churches and monasteries, including an especially large gift—two thousand rubles—to the Vladimir Mother of God church in Vologda to underwrite construction of a new stone church and stone bell tower.[23]

What the testament does not mention, however, is the parsuna that concerns us here. Although men like V. V. Golitsyn, with whom Fetiev was friendly and to whom he bequeathed some valuable items, clearly enjoyed possessing portraits of themselves and others of their contemporaries (a practice probably learned from foreigners they encountered in Muscovy),[24] Fetiev evidently did not absorb that particular interest, although in other respects he was clearly "consuming" western culture.[25] For example, like Golitsyn, Fetiev had mirrors on his walls, and therefore, like his European colleagues, Fetiev had frequent occasion to view and consider his "self."[26] It may be, as Gennadii Vdovin has proposed, that mirrors are closely connected to the development of portraits: "the depiction, being equal to the one being depicted, replaced the original."[27] But if Fetiev's testament is to be believed, he did not own a portrait of himself. This circumstance argues therefore that the parsuna was done after his demise, and not before.[28]

Although the full history of Russian commemorative portraits remains to be written, it is clear that, by the time of Fetiev's death, portraits of the dead (or dying) in Muscovy were being painted—on canvas and in oil (like Fetiev's). Perhaps the best-known instance is the 1694 portrait of Natalia Naryshkina, probably done by Mikhail Choglokov.[29] Despite being painted at death, portraits like this one did not represent the deceased in repose on a deathbed; instead, they depicted a living subject. Furthermore, whereas an icon might be destined to stand over the coffin of the deceased, increasingly these commemorative portraits found a secular use, often hanging alongside images of kin and kings in the houses of the Muscovite and later Petrine elites.[30] These "galleries of kin" (as one historian has called them) allowed the Muscovite upper crust to imitate European (especially Polish) aristocrats.[31]

Fetiev's portrait, as noted above, had a different destiny, finding a home in the church sacristy. This indicates that its purpose had been to commemorate the church's benefactor.[32] If so, then the picture might well speak as a remembrance of a generous donor, whose image was—until 1927—always contextualized by the church in which the painting hung. We might easily imagine, therefore, that most eighteenth- and nineteenth-century parishioners of this church saw in Fetiev's portrait not so much a particular, real person—as he might appear in a "gallery of kin"—but rather an abstraction, a symbol of generosity and faithfulness. And churchmen who installed the portrait in the sacristy might well have intended exactly that result, a conclusion that seems logical, and perhaps inevitable; yet the image itself offers little encouragement to such a reading.

Even the staunchest proponents of the historical value of "visual culture" allow that "images are more open to interpretation than texts are." Moreover, the "inherent ambiguities of visual address" allow multiple messages to be expressed.[33] How then can the historian be confident in any reading of such a text?

In his analysis of what he calls the "visual dominant," Marcus Levitt affirms that a picture may "speak a thousand words, but only to those who understand its language." Visual evidence, he continues, "does not stand alone, but is always . . . culturally mediated and historically contingent, and language is the primary and necessary vehicle of this mediation."[34] In other words, to read visual evidence, the historian must situate the image in cultural and historical context.

The history of portrait-painting in eighteenth-century Russia offers some hope for translating Fetiev's portrait. As James Cracraft noted, personal portraits became ever more common among the late Muscovite elite, a trend he attributed to Muscovites' increasing obsession with honor and social standing.[35] Early *parsuny*, he argued, were part of this cultural trend, which explains why these portraits were executed in a "style that conveyed the actual appearance of the subject much less than it vaunted the splendor or gravity of his or her dress and surroundings."[36] Here Cracraft has in view paintings like that of V. F. Liutkin (1697) in which the standing, full-body subject is surrounded by evidence of wealth and accomplishment; a cartouche with a Latin (!)

inscription identifies the subject, his age, and date of the painting.[37] At about this same time Archbishop Afanasii had a portrait of himself painted, and he evidently sat for the artist, who, "looking at him, the archbishop, painted every likeness of his person" (*smotriuchii na nego, arkhiereia, obrisoval vse podobie sushchee litsa*).[38]

The so-called *Preobrazhenskie* portraits—painted at Peter's command only a few years after the Liutkin portrait—offer a variant portrayal: like Fetiev's image, these portraits are natural and simple in design, deprived of the surrounding particulars so common in European portraits (and in those of grandees like Liutkin). However, they bore the peculiar addition of the name or title (in Russian) of the person being represented—in other words, they include a verbal gloss on the visual.[39] A reflection of Peter's increasing turn to Western influences (Peter had portraits of himself and of Catherine painted during their 1717 sojourn in Europe), these early pictures participate in a century-long preoccupation with western-style portraits, an enthusiasm that soon embraced Russia's merchant estate.[40]

By the late eighteenth century, Russian merchants had fully adopted this form of representation.[41] Yet these late eighteenth- and early nineteenth-century portraits are, in contrast to their Petrine parallels, relatively complex compositions, often including in the subject's frame distinctive markers that identify the person's location and accomplishments.[42] Indeed, Ransel argues that the particularities of merchant portraits—not only the beards, haircuts, and dress, but also "the abacuses, letters, inkstands and medals—set them apart from the peasantry by signifying their greater education and from the clergy by underscoring their professional status. . . ."[43]

Very little of this can be found in Fetiev's seventeenth-century portrait. Presenting its subject without any identifiable background, and providing only a half-body representation, the Fetiev portrait seems stubbornly incommunicative. No verbal gloss adds to the darkened background, nor does the Vologda gost' hold or foreground any of the indications of rank and wealth that Petrine grandees or even eighteenth-century merchants had deployed in their portraits. Fetiev is dressed in what appears to be a *feriaz'* or *ferez,* distinguished from other

Muscovite caftans by the fact that it was slipped over the head, and therefore had only a few buttons and fasteners.[44] A collar, which might have been fur, helps dress up the bright, red garment with its beautifully crafted, silver gilded buttons. The subject's clothing calls to mind the 1677 inventory of Fetiev's property, which listed a "man's red silk ferez" as well as "cotton *ferezy* with squirrel" and a "purple caftan with silver buttons."[45] The same record reports that Fetiev had a large collection of buttons—forty-nine "old silver" buttons, forty-one new, silver-filigree (*voliachnye*) buttons; twenty-one gilded, silver buttons, and five cloisonné buttons, so that any of these might have been added to a ferez in the years after 1677.[46] Fetiev's will does not mention a ferez, but does provide a long list of caftans, almost all of which he bequeathed to his son-in-law. Some of these, too, are similar to the garments depicted in the painting; for example, the will mentions "a red silk coat with silver embroidery at the top"; several others had fur collars like the coat in Fetiev's portrait.[47]

Could it be that the very thing that draws the viewer's attention—Fetiev's clothing—is itself key to reading the portrait? Robert Tittler noted that, in civic as well as in the so-called personal portraits of early modern England, "clothing possessed an agency appropriate to a particular task. . . . In portraits like this the notion of character has been transferred from the potential subtleties of expression and pose to the raiment itself, a symbolic but effective communication of the portraits' intent."[48] Much the same has been said about eighteenth-century Russian merchant portraits in which clothing (along with jewelry and other ornament) served to define the rank of the subject.[49]

Writing about the seventeenth century, L. A. Chernaia maintains that, if earlier artists were obliged to use their art to penetrate the internal or spiritual and thereby reflect the invisible and eternal, by the seventeenth century that expectation had changed. "The seventeenth century was a time of crisis for the old conception of a person and the formulation of a new [conception]." Indeed, she continues, with the increased valorization of reason, the "rehabilitation of 'external wisdom' was accomplished at the same time as the justification of the 'external person' as a whole, and most of all, the body—sinful flesh."[50]

For artists like Ushakov, then, the goal was "to become a second mirror, to depict all that was visible."[51]

Fetiev's seventeenth-century parsuna, perhaps precisely because of its apparent silence, obliges the viewer to focus upon the external, the "historically concrete" aspects of the subject. As one scholar has remarked,

> The carefully depicted, rich clothing and its accompaniment unmistakably testifies to the social status of the subject, and the face of the hero, in spite of the stiffness of expression, already distinguishes it from individuals on icons. Fetiev is depicted as representative of a merchant estate, and, at the same time, as a person having given service to the church.[52]

Examination of the cultural and specific context of Fetiev's portrait seems to point to at least two messages. If not depicted full-body in the midst of his enormous wealth, Fetiev's image is nonetheless a rich one, revealing him in highly ornate dress that speaks—or at least whispers—of worldly success. On the other hand, the tempered expression of social status and the fact that the portrait was evidently painted for the Church of the Mother of God point to a different message more closely related to death and memorialization. As Robert Tittler observed, writing about early modern England, memorial portraits might have served as "post-Reformation surrogate[s] for the traditional anniversary and obit prayers for the dead, and the periodic reading out from the parish bede roll the names of the departed souls. Both traditions had allowed the parish to retain in its collective memory the 'virtual' presence of the deceased."[53]

Muscovy certainly had a well-developed culture of commemoration, and Muscovite Christians actively participated in a culture of remembering the dead, making donations to church institutions in return for regular prayers of remembrance.[54] As already noted, Fetiev himself participated vigorously in this culture, making donations to numerous church institutions in exchange for memorial prayers. Fetiev's portrait seems to participate in that same tradition, if imperfectly. Perhaps, as Tittler found for England, the Muscovite merchant's portrait hanging in the church sacristy provided a kind of virtual presence of the deceased donor, implicitly reminding clergy of the duty to pray for him. On the other hand, without even a name inscribed onto the canvas and in the absence of any other indicator of rank or profession, the picture invites a more anonymous reading, the viewer inescapably attracted to the subject's face and eyes.

Can a picture speak? Most certainly, especially when, as Gary Marker has shown with his analysis of the Catherine icon and the numerous texts that emanated from the Petrine court and valorized Saint Catherine, cultural context provides an amplifying vocabulary.[55] In other cases, as in the parsuna of Gavrila Fetiev considered here, the ambiguities of visual address—even when fully contextualized—allow multiple readings, and complicate our understanding.

NOTES

1 My thanks to Gail Lenhoff and participants of the 16th Annual UCLA Early Modern Slavic Studies Workshop (February 8, 2013) for their comments on an early version of this essay, and to Ann Kleimola and my fellow co-editors for help in making the article better.

2 Gary Marker, "An Icon of Female Authority: The St. Catherine Image of 1721," in *Picturing Russia: Explorations in Visual Culture*, ed. Valerie A. Kivelson and Joan Neuberger (New Haven: Yale University Press, 2008), 63, 65.

3 The author of seven books and a host of other publications, Painter is renowned for her biographies of Sojourner Truth and Hosea Hudson, her history of the US South, and most recently, *The History of White People* (New York: W. W. Norton, 2010). After retiring from Princeton University, Painter has pursued a second career as an artist; for more on her art, go to http://www.nellpainter.com/assests/pdfs/NellPainter__ArtistCV.pdf (accessed July 22, 2014).

4 Nell Painter, "What's It Like to Leave Scholarship for Painting," *Perspectives on History* (May 2013), 30-31.

5 Peter Burke, *Eyewitnessing* (Ithaca: Cornell University Press, 2001), 14. On the other hand, discussing the "inherent ambiguities of visual address," Kivelson and Neuberger point out that "because words bear only an abstract and conventional relation to the objects they signify, images can seem more fixed in meaning" (Valerie A. Kivelson and Joan Neuberger, "Seeing into Being: An Introduction," in *Picturing Russia: Explorations in Visual Culture*, ed. Valerie A. Kivelson and Joan Neuberger [New Haven: Yale University Press, 2008], 8).

6 Kivelson and Neuberger, "Seeing," 2.

7 "Stuff Matters: Office Hours with Aden Kumler," *The Core: Supplement to the University of Chicago Magazine,* Summer 2014, 7.

8 Lindsey Hughes, "Cultural and Intellectual Life," in *The Cambridge History of Russia*, ed. Maureen Perrie et al. (Cambridge: Cambridge University Press, 2006), 2:650-52.

9 A great deal has been written about parsuny, but a good starting point is A. Novitskii, "Parsunnoe pis'mo v Moskovskoi Rusi," *Starye gody*, 1909, no. 3, 384-401.

10 In a very detailed nineteenth-century description of the church and its property, Ivan Suvorov relegates the portrait to a footnote, providing only a physical description and noting that the "date of the portrait is unknown" ("Tserkov' presviatyia Bogoroditsy Vladimirskiia v Vologde," *Pribavleniia k Vologodskim eparkhial'nym vedomostiam*, 1873, no. 1, 28).

11 VOKM 2797; M. E. Daen, "Neizvestnyi russkii khudozhnik vtoroi poloviny XVII veka. Portret Vologodskogo gostia G. M. Fetieva. Konets XVII veka," in *Russkii istoricheskii portret. Epokha parsuny* (Moscow: Khudozhnik i kniga, 2004), 148; A. A. Rybakov, *Khudozhestvennye pamiatniki Vologdy XIII-nachala XX veka* (Moscow: Khudozhnik, RSFSR, 1980), color plate no. 129, 309; *Nikolai Vasil'evich Pertsev: Katalog restavratsionnykh rabot*, ed. I. A. Boguslavskaia (Saint Petersburg: Khudozhnik Rossii, 1992), 93 (my thanks to A. M. Kleimola for providing me with this reference).

12 On the overlap between icon and parsuna and the early development of portraits, see I. L. Buseva-Davydova, "Nekotorye problemy atributsii parsuny," in *Russkii istoricheskii portret. Epokha parsuny. Materialy konferentsii* (Moscow: Gosudarstvennyi istoricheskii muzei, 2006 = Trudy Gosudarstvennogo istoricheskogo muzeia, vyp. 155), 38-53. For a persuasive pre-history of *parsuny*, see B. L. Fonkich, "Nekotorye dannye o nachale svetskogo portreta v Rossii," *Arkhiv russkoi istorii*, 1992, no. 1, 133-41.

13 Rybakov, *Khudozhestvennye pamiatniki*, 29.

14 E. S. Ovchinnikova, *Portret v russkom iskusstve XVII veka. Materialy i issledovaniia* (Moscow: Iskusstvo, 1955), 101; M. S. Cherkasova, "Portret G. M. Fetieva. Kommentarii istorika," *Sbornik nauchnykh dokladov po materialam konferentsii "Novye otkrytiia portretnogo iskusstva Severo-Zapada XVII-nachala XX v."* (Vologda: Vologodskii gosudarstvennyi istoriko-arkhitekturnyi i khudozhestvennyi muzei-zapovednik, 2006), 136.

15 The standard biography for a long time belonged to E. A. Zaozerskaia, "Vologodskii gost' G. M. Fetiev (Iz byta torgovykh liudei XVII v.)," *Zapiski istoriko-bytovogo otdela gosudarstvennogo russkogo muzeia* 1 (1928): 195-212. More recently M. S. Cherkasova has added considerable detail: "Novye dannye o deiatel'nosti vologodskogo gostia G. M. Fetieva," in *Torgovlia, kupechestvo i tamozhennoe delo v Rossii v XVI-XVIII vv. Sbornik materialov mezhdunarodnoi nauchnoi konferentsii (Sankt-Peterburg, 17-20 sentiabria 2001 g.)* (Saint Petersburg: Izdatel'stvo S.-Peterburgskogo universiteta, 2001), 95-102; idem, "Fetiev, Gavrila Martynovich," in *Vologda v minuvshem tysiacheletii: Chelovek v istorii goroda* (Vologda: Drevnosti Severa, 2007), 36-37 (and reproduced online at http://www.booksite.ru/lichnosty/index.php?action=getwork&sub=about&pid=206 [accessed July 1, 2014]).

16 *Pistsovye i perepisnye knigi Vologdy XVII-nachala XVIII veka*, (Moscow: Krug, 2008), 1:41. On Fetiev's father, see L. A. Timoshina, "Rasselenie gostei, chlenov

gostinnoi i sukonnoi soten v russkikh gorodakh XVII v.," in *Torgovlia i predprinimatel'stvo v feodal'noi Rossii. K iubileiu professora russkoi istorii Niny Borisovny Golikovoi* (Moscow: Arkheograficheskii tsentr, 1994), 132.

17 See, for example, "Khramozdannaia gramota Preosv. Markella, arkhiepiskopa Vologodskago i Velikopermskago, na postroenie v Vologde novoi dereviannoi Vladimirskoi tserkvi, 1652," in Suvorov, "Tserkov' presviatyia Bogoroditsy Vladimirskiia v Vologde," *Pribavleniia k Vologodskim eparkhial'nym vedomostiam*, 1873, no. 2, 62-63; Cherkasova, "Novye dannye," 96; *Tamozhennye knigi Moskovskogo gosudarstva XVII veka,* 3 vols. (Moscow: AN SSSR, 1950-51), 3:475, 478, 499, 502, 612, 613, 615.

18 *Rossiiskoe zakonodatel'stvo X-XX vekov*, 9 vols. (Moscow: Iuridicheskaia literatura, 1984-94), 4:136; also available on-line at http://www.hist.msu.ru/ER/Etext/novotorg.htm (accessed July 3, 2014).

19 Zaozerskaia, "Vologodskii gost'," 206-208; T. V. Starostina, "Ob opale A. S. Matveeva v sviazi s sysknym delom 1676-1677 gg. o khranenii zagovornykh pisem," *Uchenye zapiski Karelo-Finskogo gosudarstvennogo universiteta* 2, no. 1 (1948), 44-89 (74-77 on Fetiev; my thanks to Martha Lahana for this reference).

20 *Moskovskaia delovaia i bytovaia pis'mennost' XVII veka* (Moscow: Nauka, 1968), 213-17; "1677 fevralia 3. Rospis' imushchestva gostia G. Fetieva," in *Privilegirovannoe kupechestvo Rossii vo vtoroi polovine XVI-pervoi chetverti XVIII v. Sbornik dokumentov* (Moscow: ROSSPEN, 2004), 268-73 (which reproduces Rossiisskii gosudarstvennyi arkhiv drevnikh aktov, f. 210, Belgorod stol, no. 1360, ll. 93-120).

21 Because the last part of Fetiev's testament is dated late December, 1683, most historians have assumed that Fetiev died in 1683, even though no document so far cited goes any further than to identify the Russian year (6192), which stretched from 1683-1684 (see "Izvestie o smerti Kholmogorakh i pogrebenii v Vologde torgovago gostia Gavrila Martinovicha Fetieva," *Pribavleniia k Vologodskim eparkhial'nym vedomostiam,* 1873, no. 5, 205-206). However, already in her 1928 article, Zaozerskaia correctly noted—without citing her source—that Fetiev had died January 6, 1684 ("Vologodskii gost'," 198). Zaozerskaia must have accessed the *chinovnik* of the Kholmogory Resurrection Cathedral, which documents that Fetiev died January 6, 1684 at the palace of Archbishop Afanasii; the funeral mass was sung January 8, and the *panikhida* observed on January 15. See Aleksandr Golubtsov, *Chinovniki Kholmogorskogo Preobrazhenskogo sobora* (Moscow: Imp. Obshchestvo istorii i drevnostei rossiiskikh pri Moskovskom universitete, 1903), 178-79 (I thank A. M. Kleimola who discovered and shared this find with me).

22 "Spisok s dukhovnoi torgovago gostia Gavrily Martinova Fetieva," *Otechestvennye zapiski*, no. 106 (February 1829):170-202; Iv. Suvorov, "Dukhovnoe zaveshchanie torgovago gostia Gavriila Martinovicha Fetieva, 1683 goda," *Pribavleniia k vologodskim eparkhial'nym vedomostiam*, 1873, no. 3, 93-111; ibid., no. 4, 151-61; ibid., no. 5, 200-205. The testament has subsequently attracted several commentators, but one of the earliest was Vl[adimir] Trapeznikov, "Rastsvet g. Vologdy i zaveshchanie Vologodskogo gostia Fetieva, kak pamiatnik byloi kultury," *Izvestiia Vologodskogo obshchestva izucheniia severnogo kraia* 4 (1917): 56-61.

23 The gift was one of the largest charitable bequests recorded in Muscovy; for comparisons see Daniel H. Kaiser, "Testamentary Charity in Early Modern

Russia: Trends and Motivation," *Journal of Modern History* 76 (2004): 1-28. For a nineteenth-century description of the church and bell tower that Fetiev financed, see Ivan Suvorov, "Tserkov' presviatyia Bogoroditsy Vladimirskiia v Vologde," *Pribavleniia k vologodskim eparkhial'nym vedomostiam,* 1872, no. 24, 736-41. Even before endowing the new building and bell tower, Fetiev had made numerous other gifts to the church, including a silver chalice, discos (paten), asterikos, a spoon, and cups that he donated in 1677, perhaps on the heels of his encounter with the Matveev investigation (Ivan Suvorov, "Tserkov' presviatyia bogoroditsy Vladimirskiia v g. Vologde (prodolzhenie)," *Pribavlenie k vologodskim eparkhial'nym vedomostiam*, 1873, no. 1, 25).

24 The 1689 inventory of Vasilii Golitsyn's property reported that he owned a dozen parsuny, most depicting Russia's past sovereigns, along with three pictures of unspecified kings; he also had one of himself. See *Rozysknye dela o Fedore Shaklovitom i ego soobshchnikakh* , 4 vols. (Saint Petersburg: Arkheograficheskaia kommissia, 1884-93), 4:3, 10. Likewise, Archbishop Afanasii in whose presence Fetiev died and who was often in Fetiev's company, owned numerous framed pictures. A 1702 inventory of Afanasii's property reported eighteen framed Russian and foreign prints in the archbishop's dining room and another six framed pictures in the foyer (*seni*) (*Arkhiepiskop Afanasii i religiozno-kul'turnoe prostranstvo Nizhnego Podvin'ia (konets XVII-XX vv.)* [Archangel: Pomorskii universitet, 2008], 177-78). Collections like these became more common in the early eighteenth century; see I. V. Saverkina, *Veshch' v kul'ture Rossii vtoroi poloviny XVII-pervoi treti XVIII veka* (Saint Petersburg: Sankt-Peterburgskaia gosudarstvennaia akademiia kul'tury, 1995), 78-84 (my thanks to A. M. Kleimola who shared photocopies of these two titles with me).

25 On more examples of Fetiev's western tastes, see Zaozerskaia, "Vologodskii gost'," 202-205.

26 According to the 1689 inventory, Golitsyn had five mirrors alone on the walls of his *bol'shaia stolovaia polata* (*Rozysknye dela*, 4:4). The 1677 inventory of Fetiev's property identified two mirrors on the walls as well as a "large wall mirror" that was stored in a trunk ("1677 fevralia 3," 270).

27 Gennadii Vdovin, *Stanovlenie "Ia" v russkoi kul'ture XVIII veka i iskusstvo portreta* (Moscow: Nash dom/L'Age d'homme, 1999), 166. Vdovin developed further his ideas about the emergence of self in eighteenth-century Russia in *Persona. Individual'nost'. Lichnost'. Opyt samopoznaniia v iskusstve russkogo portreta XVIII veka* (Moscow: Progress-Traditsiia, 2005). For a different take on the same subject, see Daniel H. Kaiser, "Discovering Individualism Among the Deceased: Gravestones in Early Modern Russia," in *Modernizing Muscovy: Reform and Social Change in Seventeenth-Century Russia*, ed. Jarmo Kotilaine and Marshall T. Poe (London: RoutledgeCurzon, 2004), 433-59.

28 Without citing any evidence, several scholars have asserted confidently that the portrait was done posthumously (L. Iu. Rudneva, "O zhivopisnoi parsune poslednei treti XVII veka i ee traditsiiakh v XVIII veke," in *Russkii istoricheskii portret. Epokha parsuny,* 46; O. V. Aleksandrova, "Kupecheskii portret kak zhanr russkoi zhivopisi: Vvedenie," kandidatskaia dissertatsiia, Saint Petersburg, 2006, available on-line at http://www.dissercat.com/content/kupecheskii-portret-kak-zhanr-russkoi-zhivopisi [accessed July 3, 2014]). Perkhavko follows a more unusual

route to reach the same conclusion, arguing that a sketch of Fetiev, published as an insert to Trapeznikov's 1917 article, actually served as an artist's draft for the parsuna, and was enclosed with an early copy of Fetiev's testament, implicitly confirming that the portrait was done posthumously (V. B. Perkhavko, *Srednevekovoe russkoe kupechestvo* [Moscow: Kuchkovo pole, 2012], 291, 551 [n. 171]). The published sketch bears no identifying information, but Cherkasova concludes that the sketch was done by Trapeznikov himself, and therefore has no bearing on the origins of the parsuna (M. S. Cherkasova, *Arkhivy Vologodskikh monastyrei i tserkvei XV-XVII vv. Issledovanie i opyt rekonstruktsii* [Vologda: Drevnosti Severa, 2012], 110).

29 I. I. Khilimonchik, "'. . . Obrazy sut' zhivot pamiati . . .' Atributsiia Mikhailu Choglokovu portreta tsaritsy Natal'i Kirillovny iz sobraniia GRM," in *Russkii istoricheskii portret. Epokha parsuny,* 249; for similar context, A. A. Pavlenko, "Karp Zolotarev i moskovskie zhivopistsy poslednei treti XVII v.," *Pamiatniki kul'tury. Novye otkrytiia. Pis'mennost'. Iskusstvo. Arkheologiia. Ezhegodnik 1982* (Leningrad: Nauka, 1984), 301-16.

30 Khilimonchik, "'. . . Obrazy," 249-50.

31 V. G. Chubinskaia, "Novoe ob evoliutsii russkogo portreta na rubezhe XVII-XVIII vv.," *Pamiatniki kul'tury. 1982*, 318.

32 L. Iu. Rudneva, "O zhivopisnoi parsune poslednei treti XVII veka i ee traditsiiakh v XVIII veke," in *Russkii istoricheskii portret. Epokha parsuny*, 46; Cherkasova, "Portret," 138; V. B. Perkhavko, "Kupechestvo i kul'tura russkogo goroda XVII v.," in *Stolichnye i periferiinye goroda Rusi i Rossii v srednie veka i rannee novoe vremia (XI-XVIII vv.)*, ed. V. L. Ianin et al. (Moscow: Drevlekhranilishche, 2003), 185.

33 Kivelson and Neuberger, "Seeing," 9.

34 Marcus C. Levitt, *The Visual Dominant in Eighteenth-Century Russia* (De Kalb: Northern Illinois University Press, 2011), 13.

35 James Cracraft, *The Petrine Revolution in Russian Imagery* (Chicago: University of Chicago Press, 1997), 191. To say so, however, is to imply a contradiction because of the formal abolition of the "system of places" in 1682.

36 Cracraft, *Petrine Revolution*, 192; Chubinskaia makes a similar point: "individualization of the person being depicted, which became an obligatory and inescapable trace of eighteenth-century portraiture, did not enter into the circle of concerns of the masters of *parsuna* art." In her words, the subject "of a *parsuna* was not so much depicted as signified"—reflecting wealth, class, and social status (Chubinskaia, "Novoe," 320-21). This characterization might apply as well to the parsuna of Patriarkh Nikon; see *Russkii istoricheskii portret. Epokha parsuny,* 156-59; and L. A. Korniukova and A. V. Vasil'eva, "Obraz i portret v parsune patriarkha Nikona," in *Issledovanie i restavratsiia parsuny patriarkha Nikona. Materialy nauchno-prakticheskogo seminara* (Moscow: Gosudarstvennyi istoricheskii muzei, 2006 = *Trudy Gosudarstvennogo istoricheskogo muzeia*, vyp. 157), 19-24.

37 Ovchinnikova, *Portret,* 116.

38 A second version was evidently later copied from the original. See E. I. Ruzhnikova, "O portretakh Afanasiia, arkhiepiskopa Kholmogorskogo i Vazhskogo," in *Russkii istoricheskii portret. Epokha parsuny. Materialy konferentsii,* 89-99 (90).

39 Cracraft, *Petrine Revolution*, 192-93. For two examples painted close to the time of Fetiev's death, see the portraits of Iakov Turgenev and Fedor Verigin, in *Russkii istoricheskii portret. Epokha parsuny*, 172-73, 176.

40 Cracraft, *Petrine Revolution,* 197-200. For a Russian perspective on the historical development of the portrait in imperial Russia, see G. Ostrovskii, "Portret v gorodskom narodnom iskusstve," *Iskusstvo,* 1979, no. 7, 62-69.

41 David L. Ransel, "Neither Nobles nor Peasants: Plain Painting and the Emergence of the Merchant Estate," in *Picturing Russia*, 76; Ostrovskii, "Portret," 63.

42 For more detail, see Lina Bernstein, "Eighteenth-Century Merchant Portraits in Words and Oil," *Slavic and East European Journal* 49 (2005): 407-29.

43 Ransel, "Neither Nobles Nor Peasants," 78.

44 E. V. Politkovskaia, *Kak odevalis' v Moskve i ee okrestnostiakh v XVI-XVIII vv.* (Moscow: Flinta/Nauka, 2005), 45; P. A. Savvaitov, *Opisanie starinnykh russkikh utvarei, odezhd, oruzhiia, ratnykh dospekhov i konskogo pribora* (Saint Petersburg: Tipografiia Imperatorskoi Akademii nauk, 1896), 157. On the varieties and different values of Muscovite caftans, see Richard Hellie, *Economy and Material Culture in Russia 1600-1725* (Chicago: University of Chicago Press, 1999), 380-83.

45 "1677 fevralia 3," 270.

46 Ibid., 271. Richard Hellie found that gilded silver buttons might be worth as much as 4.4 rubles each (*Economy*, 331-32).

47 "Rospis' chto po prikazu Gostia Gavrily Martinovicha rozdat' priiatelem," *Otechestvennye zapiski*, no. 107 (March 1829): 342-43.

48 Robert Tittler, *Portraits, Painters, and Publics in Provincial England 1540-1640* (Oxford: Oxford University Press, 2012), 150.

49 Ostrovskii, "Portret," 67. For more on merchant attire in the later Russian Empire and how it was posed in the new medium, photographs, see Christine Ruane, "Caftan to Business Suit: The Semiotics of Russian Merchant Dress," in *Merchant Moscow,* ed. James L. West and Iurii A. Petrov (Princeton: Princeton University Press, 1998), 53-60.

50 L. A. Chernaia, "Chelovek 'vnutrennii' i 'vneshnii' v russkoi kul'ture XVII v.," in *Russkii istoricheskii portret. Epokha parsuny. Materialy konferentsii*, 8-10.

51 Chernaia, "Chelovek," 16.

52 Aleksandrova, "Kupecheskii portret."

53 Tittler, *Portraits,* 21.

54 See Ludwig Steindorff, *Memoria in Altrußland. Untersuchungen zu den Formen christlicher Totensorge* (Stuttgart: Steiner, 1994) = Quellen und Studien zur Geschichte des östlichen Europa, Bd. 38; idem, "Pominanie usopshikh kak obshchee nasledie Drevnei Rusi i zapadnogo Srednevekov'ia," in "*Sikh zhe pamiat' prebyvaet vo veki" (Memorial'nyi aspect v kul'ture russkogo pravoslaviia): Materialy nauchnoi konferentsii 29-30 noiabria 1997 g.* (Saint Petersburg: Rossiiskaia natsional'naia biblioteka, 1997), 39-45.

55 Marker, "Icon," 63; and more fully in Gary Marker, *Imperial Saint: The Cult of St. Catherine and the Dawn of Female Rule in Russia* (DeKalb: Northern Illinois University Press, 2007).

Tracking the *Travels* of Adam Olearius

Nancy S. Kollmann
(Stanford University)

I am a big fan of Gary Marker's first book—a study of printing and publishing in Russia's eighteenth century. There he showed how Russia's reading public took shape and how its interests changed, moving steadily towards belles-lettres and secular philosophy with a good dose of lowbrow adventure tales and garishly illustrated romances. So Gary understands the early modern publishing world, with its penchant for illustration and its dynamism, which is what this paper is about. It stems from an encounter I had in Houghton Library with a curious version of Adam Olearius' *Travels* to Russia and Persia.

Students of early modern Russian history are unavoidably fast friends with Adam Olearius (1599-1671). His account is fascinating and is one of the few to provide contemporary illustrations, problematic as they may be. Olearius served Duke Frederick III of Schleswig-Holstein, who was endeavoring to win a monopoly for Holstein on trade to Persia, for which he needed Russian permission for transit travel. Frederick sent two embassies—to Moscow in 1633-35 and through Russia to Persia in 1635-39—and Olearius served on both. He returned briefly to Russia in 1643. In 1647 Olearius published an account of his voyages, as he said, upon the urging of friends (a common trope in introducing such books). The 1647 edition appeared at the Schleswig press—a handsome volume in 536 folio pages with about 70 copper engravings approximately evenly divided between the Russian and Persian parts of the account (plus nine dedicatory portrait engravings). Olearius' images were primarily ethnographic scenes of daily life and panoramic cityscapes, with three large maps (the cities of Moscow and Ardabil, and a map of Persia celebrated as including the first accurate depiction of the Caspian Sea).[1] In 1656, noting that the 1647 edition was sold out and that he had had time to prepare material and images that had not made it into the first edition, Olearius published an even more lavish volume, a folio edition of 766 pages with about 120 illustrations, including around 70 in the Russian portion; in addition to more ethnographic scenes and cityscapes, it added a large map of the course of the Volga River.[2] Olearius' intent in both these editions was to illustrate daily life and mores, as well as to share his scientific and geographic expertise.

Olearius was a distinguished scholar in the late Renaissance tradition of the humanist scientist. A linguist, theologian, and geographer, after his Russian and Persian travels Olearius served Duke Frederick as counselor, court mathematician, and antiquarian, as well as curator of the duke's library and *Kunstkammer*. Fascinated with Persia, Olearius translated a classic Persian collection of verse and stories (Sa'di's *Gulistan* or *Rose Garden*), prepared Persian-Latin and Latin-Persian-Turkish-Arabic-Hebrew dictionaries, expanded the duke's cabinet of curiosities (including flora and fauna he collected in Russia and Persia), corresponded with scholars throughout Europe, and amassed a library of over twenty-four hundred volumes, including rare Persian manuscripts. He also built scientific instruments, including an astrolabe, a microscope, a telescope, and the Great Celestial Globe that the duke of Gottorp gave to Peter I in 1713.[3]

Olearius was an inveterate promoter of information about Persia, India, and points east, areas on which Duke Frederick had set his sights for trade. Olearius managed the publication of several works related to these areas at the Schleswig press. He personally oversaw reprinting or revisions of his 1656 edition (in 1661, 1663, and 1671) and included in all his editions an account of travel to Madagascar and India by his friend John Mandelsloh that Olearius himself had edited.[4] In 1654 he published his translation of the *Gulistan* and in 1666 Heinrich von Uchteritz's account of Barbados; in 1669 Olearius edited a Schleswig publication of Jürgen Andersen and Volquard Iversen's travels to India and the Spice Islands. Trade was not his only motivation; this was a time when Europeans were fascinated by foreign travel, presaging Enlightenment universalism. One contemporary French writer asserted that travel accounts were "more popular than the novel," and Olearius strikes notes of edification and entertainment in introducing his 1663 edition, justifying travel accounts as a way for those at home to learn lessons from other societies and to virtually enjoy a society through the eyes of a faithful observer like himself.[5]

Olearius' account is one of the more valuable foreigners' accounts of Russia, despite his evident prejudices. He perpetuated the trope of Russia as a despotism and brought a Reform Protestant moralizing to his commentary. Condemning Russians' crudeness and barbarity, he scathingly described drunkenness and sexual debauchery, uncleanliness, foul language, and street fighting. At the same time, nothing human was foreign to him, and his book is a wide-ranging ethnography of Russian society, politics, and religion. He declared that he would only present information that he personally saw or could verify: "I present here a true and exact description of that state and also of other countries, regions, and peoples, which we visited, in the very view and condition in which we found them in the present time."[6] So, modern-day readers, reading critically, can learn a lot about Muscovy from Olearius' encyclopedic account.[7]

A fascinating aspect of his account is the illustrations, whose veracity Olearius personally vouched for. In the 1647 edition he wrote,

> As for the copper engraved pictures of this edition, one should not think that they are, as is sometimes done, taken from other books or other engravings. Rather, I myself drew the majority of them from life (some of them—by our former doctor G. German, my close friend). Then they were turned into a final form with the help of the

> excellent artist Avgust Ion, who many years ago taught me drawing in Leipzig. For that they used models, dressed in national costumes that I brought here. So that, however, during the work of engraving no degree of accuracy would be lost, for a long time I kept three engravers, not without great expense, at my house. They were to work under my direction.[8]

Nevertheless, Olearius' engravers took what he told them and interpreted it using the conventions of early modern European engraving; these pictures are a few problematic steps removed from direct eyewitness.[9]

What concerns us here is the fate of Olearius' *Travels* in translation. Marshall Poe has detailed the many languages and editions the most popular European travel accounts to Russia appeared in early modern Europe.[10] I had blithely assumed that such translations represented the same texts (and illustrations) as the originals. An afternoon in the Houghton Library at Harvard disabused me of this idea and piqued my curiosity about the uses to which travel accounts were put in early modern Europe.

Houghton Library possesses a Dutch translation of Olearius' 1647 edition by Dirck von Wageninge, published in Utrecht in 1651. Looking at it *de visu* when researching Olearius' images of punishment was eye-opening. This is a tiny book (about five and a half inches tall) that would fit into a pocket or satchel; produced in duodecimo in 925 pages of thickly packed text and scant margins, it is small and fat. It seems to contain the full text of Olearius' 1647 edition, including the Russian and Persian parts and John Mandelsloh's letters. But the illustrations are greatly pared down—only four of the nine dedicatory portraits are included, and of the travel illustrations, only six of the 1647's seventy illustrations appear. Distributed through the text, they form three matched pairs: the Russian and Persian alphabets and numerals, portraits of Tsar Mikhail Fedorovich and the Safavid Shah Safi, and images of diplomatic receptions by these two rulers. Out of Olearius' compendious folio volume, this editor has crafted a handy travel guide for a diplomat or merchant; recall the Dutch Republic's aggressive trade across the Middle East and Asia at the time.[11]

Translations of Olearius had a life of their own, apparently, and I became curious to see what others were like. Surveying the major early modern translations, Olearius' *Travels* emerges as a malleable object, the text being excerpted or edited, the illustrations and maps omitted, pared down, or redone, all to suit the perceived readership in a given place and later time.

Let's start with the 1647 edition. Interest was fierce in Olearius' book as soon as it appeared in the Dutch republic; in 1651 three different versions came out. In addition to the diminutive Utrecht one, in Amsterdam, two publishers put out rival versions, one in quarto and a smaller one in octavo. I have been able to look at the quarto, published by Hartgers.[12] This is an entirely different presentation than the Utrecht translation. It appears to include the Russian and Persian travels, but has little interest in imagery. Its title page dedicates the top half to a banner, held by stereotypic Russian and Persian figures, on which the title appears; the bottom half is a truncated version of Olearius' image of the Moscow diplomatic audience. Otherwise, the book seems to select a random group of only five images—a storm at sea in Livonia, Russian burials, Cheremis pagan rites, a market in Persia, and men shooting a cannon and crossbow in a Persian square. These are scattered through the 134-page book. I am unable to tell whether the few introductory remarks spell out who the editor thought his audience would be; clearly, rather than a book for travel, this one seems to be a book for reading.

A French translation quickly followed the Dutch; in 1656 Abraham de Wicquefort published the 1647 edition in Paris. A medium-sized book in quarto (about eight and a half inches tall) in 543 pages, it includes the full account and Mandelsloh's letters, but no illustrations, not even the dedicatory portraits of Olearius' patrons. De Wicquefort presents his work to an audience interested in learning about exotic peoples and lands. "Urged by his friends" to translate this "excellent and very interesting" work, de Wicquefort assures his readers that Olearius will accurately teach them the geography of lands that are currently "very confusing." He praises Olearius the linguist, mathematician, and geographer for knowing the languages of the Muscovites and "Arabs" (Persian, actually), for interviewing locals and reporting eye-witness observations, for citing true latitudes and longitudes, and for providing maps of rivers, towns, and regions that are so good that all contemporary maps should be revised on their basis. For de Wicquefort, this work appeals to general interest readers and practical travelers. [13]

Olearius' 1656 German edition proliferated in translation. All the German reprints and editions produced in Olearius' lifetime used his 1656 text and the original copper engraving plates.[14] Its first translation, into Italian, appeared in 1658 in Viterbo. In quarto, this version included only the parts relevant to Russia (Books I and II, interestingly omitting three chapters on religious rituals) and was published with the first appearance of Rafaello Barberini's account of visiting Moscow at the start of the Oprichnina (1564-65). It reproduces only four of Olearius' engravings, crudely copied: the reception in Moscow, a grand religious procession, a panorama of the city of Novgorod, and the map of Moscow. Dedicating the book to the "Cardinals of the Congregation of the Propagation of the Faith," the editor expresses the hope that this volume will aid in the propagation of the faith in "Moscovia," by which he might have meant to reference the struggles of the Uniate Church (established by the Orthodox-Vatican Union of Brest, 1596) to survive and expand in Ukraine and Belarus'.[15]

Italian was quickly followed by French: in 1659 the translator of Olearius' first edition, Abraham de Wicquefort, published in Paris a translation of the 1656 edition. This became the basis of Paris editions of 1666 and 1679. A medium-sized book in quarto, this version liberally revised Olearius' text. John Emerson critiques de Wicquefort for omitting key introductory parts of Olearius' text, rearranging material, and adding information from other sources without identification. In addition, de Wicquefort dispensed with all but one of Olearius' illustrations—the immense map of the Volga—and added two maps in French of Livonia and "Moscovie" (European Russia).[16] De Wicquefort praises the map of the Volga for giving would-be French travelers essential information theretofore unknown. His introduction makes clear that his purpose was also to produce a good read. Of all the genres of philosophy, history, the novel, and the travel account, de Wicquefort wrote, the travel account is the most edifying and most entertaining: "in seeing the customs and cities of diverse peoples one can understand their spirit, and one acquires much enlightenment and prudence . . . one takes part in the pleasure that charms voyagers and . . . an infinity of dangers, fatigues, and inconveniences that accompany them."

Entertainment was not the only goal of such translations, however, as the English versions attest. Editions published in London in folio in 1662 and 1669 were based on de Wicquefort's 1659 Paris text and restored some illustrations from the 1656 German version. The 1662 edition translated into English the maps in the French edition (Livonia, European Russia, the course of the Volga), but returned to Olearius to add his map of Persia, to craft a frontispiece with five of the nine dedicatory portraits (Crusius, Bruggemann, Olearius, Duke Frederick, and Mandelsloh), and to reproduce the portraits (slightly redone) of Tsar Mikhail Fedorovich and the Persian Shah Safi.[17] The English 1669 edition made minor textual corrections and was simpler in illustration, with only the maps of European Russia, the Volga, and Persia, and the portrait of the Shah.[18]

John Davies saw his goal differently than did his French predecessor. He included an English version of de Wicquefort's introduction where the French translator presents travel accounts as edifying and entertaining; like de Wicquefort, Davies also praises Olearius for accuracy and expertise, citing his long-time first-hand experience in these countries, his scientific knowledge of geography and mathematics, and "his acquaintance with the languages of the countries, through which they travelled." But his dedication strikes a more nationalistic and utilitarian note than had that of de Wicquefort. Presenting his work to "The Governour and Fellowship of English Merchants, for discovery of new Trades, in Muscovy, Russia, etc.," Davies justified its worth this way:

> The more reasonably at this time, inasmuch as this Kingdom, especially this city, begins to disperse its industrious inhabitants, and spread the wings of its trade into the most remote cantons of the world. Which that it may do, till its wealth at home and honour

abroad be so highly improved as that this corner of the universe may give laws to the noblest parts thereof.[19]

Entertainment and edification, trade and travel were all notes struck by the last full editions of Olearius in translation. Long after Olearius' original publications, de Wicquefort's French translation was edited and published in Leiden by the prolific scientific editor and publisher Peter van der Aa in 1718 and 1719. In folio with copious maps and engravings, these editions were predecessors to the lavish version that van der Aa produced in 1727 in Amsterdam in collaboration with an eminent scientific publisher, Michel Charles de Ce'ne.[20] De Ce'ne explained in his introduction that all previous editions had omitted Olearius' maps and images, usually "to save costs," but that Olearius' illustrations were essential for understanding the text and many would be included in his edition. He uses the de Wicquefort translation, praising its "beauty, elegance and [the] general esteem in which it is held," but notes that van der Aa and he have added a new index, topics in the margins, more material from the Olearius original, and new headers, all for the reader's convenience.

Van der Aa and de Ce'ne produced something in the spirit of Olearius' intentions. Admittedly, in de Wicquefort's translation they used what Emerson considered a bowdlerized text, but they respected the author's scientific goals by updating Olearius' work. These two men used their connections with geographers to add several new maps (at least eleven in the Russia section of the book), including some of areas not so relevant to Olearius' journey as to the dedicatee, King Frederick IV of Norway and Denmark (maps of Denmark, Poland, and Royal Prussia). The edition includes copies—often more decorative, often substantively altered—of about forty of the approximately seventy images in the Russian part of the book, a representative sample of Olearius' ethnographic images and cityscapes. It also adds six new pictures of Russian peasants and clerics, not included in editions that Olearius oversaw. Where they came from I have not been able to establish, but they are of a sort as would have been included in the popular European genre of costume book.[21] All in all, this lavish folio edition should have appealed to those interested in foreign lands and exotic images, vicariously tracing on updated maps imagined routes east.

In addition to van der Aa's efforts in Leiden and Amsterdam (1718-27), a flurry of activity in the 1690s continued to disseminate Olearius' work. In 1696 the major accounts that Olearius had published—his *Travels*, his translation of the Persian *Gulistan,* Mandelsloh's letters, and the Andersen and Iversen account—were published in a large folio collection "edited by the world-renowned Adam Olearius."[22] In this form, his work spoke to a German audience for at least another century: at the end of the eighteenth century German romantics—Herder, Schiller, Goethe—reported reading these accounts of the exotic East.[23]

Image erroneously attributed to Olearius, one of six new pictures of Russian peasants and clerics added to the edition put out by Peter van der Aa and Michel Charles de Ce'ne in 1727 (http://commons.wikimedia.org/wiki/File%3AOlearius_peasants.jpg). Freely adapting and modifying Olearius' work, they included updated maps and images not in the original edition.

The 1696 edition in turn brought Olearius to Russia. The Library of the Academy of Sciences in the 1720s owned publications of several foreign travel accounts, including an unidentified edition of Olearius' *Travels*.[24] Apparently, at least one translation of the 1696 Hamburg edition was made in Russia at this time as well. A. I. Sobolevskii dates two manuscripts to the late seventeenth century: one (BAN 34.3.1) includes the entire *Travels*, with the addition of a translation of Nicholas Sanson's travels to Persia. This resides in the Academy of Sciences in Saint Petersburg; it is in folio in 760 pages in chancery cursive and was purchased in 1763 in Moscow from a private collector, I. Il'in.[25] The other (GPB F IV 15) contains only Olearius' Books 5 and 6 (concerning Persia), but the pagination suggests that the manuscript originally included the entire *Travels*. Sobolevskii does not clarify if one is a copy of the other or if they are separate translations. Sobolevskii also cites a manuscript translation of the other works in the 1696 Hamburg edition, not including the *Travels*.[26] But the Persian focus and timing of the creation of these manuscripts—when Peter the Great was focused on the Black Sea coast and Persia (Russia held Azov from 1696 to 1711 and extensive parts of the western and southern Caspian shore, with Derbent and Baku, from 1722 to 1732)—suggest that these translations might have been associated with Russia's Foreign Affairs Chancery, which had been importing and translating news from Europe since the mid-seventeenth century. The Saint Petersburg manuscript, alas, includes no illustrations.[27]

There was clearly a European readership for Olearius, particularly among those interested in Persia. Editors chose him to present an entertaining book, to appeal to people's interest in exotic lands, and even to aid real travelers and traders. And they did not mangle his text as badly as they might have. Olearius, that energetic publisher, would have been pleased to see his work disseminated. But he would have been disappointed, as were Peter van der Aa and Michel Charles de Ce'ne, at the fate of his illustrations, which were generally not reproduced in translations. Olearius would have agreed with them that the images are essential for understanding the text; he had worked hard to ensure that they represented what he wanted to convey and he made sure that the editions that appeared in his lifetime included all of them. We will leave for a later article how exactly those images shaped an impression of Russia, and conclude by reflecting on how fertile a genre travel literature was for the early modern reading public.

NOTES

1 Adam Olearius, et al., *Offt begehrte Beschreibung Der Newen Orientalischen Reise, So durch Gelegenheit einer Holsteinischen Legation an den König in Persien geschehen: Worinnen Derer Oerter vnd Länder, durch welche die Reise gangen, als fürnemblich Rußland, Tartarien vnd Persien, sampt jhrer Einwohner Natur, Leben vnd Wesen fleissig beschrieben, vnd mit vielen Kupfferstücken, so nach dem Leben gestellet, gezieret ; Item Ein Schreiben des WolEdeln [et]c. Johan Albrecht Von Mandelslo, worinnen dessen OstIndianische Reise über den Oceanum enthalten ; Zusampt eines kurtzen Berichts von jetzigem Zustand des eussersten Orientalischen KönigReiches Tzina* (Schleßwig: ZurGlocken, 1647); for the microfiche of the 1647 edition, see Axel Frey and Leopold Hirschberg, *Bibliothek der deutschen Literatur: Mikrofiche-Gesamtausgabe nach den Angaben des Taschengoedeke* (München: K.G. Saur, 1990), fiche 21: 9454-56; for the 1647 edition online, see Adam Olearius, et al. *Offt begehrte Beschreibung Der Newen Orientalischen Reise. . . .* (Wolfenbüttel: Herzog August Bibliothek, 1647), Wolfenbütteler Digitale Bibliothek http://diglib.hab.de/drucke/263-1-hist-2f/start.htm_(accessed September 10, 2014). I consider the Russia part to extend to the account of the city of Samara, through Book 4, chap. 7 of the 1656 edition.

2 For a modern facsimile of the 1656 edition, see Adam Olearius, *Vermehrte newe Beschreibung der Muscowitischen und Persischen Reyse,* ed. Dieter Lohmeier (Tübingen: Niemeyer, 1971). Also available on fiche in Frey and Hirschberg, *Bibliothek der deutschen Literatur,* fiche 21: 9457-60.

3 Elio Christoph Brancaforte, *Visions of Persia: Mapping the Travels of Adam Olearius* (Cambridge: Harvard University Department of Comparative Literature, 2003), 5-25.

4 The 1661 and 1671 editions survive in very few copies; Pavel Barsov does not consider them true editions: Pavel Barsov, "Podrobnoe opisanie, puteshestviia Golshtinskogo posol'stva v Moskoviiu i Persiiu v 1633, 1636 i 1638 godakh . . . ," *Chteniia v imperatorskom obshchestve istorii i drevnostei rossiiskikh pri Moskovskom universitete,* nos. 1-4 (1868), ix-x. For full publication data, see ibid., nos. 1-4 (1868); ibid., nos. 1-4 (1869); and ibid., no. 1 (1870); and separately *Podrobnoe opisanie puteshestviia Golshtinskogo posol'stva v Moskoviiu . . .* (Moscow: Universitetskaia tipografiia, Katkov i ko., 1870).

5 On the 1663 introduction, see Barsov, "Podrobnoe opisanie," 7. On the publishing history of the *Travels*, see John Emerson, "Adam Olearius and the Literature of the Schleswig-Holstein Missions to Russia and Iran, 1633-1639," in *Etudes safavides*, ed. Jean Calmard (Paris: Institut français de recherche en Iran, 1993), 31-55; and Barsov, "Podrobnoe opisanie," iii-xii. On Olearius' publication of travel literature, see Jürgen Andersen and Volquard Iversen, *Orientalische Reise-Beschreibungen*

in *Der Bearbeitung von Adam Olearius, Schleswig, 1669*, ed. Dieter Lohmeier (Tübingen: Niemeyer, 1980), 14-15, 221 For Uchteritz's account, see A. Gunkel and J. S. Handle, "A German Indentured Servant in Barbados in 1652: The Account of Heinrich von Uchteritz," *Journal of the Barbados Museum and Historical Society* 33 (1970): 91-100.

6 Barsov, "Podrobnoe opisanie," 7.

7 For modern translations, see (with selected Russian sections into English from the 1656 edition) Adam Olearius, *The Travels of Olearius in Seventeenth-Century Russia*, ed. and trans. Samuel H. Baron (Stanford: Stanford University Press, 1967); the entire text into Russian from the 1663 German edition, Barsov, "Podrobnoe opisanie"; primarily the Russia sections into Russian, using an edition close to that of 1656, Adam Olearius, *Opisanie puteshestviia v Moskoviiu*, trans. A. M. Loviagin (reprint of Saint Petersburg, 1906 edition) (Smolensk: Rusich, 2003).

8 Olearius, *Opisanie puteshestviia*, trans. Loviagin, 14-15.

9 Lohmeier remarks on how some illustrations in the Andersen and Iversen account of 1669, under Olearius' supervision, were based on stock European engravings: *Orientalische Reise-Beschreibungen*, 22. In Olearius' *Travels*, this is less pronounced; the tropes are more subtle.

10 Marshall Poe, *A People Born to Slavery: Russia In Early Modern European Ethnography, 1476-1748* (Ithaca: Cornell University Press, 2000).

11 Adam Olearius, Johan Albrecht von Mandelslow, and Dirck van Wageninge, *Beschrijvingh vande nieuwe Parciaensche ofte orientaelsche reyse, welck door gelegentheyt van een Holsteynsche ambassade, aen den koningh in Persien gheschiet is: waer inne de ghelegentheyt der plaetsen en landen, door welcke de reyse gegaen is* (Utrecht: Lambert Roeck, 1651).

12 Adam Olearius, *Persiaensche reyse, uyt Holsteyn, door Lijflandt, Moscovien, Tartarien in Persien. Door Philippus Crusius, en Otto Brughman, gesanten, des Doorl: Hoogh: Heere, Heer Frederick* (Amsterdam: Hartgers, 1651). Available online at Munich Bayerische Staatsbibliothek Digital.

13 Adam Olearius, Johann Albrecht von Mandelslo, and Abraham de Wicquefort, *Relation du voyage de Moscouie, Tartarie, et de Perse: fait a l'occasion d'vne ambassade, enuoyée au grand-duc de Moscouie, & du roy de Perse, par le duc de Holstein depuis l'an 1633 iusques en l'an 1639* (Paris: Chez Geruais Clouzier, 1656). Online at Munich Bayerische Staatsbibliothek Digital and also as a Google EBook.

14 Emerson, "Adam Olearius and the Literature," 31-55. On the 1661 and 1671 printings, see note 4 above. The 1663 edition: Olearius, Adam. *Adam Olearii Auszfuehrliche Beschreibung der kundbaren Reyse nach Muscow und Persien, so durch Gelegenheit einer holsteinischen Gesandschafft von Gottorff auß an Michael Fedorowitz den grossen Zaar in Muscow, und Schach Sefi Koenig in Persien geschehen: worinnen die Gelegenheit derer Orter und Länder, durch welche die Reyse gangen, als Liffland, Rußland, Tartarien, Meden und Persien . . . zu befinden* (Schleswig: [Holwein?], 1663). Online Wolfenbütteler Digitale Bibliothek (WDB).

15 Adam Olearius and Raffaello Barberini, *Viaggi di Moscovia de gli anni 1633. 1634. 1635. e 1636.: libri tre cavati dal Tedesco* (Viterbo, 1658). Available online at Munich Bayerische Staatsbibliothek Digital and also as a Google EBook. Thanks to Chris Babich for translating the Italian editor's introduction. On the Uniate Church at this time, see Barbara Skinner, *The Western Front of the Eastern Church:*

Uniate and Orthodox Conflict in Eighteenth-Century Poland, Ukraine, Belarus, and Russia (DeKalb: Northern Illinois University Press, 2009).

16 I have been unable to see the 1659 and 1679 French editions. For the 1666 edition, see Adam Olearius, Abraham von Wicquefort, and Johann Albrecht von Mandelslo, *Relation du voyage d'Adam Olearius en Moscouie, Tartarie, et Perse: augmentee en cette nouuelle edition de plus d'vn tiers, & particulierement d'vne seconde partie: contenant le voyage de Jean Albert de Mandelslo aux Indes Orientales* (Paris: Chez Iean du Puis, 1666). Available as a Google EBook (maps not visible) and fully scanned on Gallica, the French national digital catalog, http://gallica.bnf.fr/ark:/12148/bpt6k118549z (accessed September 9, 2014).

17 1662 English version, see Adam Olearius, Johann Albrecht von Mandelslo, and John Davies, *The Voyages & Travels of the Ambassadors Sent by Frederick Duke of Holstein, to the Great Duke of Muscovy, and the King of Persia: Begun In the Year M.DC.XXXIII, and Finish'd In M.DC.XXXIX: Containing a Compleat History of Muscovy, Tartary, Persia, and Other Adjacent Countries . . .* (London: Printed for Thomas Dring and John Starkey . . ., 1662).

18 For the 1669 English version, see Adam Olearius, Johann Albrecht von Mandelslo, and John Davies, *The Voyages and Travells of the Ambassadors Sent by Frederick, Duke of Holstein, to the Great Duke of Muscovy and the King of Persia . . .*, second edition, corrected (London: Printed for John Starkey and Thomas Basset . . ., 1669).

19 1662 English version, unpaginated "Dedication" in the front matter.

20 Barsov praises the 1727 as more expanded and luxurious than the 1718 and 1719 editions: "Podrobnoe opisanie," xi-xii. For the 1718 edition, see Adam Olearius, *Voyages très curieux et très renommez faits en Moscovie* (Leide: P. Vander Aa, 1718); for that of 1719, see Adam Olearius and Abraham de Wicquefort, *Voyages très-curieux & très-renommez faits en Moscovie, Tartarie et Perse* (Leide: P. Vander Aa, 1719); for the 1727 edition, see Johann Albrecht von Mandelslo, Adam Olearius, and Abraham de Wicquefort, *Voyages celebres & remarquables, faits de Perse aux Indes Orientales* (Amsterdam: M.C. Le Céne, 1727). Barsov mentions later French editions that I have not tracked down: The Hague, 1727; Amsterdam, 1732; Paris, 1759.

21 They are not in the 1656, 1663, or 1696 Olearius editions. I have not seen the 1661 and 1671 versions, but they are unlikely to be different. These new images are not based on Augustin von Meyerberg's images.

22 Adam Olearius, Johann Albrecht von Mandelso, Jürgen Andersen, and Volquard Iversen, *Des Welt-berühmten Adami Olearii colligirte und viel vermehrte Reise-Beschreibungen bestehend in der nach Muszkau und Persien: wie auch Johann Albrechts von Mandelslo Morgenländischen, und Jürg: Andersens und Volq: Yversens Orientalische Reise: : mit angehängter Chinesischen Revolution, und wie solch mächtiges Reich vor kurtzen Iahren von den Tartarn überwältiget und eingenommen: auch: wie der flüchtende chinesische Mandarin und See-Räuber Coxinga, die von den Holländern besetzte Insul Formosa angefallen und erobert: : nebenst beygefügtem Persianischen Rosen-Thal und Baum-Garten: . . . durchgehends mit vielen, meist nach dem Leben in Kupffer gestochenen Figuren, Abbildungen und Land-Taffeln geziehret* (Hamburg: In Verlegung Zacharias Herteln und Thomas von Wiering, 1696). On microfilm, see Kurt von Faber du Faur, *German Baroque Literature* (New Haven: Research Publications, 1970), reel 65, no. 326.

23 Lohmeier in Andersen and Iversen, *Orientalische Reise-Beschreibungen*, 22.

24 *Istoricheskii ocherk i obzor fondov Ruskopisnogo otdela Biblioteki Akademii nauk. Vol. 1. XVIII vek* (Moscow-Leningrad: Izd. Akademii nauk SSSR, 1956), 168, 260, 337.

25 For a description of the complete manuscript, see BAN 34.3.1: Istoricheskii ocherk, 450, no. 10; Sobolevskii on these manuscripts: *Perevodnaia literatura Moskovskoi Rusi XIV-XVII vekov. Bibliograficheskie materialy in Sbornik Otdeleniia russkogo iazyka i slovesnosti Imp. Akademii nauk*, vol. 74, no. 1 (1903): 69-75. Sobolevskii reports that Sanson's book (*Voyage ou relation de l'état present du royaume de Perse: avec une dissertation curieuse sur les moeurs, religion & gouvernement de cet état* [Paris: Chez la veuve Mabre Cramoisi, 1695]) was translated into Russian from a German version of the French: *Perevodnaia literatura,* 70.

26 For the partial manuscript, see (National Library of Russia GPB F IV 15): Sobolevskii, *Perevodnaia literatura*, 74; for the manuscript of the Russian translation of 1696 Hamburg edition, not including Olearius' *Travels*, see (National Library of Russia GPB F XVII 4): Sobolevskii, *Perevodnaia literatura,* 75.

27 Correspondence with BAN Senior Archivist Vera G. Podkovyrova, March 27-28, 2014.

Catherine the Great and the Art of Collecting: Acquiring the Paintings that Founded the Hermitage

Cynthia Hyla Whittaker
(Baruch College and Graduate Center, City University of New York)

Catherine II of Russia was one of the greatest rulers of her time. Even in an age of enlightened monarchy, she stands out for her political, military, and cultural achievements. Fittingly, she has been the subject of any number of biographies that follow her from her birth in 1729 in an insignificant German principality to her move to Russia in 1744 to marry the heir to the throne, and then her seizure of that throne for herself. She then ruled from 1762 until her death in 1796. In a curious omission, no biographer has told the story of why or how Catherine subsequently became "one of the greatest art collectors of all time."[1]

What motivated this German princess from the backwaters of Anhalt-Zerbst to become the Maecenas of her day? Family background offers no hint of interest or wherewithal to stimulate any concern with the arts. Catherine's *Memoirs*, describing her eighteen years as the wife of the heir in the Russian court of Empress Elizabeth (r. 1741-1761), recount her enthusiasm for ancient and modern literature, politics, and philosophy, but evince none for art.[2] Even after she seized the throne from her husband, Peter III (r. December 1761-June 1762), no one would have expected a female ruler to direct her time and resources toward art collecting, since for centuries it had been almost exclusively a male preserve.[3] Moreover, Russia remained a relatively backward eastern realm with seemingly too little sophistication to venture into the highly competitive European art market. Despite all this, only two years after ascending the throne, Empress Catherine consciously embarked on the most audacious program of acquisitions the world had then seen. By her death in 1796, she had accumulated a monumental four thousand paintings that remain the core of the Hermitage, one of the greatest museums in the world today.

Catherine's primary motivation for collecting art was based on *raison d'état.* The chief objective of the empress's entire reign was to bring to fruition Peter the Great's (r. 1689-1725) plan to transform Russia into a westernized country with international stature, not only in respect to its political and military standing but also as a seat of culture. An emphasis on the arts indeed signaled—in the words of Denis Diderot, one of the century's most influential philosophes—"a people's rise out of barbarity and into a people enlightened, powerful, and thriving."[4]

By the eighteenth century, paintings, especially those of the old masters, had achieved a primacy over other art forms. The acquisition of a collection, especially one that was large or significant, carried great prestige because it suggested cultivated taste and national vigor. Rulers came to use their paintings as an integral part of the presentation of royal authority. In truth, a collection impressed, conveyed splendor, indicated wealth, enhanced prestige, glorified the dynasty—and refuted charges of backwardness. When receiving domestic or foreign delegations, monarchs, Catherine included, could have their paintings serve as a backdrop, basking in the reflected glory of the old masters with their depictions of the great men and women of the Bible, mythology, and history.[5]

Collecting demanded money, so the expense involved also served to project an image of fiscal strength. Fending off criticism of self-aggrandizing extravagance, rulers alluded to Aristotle's theory of magnificence: namely, that expenditure connected with "public-spirited ambition" is a virtue.[6] Catherine intoned in her Nakaz, or Instruction: "Decency requires that Affluence and Magnificence should surround the throne . . . and for all of which, *Expense* is not only *necessary* but highly *useful.*"[7]

A great collection would not only raise Russia's standing in Europe, it could also contribute to Catherine's very real need to establish her own legitimacy as a monarch and to present an image of stability both at home and abroad. As is well known, she usurped the throne from a perfectly legal ruler, who died under mysterious circumstances ten days later, recalling earlier brutal shifts of power in Russia. Scandal naturally ensued, which made the country seem like a banana republic *avant la lettre*.[8] Immediately after taking the throne in June of 1762, Catherine issued a series of manifestoes to justify her seizure and orchestrated a lavish eight-day coronation in September to reinforce her claims.[9]

In establishing her legitimacy, both at the beginning of and throughout her thirty-four years as ruler, Catherine courted the philosophes—the high priests of public opinion—seeking to gain their approval as an "enlightened" monarch in that Age of Enlightenment. As her reign progressed, Catherine's deeds in fact conformed to the three criteria by which the philosophes judged eighteenth-century monarchs. Conquest and expansion figured prominently. The empress moved her empire both south to the Black Sea and west into Central Europe, claiming victories in the Turkish and Swedish wars, all the while cementing Russia's hold over its eastern expanse to the Pacific. Second, philosophes commended hard-working rulers who strove to introduce modern, secular, rational practices into their realms. The empress produced thousands of pieces of legislation in her efforts to reform the creaky machinery of the Russian government in fields as varied as education, the judiciary, public health, and the bureaucracy. To great acclaim, she proposed a new set of laws for Russia in 1767 that

***Portrait of Catherine II* by Aleksei Antropov, one of many commissioned after the coronation to trumpet the empress's legitimacy by showing her in all her majesty with throne, orb, scepter, four crowns, and the sash of the Order of Saint Andrew, worn only by royalty.[10]**

was translated into every European language and deemed so "liberal" that the French authorities stopped the document at the border.

The third criterion was involvement with the arts, and Catherine vigorously championed them. Indeed, the empress became eulogized as Minerva, who symbolized at once military prowess, legislative wisdom, and patronage of the arts.

***Catherine II as Minerva*, a cameo engraved by the empress's daughter-in-law, Grand Duchess Maria Feodorovna.[11]**

While Catherine excelled as a collector of paintings, she was extensively involved with the other arts as well. Her literary forays certainly command serious attention. The empress figured as one of the most prominent Russian writers in her century and one of the most prolific author-monarchs of all time. She wrote laws, of course, but she also wrote in all other literary forms at a time when Russian literature was still in its infancy. She penned splendid memoirs, collaborated on a text in linguistics, founded journals, and published polemical works, educational essays, and a history of Russia; she also wrote libretti for operas and corresponded tirelessly in three languages (German, French, and Russian). The fairy tales that she wrote for her grandsons became the first works of children's literature ever published in Russia. Catherine also wrote about two dozen plays and built public and private venues where dramas could be produced; she also founded the Imperial Theatrical School to train actors and directors. Her personal love of theater led her to build an exquisite structure within the Winter Palace to stage plays and operas for herself and the court.

Catherine's theater in the Hermitage, designed by the famed architect Giacomo Quarenghi and modeled after the Renaissance Palladian theater in Vicenza.[12]

As just intimated, another of Catherine's public passions was building. The empress confessed to her longtime correspondent and friend, the philosophe Friedrich Melchior Grimm: "I am passionately interested in books on architecture; they fill my room, but even that is not enough for me."[13] The empress didn't just want to read about architecture: she wanted to build, and build she did. Like other monarchs of the era, she believed that "building was part of the profession of ruler on a par with statecraft, warfare, ceremonies. . . ."[14] Her construction projects became the visible embodiments of her legitimacy and her enlightenment, just as Peter regarded Saint Petersburg as the physical embodiment of his quest to westernize Russia. Upon coming to the throne, Catherine immediately began renovating the imperial estates as well as the capitals of Moscow and Saint Petersburg. She then proceeded to guide the remodeling of 200 older towns and found 216 new ones—and all according to the neoclassical styles prevalent in the rest of Europe.[15]

As was evident in regard to the theater, Catherine's passions for building and the arts often merged. Early in her reign, the empress awarded a charter to the Academy of Fine Arts in order to encourage the dissemination of the latest knowledge of architecture, painting, sculpture, and the graphic arts. She then gave it a permanent president and erected a new building in the neoclassical style, still standing today.

Most famously, the empress built an addition to the Winter Palace, called the Hermitage, as her living quarters and as a repository and showcase for her collections.[17] She needed the space, since Catherine collected on a grand scale. Late in life, she crowed to Grimm, that besides her paintings,

> [M]y museum in the Hermitage consists of 38,000 volumes, four rooms filled with books and engravings, 10,000 cut gemstones, nearly

A photograph of the Academy of Fine Arts, called one of the most elegant structures in Saint Petersburg and one that immediately brought new prestige to the fine arts of architecture, painting, and sculpture.[16]

> 10,000 drawings, and a natural history collection that occupies two large halls.[18]

When writing to Grimm, she forgot to mention her sixteen thousand coins and medals, her sculptures (including a Michelangelo), and her collections of silver, jewels, furniture, glass, tapestries, ceramics, mosaics, and porcelain.

Catherine consciously presented the Hermitage to her own subjects and the rest of the world as proof of Russia's enlightenment, sophistication, and wealth—the signs of a great power. The art objects that filled the cases and lined the walls of the Hermitage were intended to dazzle courtiers and friends. The Hermitage gave Catherine great personal pleasure as well. She liked to stroll along the corridors or sit in her library and admire her treasures, something she often did during the day to take a break from official business. She wrote to Grimm:

> Do you want to know how I spend my days . . . ? I wake up in the morning at six and right after coffee I run to the Hermitage and sit down in my small study. . . . Having finished with all the morning reports, I go back to the Hermitage. When I take my exercise, I look at the paintings. . . . After dinner I go again . . . to the Hermitage in order to walk by my engraved stones.[19]

In terms of her collections, so great was Catherine's reach that one French scholar has described Catherine's acquisitions as "the most remarkable artistic achievement of any eighteenth-century sovereign."[20] In this regard, she bears resemblance to the Medicis, but they worked at collecting for three centuries, while she had only three decades. With all these visible manifestations of her artistic pursuits, Catherine secured the reputation throughout Europe to which she had aspired.

Catherine's greatest artistic achievement, however, remains her art collection. When the empress entered the art market, rulers were vying for a limited number of masterworks. With that, an art war erupted among the courts of Europe, and Catherine eagerly joined the fray. She understood how important her participation was both for promoting her own legitimacy and for elevating Russia's status among the other

***Catherine II as Patroness of the Arts*, by Stefano Torelli, 1770. The arts represented include writing, theater, painting, and architecture.**[21]

nations of Europe. Besides, it turned out that she loved art and developed the insatiable greed of an avid collector—she admitted that she had become a "glutton" when it came to art and often accused herself of succumbing to a "mania," an "abyss," a "fever," a "disease," and an "addiction like drinking." More confidentially, she admitted that she collected on a grand scale because she loved outwitting and outbidding other monarchs in the Europe-wide art wars.[22]

Catherine was energetic and passionate about whatever she did and, predictably, became intimately involved with the process of putting together an art collection. She quibbled about prices, always demanded a second or third opinion, and pored over sales catalogues to make her choices.[23] When shipments arrived, she grew as excited as a child at Christmas and personally oversaw the unpacking, at first letting no one else see her prizes: "Only I and the mice can admire all this."[24] The empress also knew what she wanted. She wrote to her envoy and art agent in Naples, Prince Nikolai Iusupov: "Don't send me pictures of subjects that are sad or too serious, but I love Angelica Kauffmann [a leading artist located in Rome and an international celebrity] and have her do a picture based on themes from Homer." When she received the Kauffmann picture, she was thrilled: "I cannot walk by without stopping so that I might take pleasure in it."[25]

Sometimes, an agent would disappoint, and Catherine would get irate. She complained to Grimm about the inferiority of a group of paintings that her agent in Rome, the "divine" Johann Reiffenstein (the sobriquet she bestowed upon him) had purchased from the famed English broker, Thomas Jenkins: "Some are good," she said,

> but the rest are but wretched scrawls. . . . Damn! It is incredible how the divine one let himself be deceived this time. Please tell him clearly that he is to buy nothing more from Mr. Jenkins: it is scandalous to pass off such miserable works. . . . We are quite dismayed to see such daubs. [26]

Grimm once asked her how she had developed her eye, and she responded: "Read the descriptions of the paintings which the antique dealers are selling. By constantly studying catalogues of the paintings which I purchase, I have learned to . . . see."[27] Indeed, absent images, these catalogs were rich in detail; they described each painting's size, provenance, condition, colors, background, estimated worth, and even the placement of arms and feet or the tilt of the head. [28]

Like the other monarchs of the time, Catherine used an extensive network of ambassadors, dealers, and correspondents to help her build collections. Often, artists with good taste but mediocre talent abandoned painting for the more lucrative profession of obtaining old masters for new monarchs. All these agents acted as art spies in the various countries that boasted of good art—in particular the Netherlands, France, and Italy—and informed their monarchs of impending sales, recent deaths, impoverished heirs, and new talent.[29] As Voltaire quipped, they are "the spies of merit and misfortune."[30]

Her stable included an array of experts, both Russian and foreign. Prince Dmitri Golitsyn was well connected and well respected in the intellectual and artistic circles of Europe. He was relentless in his search for art for the empress while serving in the embassies to Paris and The Hague. It was said of him: "No one could compete with Golitsyn at auctions."[31] Of course, he had the wealth of an empire behind him. Ivan Shuvalov had been Empress Elizabeth's favorite and was in charge of the arts for much of her reign. He was the first to extol the new Empress Catherine, with not much proof, as a "zealous protector of the arts and sciences."[32] Once he took up residence in Italy, he put his deep knowledge of the art market to work as Catherine's art agent.

Among the foreigners, Diderot, one of Catherine's earliest advisors, actively scoured the art markets in Paris for her in the 1760s and 1770s, and the commissions she paid him helped support him as a writer. Johann Reiffenstein resided in Rome and was one of the best brokers in Europe, making spectacular acquisitions for the empress over the course of twenty years until his death. He was so relentless in his hunt that Grimm jested: "I spoke with the divine Reiffenstein, and it seems that he wants to transport Rome in its entirety to Saint Petersburg."[33] Grimm himself, Catherine's lively correspondent about all things artistic, figured as one of her closest advisors and most zealous agents.[34] Étienne Falconet, the French sculptor whom Catherine brought to Russia to create a monument to Peter the Great, also corresponded with the empress, relentlessly advising her on all the arts.[35]

Catherine's first major foray into the art market proved a brilliant move.[36] Two years into her reign, a Berlin dealer, Johann Gotzkowski, approached the Russian ambassador to Prussia with a stunning group of old masters that he had been collecting for Frederick the Great. The king claimed that the debts incurred during the recent Seven Years War prevented him from purchasing the collection, and the dealer offered it to Catherine, even though Russia had fought in that war as well. With a show of bravado, the empress snatched up the 225

***Young Man with a Glove*, Frans Hals**

paintings that had been destined for Sans Souci. As was the style at the time, the collection consisted almost entirely of Flemish and Dutch paintings. The undisputed masterpiece among them was by Frans Hals, *Young Man with a Glove*.[37]

With this purchase, she accomplished several aims at once: she acquired the first set of important paintings for the Hermitage, dealt a psychological blow to Frederick (with whom she consciously competed), and, to the astonishment of the European elite, this former German princess, usurper of a throne, ruler of what was considered a cultural backwater, had suddenly become a major opponent in the art wars being played out in European courts.

With extraordinary speed, Catherine built a royal gallery that rivaled any in Europe. Soon after the Gotzkowski coup, Golitsyn arranged the purchase of Rembrandt's *The Return of the Prodigal Son*, a gem of the Hermitage's collection.[38] In fact, of the twenty-two Rembrandts hanging in the Hermitage, the empress collected sixteen.

***Return of the Prodigal Son,* Rembrandt**

Catherine began shocking European courts with her spending, even while Russia was fighting a costly war in Turkey and participating in the partition of Poland. In a standard pattern, she increased her acquisitions during wartime, probably to astound and stagger allies and enemies alike with Russia's seemingly bottomless treasury. She boasted to Voltaire: "You have heard correctly, Sir, that this spring I raised the pay of all my military officers . . . by a fifth. At the same time, I've bought the collection of paintings of the late M. de Crozat [more about that later], and I am in the process of buying a diamond bigger than an egg."[39]

Ambassadors, envoys, dealers, and friends all helped Catherine acquire the collections of connoisseurs throughout Europe, often from under the noses of their rulers. In the 1760s and 1770s—at the height of her buying frenzy—Golitsyn secured the 320 paintings of the noted collector, Jean de Julienne, and the small but superb holdings of the Sardinian Charles-Joseph, Prince de Ligne. Next, Golitsyn succeeded in buying the fabled collection of the Austrian minister, Johann-Philip Cobenzl, which also featured 6,000 old master drawings, immediately making the Hermitage's collection one of the best in the world, a distinction it still holds today.[40]

Simultaneously, Diderot, working with Falconet, acquired the forty-six paintings of Louis-Jean Gaignat, secretary to Louis XV, which included Murillo's masterpiece, *The Seated Virgin*.[41] Soon after, an agent in Amsterdam—in a "masterstroke," according to contemporaries—purchased the magnificent collection of Count Heinrich von Brühl, a minister of Augustus II, king of Poland and elector of Saxony, with whom he shared a love of art, creating in Dresden one of the finest galleries in Europe. The six hundred paintings included Rembrandts, Rubens, and two of the best landscapes ever created by Ruisdael.[42]

Early in the 1770s, the empress acquired the superb cache of three hundred paintings amassed by the Dutch merchant, Gerrit Braancamp. In a terrible blow to the art world, the ship carrying the collection to Saint Petersburg was lost in the Baltic. Catherine was philosophical: "Well, there goes 60,000 *écus* [about a half million dollars]."[43] At roughly the same time, Diderot and Golitsyn orchestrated the purchase of the cabinet of the Duke de Choiseul. As the French foreign minister, he had been the empress's mortal enemy and also her keenest competitor at art auctions, so his fall from power and need to sell his precious collection gave Catherine double satisfaction.[44] In the 1780s, it took Grimm five years to negotiate the sale of the 119 pictures of Count Baudouin, "one of the best and most famous in Paris," a coup that left other bidders "green with envy."[45]

Catherine also added to her collection through individual purchase and commissions. For instance, she acquired two paintings by Van Loo from her correspondent, the famed *salonnière,* Madame Marie-Thérèse Geoffrin.[46] Following the advice of Diderot and Falconet, Catherine commissioned paintings from such eighteenth-century luminaries as

Chardin, Greuze, Vernet, Vigée Le Brun, and Mengs, who was probably the most distinguished painter in Europe at that time.[47] After long negotiations, conducted with the assistance of Ambassador Simon Vorontsov, Catherine commissioned three paintings from the eminently popular Sir Joshua Reynolds. She picked themes for two of these, while he chose to paint an allegory of the empress's struggle to make Russia a great power for the third, resulting in *The Infant Hercules Slaying Serpents*.[48]

When the empress could not buy something she wanted, she had it copied.[49] One commission—typical of her swagger, style, and determination to get what she wanted—occurred in September, 1778. Depressed and suffering from a headache because of the rain and gray waters of the Neva, she came upon some long-forgotten books of engravings copied from Raphael's famous *loggia* in the Vatican. This long, vaulted space contains fifty-two frescoes depicting scenes from the Old and New Testament, interspersed with drawings of real and

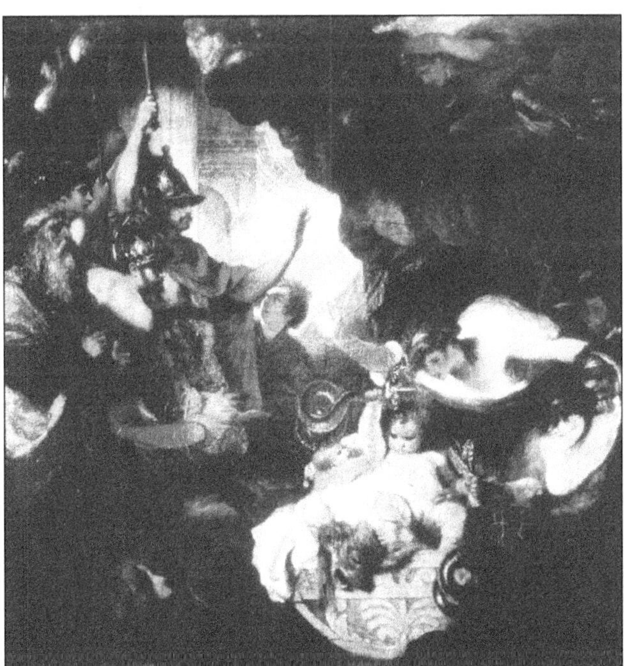

***The Infant Hercules Slaying Serpents*, Sir Joshua Reynolds**

imagined creatures inspired by fragments from Nero's palace. Perusing the books brought Catherine immediate relief. That night, she wrote Grimm that she wanted a duplicate of the *loggia*: "I won't have any rest or peace until this is done." Grimm quickly contacted "the divine" Reiffenstein in Rome, who then consulted with Mengs, a favorite artist of Catherine who had experience copying Raphael. Mengs recommended his best student, Christopher Unterberger, and his team took five years to complete the work. Quarenghi, Catherine's favorite architect, was commissioned to build an edifice to house the loggia, and the project was finally finished, nine years after the empress thought of it.

The *Loggia*, Hermitage, Quarenghi

It remains one of the most beautiful spaces in the Hermitage, and one of the few still identical to the way it was in Catherine's time.[50]

However, the two biggest prizes among the empress's acquisitions were the Crozat and Walpole collections, whose purchase caused a sensation throughout Europe. They beautifully illustrate Catherine's art of collecting.

It seems clear that Catherine liked what we call today blockbuster purchases. They aroused awe and envy, brought Europe-wide publicity, and challenged the stereotype of Russia's cultural backwardness. Pierre Crozat's was widely regarded as the most important private collection in France. The galleries of the king and his brother offered competition, but they were open only to courtiers. The Crozats, in contrast, had opened their doors to amateurs and the curious, even preparing a catalog for visitors; therefore, the collection came to be seen as a public asset rather than private property.[51] Crozat had made a fortune at the turn of the century in banking; he then used that fortune to amass a collection of paintings, drawings, engraved stones, and statuary, and to build an elegant mansion to house his treasures. The collection included four hundred canvases representing the Flemish, Dutch, Italian, and French schools of European art, making it the most comprehensive in France.[52]

Hearing that Crozat's heir had died, Diderot went to work. He convinced the next generation that the current financial crisis in France and another impending art sale signaled an unpropitious time to put the paintings up for public auction. He suggested that selling the collection en bloc to the empress of Russia would prove more profitable. And, the heirs would receive their money immediately. Diderot then embarked upon two years of negotiations on Catherine's behalf. First, he invited François Tronchin—a banker, brilliant collector, correspondent of Catherine, and a genuinely decent man—to come to Paris from Geneva, prepare a detailed catalogue, and estimate the worth of the collection. Tronchin was assisted by two experts, one hired by the heirs and another hired by Diderot; they agreed to a price of 460,000 livres (about $3.5 million today). The empress and the heirs accepted the price, and Diderot signed the contract for the empress. Next, Tronchin oversaw the packing of the seventeen crates and their loading onto ships. The process of crating and shipping carried a great deal of stress, since only a few months before, the Braancamp disaster had occurred. To Catherine's glee, the Crozat collection arrived safely. She sent Tronchin a thank you note accompanied by a sack of sable furs.[53]

An outcry followed the sale. The person who acted as the director of fine arts in France moaned: "I had to stand by and see these treasures go abroad, for want of the funds necessary to buy them on the king's behalf." Diderot reported being attacked from all sides:

> The collectors, the artists, and the rich are all up in arms. . . . So much the worse for France, if we sell our pictures in time of peace, whereas Catherine can buy them in the middle of a war. Science, art, taste, and wisdom are traveling northward, and barbarism and all it brings in its train, is coming south."[54]

Others complained: "Diderot every day dreams up plans to enrich Russia at France's expense."[55] One French scholar, one hundred fifty years later, still found the sale humiliating and complained about Diderot "vandalizing" France by sending French treasures to the Russian throne.[56] Robbing us of any sympathy we might have for this argument, an eighteenth-century French art connoisseur complained: "If we do not take precautions, foreigners will succeed in stripping us of all our excellent paintings which have been the glory of our country and which were procured in Italy only after great effort and cost."[57] Thus, the Russian barbarians did unto the French as they had done unto the Italians. Nonetheless, with this sale, Catherine had clearly won a major battle in the European art wars—she would win another seven years later

In 1779, the empress's purchase of the Walpole collection repeated the earlier feat and repercussions of the Crozat sale. While the Crozat collection was considered the most important in France, Walpole's held the same distinction in Great Britain. Sir Robert Walpole, Britain's first prime minister, successfully speculated in South Seas companies and used his fortune to amass old masters at the same time that Crozat had been building his own collection. Sir Robert, also like Crozat, built an edifice to house his collection, though it found a rural setting. Houghton Hall still stands as a magnificent Palladian country home in Norfolk and is now a museum. Sir Robert died deeply in debt; his son died six years after that, even more in debt; the grandson—dubbed the "mad earl"—added to the indebtedness and preferred horses and pedigree dogs to high art. Clearly, the collection was going to be sold.

The mad earl met personally with Catherine's ambassador to England, who wrote to Catherine that "it is worthy, in the opinion of every connoisseur, of belonging to the greatest of monarchs." Working with great secrecy, the earl then hired James Christie, who had just founded a new auction house, to estimate the worth of the paintings. Catherine, as was her habit, wanted additional opinions: three painters, including Benjamin West, who was the most respected art critic of his era, examined the collection and provided appraisals.

A catalog was sent to Catherine with each of the 204 paintings priced separately, for a total cost of £40,550 ($4.1 million today).[58] Tastes, of course, change. It is fascinating to note that the canvas of a painter not much esteemed today, Guido Reni's *The Fathers of the Church Disputing the Doctrine of the Immaculate Conception*, fetched £3,500 ($350,000), while a Rembrandt, the acclaimed *Abraham's Sacrifice,* was tagged at only £300 ($30,000). Portraits were considered more of a craft than an art, and so Catherine purchased a number of Van Dycks for only £40 ($4,000) each. One hundred and fifty years later, Andrew Mellon would buy some of them from the Soviet government at a thousand times that price, and they eventually became part of the National Gallery in Washington, D.C.[59] When the sale was finalized, as a token of her appreciation, Catherine sent the mad earl a larger-than-life portrait of herself that still hangs in majesty in Houghton Hall.[60]

Catherine's purchase was widely regarded as the sale of the century, and it made Christie's reputation. However, it was considered, even by him, a national tragedy, and a sign of the decline of the empire; people grieved that "Russia is sacking our palaces and museums."[61] Publications spoke of "dishonour" and "disgrace" and "a general dissatisfaction and regret."[62] One wit commented, "To be sure, I should wish they were rather sold to the Crown of England than to that of Russia, where

Saloon of Houghton Hall

they will be burnt in a wooden palace on the first insurrection."[63] Much like the reaction to the Crozat sale, one letter to the editor of *The European Magazine*, complained:

> Gentlemen, the removal of the Houghton Collection of Pictures to Russia is, perhaps, one of the most striking instances that can be produced of the decline of the empire of Great Britain, and the advancement of that of our powerful ally in the North. That so noble a collection could not be retained in England, is very humiliating and deplorable. . . .[64]

Catherine continued to practice her art of collecting until her death. She enjoyed it, certainly, including all the controversy that her purchases generated. Today, in the Hermitage, in the room devoted to seventeenth-century French art, the empress collected thirty-one of the sixty-one paintings and twenty of the thirty-two in the Flemish room. In the Rubens room, there are thirty-seven paintings hanging; Catherine collected twenty-eight of them. There are twenty-six Van

Dycks hanging in the Hermitage; Catherine collected twenty-three of them. On a wall of the celebrated "small" paintings of the Flemish school, Catherine collected thirty-one of the thirty-five. It was an unparalleled achievement in the history of art.

From the historical point of view, the empress understood that, in the eighteenth century, a great art collection was as much a sign of power as a great army. She wanted and got both, because both worked toward her final aim: the transformation of Russia from a political and cultural backwater into a full-fledged partner in the state affairs and artistic trends of Europe.

NOTES

1 Geraldine Norman, "Catherine's Life," in *Treasures of Catherine the Great*, ed. Mikhail B. Piotrovski (New York: Henry N. Abrams, 2000), 29. The most recent biography devotes thirteen pages to her role in the arts: Robert K. Massie, *Catherine the Great: Portrait of a Woman* (New York: Random House, 2011), 519-33; and the most thorough, fifteen: Isabel de Madariaga, *Russia in the Age of Catherine the Great* (New Haven: Yale University Press, 1981), 327-42.

2 *The Memoirs of Catherine the Great*, tr. Mark Cruse and Hilde Hoogenboom (New York: Modern Library, 2005), *passim*.

3 For the few exceptions, see the slim volume edited by Susan Bracken, Andrea M. Galdy, and Adriana Turpin, *Women Patrons and Collectors* (Newcastle upon Tyne: Cambridge Scholars, 2012). The introductory essay by Sheila ffolliott is especially useful. As a rule, women collected jewelry or design objects.

4 From an unpublished letter of Diderot to John Wilkes, in Jonathan G. W. Conlin, "High Art and Low Politics: A New Perspective on John Wilkes," *The Huntington Library Quarterly* 64, no. 3-4 (2001), 367.

5 See Jonathan Brown, *Kings and Connoisseurs: Collecting Art in Seventeenth-Century Europe* (Princeton: Princeton University Press, 1995); Francis Henry Taylor, *The Taste of Angels: A History of Art Collecting from Rameses to Napoleon* (Boston: Little, Brown, 1948). Catherine certainly engaged in this practice. Taylor, *Taste*, 526.

6 Aristotle, *The Nicomachean Ethics*, tr. David Ross (Oxford: Oxford University Press, 1988), 87.

7 *Catherine the Great's Instruction (Nakaz) to the Legislative Commission (1767)*, ed. Paul Dukes (Massachusetts: Oriental Research Partners, 1977), 114 (article 579) (translation somewhat altered by author).

8 For just two descriptions of how the news was received in the salons of Paris, see Janet Aldis, *Madame Geoffrin: Her Salon and Her Times, 1750-1777* (London: Methuen & Co., 1905), 348; Alphonse Fortia de Piles, *Voyage de deux français en Allemagne, Danemarck, Suède, Russie et Pologne, fait en 1790-1792*, 5 vols. (Paris: Desenne, 1796), 4:177-80.

9 See Cynthia Hyla Whittaker, *Russian Monarchy: Eighteenth-Century Rulers and Writers in Political Dialogue* (DeKalb: Northern Illinois University Press, 2003), 99-106; Richard S. Wortman, *Scenarios of Power: Myth and Ceremony in Russian Monarchy*, 2 vols. (Princeton: Princeton University Press, 1995), 1:110-46.

10 A. P. Antropov, *Portrait of Catherine II,* before 1766, from a postcard.

11 Yulia Kagan and Oleg Neverov, "An Imperial Affair," *Treasures*, 99.

12 From the collections of the New York Public Library, with permission .

13 Quoted in Anna Trofimova and Valery Shchevchenko, "The most perfect Beauty . . .," in Piotrovski, *Treasures*, 135.

14 Samuel John Klingensmith, *The Utility of Splendor: Ceremony, Social Life, and Architecture at the Court of Bavaria, 1600-1800,* ed. Christian F. Otto and Mark Ashton (Chicago: University of Chicago Press, 1993), xv.

15 The two most recent studies are: George E. Munro, *The Most Intentional City: St. Petersburg in the Reign of Catherine the Great* (Madison: Fairleigh Dickinson University Press, 2008); Alexander M. Martin, *Enlightened Metropolis: Constructing Imperial Moscow, 1762-1855* (Oxford: Oxford University Press, 2013).

16 *Vidy Peterburga* (Saint Petersburg: Izd. Iv. Iv. Perevoznikova, 1901), n. 25. For an eighteenth-century estimate of the beauty and impact of the academy, see Fortia de Piles, *Voyage*, 3:188-92.

17 See the superb article by Katia Dianina, "Art and Authority: The Hermitage of Catherine the Great," *Russian Review* 63 (2004): 630-54.

18 *Pis'ma Imperatritsy Ekateriny II k Grimmu (1774-1796)*, ed. Ia. Grot (Saint Petersburg: Tip. Imp. Akademii nauk, 1878, *Sbornik imperatorskogo russkogo istoricheskogo obshchestva*, vol. 23), 40.

19 As quoted in M. I. Maksimova, "Imperatritsa Ekaterina Vtoraia i sobranie reznyk kamnei Ermitazha," *Sbornik Gosudarstvennogo Ermitazha* 1 (1921): 51. Also see Geraldine Norman, "Catherine's Collections," in *The Hermitage: The Biography of a Great Museum* (New York: Fromm International, 1997), 21-36.

20 Louis Réau, *Catherine la Grande, Inspiratrice et Mécène des arts* (Paris: Editions Le Calame, 1912), 7.

21 Stefano Torelli, *Catherine II as Minerva, Patroness of the Arts,* 1770, State Russian Museum, Saint Petersburg, as reproduced in *Catherine the Great: Art for Empire,* ed. Nathalie Bondil (Ghent: Snoeck, 2005), 40. On Torelli's remarkable career in Russia, see Irene Graziani, *La bottega dei Torelli: Da Bologna alla Russia di Caterina la Grande* (Bologna: Abe Books, 2005).

22 On her voraciousness, see Bondil, "'Gluttony' in the Fine Arts: Did Catherine II have Taste?" *Catherine the Great: Art for Empire*, 169-177. Her great rivals, besides Frederick II of Prussia, included the kings of Poland and Sweden: *Catherine the Great & Gustav III,* ed. Magnus Olausson (Stockholm: Nationalmuseum, 1998).

23 Dozens of archival sources attest to Catherine's "system" of collection: Rossiiskii gosudarstvennyi arkhiv drevnykh aktov (hereafter RGADA), f. 17, op. 1: ed. khr. 274 (1765); ed. khr. 276 (1768); ed. khr. 282 (1779); ed. khr. 283 (1780); ed. khr. 286 (1788) and also f. 1263, op.l , ch. 1, ed. khr. 1113-1116 (1765-1768) and ed. khr. ed. khr. 590 (1775).

24 Quoted in Pierre Descargues, *The Hermitage*, tr. Katharine Delavenay (London: Thames and Hudson, 1956), 8-29.

25 RGADA, f. 1290, op. 2, ch. 1, ed. khr. 70. I have not been able to locate this painting; the staff at the Hermitage were also stumped. At this time, "history paintings" were in vogue along with large canvases depicting biblical, historical, or mythological scenes. See Richard Stites, *Serfdom, Society, and the Arts in Imperial Russia: The Pleasure and the Power* (New Haven: Yale University Press, 2005), 300.

26 27 September 1781, *Pis'ma Imperatritsy Ekateriny II k Grimmu (1774-1796)*, 221. On Catherine and Reifffenstein, there is a good set of archival documents in RGADA, "Pis'ma barona Reifenshteina o kartinakh," f. 17, op. 1, ed. khr. 281 (1779-1791), especially ll. 2-3 (September 27, 1780).

27 *Pis'ma*, 23 (1879): 40.

28 These catalogs were first issued by the Dutch in the early seventeenth century and rapidly became de rigueur: Clara Bille, *De Tempel der kunst of Het Kabinet van den Heer Braamcamp*, 2 vols. (Amsterdam: J. H. de Bussy, 1961), 1:234-237. Also see Pomian Krzysztof, *Collectors and Curiosities: Paris and Venice, 1500-1800*, tr. Elizabeth Wiles-Portier (Cambridge: Polity Press, 1987), 141-143.

29 See Descargues, *Hermitage*, 23-24.

30 Quoted in Henry Tronchin, *Le Conseiller François Tronchin et ses amis, Voltaire, Diderot, Grimm, etc.* (Paris: E. Plon, Nourrit, 1895), 288.

31 Quoted in Colin Eisler, *Paintings in the Hermitage* (New York: Stewart, Tabori & Chang, 1990), 10.

32 Denis Diderot, 20 August 1762, *Correspondance*, 16 vols., ed. Georges Roth (Paris: Éditions de Minuit, 1955-70), 4:174.

33 2 February 1779, *Correspondance artistique de Grimm avec Catherine II*, ed. Louis Réau (Paris: Daupeley-Gouverneur, 1932), 47. At his death, Grimm wrote Catherine: "The divine Reiffenstein of Rome exists no longer. Knowing the scrupulous exactitude of this excellent man, I have no doubt that he found the time before his death to dispatch the two paintings of Teresina de Maron," (ibid., 192; 10 November 1793).

34 They corresponded without interruption from 1774 to Catherine's death in 1796, except for the year he spent in Saint Petersburg, when they saw each other twice a day: Grimm, "Mémoire historique sur l'origine et les suites de mon attachement pour l'Impératrice Catherine II jusqu'au décès de sa Majesté Impériale, 1797," in *Correspondance littéraire, philosophique et critique par Grimm, Diderot, Raynal, Meister, etc.* 16 vols. (Paris, 1877-1882), 1:12-21.

35 See *Correspondance de Falconet avec Catherine II, 1767-1778*, ed. Louis Réau (Paris: E. Champion, 1921). Also see Alexander M. Schenker, *The Bronze Horseman: Falconet's Monument to Peter the Great* (New Haven: Yale University Press, 2003).

36 An excellent study of this period is Natalia Gritsai, "Catherine II's Collection of Paintings," in Olausson, *Catherine the Great*, 397-421.

37 Frans Hals, *Portrait of a Young Man with a Glove*, 17th century, in Piotrovski, *Treasures*, 25. On the collection, see Descargues, *Hermitage*, 22.

38 Rembrandt van Rijn, *Return of the Prodigal Son*, 1668/9, in *The Hermitage: Selected Treasures from a Great Museum* (Leningrad: Booth-Clibborn Editions, 1990), 78; Descargues, *Hermitage*, 25.

39 Catherin II to Voltaire, 1 September 1772, *Correspondence*, 168, as quoted in *Documents of Catherine the Great: The Correspondence of Voltaire and the*

Instruction of 1761, ed. W. F. Reddaway (Cambridge: Cambridge University Press, 1931).

40 Bille, *De Tempel*, 231; V. F. Levinson-Lessing, *Istoriia kartinnoi galerei Ermitazha (1764-1917)* (Leningrad: Iskusstvo, 1985), 67. On the Julienne collection, see the beautiful volumes of Emile Dacier and Albert Vuaflart, *Jean de Julienne et les graveurs de Watteau au XVIIIe siècle*, 3 vols. (Paris: Pour les membres de la Société, 1929), 3:26-26A; Watteau was a favorite both of Catherine and Frederick the Great.

41 Taylor, *Taste*, 526-31.

42 Heinrich von Brühl, *Recueil d'estampes gravées d'après les tableaux de la galerie et du cabinet de S. E. M. le comte de Brühl (Description des tableaux, etc.)* (Dresden, 1754).

43 Charles Blanc, *Le Trésor et la curiosité*, 2 vols. (Paris: Renouard, 1857), 1:463-80; Bille, *De Tempel* 1:39, 47, 219-24.

44 Étienne-François, duc de Choiseul, *Recueil d'estampes gravées d'après les tableaux du cabinet de Monseigneur le duc de Choiseul, par les soins du Sr. Basan . . .* (Paris: L'auteur, 1771).

45 Descargues, *Hermitage*, 44-45.

46 *Correspondance littéraire, philosophique et critique de Grimm et de Diderot*, 15 vols. (Paris: Furne, 1829-31), 8:102-103.

47 Eisler, *Paintings*, 24-26.

48 RGADA, f. 17. op. 1, ed. khr. 287 (1789); Gerard Reitlinger, *The Economics of Taste: The Rise and Fall of the Picture Market, 1760-1960* (London: Barrie & Rockliff, 1961), 73; J. S. G. Simmons, "Samuel Johnson 'On the Banks of the Neva': A Note on a Picture by Reynolds in the Hermitage," in *Johnson, Boswell and Their Circle* (Oxford: Clarendon Press, 1965), 208-214. The picture is reprinted in *The Hermitage: The History of the Buildings and Collections,* tr. Paul Williams (Saint Petersburg: Alfa-Colour Art Publishers, 2000).

49 Germain Bazin, *The Museum Age*, tr. J. Cahill (New York: Universe Books, 1967), 124.

50 A. T., "Materialy dlia istorii tsarskikh sobranii," *Starye gody* (Jul-Sep 1913), 34-38; Catherine is quoted on page thirty-six. Examination of the books reveals their sumptuousness. Also see Regina Kogan et al., *The Hermitage* (Saint Petersburg: Alfa-Colour, 1998), 86-88. The copy is from the collections of the New York Public Library with permission: T. M. Sokolova, *Zdaniia i zaly Ermitazha* (Leningrad: Avrora, 1973), 130-33.

51 A good introduction to this collection is Hélène Meyer, "La collection de Louis-Antoine Crozat, baron de Thiers," *L'Age d'or flamand et hollandaise: Collections de Catherine II. Musée de l'Ermitage, Saint-Pétersbourg* (Dijon: Musée des beaux-arts de Dijon, 1993), 49-56.

52 Descriptions of the collection are located in *Catalogue des tableaux de Cabinet de M. Crozat, baron de Thiers* (Paris: DeBure, 1755); Pierre Jean Mariette, *Description de la collection Crozat* (Geneva: Minkoff Reprint, 1973, a reprint of a book published in Paris in 1741); and Margret Stuffman, "Les Tableaux de la collection de Pierre Crozat," *Gazette des beaux-arts* 110 (July 1968): 11-144.

53 On the negotiations, consult Maurice Tourneux, *Diderot et Catherine II* (Paris: Calmann-Lévy, 1899), 46-47; and "Diderot et le Musée de l'Ermitage," *Gazette*

des beaux-arts 29, no. 490 (April 1898), 333-43. Also see Tronchin, *Tronchin*, 307-31.

54 Quoted in Pierre Descargues, *Hermitage*, 35.

55 Quoted in Tourneux, "Diderot," 386.

56 Réau and Georges Loukomski, *Catherine la Grande: Inspiratrice d'art et Mécène* (Paris: Éditions Le Calame, 1930), 56.

57 As quoted in Bazin, *Museum Age*, 114.

58 Larissa Dukelskaya, "The Houghton Sale and the Fate of a Great Collection," *A Capital Collection: Houghton Hall and the Hermitage*, ed. L. A. Dukelskaya and Andrew Moore (London: Yale University Press, 2002), 65-69; Moore, "The Sale to Catherine the Great," in Moore, ed., *Houghton Hall: The Prime Minister, the Empress, and the Heritage* (London: Wilson, 1996), 56-64 and 151-52.

59 "Authentic Catalogue of the Houghton Collection of Pictures," *The European Magazine* 1 (February 1782); Reitlinger, *Economics*, 21-22; Algernon Graves, *Art Sales: From Early in the Eighteenth Century to Early in the Twentieth Century*, 3 vols. (London: Graves, 1918-1921).

60 In Moore, *Houghton Hall*, 118.

61 Jonathan Conlin, "Raiders of the Lost Art," *History Today* 53 (2003): 2.

62 Dukelskaya, "The Houghton Sale," 57, 70-71.

63 Quoted in Dukelskaya, "The Houghton Sale," 70. Ironically, if they had stayed at Houghton Hall, they would have been burned in a fire that leveled the picture gallery in 1789.

64 "To the Editors of the European Magazine," *The European Magazine* 1 (February 1782): 95-96. These kinds of controversy are still with us; in 2006, the British government barred the export of a Constable landscape and began raising the $5.3 million needed to keep it in England. Happily, sixty of the old masters returned to the rooms in which they originally hung for an exhibition at Houghton Hall that took place from May 17 to September 29, 2013. It was sponsored by the Hermitage, Houghton Hall, and the Royal Academy of Arts.

Rozanov's Peter

Simon Dixon
(University College London)

Peter I remained a living presence in the final years of the old regime, not because his features adorned the five-hundred-ruble note (a denomination beyond the reach of all but the wealthiest Russians), but because his role in Russia's historical development still inspired a potent mixture of veneration and vilification from historians and writers alike. The sheer volume of their output prompted Nicholas Riasanovsky, Gary Marker's Berkeley adviser, to acknowledge that even his magisterial survey of Peter's posthumous reputation was not a comprehensive account.[1] Marker made his own contribution to the subject in an essay on Sergei Mikhailovich Solov'ev (1820-79) in which he sought to reconcile the historian's lofty view of the tsar as Mosaic patriarch, "grappling to lead his tribe to . . . a historicised promised land of law, order, and civility," with his conviction that the Russian peasantry remained confined, even in his own day, to an inebriated slough of despond. According to Marker, the key to the conundrum lay in Solov'ev's portrayal of the tsar as "an elemental, almost superhuman, virile life force," symbolically "deflowering" the virgin Russian land (and trampling his recalcitrant subjects) in order to give birth to his radical vision. In Solov'ev's interpretation, Marker suggested, Peter had literally fathered the modern Russian state. This, to quote a characteristically arresting phrase, was a case of "testosterone as *zakonomernost'*."[2]

Sexual imagery is more often associated not with Solov'ev, but with one of the last students to hear him lecture at Moscow University: Vasilii Rozanov (1856-1919). As Andrei Belyi remarked in 1910, Rozanov had but "one idea" and he "demonstrated it on multiple occasions in diverse ways":

> From the male seed is formed the world, history, the fate of nations; childbirth is equivalent to the creation of the world; the sexual act is equivalent to literary creativity; everyday life [*byt*] emerges from the seed; history, from everyday life.[3]

As we shall see, Rozanov's big idea had relatively few implications for his image of Tsar Peter. Neither was there anything carnal in his impression of Solov'ev, who evidently displayed the same dispassionate exterior to his students as he did to his own family. "Peacefulness," Rozanov recalled in 1916, was Solov'ev's "prevailing feature . . . he lectured neither loudly nor quietly: middling." Nevertheless, according to Rozanov, he was capable of the sort of conceptual insight more reminiscent of Tartu-style semiotics than of an acknowledged master of narrative history:

> I remember his explanation of "the change in dress under Peter the Great." "Everyone thinks this a trifle, and superfluous—a surface phenomenon; but that was not so, gentlemen (he was addressing students)! Every form of dress is always a flag, a symbol, a banner around which uncoordinated people gather, and which unites them into an amalgamated mass. And to Peter, considering the task of his reforms, it was natural to snatch this banner from the hands of the enemy and to stamp on his feet." Since I had never read and never heard such an explanation, I was amazed.[4]

Unlike Solov'ev, Rozanov made no original contribution to historical knowledge. Neither have his views on Peter influenced subsequent historical scholarship. Nevertheless, they reached a wide readership among his contemporaries: the circulation of *Novoe vremia*, whose staff Rozanov joined in 1899, grew from sixty thousand in 1905 to two hundred thousand in 1914, when *Russkoe slovo*, which published him between 1905 and 1911, was selling six hundred thousand copies a day.[5] And while we may learn nothing about Peter from Rozanov—one reason, perhaps, why Riasanovsky made no mention of him—his image of the tsar helps us to reconsider his own place on the spectrum of Russian conservative thought.

By claiming to be simultaneously conservative and revolutionary, Rozanov merely multiplied the number of his adversaries. "'The Left,'" as Filosofov put it, "cannot forgive his reactionary origins in the ranks of the most malicious and spiteful epigones of Slavophilism," while "'the Right' hates him as an anarchist who shakes the sacred foundations of the state system: the church, marriage, and the family."[6] Both sides were alienated by Rozanov's repeated disavowals of the sincerity of political convictions. Struve may have been among the self-styled black hundredist kadets in the Second Duma, who signalled their independence from the party line by negotiating with Stolypin, but that did not reconcile him to Rozanov's apparent lack of ideological commitment.[7] He refused to publish *"Oslabnuvshii fetish" (Psikhologichekie osnovy Russkoi revoliutsii)* ("The weakened fetish": Psychological foundations of the Russian revolution, 1906) on the grounds that it was unprincipled and immoral, in a period of political upheaval, for a writer to strive purely for literary effect.[8] All the more unfortunate, then, that the few modern studies of Rozanov's politics should have relied so heavily on his last three books: *Uedinennoe* (Solitaria, 1912), *Opavshie list'ia* (Fallen Leaves, 1913-15), and *Apokalipsis nashego vremeni* (The Apocalypse of Our Times, 1917-18).[9] While these celebrated experiments in formlessness doubtless constitute his most important literary legacy, they have also encouraged the misleading belief that Rozanov's penchant for aphorism generally prevented him from seeing the big picture.[10] Though Rozanov was not a systematic thinker, the fact that he expressed his most penetrating insights in seemingly casual observations about domestic trivia did not render him incapable of generating recurrent patterns of thought. Of the many such patterns traceable through the vast corpus of his journalism (he wrote over sixteen hundred articles for *Novoe vremia* alone), only the most obvious and most repellent—anti-Semitism—has attracted critical attention.[11] Another—Rozanov's image of Peter the Great—is the subject of this essay.[12]

Contemptuous of the inflated footnote from an early age, Rozanov was never a professional scholar and produced no recognizable work of history.[13] Nevertheless, fascinated by the subject from childhood, he studied it at university between 1878 and 1882, taught it over the following decade at three provincial schools, and repeatedly reflected, in the course of his subsequent career as a writer, on the philosophy of history and on Russia's historical development. Among historians, not only Solov'ev but also his successor, Vasilii Kliuchevskii, made a lasting impression.[14] A third Moscow professor, Solov'ev's disciple Vladimir Ger'e (Guerrier), having tried in vain to persuade Rozanov to stay on as a research student, remained in correspondence with him for thirty years.[15] It is hardly surprising that Rozanov, inspired by such mentors as these, should have believed in the transformative role of great men, or that Peter I should have ranked high among their number. In his final undergraduate year, Rozanov wrote a dissertation, now lost, on Prince M. M. Shcherbatov (1733-90), a critic of Petrine morals who admired the tsar's reforms.[16] In 1895, reviewing Barsukov's life of Mikhail Pogodin, which Rozanov admired for its unpremeditated stream of consciousness, he quoted approvingly from descriptions of Peter as a "human god."[17]

The question was not whether such colossal figures existed, but how they came into being—and here Rozanov had a provocative suggestion to make. In an essay first published in *Russkoe obozrenie* in 1895, re-issued separately that year and reprinted in *Priroda i istoriia* (Nature and History) in 1900, he developed what proved to be a lasting interest in the "accumulation" and "discharge" of "energy" in great men. It was no coincidence, Rozanov claimed, that so many had been at their most creative in early adulthood:

> It is as if some deep and hidden fluctuation [*kolebanie*] takes place in the organism of the man of genius at the time when people ordinarily experience physical (sexual) maturity; will he become, like the common run of mankind, merely the continuer of his own kin [*rod*],

> or will he create miraculous works in the sphere of thought, art, or politics? All this is determined at that moment, and remains hidden until the said fluctuation has been resolved. What brings about this resolution, we cannot even guess. But it happens nevertheless; [a man's] entire organic energy, having reached the point of complete internal accumulation and being ready to be communicated to his descendants, is instead transformed into something mental; and the genus [*rod*] in it dies out at the same time as magical plans for future creations arise.[18]

Looking back on this theory in 1913, Rozanov still found it not only "justifiable" with reference to the individuals he had named (in addition to Peter, they included Caesar, Raphael, Descartes, and Mozart, among others), "but almost true in general." Now, however, the elusive discharge was said to resemble not so much a bodily fluid as electricity.[19]

In the intervening two decades, Rozanov had occasionally referred to "historical 'electricity'" as a power that, "being invisible, moves everything that can be seen."[20] In general, though, his early preoccupation with the cyclical rise and fall of nations, inspired by Leont'ev, had given way to the view expressed in *Apokalipsis nashego vremeni* that Russian history, at least, was better interpreted not in terms of process, but as a series of pivotal moments.[21] Peter's reign was plainly one of these. It was also central to a further distinction: "There is passive history and there is active history; the first forms everyday life [*byt*], but only the second starts events."[22] Whereas pre-Petrine Muscovy represented the epitome of "the passive ideal," "what, on the other hand, was Peter's personality, if not an infinity of actions, infinite activity?!"[23] After 1905, the fruits of the tsar's restless urgency could no longer be dismissed as a purely historical phenomenon. In his New Year's message for 1907, Rozanov told readers of *Novoe vremia* that they were "living through a second 'epoch of reforms,' as S. M. Solov'ev called the reign of Peter the Great. It will drag on for more than a single decade. In it, Russia's entire internal organism is being reshaped."[24]

"In discussing literary or public men," as Gollerbakh observed, Rozanov "was above all interested in the personality, in the 'physiognomy' of the man."[25] Peter was a case in point, and Rozanov was more alert to the tsar's peculiarities than any member of his generation save, perhaps, Valentin Serov, whose portraits he admired.[26] He highlighted the tsar's extraordinary features in a review of Merezhkovskii's *Tsarevich Aleksei*:

> Peter was unusual even in physical terms: not only because of his huge height and strength, but also, for example, by virtue of those chubby, almost spherical cheeks, together with the delicate, strange, unprecedented dimple on his chin (I have never seen one on a man). Besides the terror in him there was also a mysterious charm [*tainstvennoe ocharovanie*]. In a word, this was an unusual person from birth.[27]

Birth was especially significant, for if Solov'ev implied that Peter was the father of the Russian state, Rozanov believed that Natal'ia Kirillovna Naryshkina was "the real 'mother of modern Russia.'" As a committed geneticist, he was bound to think nurture inferior to nature: Peter's "upbringing, the German suburb and so on" were merely "helpful circumstances, and not fundamentally creative."[28] But there was more to it than that, because Rozanov was convinced that genius usually passed down the female line: "We recall Napoleon I and our own Peter. Here lies the explanation why the majority of dynasties are interrupted following the reigns of rulers of genius, and 'troubles' begin."[29]

Peter I's death had not led to a time of troubles because his reforms had altered the course of history. At his most triumphalist, Rozanov presented Peter in even more explicitly Mosaic terms than had Solov'ev:

> "The phenomenon of Peter" in our history amounts in sum and essence to the appearance of a huge personality, which took the place of the nation and compelled the whole of Russia to live not so much a mechanical-historical life as a personal-biographical one for twenty-five years. All Russia turned as if into an individual person [*litso*], a personality [*lichnost'*], and experienced a sort of "C-major" by Tchaikovsky. This was a secular form of prophecy or lawgiving, as in the case of Moses (a change in the entire course of history, the definition of the whole future fate of a people).[30]

Faced with such a passage, one can easily see why Rozanov should have been portrayed as an admirer of Peter's reforms.[31] However, on closer investigation, his thoughts prove to have been characteristically ambivalent, complicated not only by his own sensitivity to paradox, but also by widespread scepticism about Peter among Rozanov's fellow conservatives.

His reverence for Peter certainly set Rozanov at odds with members of the "Slavophile colony" employed in the 1890s under the patronage of the state comptroller, Tertii Filippov. Recruited to this coterie in March, 1893, Rozanov was both amused and disconcerted to find that his immediate superior, the poet and journalist Afanasii Vasil'ev, wore Muscovite clothes in the privacy of his own home, and "some sort of yellow knee-boots. . . . And when in the course of conversation I mentioned 'Peter the Great,' not remotely emphasizing *the great*, he sharply interrupted me: Why do you say *the great*—he is Petrushka, a rebel, and repulsive' (i.e., he abolished Russian dress)."[32] Still more offensive to Filippov's circle was Peter's treatment of the Russian Orthodox Church. Regarding his office as a consolation prize, accepted in 1889 once it was clear that his rival Konstantin Pobedonostsev would hold on to the coveted post of synodal chief procurator, Filippov never lost interest in matters ecclesiastical. For him, the church reforms imposed by Peter and Feofan (Prokopovich) were nothing less than "satanic," and it was inconceivable that any right-thinking person should sympathize with them. "What kind of conservative," he complained with reference to Mikhail Katkov, "is an opponent of the church and a friend of Feofan?"[33]

This was precisely the sort of question that Rozanov felt obliged to answer, not so much to mollify Filippov as to salve his own conscience, troubled by the sense that he did not think as a true Slavophile ought. On one point, he would make no concession. For Rozanov, Peter's attack on monasticism was justified in principle because monasticism glorified the ultimate enemy by promoting celibacy at the expense of procreation and valuing death over life:

> The fact is that in monasticism there is no *energism to activity*, and "denial of the world," "escape from the world" is always its root, unchanging, eternal, essential. . . . In the final analysis, "monasticism," being a "psychic miracle," nevertheless incorporates at its

> root a kind of "incineration" of everyday existence [*bytiistvo*] and of everyday things (hence the storm against it by Peter the Great, indeed by all *energetic* people).[34]

However, as far as Peter's remaining church reforms were concerned, matters seemed more complex, prompting Rozanov to develop a number of stratagems in defence of his support for the tsar.

First among these was the claim that the most flagrant abuses afflicting the modern church were a distortion of Peter's original intentions. Rozanov believed, for example, that the tendency to demote strong-minded bishops to less prestigious sees—a feature of the second half of the nineteenth century, when "talents were trampled underfoot; energy was dissipated"—would not have crossed the tsar's mind.[35] For such offences Rozanov plausibly blamed interfering chief procurators. On the other hand, a genius such as Peter would not have wasted time consulting his prelates on such "trivia" as "legal separation for married couples" (a cause especially dear to Rozanov's heart), because his "vast common sense" would have told him that this was a question of "national [*narodnyi*] improvement, the regulation of daily life," rather than a matter for the church.[36] No less controversially, Rozanov insisted that Peter had never intended to impose foreign norms on Russia. "He simply strove for what was 'better,' 'livelier,' and 'faster': it was purely coincidental that, in his time, 'better,' 'livelier,' and so on were to be found in the West." Had the West in itself been a point of principle for the tsar, he would "certainly, by virtue of his irrepressibility, have broken the very faith—not only broken the church's institutions, but replaced one set of saints with another." In fact, Peter had done nothing of the sort, because "he deeply worshipped the Russian saints" and "was altogether a firmly convinced Russian [*voobshche krepko russkii chelovek*]." Once again, a charge commonly made against the tsar reformer would, according to Rozanov, have been better levelled at his successors on the throne:

> The essence of Peter's reforms consisted in eternal *activity, unstoppingness* [*ne ostanavlivaemost'*], and if they had preserved this essential feature, they would not have fallen sick, not have been blunted. Whereas under his incapable successors, they were interpreted—and interpreted in a real way, in real institutions—as some sort of foreign

> conquest of Russia, as a kind of indispensable assimilation of western "forms," when it was not at all a matter of form, but of activity, of the awakening of a spirit.[37]

This last argument, advanced on the 150th anniversary of Lomonosov's death in 1915, was consistent with the case Rozanov had made as early as 1892 that Peter's greatness lay not so much in his success as in his method, which had given rise, by encouraging unfettered individuality, not only to writers such as Lomonosov, but ultimately, by implication, to Rozanov himself, another northern provincial cast from the same imaginary rugged mold:

> Full of inexhaustible energy and life . . . by his nature alone [Peter] tore asunder and mangled all the established relationships, the entire intricately contrived pattern of our old way of life and, himself eternally free, gave inner freedom to his people. In matters great and small . . . he taught his contemporaries what was simple and natural and by this means opened up a new era in our history, having made possible in it the manifestation of all man's spiritual gifts, all his capabilities, both brilliant and deformed.[38]

Finding his own creativity stifled by Filippov and his acolytes, Rozanov moved in May, 1899, to *Novoe vremia*, whose publisher, Aleksei Suvorin, was prepared to grant a degree of intellectual freedom (and handsome material rewards) to a writer whose increasingly scandalous reputation promised a growing readership for his newspaper. Here too, however, Rozanov's admiration for Peter was to prove a hostage to fortune. First coined by Count Sergei Uvarov in 1832, "Orthodoxy, autocracy and nationality" proved a convenient slogan for a range of emergent right-wing groups after 1900. However, whereas ideologists of "Official Nationality" under Nicholas I had treated Peter with "blind veneration,"[39] their twentieth-century successors were more critical. Following the lead of the former terrorist, Lev Tikhomirov, whose *Monarkhicheskaia gosudarstvennost'* (The Monarchist State System) appeared in 1905, populist and elitist rightists alike portrayed Peter's reign as the boundary between authentic Muscovite "autocracy," understood as a form of benevolent paternalism, and a novel type of impersonal "absolutism" driven by malign bureaucrats.[40] When neo-Slavophile leaders launched a vain appeal for the restitution of a pre-Petrine *zemskii sobor* in the aftermath of Bloody Sunday (January 9, 1905), they therefore had two aims in mind: to privilege the consultative principle over incipient demands for popular representation and to undermine Russia's leading bureaucratic modernizer, Sergei Witte, whose burgeoning reputation on the right as a traitor to the tsar was soon to be confirmed by the promulgation of the October Manifesto.[41] All the more striking, then, that Rozanov, no uncritical admirer of bureaucracy, should have been so positive about Witte and so sceptical about Orthodoxy, autocracy and nationality.

A mathematician by training and a financial specialist by vocation, Witte scarcely counted in Rozanov's mind as a member of the intelligentsia; neither was he a remotely spiritual man. Yet he more than compensated for any lack of ideological commitment [*bezideinost'*] by unbounded reserves of energy. Indeed, in comparing him to Peter I, Rozanov suggested that "an unbiased observer" would "find no more interesting, more attractive figure than Witte in the whole of the nineteenth century, and none more capable of arousing rapture and admiration":

> He never knew tiredness! . . . He never experienced failure, disappointment, fear, bewilderment, dismay. There was a fragment in him of Peter the Great, similarly disinclined to dwell on "philosophical thoughts." At any rate, not a single person from the eighteenth century, the nineteenth, or this first decade of the twentieth so resembles Peter, is so kindred to him in his whole make-up, even in bone, nerve and muscle, as Witte.[42]

Two qualities above all recommended Witte to Rozanov in this article: his apparently infinite capacity for innovation—"each morning of every day, something new"—and the ability to see his initiatives through to a successful conclusion. The implied contrast with the ineffectual, backward-looking neo-Slavophiles was obvious—and it serves as a warning against any temptation to define too precisely the oscillation of Rozanov's political ideas. Fateev, for example, claims that the year 1909, when Rozanov split with Merezhkovskii and published a series of articles condemning terror in *Novoe vremia*, marked "a final return to the conservative political views" that would dominate his journalism down to the February Revolution.[43] Yet Rozanov's paean to Witte, written in the summer of 1910, could never have been published in the right-wing press, not least because of its unflattering comparisons with Pobedonostsev. Instead it appeared, under the widely recognized pseudonym V. Varvarin, in *Russkoe slovo*, whose editor, seeking a middle ground between the revolution and the right, had pledged to eschew "all that is dark and gloomy."[44] Not content with praising Witte, Rozanov had already questioned the political utility of Orthodoxy, autocracy and nationality in an unsigned article published two years earlier in *Novoe vremia*. Without directly naming Uvarov's slogan, he left no doubt about its limitations:

> It offers much for dreams; it is the incarnation of political romanticism, but it offers little for healthy, sober policy. It is neither compass nor rudder. Peter the Great, the founder of modern Russia, would not have known what to do with these principles, and managed without at least two of them completely unceremoniously—and Peter not only was, but remains the leader of practical Russia, moving forward, building, and constructing.[45]

Epitomized in a casual reference to Katkov—"the great political practitioner, a real 'Peter the Great' of journalism"[46]—Rozanov's persistent association of the tsar with constructive practical achievement points towards a feature of his politics that is easily underestimated.[47] "Conservatism," Struve remarked in his review of *Sumerki prosveshcheniia* (The Twilight of Education, 1899), "may be either an entire cultural world-view, as with the Slavophiles, or a narrow tendency in practical politics, as with Katkov."[48] For Struve, as for most subsequent commentators, Rozanov belonged firmly in the Slavophile camp. By temperamental disposition, all his closest conservative contacts—Strakhov, Leont'ev, Filippov, and Florenskii—were indeed contemplative neo-Slavophiles. And yet part of him was drawn ineluctably towards *gosudarstvenniki* such as Katkov and Witte, proponents of the sorts of technological advance that Rozanov regularly urged Russia to adopt in order to rescue its economy from the clutches of foreign and Jewish capital.[49] Filippov, by contrast, personified an extreme case of the inertia Rozanov despised. Twenty years after their first meeting in 1893, he claimed even at that initial encounter to have sensed his new patron's deathly immobility:

> Life is jokes, smiles, witticisms; at any rate, life is movement. Here, in the silent reception room (no-one [else] was there) and especially in the figure silently bowing towards me, I saw and sensed such a denial of *movement*, such a prohibition, *bordering on the infernal*, on joking, speaking and moving, that I felt I was dying, and indeed made a move—sprang from the grave.[50]

Though it was less extreme, Rozanov sensed a similar lack of creativity in the sort of bureaucrat, exemplified by Speranskii, who had been educated in the seminaries. There were, he acknowledged, "no more steadfast, hardy, logical, quick-witted, and subtly intelligent people in service than the seminarians." Such people were admittedly "more systematic than the creators." But they could never "lead the state to anything new":

> A minister drawn from the ranks of the seminarians always smells more of a bureaucrat. Peter the Great is the complete negation of seminarism; Speranskii struck down Peter's impulse with his institutions and entirely extinguished our political creativity.[51]

In addressing a readership of statist nationalists, Rozanov could always resort to the claim that "of all Peter the Great's creations, only the army emerged as hardy and fine, active and linked to the people [*narodna*]":

> To the main motive for reform in Russia—the motive of self-preservation—this reform responded with a firm, skilful "yes." All the rest of his reforms were not created with the same consciousness of need, with the same animation, the same hopes and fear, with the poetry of personal exertions and popular expectations—were not forged in the labors and disasters of the Great Northern War. And all the rest—for the most part the fruit of imitation—is flabby, has no value . . . Peter did not insist on the rest.[52]

Shifting his emphasis for a commemoration of Suvorov in 1900, Rozanov argued that "Peter's very reforms were, in essence, a military phenomenon, and not a phenomenon of the civic order. . . . Peter the warrior" could be found in all his "movements and speeches." From this flowed "the heroic stream of history" and the "heroic genius of the people."[53] It was but a short ideological step from such claims to the Poltava bicentenary, when Rozanov placed alongside Peter, "the founder of everything in Russia," not only Pushkin, "the highest phenomenon in our modern history," but the common soldier, "the spokesman and representative of the common people"; for "the battle of Poltava was a battle of the Russian people [*narodnyi, russkii boi*]. And we celebrate this day of the people."[54]

How different it would all seem in the aftermath of the February Revolution! In March, 1917, after a sleepless night reflecting on Russian history, all Rozanov could see was "weakness, weakness, weakness." Suvorov, portrayed in 1900 as "an historical necessity," now appeared to be "the sole really attractive personality in 'Russia's military annals.'" Aleksandr Nevskii, Vladimir Monomakh, Dmitrii Donskoi, and Ermak were the stuff of "myth, rather than history." Poltava looked different, too: Peter I was "a coward" who, "apparently, ran away (on the whole, Menshikov was the victor at Poltava)." And all this was emblematic of a still wider point. "Strictly speaking," Rozanov told Florenskii, "Russian history, flabby and loveable, ended with Aleksei Mikhailovich. Ended and *ceased*. Peter marks the beginning of imitation: of the Germans, the Dutch, the French, and the English."[55]

Here was an incontrovertible expression of the anxiety that had troubled Rozanov from the start. Even when acknowledging Rozanov's "striking and fresh idea" that the Westernizers might have been more authentically "pre-Petrine people" than the Slavophiles, Strakhov had warned him in 1890 that Westernism nevertheless incorporated "the worst features of the Russian soul" and that "nihilism was its logical fruit." "This," Rozanov reflected on publishing their correspondence in 1913, was "deep": "'nihilism,' of course, was already contained *implicite* even in the reform of Peter the Great."[56] For one who never abandoned his obsession with the radical "men of the sixties," this was an unnerving thought, and it surfaced in recurrent warnings about the gap dividing the intelligentsia from the *narod*. Until 1861, when serf emancipation threw a "bridge of hope" over the chasm, it had become progressively wider and deeper since Peter's reign. Emancipation, however, proved in this respect to be a false dawn. Even in 1904, the *narod* remained "the instinctive custodian" of "Russian justice," while the intelligentsia "alas, with few exceptions," had forgotten it "from the time of Peter" and lived "an alien, western [life]."[57] "'Peter's cause' got stuck"—and was still "stuck," Rozanov claimed in 1908—because the tsar, "like contemporary nihilists, approached the *narod* only from the outside, in material terms." In his "struggle with 'the old,'" Peter had "not conquered the popular soul, but merely attacked and abused it"—and the popular soul had withstood his onslaught "for the simple reason that it was deeper than the Petrine soul, just as it is deeper than the soul of the contemporary nihilists." Russia's educated classes could complete Peter's work only by entering the soul of the people, where they would find "a great deal to learn."[58] It was a forlorn hope. "We are living through a crisis of Westernizing ideas," Florenskii told a depressed Rozanov in August, 1917. "If Russia is not to perish, it must overcome Westernism. But, alas, whatever happens, the intelligentsia will not betray its arrogance. It is unable to repent."[59]

To some extent, the generally acknowledged pessimism and conservatism of Rozanov's latter years is reflected in changing perceptions of the tsar reformer. In 1915, reading Leskov on retirement, he was prompted to reassess even Peter's most fundamental virtue: his unceasing activity. Retirement, Rozanov reflected, was a state of being "outside history." Peter, on the other hand, had "taken Russia into history," and "lack of sedentariness [*nepodsidchivost'*]" was "his most intolerable feature," which "Russians could in no way recognize as 'Russian.'" Oblomov came to mind. "'What sort of Russian is eternally running about, in a rush, in a hurry.' Really, it is not national [*natsional'no*]."[60] A year later, the same idea recurred. Peter "would have achieved immeasurably more personal greatness and immeasurably more historical success had he not been in such a rush and such a hurry," and in particular had he absorbed "the spirit of the church and the strength of the church."[61]

Rozanov's mind, however, rarely worked in straightforwardly linear ways. He was closer, intuitively, to that earlier conservative,

Apollon Grigor'ev, who considered it a general rule that all Russians were "half little Peter the Greats and half followers of Oblomov."[62] Certainly Rozanov retained even in his final years a powerful and disturbing sense of the ambivalence of historical change. It was "*terrible*," he reflected in 1913, that "an *indelible* 'yes' and 'no'" should "hang over the most important moments in history, the most tormented minutes in the life of humanity." Peter's reforms, incorporating both "hell" and "paradise," were no exception.[63] A cynic might say that Rozanov manipulated both poles at will, according to the needs of a particular argument or the prejudices of his readers. There is doubtless some truth in that. But it was the larger point that haunted him, as he showed in a review of Natal'ia Manaseina's *Tsarevny* (1915), a novella from the era of Tsar Aleksei Mikhailovich, "which silently and piously brought Muscovite Rus' to an end and was so roughly, cruelly swept away by Peter's 'pogrom.'" For Rozanov, this historic collision was above all a clash of values: "an encounter between energy and silence, storm and repose: in essence, between monastery and city, between wisdom and journalism." Crucially, he believed that both sides of the binary were necessary "for history and for man," because, should he fail to assimilate them, this "incomplete" and "calamitous creature," trapped in a ceaseless tug-of-war between city and monastery, would be unable to escape the eternal ambivalence that so obviously afflicted Rozanov himself: "Where I *deny*, so there I *confirm*."[64]

NOTES

1 Nicholas V. Riasanovsky, *The Image of Peter the Great in Russian History and Thought* (New York: Oxford University Press, 1985), vii.

2 Gary Marker, "Solov'ev's Peter: *Otets otechestva, otsovtsva, i muzhestva*," in *Reflections on Russia in the Eighteenth Century*, ed. Joachim Klein, Simon Dixon, and Maarten Fraanje (Köln: Böhlau, 2001), 73-83, quoted at 77, 80.

3 Andrei Bely, "V. Rozanov, *Kogda nachal'stvo ushlo . . . 1905-1906 gg.*," *Russkaia mysl'*, November 1910, 374-75. The stimulating study by Adam Ure, *Vasilii Rozanov and the Creation: The Edenic Vision and the Rejection of Eschatology* (New York and London: Continuum, 2011), can be read as a series of variations on this theme, transposed into an overtly religious key.

4 "Eshche—Pamiati russkogo istorika (O S.M. Solov'eve)," in V. V. Rozanov, *V chadu voiny: Stat'i i ocherki 1916-1918 gg.*, ed. A. N. Nikoliukin (Moscow: Respublika, 2008), 218. Rozanov exploited this idea without acknowledgement in "Dva slova o mundire uchitelei," *Novoe vremia*, June 20, 1901, in V. V. Rozanov, *Iudaizm. Stat'i i ocherki 1898-1901 gg.*, ed. A. N. Nikoliukin (Moscow: Respublika, 2009), 629-31. Whereas Rozanov consistently referred to "Peter's reform" in the singular, I have followed conventional English usage by using the plural throughout.

5 Caspar Ferenczi, "Freedom of the Press under the Old Regime, 1905-1914," in *Civil Rights in Imperial Russia*, ed. Olga Crisp and Linda Edmondson (Oxford: Clarendon Press, 1989), 205. By comparison, the average circulation of *Rech'* in this period was only seventeen thousand (ibid., 206).

6 D.V. Filosofov, *Slova i Zhizn': Literaturnye spory noveishago vremeni (1901-1908 gg.)* (Saint Petersburg: Tipografiia Akts. Obshch. tip. Dela, 1909), 148. Even Rozanov's radical friends were ultimately disillusioned by his loyalty to the anti-Semitic *Novoe vremia*.

7 The remaining black hundredist kadets were S. N. Bulgakov, V. A. Maklakov, and M. V. Chelnokov. See S. N. Bulgakov to A. S. Glinka, 27 May 1907, in *Vzyskuiushchie grada: Khronika chastnoi zhizni russkikh religioznykh filosofov v pis'makh i dnevnikakh*, ed. V. I. Keidan (Moscow: Iazyki russkoi kul'tury, 1997), 145, 147, n. 7.

8 P. B. Struve, "Bol'shoi pisatel' s organicheskim porokom," *Russkaia mysl'*, November 1910, 138-46, esp. 141-42.

9 Renato Poggioli, *Rozanov* (London: Bowes & Bowes, 1962), 63-72; Heinrich A. Stammler, "Conservatism and Dissent: V. V. Rozanov's Political Philosophy," *Russian Review* 32 (1973): 241-53.

10 See, for example, G. V. Florovskii, *Puti russkogo bogosloviia*, 2nd ed. (Paris: YMCA, 1981), 459.

11 Laura Engelstein, *The Keys to Happiness: Sex and the Search for Modernity in Fin-de-Siècle Russia* (Ithaca: Cornell University Press, 1992), 298-333; Henrietta Mondry, *Vasily Rozanov and the Body of Russian Literature* (Bloomington: Slavica, 2010).

12 I owe a clear debt to A. N. Nikoliukin's multi-volume edition, which, for all its idiosyncrasies, has collected Rozanov's scattered journalism, including hundreds of articles published anonymously. For a critique of Nikoliukin's own politics, see Mondry, *Vasily Rozanov*, 138-42.

13 For withering remarks on "scholarly apparatus," see the undated letter to Strakhov (after June 19, 1888) in V. V. Rozanov, *Literaturnye izgnanniki: N. N. Strakhov. K. N. Leont'ev*, ed. A. N. Nikoliukin (Moscow: Respublika, 2001), 175.

14 In Rozanov's view, Kliuchevskii was not merely "a Russian historian"; he ranked "among the *memorable* people of the Russian land." See V. V. Rozanov, *Sakharna*, ed. A. N. Nikoliukin (Moscow: Respublika, 1998), 262.

15 "Nepopuliarnyi nastavnik i ego vernyi uchenik: Perepiska V. Ger'e i V. Rozanova," *Rossiia* 19, no. 5 (September-October, 2003): 156-87.

16 V. G. Sukach, *Vasilii Vasil'evich Rozanov: Biograficheskii ocherk; Bibliografiia 1886-2007* (Moscow: Progress-Pleiada, 2008), 12.

17 V V Rozanov, *Religiia i kul'tura. Stat'i i ocherki 1902 1903 gg.*, ed. A. N. Nikoliukin (Moscow: Respublika, 2008), 68; "Kul'turnaia khronika russkogo obshchestva

i literatury za XIX vek," first published in *Russkii vestnik*, October 1895. The notion stemmed from Lomonosov, consistently represented by Rozanov as Peter's closest spiritual descendant.

18 "Krasota v prirode i ee smysl'," in V. V. Rozanov, *Priroda i istoriia: Stat'i i ocherki 1904-1905 gg.*, ed. A. N. Nikoliukin (Moscow: Respublika, 2008), 43-103, esp. 89-95, quoted at p. 94, was written in response to Vladimir Solov'ev, and through him to Darwin.

19 V. V. Rozanov, *Literaturnye izgnanniki. Kniga vtoraia. P. A. Florenskii, S. A. Rachinskii, Iu. N. Govorukha-Otrok, V. A. Mordvinova*, ed. A. N. Nikoliukin (Moscow: Respublika, 2010), 629-30.

20 V. V. Rozanov, *Kogda nachal'stvo ushlo . . . 1905 i 1906 gg.*, ed. A. N. Nikoliukin (Moscow: Respublika, 2005), 149.

21 Compare V. V. Rozanov, *Esteticheskoe ponimanie istorii*, ed. A. N. Nikoliukin (Moscow: Respublika, 2009), 89, and Rozanov, *Priroda i istoriia*, 81 ff., with Rozanov, *Apokalipsis nashego vremeni*, ed. A. N. Nikoliukin (Moscow: Respublika, 2000), 330.

22 Rozanov, *Iudaizm*, 186; "Putanye idei," *Novoe vremia*, June 1, 1899.

23 Rozanov, *Iudaizm*, 350, 352; "Passivnye idealy," *Novoe vremia*, January 11, 1900.

24 V. V. Rozanov, *Russkaia gosudarstvennost' i obshchestvo. Stat'i 1906-1907 gg.*, ed. A. N. Nikoliukin (Moscow: Respublika, 2003), 241; "Na novyi god," *Novoe vremia*, January 1, 1907.

25 V. V. Rozanov, *Solitaria*, with an abridged account of the author's life, by E. E. Gollerbach, trans. S. S. Koteliansky (London: Wishart, 1927), 39.

26 Rozanov praised "Peterburg," a poem by S. M. Solov'ev's daughter, Poliksena, as "physiognomic, like a Serov portrait" (V. V. Rozanov, *Terror protiv russkogo natsionalizma. Stat'i i ocherki 1911 g.*, ed. A. N. Nikoliukin [Moscow: Respublika, 2011], 83; "Literaturnyi rod Solov'evykh," *Novoe vremia*, April 14, 1911).

27 Rozanov, *Priroda i istoriia*, 273; "Tsarevich Aleksei," *Novoe vremia*, January 5, 1904.

28 Ibid.

29 Rozanov, *Religiia i kul'tura*, 211; "Embriony," first published in *Religiia i kul'tura* (1899).

30 Rozanov, *Kogda nachal'stvo ushlo*, 41; "Gosudarstvo i obshchestvo," *Novoe vremia*, March 3, 1905.

31 Ure, *Vasilii Rozanov*, 233.

32 Rozanov to S. A. Rachinskii, 11 August 1895, in Rozanov, *Literaturnye izgnanniki. Kniga vtoraia*, 515 (here and elsewhere, unless otherwise indicated, emphasis in the original).

33 Filippov to Leont'ev, 3 October 1888 and 1 December 1885, in *Proroki vizantizma: Perepiska K. N. Leont'eva i T. I. Filippova (1875-1891)*, ed. O. L. Fetisenko (Saint Petersburg: Pushkinskii Dom, 2012), 508, 307.

34 Rozanov, *Literaturnye izgnanniki*, 380, note on a letter from Leont'ev; Belyi classified Rozanov as "the most *bytiistvennyi* writer of our times" ("V. Rozanov, *Kogda nachal'stvo ushlo*," 374).

35 Rozanov, *Russkaia gosudarstvennost' i obshchestvo*, 204; "Vybornye episkopy v russkoi tserkvi," *Novoe vremia*, November 26, 1906, unsigned.

36 V. V. Rozanov, *Zagadki russkoi provokatsii. Stat'i i ocherki 1910 g.*, ed. A. N. Nikoliukin (Moscow: Respublika, 2005), 389, 391; "Zaputavsheesia delo (K zakonoproektu o razdel'nom zhitel'stve suprugov,") *Novoe vremia*, November 5, 1910.

37 V. V. Rozanov, *O pisatel'stve i pisateliakh*, ed. A. N. Nikoliukin (Moscow: Respublika, 1995), 612-13; "Lomonosov: Ego lichnost' i sud'ba (4 aprelia 1765 g.—4 aprelia 1915 g).," *Novoe vremia*, April 4, 1915.

38 Rozanov, *Esteticheskoe ponimanie istorii*, 102-104. The passage was taken from Rozanov's "Teoriia istoricheskogo progressa i upadka," *Russkii vestnik*, February-March 1892, later re-cycled as "Zametki ob istorii," an appendix to *Priroda i istoriia*. See Rozanov, *Priroda i istoriia*, 259.

39 Riasanovsky, *The Image of Peter the Great*, 108.

40 I. V. Omel'ianchuk, *Chernosotennoe dvizhenie v rossiiskoi imperii, 1901-1914* (Kiev: MAUP, 2007), 267-68, 270.

41 See, for example, A. A. Kireev, *Dnevnik 1905-1910*, ed. K. A. Solov'ev (Moscow: ROSSPEN, 2010), 25 (January 19 and 22, 1905), 27 (January 24) and passim.

42 Rozanov, *Zagadki russkoi provokatsii*, 211; "Vitte i Pobedonostsev (K nedavnemu iubileiu gr. S. Iu. Vitte)," *Russkoe slovo*, June 16, 1910.

43 Valerii Fateev, *S russkoi bezdnoi v dushe: Zhizneopisanie Vasiliia Rozanova* (Saint Petersburg: Kostroma, 2002), 424-25.

44 V. Doroshevich to I. D. Sytin, 2/15 November 1905, in Ivan D. Sytin, *My Life for the Book: The Memoirs of a Russian Publisher*, trans., ed. Charles A. Ruud and Marina E. Soroka (Montreal: McGill-Queen's University Press, 2012), 139.

45 V. V. Rozanov, *V nashei smute. Stat'i 1908 g.*, ed. A. N. Nikoliukin (Moscow: Respublika, 2004), 167; "Uroki gosudarstvennogo samosoznaniia," *Novoe vremia*, May 7, 1908, unsigned.

46 Rozanov, *V chadu voiny*, 405; "P.A. Florenskii ob A.S. Khomiakove," *Kolokol*, October 14 and 22, 1916.

47 Peter "knew only the precise, the imminent, the tangible, and the practical" (Rozanov, *O pisatel'stve i pisateliakh*, 609). In a similar vein, in a manuscript dating from 1914, Rozanov ascribed Belinskii's "transition from aesthetic to business-like, 'realist' evaluations" to the critic's essential "*practicality* (as with Peter the Great)." See "Inache ia postupit' ne mog," in V. V. Rozanov, *Na fundamente proshlogo: Stat'i i ocherki 1913-1915 gg.*, ed. A. N. Nikoliukin (Moscow: Respublika, 2007), 412.

48 P. B. Struve, "Romantika protiv kazenshchiny," in *V. V. Rozanov: Pro et contra*, ed. V.A. Fateev (Saint Petersburg: Izdatel'stvo Russkogo Khristianskogo gumanitarnogo instituta, 1995), 1:362.

49 See, for example, "Ob'edinenie praktiki i znaniia," *Novoe vremia* , January 5, 1900, in Rozanov, *Iudaizm*, 328-30.

50 Rozanov, *Literaturnye izgnanniki*, 133.

51 Rozanov, *Iudaizm*, 758; "Soslovnoe li tol'ko bezvkusie?" *Novoe vremia* , December 23, 1901. The article was reprinted with minor revisions in V. V. Rozanov, *Okolo tserkovnykh sten*, ed. A.N. Nikoliukin (Moscow: Respublika, 1995), 148, under the title "Talantlivost' i bestalantnost' v dukhovenstve," whose first publication Nikoliukin was naturally unable to trace.

52 V. V. Rozanov, *Vozrozhdaiushchiisia Egipet*, ed. A.N. Nikoliukin (Moscow: Respublika, 2002), 342; "Mechta 'dukhovnykh khristian,'" first published in *Russkoe obozrenie*, November 1896 and reprinted in *Apokalipsicheskaia sekta (Khlysty i skoptsy)* (1914). The same passage also appeared in "Psikhologiia russkogo raskola," *Religiia i kul'tura* (1899).

53 Rozanov, *Iudaizm*, 440; "O Suvorove," *Novoe vremia*, May 8, 1900.

54 Rozanov, *Staraia i molodaia Rossiia*, 213-15; "Dvukhsotaia godovshchina Poltavskogo boia," *Novoe vremia* , June 27, 1909, unsigned. Right-wing political parties adopted the Poltava anniversary as a major popular festival.

55 Rozanov to Florenskii, 3 March 1917, in Rozanov, *Literaturnye izgnanniki. Vtoraia kniga*, 396-97.

56 Strakhov to Rozanov, 13 September 1890, in Rozanov, *Literaturnye izgnanniki*, 68 and n. 2.

57 Rozanov, *Priroda i istoriia*, 317; "Kto my takie?" *Russkaia Pravda*, Moscow, April 4, 1904, unsigned.

58 V. V. Rozanov, *Okolo narodnoi dushi. Stat'i 1906-1908 gg.*, ed. A.N. Nikoliukin (Moscow: Respublika, 2003), 300-301; "Okolo narodnoi dushi," *Novoe vremia*, April 20, 1908.

59 Florenskii to Rozanov, 8 August 1917, in Rozanov, *Literaturnye izgnanniki. Vtoraia kniga*, 192, a reply to Rozanov's letter of July 29 (ibid., 408-11).

60 V. V. Rozanov, *Mimoletnoe 1914 god. 1915 god*, ed. A. N. Nikoliukin, 2nd ed. (Moscow: Respublika, 2011), 514, May 29, 1915.

61 Rozanov, *O pisatel'stve i pisateliakh*, 639, "'Sviatost' i 'genii' v istoricheskom tvorchestve," *Kolokol*, May 6, 1916.

62 Apollon Grigor'ev, *Vospominaniia*, ed. V.F. Egorov (Moscow: Nauka, 1988), 13.

63 Rozanov, *Literaturnye izgnanniki*, 102.

64 Rozanov, *Na fundamente proshlogo*, 553; "N. Manaseina. Tsarevny. Istoricheskaia povest'," *Novoe vremia*, November 19, 1915.

The Question of Women in Power in the Eighteenth Century

E. V. Anisimov
*(National Research University Higher School of Economics, Saint Petersburg)**

In Russia the question of women in power is indeed serious and, as we know, not resolved even today. We can count on the fingers of merely one hand the number of prominent Russian women politicians. And in the eighteenth century we run into a striking paradox: the norms of the *Domostroi*, the sixteenth-century guide to patriarchal family governance, reigned everywhere, and Russian society simply regarded women as second-class beings; at the same time, women ruled the exceedingly powerful empire almost without interruption for nearly seventy-five years. Moreover, these women came from a class possessing few rights: widows (Catherine I, Anna Ivanovna, and Catherine II) and unmarried women (Elizabeth). We know that in the ancient world this class was regarded as liminal: they were generally expected to marry or take the veil. In rare cases, women of this status succeeded in maintaining their rather high position at court and in society: for example, the boyarina (Feodosia) Morozova, the regent Sofiia (Peter the Great's half-sister), Natal'ia Alekseevna (Peter's sister), Ekaterina Dashkova, and others.

Without a doubt, the idea of woman as an incomplete being originated in pre-Petrine Russia, and the church regarded woman as a sinner, even "a vessel of sin."[1] This conception exerted important influence in the perception of women.

The incapacity of women in matters of mind and will, and particularly in tasks such as the management of the state, was a matter of broad social and intellectual consensus in the eighteenth century. Immediately after the selection of Anna Ivanovna, the duchess of Courland, to become empress in February, 1730, V. N. Tatishchev drafted a document that was discussed by the nobility. It stated:

> Regarding her Highness the Empress, although we are indeed sure of her wise, moral, and orderly government, however as *she is a female, too much work is incommodious* [here and elsewhere below, emphasis is the author's], all the more as laws are lacking. For this, until the Almighty grants us a male on the throne it is necessary to create something to aid her Highness.[2]

Out of this in 1731 came the Cabinet of Ministers.

Tatishchev and his colleagues traveled a well-trodden path. Back in 1726, a similar body had been created under the first female ruler, Catherine I—the Supreme Privy Council. The draft document that created this body, "Opinions Not in the Decree about the New Privy Council," written by Catherine's son-in-law, Charles Frederick, duke of Holstein, stated that the council was established for the sole purpose of "relieving the heavy burdens of government." Catherine's decree of January 1, 1727, made it even clearer: "We created this council to be supreme *and at our side* [*pri boku nashem*] *only to assist and relieve Us* in the heavy burden of administration by its faithful counsel and its dispassionate pronouncement of opinions in all affairs of state."[3] The point of these passages is obvious: due to her weak nature, a woman is predestined to be imperfect and is incapable of bearing the burden of power, and for this reason requires the assistance and counsel of men.

The story of Catherine I is remarkable, for it develops an original conception of the transference onto her, as Peter the Great's wife, of the especially masculine virtues of her great consort. This should have raised her status in the eyes of society and made her a valuable heir to the throne. As is well known, in 1714 Peter created the highest women's honor, the Order of Saint Catherine. The first member of this order, which had upon its badge the inscription "Her work matches her husband's," was the Tsaritsa Catherine. Catherine famously showed her courage during the Pruth campaign of 1711 when the Russian army, along with the tsar and his wife, was surrounded, and when many thought that the army would be vanquished after the collapse of negotiations. Catherine insisted on continuing the negotiations and, according to legend, bribed the Turkish commander with all the jewels the tsar had given her.[4] Awarding this order to his wife on November 24, 1714, Peter stated that the order "was created to commemorate Her Highness's presence in the battle with the Turks at Pruth, where at a dangerous moment she was regarded by everybody not as a wife [that is, as a woman] but rather as a man."[5] Later, in a decree of 1723 concerning the coronation of Catherine, Peter again recalled the ill-fated Pruth campaign and the courage of his comrade in arms, who behaved not as a weak, cowardly woman, but with the courage, composure, daring, and intellect of a man.

The first-class court flatterer, Archbishop Feofan Prokopovich, boldly went further in his praise of Catherine's qualities. In a solemn address at the coronation of Catherine on May 7, 1724, he not only played upon the Pruth incident, which everybody surely had become sick and tired of hearing rehashed, but went further, and dared to incur the anger of the sovereign when, in comparing Catherine to the celebrated, pious, and saintly women of antiquity (Helen, Pulcheria, Eudoxia), he favored his empress over these saintly women. Apparently to the great surprise of the orator, Empress Catherine combined qualities that could not be possessed by one woman: love of God, love of husband and family, and also love of the fatherland. To Prokopovich this combination was unusual. In the case of Catherine, according to Prokopovich, "female flesh does not diminish generosity." In a word, the most to which even the greatest woman can aspire is to be like a man.

A few months after Catherine's coronation, on March 10, 1725, Prokopovich, in his famous eulogy to Peter the Great, addressed the widow and stated, "the entire world is witness that the female sex has not prevented you from being like Peter the Great." In the context of the eulogy, this statement suggested that a novel reincarnation had occurred: Peter's crown, spiritual virtues, and energy had passed to his spouse. Prokopovich called on all to rally around the crown and comfort "the sovereign and our mother, and console yourselves in the certain knowledge that *Peter's spirit lives in the monarch before us* as if Peter had not entirely left us."[6] However, as we see from the later history of the Supreme Privy Council, there was no reincarnation, and an ancillary male institution was considered necessary "at the side" of the new sovereign.

But the fact remained that a woman had come to power; she was the autocrat and ruled as best she could. What happened in society, in people's consciousness? Undoubtedly, some people came to terms with this fact, as they would come to terms with any other ruler, whether valiant warrior or total idiot. But others never forgot that a woman was on the throne and commented on this state of affairs incessantly.

At the court and among the elite, some thought a female ruler temporary and contingent. Under the pressure of misogynistic public opinion, the empresses committed certain public acts that demonstrated their firm intention to transfer power without fail, if not now then in the future, to a male heir. For example, Catherine I appointed Peter, the son of Tsarevich Alexis, as heir. But this tendency was manifested even more blatantly and humorously under Anna Ioannovna, who in 1731 forced the entire country to swear a loyalty oath to the unborn male child of a future marriage of her still-minor niece, Anna Leopoldovna, and an unknown foreign prince. As it happened, fortune smiled on Anna and, indeed, nine years after this oath a boy, Ivan Antonovich, was born.

The problem of succession was no less serious for the next empresses. Elizabeth Petrovna, who came to power because of a conspiracy, actively invoked the idea of the reincarnation of her father, Peter the Great, just as her mother Catherine had done before her; she tried to persuade the Guard regiments (and then society at large) that with her accession to power, Peter's symbolic body would be reborn without fail. However, in addition to her efforts to convince her skeptical subjects of this reincarnation, at the beginning of her reign she declared her heir to be Peter the Great's grandson and her own nephew, Karl Peter Ulrich (Peter Fedorovich). He was kept under close supervision, in a virtual golden cage.

The dynastic question became especially acute for Catherine II. Right up to the death of Elizabeth, the ambitious grand duchess Catherine did not figure in the calculations of Bestuzhev-Riumin, the Panins, the Shuvalovs, and other courtiers as a sovereign in her own right, but only as the wife of the appointed heir and, potentially, as a regent for the minor Paul Petrovich. But when she became the autocrat following a coup, members of the elite apparently were willing to extend her term until the heir turned seventeen. This expectation permeated every step of Nikita Panin, Paul's tutor, and even Paul himself prepared to ascend the throne upon reaching the age of majority. But by the beginning of the 1770s, Catherine had so consolidated her position that she was able to neutralize the efforts of Nikita Panin and others, which were directed at the accession of Paul to the throne. This torpedoed the relationship between mother and son for years to come.

It is important to note that marriage constantly hung like the sword of Damocles over female empresses. Outside marriage, their very existence was shameful. Would-be husbands of crowned widows and girls appeared all the time. At the beginning of the reign of Anna Ioannovna, for instance, a Portuguese prince appeared in Russia with the intention of marrying a Russian tsaritsa. A flock of potential grooms hovered around the lovely Elizabeth, and various marriage combinations involving her were much discussed in the early years of her reign. However, after everyone found out about Elizabeth's secret marriage to Aleksei Razumovskii, such conversations stopped.

Empress Catherine the Great was in an extremely difficult position when she came to power. On the one hand, Grigorii Orlov longed to marry her, a union in principle condemned by society. On the other hand, society fussed about a formally single empress. One of the first open conspiracies showed that the nobility discussed an ideal solution to the problem of female rule—to marry Catherine to "Little Ivan," the former emperor Ivan Fedorovich, imprisoned in the Shlisselburg Fortress. It is quite possible that the discovery of this plan for such an impossible and, for Catherine, shocking union decided the fate of Ivan Antonovich, who was killed in August, 1764, by his guards.

Nevertheless, in the consciousness of the elite the negative aspects of female rule were allayed by many circumstances. First, society then generally acknowledged a woman ruler's humaneness. This conviction became notable in the reign of Elizabeth, who for twenty years did not sign a single death sentence, and especially in the reign of Catherine, whose humaneness and enlightened views were well known.

Second, we should, of course, not exaggerate the significance of the *Domostroi* as a generally accepted and approved norm defining the relationship of women inside the family and home. Many documents indicate the tremendous influence of women in domestic matters, both among the common people and among the elite. This was determined by many circumstances—including, for example, the character and temperament of spouses, as well as the relations of children and parents, not to mention the fact that in Russia in the seventeenth and eighteenth centuries a noblewoman legally possessed incomparably more property rights than did her European contemporaries.[7] For all the ruthlessness of political repression, the spouse of the repressed always had the right to choose whether to follow her husband into exile or to remain on the estate that was part of her dowry, and that right continued to be enshrined in law. Even the Petrine reforms, regarded as creating female society in Russia, demonstrated that it was time not to push Russian women into public but rather to restrain them from rushing into freedom. As we know, Peter authorized publication of a guide for young people, *The Honorable Mirror of Youth* (*Iunosti chestnoe zertsalo*), which had a section devoted to girls—"Girls' Honor and the Crown of Virtue" (*Devicheskoi chesti i dobrodeteli venets*). This section discussed behavior inappropriate for a proper girl, who had to be cautioned against indulging in indecency: "A scatterbrain [*razinia pazukhi*] will sit next to young lads and men, push and shove (rather than sit quietly), sing lecherous songs, make merry and become intoxicated, jump about the tables and chairs, and allow herself to be dragged around like carrion, for where there is no shame, there is no humility."[8] We know that the prohibitions against deviant behavior, which may give the impression in normative documents that such behavior did not occur, reflect actual—and even accepted—norms of conduct. Consequently, it may well be that Russian women reacted with such enthusiasm to the freedom granted them by Peter that it was necessary to immediately appeal to their modesty and moderation.

Third, and no doubt most important, the elite was reconciled to the rule of women because by its very nature the court and court life were symbolically the woman's space, as generally the home and domestic matters were (and still are) regarded and associated with women's authority, with Hestia, the goddess of home and hearth. This sphere was strictly contrasted to the field, to war, to the inherent occupation of the male warrior, the skillful fighter, the courageous warrior, and the sincere, noble knight who possessed what was then called "a soldier's coarseness." But at court other qualities and habits were required of both men and women, qualities that were ascribed primarily to women. These were the ability to be liked, to flatter one's lord (or lady)—in a word, the art of pleasing—while at the same time carrying on a constant struggle for primacy by means of intrigue, duplicity, and lies. And it was also important to concoct ways to be idle beautifully. It was important that men at court engage in women's affairs, whether this meant serving as so-called commanders of cutlets or fatted fowl, observing and participating in the frequent rituals, ceremonies, dances, and theatrical productions, or practicing the gallant, refined manner of conduct at the court in which men displayed their masculinity. It is not an accident that Elizabeth's reign developed the phenomenon of the court dandy or flirt, for in the eyes of critics like Elagin it symbolized precisely such feminine, unworthy conduct. The effeminate courtier with a beauty spot on his cheek, bows on his sword hilt, all curled and powdered, in a bright lilac or canary outfit, circles among other effeminate creatures. Thus, under the influence of a feminized court, the line between male and female conduct and appearance was consciously erased; not for nothing did Elizabeth Petrovna frequently organize cross-dressing festivities where all women wore men's clothes and all men wore women's. Of course, the empress wanted first and foremost to use this masquerade to show everyone her wonderful legs, which were usually hidden beneath her dresses, but the very idea of cross-dressing (the courtier could exhibit what sociologists call androgyny) symbolized the capacity to combine male and female qualities, in dress, behavior, or even speech. Some philologists maintain that women played a great role in the establishment of a Petersburg pronunciation, emanating from the court, and as a whole in the development of conversational Russian. Thus, women were responsible for pronouncing the unstressed vowel "o" as "a," eliding the consonants in complex combinations, spreading French pronunciation, and nearly completely driving out Church Slavonic pronunciation, alien to women, from the conversation of the secular elite.[9]

The model of the androgynous being who combined the masculine qualities of the warrior with the feminine qualities of the courtier was Field Marshal Münnich, whose masculinity was indisputable, so many were his duels and battles. Lady Rondeau, wife of the English emissary, confirmed Münnich's appeal when she wrote a correspondent in England in 1735,

> Madam, your impression of Count Münnich is quite inaccurate. You say that he has the look of a rugged soldier who has been through a lot. But he is handsome, has fair skin, is tall and well built, and his movements are soft and delicate. He is a good dancer, exudes youth in all his actions, behaves with women as one of the most gallant cavaliers of this court, and in the presence of representatives of our sex radiates gaiety and tenderness.

Lady Rondeau added that all this was still not widely recognized, for Münnich lacked moderation and appeared false through and through. Later, describing Münnich's deliberately languid gaze at ladies and the way he tenderly kissed their hands, Lady Rondeau noted that he behaved thus with all his women acquaintances. In a word, Lady Rondeau concluded, "sincerity, in my opinion, is not a quality with which he is familiar," and then quoted a pertinent verse: "Don't trust him, he is a congenital liar / Cruel, cunning, insidious, inconsistent." The Spanish ambassador, the duke of Liria, had the same opinion of Münnich: "He is a liar, two-faced, [and] appeared to be everyone's friend, but in fact was no one's friend. Attentive and polite with strangers, he was unbearable with subordinates."

There are other examples of androgynous, liminal figures in Russian history. One such was Field Marshal Kutuzov, who combined the talent of a commander with the resourcefulness and mendacity of a courtier; this made him disliked among the generals. The attraction of women at court and of society to a real man was connected to the femininity of court life. Noteworthy were the warm, friendly relations of Empress Maria Fedorovna, the second wife of Emperor Paul, who was chained to court ceremonies, with brutal, half-educated, and, accordingly, not androgynous men such as Hetman Platov and General Bagration, who deserved the aphorism of the day—"Dirt is the powder of a hero." In this sense there is no surprise in the erotic attraction of the ladies of court, and even of the empress herself, to Guard officers on duty (like the Orlovs)—reeking of sweat, radishes, and vodka,—and to coachmen, huntsmen, choristers, and servants, that is, to men outside the feminized environment of the court.

The reception of women on the throne was different among the common people than among the elite. A massive amount of material of the investigative offices shows that the population at large definitely regarded a woman on the throne as nonsense, a mistake, undesirable, condemnable. This was most vividly expressed in the widespread and (given the peculiarities of Russian life) jocular toast, regarded as felonious and insulting to the honor of the sovereign: "Long live her most gracious empress, even though she is a woman!" This sort of sentiment indicates that the Petrine transformation of gender identities occurred on the surface and did not change the traditional popular conception of women, among men and women alike, as incomplete beings, incapable and dishonest.

Women were consistently described as weak in spirit, body, and mind. One of the private utterances pertaining to the empresses, for which one could end up in the torture chambers, was the Russian aphorism that is widespread to this day: "A woman has more hair than brains." Naturally, then as now, men whose mental capacities were seriously in doubt were the ones who uttered this aphorism most often. In the eighteenth century, another aphorism was equally felonious: "Unfortunate is the home that is owned by a woman."[10] (Nevertheless, "owned," we should note!) Under the empresses one could end up in Siberia for such a saying. To call a man a "wifey" (*zhonka,* as a married woman was often called) was an insult that underscored his worthlessness and insignificance.

The expression "woman's business" that occurs frequently in investigations as a kind of generalized expression of women's function in society deliberately presupposed something frivolous, narrow-minded, ignorant, weak, and silly, that is, the utter disorganization of the matter. In 1731, when Anna Ioannovna ascended the throne, the peasant Timofei Korneev declared: "What joy. It would be better to have some boy tsar. How can an empress know what a man knows? Hers is women's business. She'll be the same kind of gossip as our shop woman. She's in the pocket of the boyars. What will she know?" Similar expressions occur in other investigations, and provide powerful support for the conclusion that common people found the notion of female rule profoundly disturbing at many levels.

> Now, a dame [*baba*] rules us . . .
> A dame runs the government and she doesn't know anything.
> A dame has more hair than brains; the ruler has no brain . . .
> It is unworthy of our great Russian state to have a dame be the ruler. . . .
> A tsaritsa sits on the throne, but she's a broad [*baba*], a slut . . .
> The devil made us bow before a dame . . . .
> Now, a war starts; is that really a woman's business – such a great state to wage war and wear the crown . . . .
> I will not take the oath because now dames have become tsar, so let the dames kiss the cross . . .
> I'll swear to a broad like I'll swear to a pig . . .
> I won't obey a dame's order . . .
> I didn't kiss the cross for her highness, the bitch . . .
> He won't become a soldier. We don't have a tsar now, so why would a dame need soldiers?
> The beggar doesn't even wear pants; how could she reward us?
> They called the sovereign a broad . . .
> Do you really serve under a bitch . . . .

> Why would a dame need a city? [about the taking of Ochakov in 1788] . . .
> Why are the bells ringing for a dame . . .

And so on, and so forth.[11]

The fact that supreme power belonged to a woman, and especially to a widow or young girl indeed further undermined the popular notion of the sacred nature of autocracy and its ritualized sanctity. This process occurred even earlier under the influence of social developments characteristic of the early modern period, even without the phenomenon of female rules: the Time of Troubles, when the holy throne of the Riurikids became a trophy for rogues. The establishment of the Romanovs, an autochthonous dynasty whose forefather Mikhail was "one of us" (if dealt another hand of cards, Prince D. Trubetskoi could have become tsar), only confirmed the process: Mikhail Romanov was summoned to be tsar by Cossacks, and therefore could not point, as could the Riurikids, to an unending line of ancestors behind him; no blood of the caesars or of Byzantine emperors flowed in his veins.

Peter the Great also undermined the sacral nature of autocracy; his reforms and behavior challenged tradition, forced people to doubt the veracity of the tsar, gave birth to the myth of the changeling, and heightened expectations of the coming of the true tsar. The appearance of Pugachev is most noteworthy: in popular consciousness he appeared in the form of the true Tsar Peter III, who by some miracle had avoided death at the hands of his wife, the fornicator and usurper.

Nonetheless, it seems to me that the era of female rule in the eighteenth century definitely destroyed the myth of the sacrality of supreme power in Russia. The idea, cherished and preserved in the middle of the century, of the autocrat as God's viceroy on earth, as a holy being, as a god on earth, stood in striking contradiction with the reality of a woman on the throne; this contradiction led to the desacralization of autocratic power in general. The root of the palace coups of the eighteenth century lay to a great degree in the Praetorian sensibilities of brutish soldiers who, while on duty, observed court life from the inside; the sentry saw and then in the barracks discussed the highly iniquitous and hardly immaculate life of women at the court. And all of this sharply lowered the sacred and inviolable nature of this power and, now and then, under various pretexts, prompted mutiny.

In the consciousness of soldiers this desacralization was, from time to time, agonizing, and expressed itself in the sharp bifurcation between the symbolic aspect of the empress as ruler and her physical body. This is illustrated by the investigation, in 1748, of the soldier Stepanov, a sentry outside the bedchamber of Empress Elizabeth. The empress and her favorite, A. Razumovskii, went by him and entered the room. A servant appeared and told the sentry that the empress had ordered him to leave his post. Stepanov started to go down the stairs but then, as he stated during the investigation, "I figured that Her Most Gracious Majesty and Razumovskii would fornicate; I heard the boards rap and then I shuddered and wanted, you know, with my sword leveled, to stab that Razumovskii, but that servant wanted to strike me with the handle of the sword, only I was frightened, you know." Later he stated that "He didn't know what frightened him and then he, Stepanov, thought of that Razumovskii and, he thought, that Razumovskii and Her Imperial Highness would fornicate." He further imagined that, "After having stabbed this Razumovskii, he, Stepanov, would inform Her Imperial Majesty that he stabbed that Razumovskii because he [Razumovskii] wanted to fornicate with her and he, Stepanov, would hope that Her Imperial Highness would not punish him, Stepanov."[12] But the sentries changed shifts and Stepanov was never able to carry out his reckless intention.

This amazing story illustrates something bigger, giving voice to all the contradictions in the reception of female rule by common people. It was not just anything that startled Stepanov, but rather the sudden strange choice, the substantial contradiction between the symbolic, sacral, and physical bodies of the empress. On the one hand, the empress was a holy, untouchable person for him, someone he was sworn to guard—even with his life—in his duty as a subject and soldier. On the other hand, he undoubtedly became witness to the sexual act between the empress and her favorite. Stepanov took this coitus as simply criminal, as rape, the sexual attack of Razumovskii on the holy person of the autocrat. And he was obliged to defend the sovereign from any kind of violence. The resulting contradiction could not be resolved in the soldier's mind and caused his confusion.

The desacralization of supreme female (and autocratic) power also occurred among ordinary people. In 1739, the case was opened of several peasants outside Moscow who, upon hearing holiday salvoes in the capital, struck up a conversation. The peasant Kirilov stated that "the cannons were booming because of some glad tidings about the health of the sovereign, our empress." Another peasant, Karpov, asked, "What kind of glad tidings?" to which Kirilov replied, "Since our sovereign has no joy and she is God on earth, so we must pray for her." To which Karpov replied coarsely, or as they said then, swore, "The whore [*rastakaia*], what kind of God on earth—she's a bitch, a broad, a human just like us: she eats bread, craps, pisses, and you can screw her." Here we touch on one more important aspect of the evaluation of women in power. This is eighteenth-century society's attitude toward sex outside of marriage as an improper, indecent act, as fornication, a punishable crime, of which, nonetheless, many were secretly guilty, including moralizers and the critics of the debauches of the empress.

The fact that eighteenth-century Russian empresses were not married added a particular sharpness and obscenity to these attitudes and judgments. "Does she have a husband? And, if not, who is [screwing] her?" This was one of the most widely discussed "problems" in society in those days. Dozens of political investigation were devoted to analyses of felonious utterances by people from various social strata on four basic topics that agitated people all over the country: first, the prior and current fornication history of the reigning empress; second, her lovers; third, secret issues of the empresses and the fate of their bastards; and fourth, the various occurrences in the bedrooms of the palace, accompanied by lurid details. In addition, it is astonishing how rapidly this rumor mill, an oral newspaper chronicling "the lives of the stars," spread over the entire country, from the Kola Peninsula to Astrakhan and from Kiev to Okhotsk.

Similar occurrences, rumors, and gossip (that frequently had, of course, a real basis in the far-from-pious lives of the Russian empresses) flooded the country, composing, in the final analysis, an image of the empresses as carousing trollops and false or illegal rulers. Moreover, the actions of the empresses became a model of deviant, negative, shameful conduct, condemned by social morals, even though this shameful conduct was widespread in society. Thus, in one incident, drunks sitting in a tavern compared the profile of Empress Anna Ioannovna on a one-ruble coin with the profile of a prostitute named Anka sitting next to them. In the time of Elizabeth, a commoner named Matrena Denis'eva from Solikamsk in the Perm region, said to her lover, "Well, we're playing around, that is, committing adultery [the investigator's clarification], just like Her Most Gracious Sovereign [unlikely that the offender spoke the empress's title] the b [bitch] . . . . She really screws around with Razumovskii." The woman Ul'iana (surname unknown) spoke even more sharply: "We sinners fornicate, but Her Most Gracious Sovereign lives in sin with Razumovskii." And, finally, the woman Elizaveta Ivanova put it most succinctly: "I am a whore, but that Most Gracious Sovereign . . . lives in sin with Razumovskii."[13]

While these women of loose morals were cynically frank in putting themselves in the same category as the empress, who had a favorite, the reaction of women of better families to the status and conduct of their happy monarchs is less well known. A few instances suggest that society women formally condemned excessive freedom in women's behavior (including sexual behavior), but the coming Age of Enlightenment, with its attendant air of tolerance and hedonism, in the second half of the eighteenth century greatly weakened the means of limiting this freedom. For a woman of society to be without an admirer, without a lover, was to be out of fashion. Likewise, the notion of marriage changed. As a heroine of one of A. P. Sumarokov's plays exclaimed, "I'm not some shopkeeper's wife who loves her husband." Society gradually became more tolerant of the multiple lovers of Catherine II, who ruled for thirty-four years surrounded by favorites, than it had been earlier of the modest amorous adventures of Anna Ioannovna or Elizabeth. But this tolerance did not influence the general public opinion, which continued to hold that a woman in power was something undesirable, threatening harm to society by imposing the rule of the passions over the rule of law or tradition. At the same time, even the shining example of the reign of Catherine II, whose capacity for the business of state was rarely doubted, did not change the widespread impression of a woman's inherent incapacity to conduct the business of state or public affairs in general (an impression, as shown above, actively supported by the so-called weaker sex itself). The end result was the 1797 law of Emperor Paul, forever closing off the path of women to the throne. This act ended the strange period of women in power in Russia, I think, forever.

NOTES

* Translated by Joseph Bradley.

1 See N. L. Pushkareva, *Chastnaia zhizn' russkoi zhenishchiny: nevesta, zhena, liubovnitsa X-XIX v.* (Moscow: Ladomir, 1997), 148-249.

2 E. V. Anisimov, *Anna Ioannovna* (Moscow: Molodaia gvardiia, 2002), 184.

3 *Sbornik Russkogo istoricheskogo obshchestva* 148 vols. (Saint Petersburg, 1867-1916), 55:93.

4 See Gary Marker, *Imperial Saint: The Cult of St. Catherine and the Dawn of Female Rule in Russia* (DeKalb: Northern Illinois University Press, 2007), 126-127.

5 E. V. Anisimov, *Zhenshchiny na rossiiskom prestole* (Saint Petersburg: Norint, 1998), 24.

6 Feofan Prokopovich, *Slova i rechi pouchitel'nye, pokhval'nye i pozdravitel'nye . . .*, 4 pts. (Saint Petersburg, 1760-1764), 1:107; 2:132-133.

7 Michelle L. Marrese, *A Woman's Kingdom: Noblewomen and the Control of Property in Russia, 1700-1861* (Ithaca: Cornell University Press, 2002).

8 *Iunosti chestnoe zertsalo, ili pokazanie k zhiteiskomu obkhozhdeniiu, sobrannoe ot raznykh avtorov* (Saint Petersburg, 1717), 12.

9 V. V. Kolesov, "Proiznoshenie petersburgskoe," *Tri veka Sankt-peterburga: Entsiklopediia v trekh tomakh,* 3 vols. (Saint Petersburg: Filologicheskii fakul'tet Sanktpeterburgskogo universiteta, 2001-), vol. 1, bk. 2, 189.

10 E. V. Anisimov, *Dyba i knut: Politicheskii sysk i russkoe obshchestvo v XVIII veke* (Moscow: Novoe literaturnoe obozrenie, 1999), 67.

11 Ibid., 64-68.

12 Ibid., 64-65.

13 Ibid., 66.

Businesswomen in Eighteenth-Century Russian Provincial Towns[1]

Alexander Kamenskii
(National Research University Higher School of Economics, Moscow)

Not many substantial studies are dedicated specifically to the gender history of Russia in the eighteenth century. In the more general works of Natalia Pushkareva and Barbara Alpern Engel, the eighteenth century is but one period in a longer chronological narrative. Essentially, the basis of the available historiography is made up of collected articles edited by Wendy Rosslyn, the monographs of Michelle Lamarche Marrese and Anna Belova, and several dozen essays, mostly by these same authors.[2] Gary Marker also contributed to scholarship on the issues at hand with an English-language edition of Anna Labzina's diary and a book on the cult of Saint Catherine.[3]

Due to the nature of the sources researchers have used, most of these works focus on women of noble origin and pay particular attention to their daily life, childhood, experiences in marriage, childbirth, and widowhood, and their general mindset. Marrese has provided the most detailed description of the economic aspects of Russian women's life in the eighteenth century. Marrese, who studied how Russian women disposed of their property, seems to have been the only historian to mention women's participation in business transactions, including money-lending. Alas, the dearth of sources did not allow Marrese to systematically compare men's and women's debts.[4]

The source material Marrese used was that provided by provincial notarial records (*krepostnye knigi*), which documented all kinds of transactions. The present essay aims to attract scholarly attention to another group of sources, never before studied from this point of view, that is, registries of contested or overdue promissory notes, which are very well known to students of economic history.[5]

According to the 1729 Statute on Promissory Notes (*Ustav vekselniy*), no witnesses or guarantees were required for a promissory note to be valid.[6] They were mostly drawn up by their immediate issuers, who had to identify themselves in the same manner as they would in any other legal documents, i.e., by indicating their rank, social position, and place of residence. But unlike all other legal documents, promissory notes were not registered at any governmental office. Needless to say, should both the creditor and the debtor be illiterate, they had no choice but to ask someone for assistance, while if they were literate they composed promissory notes themselves. That means that any personal details found in promissory notes are, in fact, an issuer's self-identification.

We have almost no original promissory notes at our disposal, as they were usually destroyed upon payment. Fortunately, numerous copies of promissory notes that were announced (protested) by creditors survived in the registries of contested or overdue promissory notes (*knigi protesta vekselei*). These books were kept, according to the 1729 statute, at various governmental institutions whose functions included resolving arguments related to monetary instruments, locating defaulters, and, in cases of bankruptcy, liquidating debtors' assets at auction. Registries of protested promissory notes incorporated copies of the original promissory notes, which, in turn, included names of creditors and borrowers, the amount loaned, the transaction place, and the due date for repayment.

I first encountered these sources when I decided to explore economic aspects of daily life in provincial Russian towns of the eighteenth century, based on the documents of the municipal magistracy of the town of Bezhetsk.[7] The archival holdings of the Bezhetsk municipal magistracy in the Russian State Archive of Ancient Acts (RGADA) contain twenty-five registers of protested promissory notes for the period between 1740 and 1775.[8] It appears that prior to that period, no such registries were kept in Bezhetsk, but this certainly does not mean that townspeople did not complete transactions, lend each other money, or complain to the magistracy of the borrower's default. They did so even before promissory notes (*vekselia*) made their first appearance in Russia: these transactions were recorded in letters of credit or bond indenture notes. A number of such cases survive in the archive of the Bezhetsk magistracy. Overall, this archive yielded information on 2,448 credit transactions completed over the period from 1696 to 1775. The assembled data were put into a database.

Since the magistracy was a governmental institution in charge of the urban population, the townspeople's lending transactions constituted the majority of those recorded in the magistracy's archive. The residents of Bezhetsk used credit in commercial operations or simply borrowed cash from each other. At the same time, 37% of all transactions involved gentry, ecclesiastics, clerks, people of various ranks (*raznochintsy*), and peasants. Most of these contracts were, of course, drawn up between males, but the total of 2,448 transactions did include 127 (5.2%) cases of women lending or borrowing money, accepting a promissory note in return for some goods, or issuing one as payment for a purchase. While research into note circulation is a prerequisite for the general study of credit in Russia in the eighteenth century, it seems worthwhile to determine specifically how active women were in this particular sphere. It must be noted that although Marrese studied notarial records for the towns of Vladimir, Kashin, and Tambov, the individual examples she cited in her book pertained predominantly to the upper classes of the Russian nobility. The Bezhetsk documents, on the other hand, shed light on the life of provincial gentry and townspeople whose financial means were naturally more limited.

The list of 127 cases in which women featured as borrowers or lenders includes 97 names, as some of these ladies took part in more than one transaction. Socially, these individuals fall into the following categories: fifty-six members of the nobility, thirty-three townspeople, four clerks' spouses, two wives of clergymen, and two of military men. Notably, not a single woman of peasant origin shows up on this list, even though peasant men featured in 13.5% of the total number of promissory notes found in Bezhetsk. Thus, male peasants' ample use of promissory notes notwithstanding, peasant wives and widows, and especially unmarried daughters, regardless of what category of peasantry they belonged to, left no evidence of commercial independence.

The number of cases involving gentry is lower than that involving peasants: 289 occurrences, or 11.8% of the total number. This certainly does not mean that nobles were less keen on promissory notes as a financial instrument. The explanation should rather be that they were more likely to do business with persons from their own milieu and, accordingly, more liable to protest unpaid notes in institutions other than the magistracy, for instance the local *voevodskaia kantseliaria*. The average amount of a promissory-note transaction involving a noble is 175.4 rubles, which is several times the average contract signed by a peasant, clerk, or clergyman.[9] Nobles borrowed money in two hundred cases and loaned cash in eighty-nine cases. Incidentally, the average amount they loaned to merchants — 116.7 rubles — was lower than the amount they typically borrowed. In other words, nobles borrowed larger sums from townspeople than they loaned them. Likewise, townspeople may be assumed to have asked nobles for credit only if they had an ongoing business relationship with them; for cash advances, it was much easier to deal with a social peer who knew the debtor and his reputation. This observation necessitates another important caveat. As George Munro remarked, "While it is *impossible* to say conclusively what purpose each note filled, circumstantial evidence indicates that for merchants at least, the vast majority was connected to buying and selling goods rather than monetary loans unrelated to a specific commercial transaction."[10] Indeed, only rarely are the concise and formulaic promissory notes, composed in strict conformity to the template included in the 1729 Statute on Promissory Notes, complemented with explicit indications that the amounts specified therein were to pay for certain goods. This is what makes the acknowledgment of a debt to a Bezhetsk merchant Ivan Omeshatov, signed in 1770 by the nobleman Fedor Myshenkov "on the orders of his mother Stefanida Andreyevna Myshenkova," stand out. According to this letter of credit, Myshenkov undertook to pay Omeshatov sixteen rubles in cash, "and in grains: a quarter of rye, a quarter of barley, and three quarters of oats." However, it was exactly because the document did not conform to the stipulations of the Statute on Promissory Notes that the magistrate did not accept Omeshatov's protest when the debt was not repaid in a timely manner. Unfortunately, we have no clue as to why Myshenkov found it necessary to mention that he was acting on his mother's orders. Most likely, he was a minor who had no right to complete transactions in his own name.

Altogether, the Bezhetsk database contains 72 promissory notes signed by noblewomen, which adds up to 23.5% of the 289 transactions involving gentry. The first of these documents is dated 1751, the last one was recorded in 1775. The average amount of these transactions is about 167 rubles, only a little less than the average sum transacted by nobles in general. At the same time, thirty-there of these cases have women lending money to merchants: thus, women make up 35% of the total number of noble creditors. The data certainly do not imply that noblewomen loaned money to townspeople more often than male aristocrats did. It is clear, nevertheless, that they did so at least as often.[11]

In three cases, the documents designated female parties to the promissory contracts as "unmarried girls" (*devitsy*); in seventeen other cases they were specified as "widows" (*vdovy*).[12] This indicates that both married and unmarried female landowners engaged in independent business activities.

As mentioned earlier, the nature of these contracts is hard to judge, as we only have indirect evidence in this respect. Large amounts specified by round numbers (fifty, two hundred, or one thousand rubles) may safely be assumed to have been cash advances, whereas the sums of 17, or 224, or 380 rubles must have been payments for certain goods. For example, during 1762 and 1763, several merchants from Tver' wrote four promissory notes to Irina Plishkina, an army captain's widow, for the sums of fifty-two, fifty-five, twenty-five, and thirty-two rubles and fifty kopecks. All of these transactions were drawn up in Tver', where the widow or, most likely, her agent, must have brought some goods for sale. The notes fail to mention what district (*uezd*) Plishkina owned land in, but the fact that all of these notes were protested in Bezhetsk probably means that this was the district center nearest to her estate. This supposition is further indirectly confirmed by another promissory note, of 1769, in the amount of three rubles and forty kopecks, issued by Plishkina herself in Bezhetsk proper for a local resident, Ivan Reviakin.

The economic activities of the Kashin landowner and college assessor's wife Anna Grigorieva seem to have been drastically different. Our database includes seven promissory notes she protested, all of them written in her name by various residents of Bezhetsk between 1769 and 1774. One of the notes is for the sum of twenty-five rubles; four are for fifty rubles each, and two for one hundred rubles each. All transactions took place in Bezhetsk proper: Grigorieva must have lived here. She appears to have loaned cash to local merchants. The fact that it was monetary loans in which she dealt is indirectly testified to by one more note. In 1775 a widowed estate-owner (*pomeshchitsa*) from Ustiug by the name of Ekaterina Nechaeva documented a promise to pay three hundred thirty rubles to Alexei Tyranov, a Bezhetsk resident who signed the note over to Anna Grigorieva: she, in turn, was the one to protest it. Tyranov apparently had good reasons to believe that this college assessor's wife, well trained in arguments over promissory notes, would be more successful in recovering the debt from the land-owner, her social peer. As for Grigorieva, she must have had sufficient means to buy out the promissory note and hoped to profit from the late payment interest.

It is worth noting that the practice of signing nobles' promissory notes issued to merchants over to other noblemen was rather widespread. It is this practice that accounts for the largest promissory-note transaction involving a noblewoman in our database. In 1770, a sergeant of the Leib Guard of the Preobrazhenski Regiment, Nikolai Strunskii, endorsed a promise to pay a Moscow merchant of the first guild, Alexei

Osorgin, the sum of two thousand rubles. The debt was to be disbursed in a year. After the due date had come and gone, Osorgin signed the promissory note over to an army captain's wife Maria Kuz'minova, who protested it in the Bezhetsk magistracy. Since no other bills of exchange mentioning this woman's name are to be found in the Bezhetsk archive, there is no reason to assume that Kuz'minova, like Grigorieva, dealt in money-lending. It is remarkable, however, that she had such a hefty sum of money at her disposal. Another army captain's wife—the widow Stefanida Tarakanova—must have been comparably wealthy. A Dmitrov merchant, Miron Nemkov, sold her a promissory note for the sum of twelve hundred rubles issued to him in 1772 by a retired lieutenant (*poruchik*) Prince Peter Ukhtomski. As for the three hundred rubles owed by a lieutenant's spouse, Matriona Tolkachiova, to the Saint Petersburg merchant Matvei Beloziorov, they were ultimately up to the Bezhetsk landowner (*pomeshchik*) Lev Batiushkov (the grandfather of Konstantin Batiushkov, the poet) to collect. In 1771 another Bezhetsk landowner, the college assessor Gavrila Maslov-Neledinskii, borrowed two hundred rubles from a Moscow-based merchant Mikhail Kurochkin. The latter signed the promissory note over to Anna Gordeeva, an army major's wife who ended up protesting it in Bezhetsk.

The largest amount of money borrowed by a noblewoman from a merchant was six hundred rubles. This is how much the Bezhetsk merchant Mikhail Reviakin loaned in 1770 to a Kashin landowner (*pomeshchitsa*), an artillery captain's widow by the name of Alexandra Berseneva. In this case, the choice of a creditor was far from accidental. Reviakin was one of the most economically active Bezhetsk residents, and monetary loans to members of the upper classes were one of his usual lines of business. In addition to Berseneva's promissory note in his name, the database contains numerous other notes he protested. For example, we have a note of 1755 in the amount of four hundred rubles signed by an Uglich landowner, an army major's widow named Vera Smolenova; there are also two notes issued in 1763 by a Secret Service (*Sysknoi prikaz*) clerk's widow, Tatiana Molchanova, worth two hundred rubles each. Further examples could be enumerated. The purposes such loans served may be gauged thanks to a somewhat extraordinary promissory note drawn up in Mikhail Reviakin's name by a Bezhetsk landowner, Sub-Lieutenant (*podporuchik*) Prokofii Fomin: in 1770, the sub-lieutenant borrowed 550 rubles "for the *purchase* from the Bezhetsk magistrate of a little village called Pechkov, with serfs."[13]

Just as unique, albeit in a different sense, is a remark included in a promissory note issued in 1756 by Daria Andreeva, a landowner and army lieutenant's wife, to Alexei Burkov, a clerk of the Bezhetsk tavern (*kruzhechnyi dvor*). She borrowed thirty rubles from him for a term of one year, "for which money a peasant Ivan Fomin, of the village of Antonovskoe of the Beletsk district, has been accepted as surety, with the provision that said Ivan Fomin would reside at Burkov's for the duration of the term."[14] The requirement to put up some collateral comes up in promissory-note transactions rather infrequently. In this case, it most likely underscores the lender's doubt in the borrower's ability to pay him back. His fears were clearly justified, as the debt was not repaid on time.

These examples show that women who took part in the promissory-note transactions preserved in the Bezhetsk archive all belonged to approximately the same stratum of the Russian gentry: their husbands' ranks placed them anywhere between the twelfth and the eighth classes of the Table of Ranks. The same is true for those male aristocrats who were actively engaged in economic activities: the greatest number of promissory notes in the Bezhetsk database involves captains, lieutenants, sub-lieutenants, and ensigns (*praporshchiki*).

Among the many Bezhetsk promissory-note transactions, only one contract had women as both parties: in 1764 Maria Koriakina, an army captain's widow and a Bezhetsk landowner, gave Anna Skobeeva, another local landowner and the spouse of a Leib Guard sub-ensign (*podpraporshchik*), a loan of fifty rubles for two months. In all the other cases, women did business with men.

Compared to noblewomen's contracts, the forty-eight promissory notes wherein women from the merchant estate acted as either borrowers or lenders present a drastically different picture. Exactly half of these—twenty-four notes—had a widow as a signatory, while twenty-three women were married to townspeople; and only one transaction involved an unmarried girl (*devka*), the daughter of a Bezhetsk merchant. Widows' active engagement in economic activities is to be expected: as is well known, on the one hand, the loss of a husband forced a widow to take his functions upon herself; on the other, it often left her with no means of support whatsoever. Not surprisingly, widows act in our sources both as borrowers and as lenders. The average amount transacted by women of this social group is, naturally, considerably lower than that by noblewomen: about twenty-five rubles. The smallest debt was two rubles and ten kopecks, and the largest, eighty rubles. However, the fifty or so promissory notes studied so far are certainly insufficient evidence to draw the conclusion that female townsfolk operated with lesser sums than their husbands. Let me quote some examples.

The name of the widow Maria Samokhvalova occurs in the Bezhetsk protested promissory-note registries starting from 1756. Her husband was killed in a drunken brawl in the same year. It looks like the widow protested the failure to repay two promissory notes right after her husband's demise. One contract was in the amount of eleven rubles and twenty kopecks, another, twenty-two rubles and twenty kopecks. Both promises were issued by Karelians (*koreliane*)—descendants of the peasants resettled into this region from Karelia back in the sixteenth century; both were for a term of nine months. After this, Samokhvalova's name disappears from the Bezhetsk protested promissory-note registers for ten years. In 1766 she shows up again and protests a promissory note for the sum of five rubles, issued to her by her late husband's younger brother Anton. Seven years later she protested a promissory note in the amount of ten rubles and thirty kopecks, signed by one of the Bezhetsk merchants. This can be seen as an indirect proof that she engaged in some petty trade. Remarkably, the latest note had a term of one year, meaning that Maria Samokhvalova was not badly in need of money. Indeed, an inventory of assets stolen from her and her husband back in 1751 testifies to their having been quite well-off.[15]

Information on protested promissory notes adds to one more family's story as described in my 2006 publication. I mean Sergei Reviakin and his mother Marfa, daughter of an ecclesiastic of the Novodevichii Monastery in Moscow. Widowed at about thirty-five years of age (her husband Vasilii died before 1747), with two children, Marfa undertook unsuccessful attempts in the early 1750s to sue her late husband's brother Luka Reviakin for a sizeable sum of money (2,629 rubles). In search of justice she turned even to the principal magistrate, but to no avail. In 1757 her elder son Ivan went to look for work in Saint Petersburg and eventually became a court lackey (*lakei*). In his passport application he stated that he was completely broke. Earlier that year, he must have engaged in petty trade, as in the same 1757 in Ustiug a local estate owner, Avdotia Nefed'eva, drew up a promissory note in his name for thirty rubles, for a term of six months. Ivan signed this note over to a second-major (*sekund-maior*), Mikhail Dosadin, but this money could no longer save him. Five years later, in 1762, his mother Marfa protested a promissory note for fifty rubles, drawn up in Ivan's name back in 1754, by his cousin Yakov Reviakin, the son of the person she had previously tried suing for money earlier. What is interesting is that Yakov, a member of one of the wealthiest Bezhetsk families (he was the elder brother of Mikhail Reviakin who, as we have seen above, loaned money to the gentry), had by this time also moved to Saint Petersburg and was "the Neva chancellery's inspector in the secretarial capacity" (*nevskoi kantseliarii v dolzhnosti sekretaria kontrolior*). Apparently, the difference between Ivan's and Yakov's starting positions determined the course of their respective careers in civil service as well.

Meanwhile, Marfa's younger son Sergei remained in Bezhetsk and acquired notoriety as one of the town's troublemakers.[16] Also in 1762, when the widow protested her elder son's promissory note for fifty rubles, she and her younger son drew up two notes of their own, for twenty-five and sixty rubles respectively, each for the term of five months each. The first of these was in the name of the same Mikhail Reviakin, who was Marfa's husband's nephew and her sons' cousin. The second note was issued to Peter Nevorotin, a resident of Bezhetsk. Soon thereafter, Marfa signed another promise to Nevorotin, also in the amount of sixty rubles and also for five months. Judging by the fact that all three promissory notes were protested, the mother and son failed to return these loans on time. However, there is no documented evidence that their assets were inventoried and sold at an auction. In 1762, their financial standing clearly took a turn for the worse. An indirect explanation of this fact can also be found in the protested promissory-note registers.

Altogether we have information on nineteen promissory-note transactions Sergei Reviakin participated in over the period between 1753 (when he was about sixteen years old) and 1774. The amounts transacted in these contracts were rather modest: from one to sixty rubles. Notably, Sergei acted as the issuer of a note, that is, a borrower, in only five cases. In all the other instances he was the creditor. It is worth noting that the first eight promissory notes issued to Reviakin (dated to the period between 1753 and 1761) featured debts from two to fifty-five rubles: he lent money to peasants five times, to local governmental clerks twice, and only once (the loan of fifty-five rubles) to a female landowner. The two subsequent transactions were the cash advances Reviakin co-signed with his mother. In 1763 Reviakin loaned ten rubles to a sacristan, Fedor Romanov, whereas in 1764 he borrowed the total of sixty rubles (in two promissory notes) from his relative Ivan Reviakin. Starting from 1766, he borrowed money only once—ten rubles from a town-dweller Alexei Dediukhin—but issued multiple loans to various individuals. However, the amounts featured in the promissory notes in his name are significantly lower than before. Small wonder, since the 1760s were exactly the time when Sergei's criminal activities peaked. A key to interpreting this data may be found in a secret denunciation submitted in 1767 by Semen Popov, a clerk, who asserted that Sergei Reviakin "does not retail anything . . . and makes do mostly with gambling"[17] In fact, the sums mentioned in the promissory notes issued in Reviakin's name could well have been gambling debts. It is plausible that in 1762 Sergei lost a lot of money in gambling, was constrained to take out loans and, since his ability to pay back was compromised in his creditors' eyes, had his mother co-signed on these loans as a guarantor of some kind.

There are promissory notes for very small amounts among the recorded transactions completed by female townsfolk. For example, in

1752 the wife of the Bezhetsk resident Yakov Repin, Avdotia, signed a promise to return three rubles and fifty kopecks within just six days. Two years later, the same individual took upon herself an obligation to repay two rubles and ten kopecks, borrowed for two months. Avdotia's name shows up in the protested promissory-note register again fifteen years later, when she borrowed three rubles, to be disbursed in three months. Quite clearly, in all three cases Avdotia had no cash to pay for some small purchases and used promissory notes instead. She likely made these purchases during her husband's absence and hoped to pay for them upon his return. We know that Yakov occasionally traveled on trade-related business thanks to an episode recorded in 1749: the magistrate received a protest on Yakov's promissory note for five rubles and sent a clerk to the delinquent's home. Avdotia Repina reported that her husband was away on a trip to the town of Ustiuzhnia Zheleznopol'skaia.[18]

One more peculiar feature of the protested promissory-note registers is worth mentioning here. These records contain valuable information on the town residents' geographic mobility. According to the law, once a protest on a promissory note was recorded, the town magistrate's clerk went to the defaulter's home for questioning. If the debtor turned out to be away, which happened not infrequently, the clerk had no choice but to speak to his household instead. Remarkably, townspeople's wives and daughters often went beyond informing the authorities of the defaulter's absence and provided details on where and for what purpose he was gone.

For instance, when several promissory notes issued by Ivan Petukhov, a Bezhetsk resident, were protested over the course of the year 1740, his wife Natalia kept telling the magistrate's clerk that her husband was not home. It was only at the end of the year that Petukhov's father specified that his son had gone "to trade in Moscow."[19] In the same year Natalia Repina stated that her husband Fedor was at a fair in the village of Porech'e.[20] In early 1749 Mikhail Degtiariov took off "to Moscow for his needs," as the magistrate's clerk was informed by Anna, Degtiariov's unmarried daughter (*devka*).[21] However, several months later, in December of the same year, when captain Polikarp Nedoveskov protested Degtiariov's promissory note for fifty-six rubles, issued a year earlier, a decemviri (*desiatski*)[22] declared that Degtiariov, along with his wife Pelageia and daughter Anna, had been "on leave" since June.[23] Degtiariov must have been back to Bezhetsk to collect his family, but nobody had attempted to recover his debts since the Statute on Promissory Notes did not make provisions for repeated searches for a defaulter.

That wives and daughters knew where their husbands and fathers were comes as no surprise. More strikingly, at times women displayed a keen awareness of their mensfolk's financial standing: quite often, not only did they avow the debt's existence, but also affirmed that a portion of it had already been repaid. For example, when in 1749 a Bezhetsk resident, Ivan Vytchikov, protested a promissory note in the amount of one hundred ten rubles, given to him by his compatriots Ivan and Ilya Tyranov, Ivan's spouse Maria reported that her husband was away, but that he had already delivered forty rubles in payment of his debt. She then requested a deferral until his return.[24]

Another Bezhetsk resident's wife—Ivan Omeshatov's spouse—did not just acknowledge that her absent husband was in arrears to a Tver' merchant Dmitri Borisov for a purchase in 1728 of "black oakum marine rigging worth twenty-two rubles" (*sudovykh snastei pen'kovykh na dvadcat' dva rubli*) (Omeshatov had paid nine rubles and sixty kopecks upfront). She also put forward a further five rubles against his balance and undertook to pay the rest later. What is remarkable in this case is that all of these events took place ten years after the transaction.[25] Such a long-standing memory of this purchase must bear witness to its importance to this family's economy.

In 1773, a local merchant, Yakov Pervukhin's widow, Daria, protested three promissory notes at once in the Bezhetsk magistrate. All three featured rather insignificant sums of money: six rubles, three rubles and eighty kopecks, and ten rubles. What makes them interesting is that the first two contracts were drawn up in the village of Valdai, by local residents: this implies that the widow had brought some goods to a local fair. Considering her willingness to wait for disbursement for six and ten months, she must not have been strapped for cash. The third defaulted promissory note in her name was written up in Bezhetsk, remarkably enough, by a priest's son. Conversely, the merchant widows Anna Ladygina and Praskovia Motovilova co-signed a promissory note for twenty-three rubles to a Bezhetsk resident, Matvei Diomin, in 1754: the women must have made a joint purchase. They undertook to return the money in ten days, but clearly overestimated their abilities.

The Bezhetsk protested promissory-note registries record few cases of women belonging to other social groups, but those that have left records are otherwise quite typical. For example, wives and widows of local clerks occasionally operated with amounts far exceeding those that women from the merchant estate dealt with. Thus, in 1755, the spouse of a scribe (*pod'iachii*) in the provincial governor's (*voevoda*) office, by the name of Natalia Smirnova, drew up a promissory note for the sum of one hundred rubles. Inversely, clerk Kuz'ma Voinov's widow Ekaterina acted as a creditor: in 1773 she received a promissory note worth thirty-two rubles and seventy kopecks (most likely, in payment for some goods), and in 1774 another one, for one hundred rubles (probably, a cash advance): in both cases the money was due in one year. Indeed, based on what is known about the Voinov family, the widow could well afford to wait. Her late husband was also engaged in promissory-note transactions, but their two sons were even more active in this respect. Like their father, Alexander and Peter Voinov worked for the office of the provincial governor (*voevoda*), with the elder one promoted in the early 1770s to the position of a provincial secretary, which corresponded to the thirteenth class according to the Table of Ranks. It is illustrative that the Voinov family members most often gave loans to others, but rarely borrowed money themselves. Indeed, it was not uncommon for the Voinovs to buy out and protest defaulted promissory notes issued by noblemen to merchants, since their official position afforded them greater opportunities to recover money from debtors of this kind. Just as telling is the fact that one of the promissory notes protested in Bezhetsk was issued in the name of Alexander Voinov's wife. The round amount featured in this contract—twenty rubles—suggests that this most likely was a cash loan for the term of three months, meaning that the official's spouse had funds of her own.

Anna, the widow of the Bezhetsk priest Iakim Pavlov, disposed of considerable assets as well: in 1768 she loaned 120 rubles to a local resident, Andrei Zagadashnikov, for a term of four months. Apparently Akulina Plotnikova, a soldier's widow, found herself in a very different situation:[26] in 1771 she twice borrowed ten rubles from one of the local residents.

The examples quoted in this essay certainly do not allow for generalizations regarding the economic activities of Russian women in the eighteenth century, but they do demonstrate the range of opportunities open to researchers concerned with this issue. The advantage of protested promissory-note registers as a source lies in the fact that this is a major data set containing multifaceted information on all regions of Russia and all the country's social strata. A study and data comparison for different regions and different periods seems to have the potential to introduce substantial corrections to accepted notions of the social history of the Russian empire.

NOTES

1 This study was carried out under the auspices of the Basic Research Program at the National Research University Higher School of Economics in 2015.

2 Natalia Pushkareva, *Women in Russian History from the Tenth to the Twentieth Century* (New York: M.E. Sharp, 1997); N. L. Pushkareva, *Chastnaia zhizn' russkoi zhenshchiny v XVIII veke* (Moscow: Lomonosov, 2012); *Women and Gender in 18th-Century Russia*, ed. Wendy Rosslyn (Aldershot: Ashgate, 2003); Barbara Alpern Engel, *Women in Russia, 1700-2000* (New York: Cambridge University Press, 2004); Michelle Lamarche Marrese, *A Woman's Kingdom: Noblewomen and the Control of Property in Russia, 1700-1861* (Ithaca: Cornell University Press, 2002); A.V. Belova, *"Chetyre vozrasta zhenshchiny": Povsednevnaia zhizn' russkoi provintsial'noi dvorianki XVIII – serediny XIX vv.* (Saint Petersburg: Aleteiia, 2010).

3 Gary Marker, *Imperial Saint. The Cult of St. Catherine and the Dawn of Female Rule in Russia* (DeKalb: Northern Illinois University Press, 2007).

4 For the preceding period, see Valerii Perkhavko, "Kupchikhi dopetrovskoi Rossii," *Voprosy istorii*, 2009, nNo. 1 (2009), 148-51. This article later became part of the book by the same author: *Srednevekovoe russkoe kupechestvo* (Moscow: Kuchkovo pole, 2012). See also Michelle Lamarche Marrese, *A Woman's Kingdom*, esp. chapter 4.

5 See George Munro, "Finance and Credit in the Eighteenth-Century Russian Economy," *Jahrbücher für Geschichte Osteuropas* 45 (1987): 552-60; Munroidem, "The Role of the *Veksel'* in Russian Capital Formation: A Preliminary Inquiry,"

in *Russia and the World of the Eighteenth Century*, ed. R. P. Bartlett, A. G. Cross, and Karen Rasmussen (Columbus: Slavica Publishers, Inc., 1988), 551-64; Munroidem, "St. Petersburg's Bills of Exchange in the Russian Economy of the Eighteenth Century," *Research in Maritime History*, no. 3 (December 1992): 99-113. In his essay on the merchants of Iaroslavl' George Munro also mentions that "women were regularly involved in providing credit through promissory notes" and gives a few examples (George Munro, "Glimpses into the Lives of the Merchants of Iaroslavl' in the Eighteenth Century," in *Eighteenth-Century Russia: Society, Culture, Economy,* ed. Roger Bartlett and Gabriela Lehmann-Carli [Berlin: Lit. verlag, 2007], 517-18).

6 *Polnoe sobranie zakonov rossiiskoi imperii*, 1st series, 40 vols. (Saint Petersburg, 1830), 8, No. 5410.

7 The first part of the project: A. B. Kamenskii, *Povsednevnost' russkikh gorodskikh obyvatelei: Istoricheskie anekdoty iz provintsial'noi zhizni XVIII veka* (Moscow: RGGU, 2006).

8 Rossiiskii gosudarstvennyi arkhiv drevnikh aktov (RGADA) f. 709 (*Bezhetskaia ratusha i gorodovoi magistrat*), op. 1, dela. 69, 98, 124, 152, 181, 217, 262, 312, 367, 414, 445, 493, 580; ibid., op. 2, dela. 622, 636, 798, 870, 902, 962, 998, 1032, 1107, 1135, 1169, 1190.

9 The average amount of a town-dweller's transaction does not tell us much, because almost every single transaction in the database of the town magistrate's records has a town resident as one of the parties to the agreement.

10 Munro, "Finance and Credit," 560.

11 Promissory notes were not the only way of getting credit in the eighteenth century Russia. With the appearance of the first Russian banks in 1754-1755 both nobles and merchants could also get loans there, but these required a deposit of estate land in the case of a noble or one of goods in the case of a merchants—which certainly was less favorable terms. Also one would not ask the bank for a loan for less than several hundred rubles.

12 The actual number of widows may have been greater.

13 RGADA, f. 709, op. 1 [2?], delo 367, fol. 55v.

14 Ibid., delo 1107, fol. 46.

15 See Kamenskii, *Povsednevnost'*, 199-200.

16 Ibid., 179-185.

17 Ibid., 184.

18 RGADA, f. 709, op. 2, d. 870, l. 3v.

19 Ibid., d. 622, fols. 3, 4, 5v.

20 Ibid., fol. 4.

21 Ibid., d. 870. fol. 1v.

22 The urban Russian population was divided into hundreds, fifties, and tens with elected *sotskie*, *piatydesiatskie*, and *desiatskie*, whose obligation it was to control the mobility of their constituency.

23 Ibid., fol. 9.

24 Ibid., fol. 3.

25 Ibid., d. 577a.

26 A "regimental court" (*polkovoi dvor*) located in Bezhetsk provided housing for retired soldiers and non-commissioned officers (*unter-ofitser*).

Dialogue and Conflict in the Ostroh Principality: The Year 1636

Giovanna Brogi Bercoff
(University of Milan)

Ostroh, the leading center of Orthodox intellectual life in the late sixteenth and early seventeenth centuries and seat of the first academic institution of the East Slavic faith, in 1636 became the theatre of a tragic clash—known as the "Ostroz'ka trahedija"—between Orthodox and Catholic believers.[1] On Easter Monday, 1636, a procession of Orthodox worshippers from Ostroh's Epiphany Church happened to cross the same bridge that Princess Anna-Alojza, the current lady of Ostroh, needed to cross on the way to her castle. The six-horse carriage carrying the princess, who was the widow of Hetman Jan Karol Chodkiewicz and granddaughter of the glorious Orthodox patron, Konstyantyn-Vasyl, was effectively prevented from crossing the bridge, and a member of her retinue, who had urged the worshippers to give way, was punched by a burgher. This act triggered a violent skirmish in which numerous people were killed, injured, or knocked into the river.

The episode prompted different accounts, influenced by the fact that Anna-Alojza was a zealous Catholic activist who, just before

Orthodox Easter, had held a notorious ceremony to re-baptize her father's bones. Significantly, the clash occurred in the tense context of the introduction of the Uniate Church to Ostroh and the resulting heightened religious intensity on both sides of the Orthodox-Uniate-Catholic religious divide. My aim is to analyze the main accounts of the event as well as a poem written by an unknown author two months later, the "Liament o prygodie neshchasnoi o zelzhyvosti i morderstvie meshchan ostrozkikh." (Lamentation for the unfortunate case of evil and the murder of the burghers from Ostroh).[2] These sources report on the tragedy from a variety of vantage points and cumulatively offer a compact case study, illustrating both the fracturing of society and the possibilities for tolerance that followed the Union.

One of the most revealing accounts appears in the so-called *Ostrozhski letopisets* (Ostroh annals), which survives in a manuscript copy of the late seventeenth century, and was only published in 1951.[3] The compiler begins with the year 1500, when the Muscovites took the so-called northern lands, and goes on to report natural disasters (earthquakes, fires, famines, and plagues), noteworthy military and political events (the Muscovites' conquest of Smolensk, marriages and coronations of Polish kings, the 1569 Union of Lublin), as well as some isolated and peculiar events, like the burning of a Jewish woman "who refused to renounce her Jewish faith," and the founding of a new sect by "Hanus' Kravec, who declared himself King of Israel." Many entries concern Tatar attacks as well as Polish and Muscovite actions against Tatars. Some disappointment tinges the matter-of-face tone when Muscovite conquests of contested cities, such as that of Smolensk in 1514, are mentioned, but in the same year, the author remarks, "our men [*nashi*] defeated Moscow in Kropivny, 80,000 [were killed]."[4] However, no emotional nuance appears when the author recounts the Polish conquest of Moscow, the coronation of the first Dimitrii, or the appearance of the second one. Whether the use of "ours" (*nashi*) is to be attributed to our compiler or comes from Bielski's chronicle (which the compiler acknowledges as a basic source) remains to be investigated, but clearly the compiler identifies with the Polish-Lithuanian Commonwealth and its king.

Although a loyal subject of the Polish king, the author must nevertheless have been a fervent Orthodox traditionalist, as becomes clearer when the account approaches events contemporary to the author. For example, the chronicler attributes the "unbelievable tempests" to Bishop Terletskyi of Lutsk, who "sowed the seeds of heresy by consenting to the new calendar, [and] the convention that took place in Brest" (1590). Similarly, the account continues, when in 1598 the Sejm approved the new calendar, "a charter [announcing the change] appeared in the [Catholic] churches, and in Jewish schools and houses, but nobody read it." Beyond the usual simplicity of narration, therefore, the reader discerns a hint of malicious satisfaction because nobody, neither Catholics nor Jews, paid any attention to this document. Against the context of the usually laconic annual entries, this four-line note seems to reflect the author's emphasis of the event.

Loyalty to the king goes hand-in-hand with local patriotism. The chronicle connects reports of natural catastrophes, famines, comets, and similarly unnatural events to deaths of members of the Ostroski family.[5] The battle of Chocim (1621) and the beginning of the reign of Ladislav IV (1635) are among the most important historical events narrated. Significantly, the manuscript ends with the painful event of 1636, the murder of the Ostroh burghers, which also marks the beginning of the domination of the Uniate Church in Ostroh.

Hetman Chodkiewicz's death in the battle of Chocim heralded a series of events considered highly inauspicious for the Orthodox community. The widow Anna-Alojza inherited her family's extensive possessions in Ostroh: "being a widow, she dominated [the country] and introduced the Jesuits, who caused much evil to the Orthodox people," the author wrote.[6] The entry describing the murder of the Uniate Bishop Iosafat Kuncewicz[7] seems to adhere simply to the facts: the compiler's empathy for the Orthodox losses (only one of four churches remained under their jurisdiction) and his outrage at the events that prompted the burgher's reaction is apparent, but not dominant (ca. 1622).[8] By contrast, the attitude toward Meletii Smotrytskyi is totally negative: the author calls him a heretic (хулник, хвальця папежскийх, кламца на святих божиих) (ca. 1629).[9] Most irritating for the author appears to be the fact that Smotrytskyi switched twice from one confession to another, back and forth![10] It is worth noting that the Cossacks' defeat of the Polish army near Pereiaslav (1630) inspires some satisfaction in the writer.

The dramatic clash of 1636 occurred in the historical context of the election of the new king, Ladislav (1632), and of the metropolitan of Kyiv, Mohyla (1633), along with the consequent resurgence and flourishing of the Orthodox Church. In these same years, however, Ostroh had a rather different experience from the rest of the Kyivan eparchy, which the chronicler blames on Anna-Alojza's fanatical behavior. The chronicle indulges in details that reveal the mentality and culture of the time: on the night between Holy Thursday and Friday, along with her Jesuit priests, the princess obliged the Orthodox priest to open the church where her father was buried. The Jesuits opened the tomb and arranged a theatrical dialogue—one Jesuit acted as a priest celebrating a baptism, the other concealed himself behind the sarcophagus. The former asked the ritual question "Aleksander, why did you come here?" The latter answered in the name of Prince Ostroski and asked for the salvation of his soul, "because I recognize that the Roman faith is the best." The mise-en-scène is dramatized by the princess washing and anointing the bones with sweet-smelling herbs. The narrative description of the skirmish on the bridge expresses deep sorrow for the losses on both sides, but does not conceal warm sympathy for the Orthodox burghers, deep pain for the citizens executed by the authorities, and ironical contempt for both the priests who fled the Orthodox procession when they saw the dangerous situation and the princess who sought shelter in the cemetery to escape being killed by angry burghers.

Our narrator also loves miracles and prodigious events, and regularly includes them. For example, the chronicle reports that, after the introduction of the Uniate rite in the Ostroh region, frog's "paws" (*lapki*) were found on one of the princess's pillows; in addition, the narrator adds that her maids of honor performed a shameful, devilish dance in the Catholic church. On the other side, the chronicle maintains that Jews, Tatars, and Poles saw candles burning for three hours over the closed castle church, a scene they attribute to Orthodox magic. The chronicle ends with a lengthy exposition of the history of the *filioque* question with reference to C. Baronius's *Annales ecclesiastici* as a source, proving that this erroneous belief did not exist until the papacy of Leo III.

The *Ostrozhskii letopisets* is a precious source for reconstructing the mentality and culture of early seventeenth-century Ukraine under Polish domination. But how helpful is it in documenting the history of the region? The evidence is not entirely reassuring. For example, instances of posthumous re-baptism of Orthodox persons into Catholicism are known from this period.[11] But doubts arise about a complete exhumation of Aleksander Ostroski's bones and the liturgical theatre the narrator describes, because in 1690, years after the 1636 drama, Aleksander's sarcophagus was still intact in the Epiphany Church. The historical accuracy of the *Letopisets* is further challenged by the identification of the dates of Catholic and Orthodox Easter: in the year 1636 the former occurred on March 23, the latter on April 27. But in the chronicle text, the Catholic and Orthodox ceremonies are joined in one Easter weekend: the bones are supposed to have been re-baptized and transferred during the night of Good Friday, while the Orthodox procession appears immediately after, on the day of the Resurrection. In point of fact, Catholic and the Orthodox Easter coincided on April 8, 1635, not in 1636 as the chronicle imagines. That the chronicle collapses this coincidence into the events of 1636 may be the effect of literary simplification, or a simple error.

Nevertheless, despite its literary imagination and a love of miraculous or magical events, the chronicle perfectly reflects the uncertainty of the first decades of the seventeenth century, when traditions underwent dramatic change and the harmony of religious coexistence in the eastern lands of the Polish Commonwealth wavered. If before the seventeenth century mixed marriages and respect for confessional differences were normal among the nobility, thereafter increasing Catholic pressure fostered intolerance and violent reactions.[12]

A completely different interpretation appears in a Jesuit source, the *Życie ku podziwieniu chwalebne*,[13] printed in Cracow at the end of the seventeenth century. In perfect hagiographic style, *Życie* portrays its subject as an ascetic heroine: she wears a rude frock, beats herself until she bleeds, and devotes her life to strengthening the Holy Union. At the same time, "The wickedness of the schismatic was horrendous." To illustrate the point, *Życie* clearly falsifies history as a means to change the narration: describing the Orthodox burghers sentenced to death after the attack of 1636 as "pale and terrorized" at the place of execution, the author reports that "she [Anna-Alojza] ordered them to be released from their chains, invited them to the dining room, and offered them food." Thus, the author continues, her generosity convinced some people to embrace the Union, although others "retained their stubborn attitude and wicked faith."[14]

The story of the tragedy of Ostroh remained deeply rooted in Ukrainian collective memory in connection with the memory of Petro Mohyla, and in the nineteenth century gave rise to serious commentary. Stepan Golubev, for instance, offered a passionate but balanced narration: he did not conceal the existence of numerous cases of Orthodox priests being forced to convert to the Uniate Church, but put the exceedingly zealous proselytism of people like Anna-Alojza in context by emphasizing that many influential magnates chose not to follow the most radical indications of the Catholic clergy (in particular, Jesuits) and preferred more pragmatic policies, permitting the coexistence of Orthodox and Uniate churches and institutions.[15]

One more very curious nineteenth-century interpretation is the lengthy, sentimental, and often contradictory account by Orest Levytskyi.[16] A pupil of the well-known historian Volodymyr Antonovych and president of the newly founded Ukrainian Academy of Sciences (from 1919 until his death in 1922), Levytskyi wrote a sort of historical novel published in the imperial, Ukrainian-oriented journal, *Kievskaia starina*. In this recounting, Anna-Alojza and her mother belong to an extraordinary cohort of women whose strong characters and humanity contributed to Ukraine's greatness. Levytskyi's highly negative attitude toward Catholicism, especially Greek Catholicism, reflects the imperial position. However, his account also reflects the pride of the Ostroskis and their original Orthodox tradition. The sins of Anna-Alojza are ascribed primarily to the Jesuits: divine justice will punish her less than the shrewd followers of Loyola. In this account, the princess appears as a victim of the Jesuit's thirst for wealth and power, rather than as a wicked person to be damned.[17]

Although the tragedy continues to resonate in Volynian historical narratives,[18] no significant new commentary on the texts has followed Zhytetskyi's literary and linguistic appreciation. Indeed, perhaps the most significant commentary on the tragedy belongs not to any modern commentator, but to the poetic "Liament" and "Prydatok," both seventeenth-century works. The former is written in uneven syllabic verse with simple, often grammatical rhymes, the latter in Sapphic stanzas.[19] I will focus here on the "Liament"; the "Prydatok" contains more realistic details, but is inspired by the same ideas.

The author of the "Liament" expresses deep sorrow and distress at the misfortune that caused the deaths of so many burghers; he also regrets the trouble that fell on people of all social classes in the community, where previously life had been harmonious and peaceful. Significantly, the author is unwilling to blame either side as being uniquely responsible for the tragedy:

> Юж я на обѣ сторонѣ правду прызнати мушу
> А похлѣбоват жадному намнѣй ся не кушу (v. 145-46).
>
> I must recognize that truth is on both sides
> And will not dare to praise either.

His most intimate empathy goes to the Orthodox, but to the Catholic princess he assigns only partial blame. Not only is she called an "honorable lady" (поцтивая матрона), but no one would have dared offend the lady's courtiers, because "who would dare to go against the sun with a spade?" (Кто ж бы ся смѣл з мотыкою на солнце порыват?) (v. 40). The poet does not dare judge whether the burghers were too arrogant or whether the nobles should be considered initiators of the fight: fate itself caused the incident that destroyed the harmony that had previously reigned in Ostroh. The Orthodox procession was organized to occur as usual on Easter Monday, but the established hour was inauspicous; it was equally inauspicious that the princess chose the same time for her drive. In the author's description, it was fate that led to the ominous encounter. Nevertheless, human responsibility might have avoided the tragedy by respecting earthly and religious law: the Orthodox should have yielded to the princess's authority, and the Catholics should have respected the divine ceremony and

> Еслы людей прынамнѣ Бога пошановат,
> Постояти было, вша конѣ моглы бы загамоват (v. 31-32).

> If people at least had honored God,
> They would have stopped, or restrained their horses.

According to the "Liament," the fundamental need to respect the religious beliefs of others has been confirmed by both pagans, "who would like to, and may even have read the honoured orator Cicero, or Jason, or the ancient Macer. . . ."[20] (хто бы хотѣл чытати красномовцу цного Цицерона, Ясона, Мрцера давного. . . .), and Christians, since Jesus reproached even Peter when he raised his sword against the Roman soldier who brought Jesus to Hannah (v. 69-74).

The "Liament" continues this theme; even as ecclesiastic leaders seemed unable to live in peace, it invoked respect for the religion of others within the Christian communities then living in the Polish-Lithuanian Commonwealth:

> Пане Боже пожался обоих прыгоды,
> Межи духовными так великои незгоды!
> Не дыв, еслы зводят бытву с посторонными,
> Але то дыв, же валіат з мещаны своими.
> Не дыво, же герезию з свѣта затумляют,
> Але дывно, же свои ж власныи члонки забывают (v. 149-54).

> Lord, have pity on both sides
> For that quarrel among religious people!
> Battles between enemies are not strange
> But it is astonishing that they fight against their own burghers.

> It is not strange that they aim at eliminating heresy
> But it is strange that they kill members of their own community.

It is no surprise that the author does not include heretics and Jews in the appeal for tolerance (Muslim infidels are not mentioned); the focus here is the passionate appeal to restore peaceful coexistence between Orthodox believers and Catholics. In this view, Poles and Ruthenians are described as bearers of the two religious communities that should put an end to their quarrels:

> През кого ж ся тое стало, нехай ся сами судят:
> Русь то, чы ляхи мои милый блудят? (v. 174-5).
>
> Who is responsible for what happened, let them judge themselves.
> Is it the Rusians, or the Poles, or both my beloved, that are in error?

No matter who was responsible for the 1636 clash, the poet continues, humility should bring Poles to respect the religious sentiments of the Rus', in the same way Ukrainians respect Polish churches:

> О великая неуваго! Хто ж до того радил,
> Абы люде з обох сторон так ганебне звадил?
> Присмотрѣмося, як свои речы оздобляемо,
> Чему собѣ теж иные лекце наважаемо?
> Так святости костельные шанумемо,
> Для чого ж и церковным тои чести уймуемо? (v. 183-88).
>
> Oh, the great impudence! Who gave this advice
> That the people of both sides should so shamefully quarrel?
> Let us consider how we take care of our things,
> Why shall we despise the others in such a way?
> We respect the holiness of Catholic churches,
> So why should Orthodox churches not be respected?

Mutual respect derives from true faith in God, because, says the author, it is impossible to love Him while hating one's neighbors; "each man should glorify God in his own way, because each man needs His holy Grace."

These thoughts and passionate prayers to God for reciprocal under standing express the most valuable fruits of the Ukrainian Renaissance. Scholars agree that the author of the "Liament" was a teacher in Ostroh, and thus represents the best of a tradition rooted among educated laypeople who recognized the high values of the Polish Commonwealth, but who also hoped for respect for their religious beliefs and the dignity of "good letters" cultivated in Ostroh or in the L'viv brotherhood. The anonymous author of the "Liament" reveals no trace of monastic fanaticism, as evidenced by his veneration of the Ostroski family. His respect for the princess in spite of her Catholic activism may be interpreted as ongoing devotion to the memory of her grandfather and father. Indeed, she had committed a horrible profanation when she transferred her father's bones to a Catholic church (no mention is made in the poem to his re-baptism). But Prince Aleksander, her father, was neither a saint nor a prophet; he was simply an honest and valorous knight, a good Orthodox Christian, who deserved respect in his eternal rest.

The poet suggests that the "honorable lady" (поцтивая матрона) of Ostroh was not herself responsible for the profanation because other devilish spirits had governed her deeds. It hardly needs saying that, according to the "Liament," these "bad spirits" are the Jesuits: all the blame is placed on them and they alone will bear the consequences of divine judgement. None of the other participants—burghers and nobles, villains and the princess—appear as actual sinners. It is fate that earns the real blame for the clash among citizens of the same community and representatives of the same "Rus' nation"—fate in the guise of a Jesuit, however.

Thus, the spirit of renaissance tradition inspires in the "Liament" a deep sense of tolerance, the poet's acceptance of positive aspects of political community within the Commonwealth, and the wish that every citizen be able to praise God following his own religious confession and tradition:

кождый своим способом хвалит Пана своего
И всякий потребует святои ласки его (v. 191-92).

Each person praises his own Lord
And each one needs His holy grace.

The spirit of the Renaissance appears also in his several references to reason as the most valuable human quality and the one that could induce people to avoid fanaticism and continue to live in peace among themselves. In his first consideration of the possible causes of the tragic clash between fellow citizens, the author includes the common-sense statement that, by nature, anger belongs to each human being and may influence one towards either good or evil:

Бо гнѣв есть у человека <на> двоя дѣленый—
Частю добрый, а частю на злое запаленый. (v. 77-78).

Anger in a man is split in two parts—
One partly for the good, and one partly for evil.

Although the burghers might have stopped the procession to give way to the princess as the greater authority in the world, their anger, the poet maintains, was justified by the need to recognize the higher value of any sacred object or act; failure to recognize this elementary human principle, which even pagans respected in antiquity, induced the burghers to strike out against the princess's retinue. Indeed, the cascade of events following the fatal collision of the two cortèges could have been avoided if reason (умысль) had prevailed:

Абысмо ся им каручы умысл свой на печы,
Завше пылне ховали . . . (v. 138-39).

Had we always maintained with prudence
Our sound thoughts . . .

Expressing his deepest sorrow and spiritual distress, the poet underlines with bitterness and irony the impossibility of convincing people to behave reasonably. The poet then prays that the Lord may have mercy on these foolish people who, on both sides, using false wisdom instead of reason, transformed the most important feast of the year into a fight:

Яко ся колвек стало и чый был початок,
Еслы ж с шляхты алболы розных небожаток
Жался Боже и их глупства и мудрых мудрости,
Же не умѣли розумом спокрыти их глупости
Тым ся раз притафило в урочыстые свята,
Же снат тая процасия на жал свады зачата (v. 41-46).

No matter how it happened and who began [the battle]
Whether nobles or commoners,
Have mercy, my God, for their stupidity and for the wisdom of wise men,
Because they could not with reason overcome the stupidity
That caused the happenings of these Holy Days,
And made the procession initiate the clash.

The inability to assign blame is intermingled with allusions to the Pauline tradition of despising earthly wisdom in favor of holy simplicity; in the poet's view, no one behaved reasonably, and the only consolation is the hope that God might be merciful to those involved.

A passionate appeal for reason also characterizes the end of the poem: in this case, reason is invoked for the administration of justice. Many individuals were arrested for having killed or beaten people during the battle, but the poet prays that their judges will be inspired by piety and compassion, that they will refuse to condemn people to death, and that, remembering the Last Judgement, they will be careful not to damn the innocent:

Тут потреба мѣти судиям доброе розезнаня.
Ґдыж ту лано невинные на суд злый скаровати,
Але ґды пред Божий прыйдет апеліоваты,
Так ся оная невынность на той час покажет:
Ґды Пан будет во час неправых на вѣки покарает (v. 218-22).

Now the judges need to have good intentions.
If innocents will be damned by bad judgement,
When they will appear before God,

Their innocence will be declared:
The Lord will then punish the unrighteous.

Human reason, righteousness in civic life, pure religious feelings, and adherence to biblical truth constitute the virtuous blend that, according to our unknown poet, ought to underpin honorable coexistence and reciprocal respect in a community intended to be a model of civil, moral, and spiritual values.

Such a community, our text suggests, was still alive in the Polish-Lithuanian Commonwealth in the first decades of the seventeenth century—at least this was the optimistic view of our poet. He probably represented the middle class, which had received a standard Orthodox education in the renaissance spirit of the Ostroh Academy and the brotherhood schools. Such people may have formed the core of a modern society tolerant enough to allow the Rus' and the Liakhs to live side by side—if not necessarily in harmony, then at least without killing one another. The tragedy of Ostroh, however, involved not only difficult relationships between Poles and Ukrainians, but also what the poet understood as the aggressive evangelism and sacrilegious actions of the Jesuits. It was, therefore, a manifestation of the extreme danger threatening civil society in the region—internecine struggles in which citizens of every rank lost their lives. The following lines show how differentiated the society that experienced the unrest of 1636 was:

. . . Як ся там посполитству тому спротивляли,
Яко тыж з обох сторон шкоды начынили.
Юж там было заровно кожному станови –
Як попови, так хлопови, ба и шляхтичови.
Досталося там дѣткам, млоденцом учтивым,
Бѣлым головам пребраным, паном и особливым,
Бо там юж сплош бито, а снат не смотрено –
Каменен ли, обухом кого ударено . . . (v. 197-204).

. . . Thus, they opposed the common people,
The two parts cause damage to one another.
It was the same for any estate,
For the priest, the peasant, even for the gentry.
All were beaten, children and good youngsters,

Honorable women, lords and commoners,
Everybody was stricken, regardless of whether
With a stone or with a firearm.

In the poet's view, the 1636 Ostroh tragedy was the result of religious intolerance, stubbornness, and lack of common sense. Still, he expresses the hope that God might bring people back to that peaceful coexistence that had characterized the Ostroh principality in the past and that was still latent within it; he hopes that his community might revive "those days of joy, of dignity, the days of great gladness" (Дьни веселые, дьни зацные, дьни великои радости, v. 1) that he sees as an idyllic paradise for the country.

The problem lies in just which country the poet has in mind. He certainly has a localist idea of this country, rather than a national (in the modern sense) one. However, it is clear that he conceives of the region as part of that larger political entity, the Polish Commonwealth, sometimes called *natio* by the poet's contemporaries. Let us remember the famous self-identification of Stanisław Orzechowski/Orixovskyj, as *gente Ruthenus, natione Polonus*. In the 1630s, at a time when periodic Cossack insurrections were already devastating the Polish Commonwealth, the Counter-Reformation had begun to invade all mental and religious spaces, and Ukrainian self-identification was increasingly modeled on religious exclusivism and ecclesiastic hierarchies, the poet of the "Liament" still hoped that God would look favorably on a state where coexistence on the basis of equal rights and reciprocal religious respect prevailed. It is remarkable that the poet conceives of a civil society made up of all classes: the sympathetic description of the losses that the tragedy brought to all components of society implied that prosperity was connected to the well-being of every segment of the population.

Thus, in addition to the importance given to individual dignity, to reciprocal religious respect, and to the overarching sacrality of divine law, the "Liament" gives a clear view into the growing importance of social differentiation and social conflict in the seventeenth-century Polish Commonwealth.

No less remarkable is the fact that, for our poet of Ostroh, self-identification is not merely religious. His links to renaissance tradition emerge in his ideal of reciprocal respect: we respect the "sacred Catholic places" (святости костелные), he asserts, and demand the same treatment for "Orthodox sacred places [literally: pride]" (церковные чести). This formula implies that civil coexistence was possible on the basis of lay principles of reciprocal respect between citizens of a recognized political entity where religion was the choice of the individual.

The hope for peaceful coexistence between Poles and Ukrainians was a long-standing utopianism. The Treaty of Hadiach (1658) was the most advanced political plan ever articulated for the realization of this utopia, but unfortunately it failed. In the second half of the seventeenth century, though in different geo-political circumstances and with different aims, Lazar Baranovych evoked this same utopian ideal in his verses. Again, in the mid-nineteenth century, Taras Shevchenko wrote one of his best poems—"To the Poles" (1848)—in which he expressed a yearning for "наш тихий рай"—"our peaceful paradise" where Cossacks and Liakhs might live together before "the gready Catholic priests and the lords differentiated and separated us" ("Неситий ксьондзи, магнати / Нас порізнили, розвели").[21] The consequences of the failure of this dream of unity in diversity envisaged by the author of the "Liament" are still quite evident, and represent one of the most typical marks of contemporary Eastern Slavic countries and peoples, as the dramatic events of 2013-2015 show all too clearly. Let us hope that Shevchenko's prayer that the Liakhs [the Poles] may offer their hands to the Cossacks "in the name of God" may become reality, not only for Poles and Ukrainians, but for the whole area for decades to come.

NOTES

1 The best commentary is P. Zhytetskyi, "Ostroz'ka trahediia," *Zapysky Naukovoho Tovarystva im. Tarasa Shevchenka* 51 (1903): 1-24.

2 I transliterate Cyrillic following the etymological orthography, though the actual Ukrainian pronunciation was certainly phonetic.

3 Gosudarstvennyi istoricheskii muzei, Muzeinoe sobranie, no. 4007; M. N. Tikhomirov, "Maloizvestnye letopisnye pamiatniki," *Istoricheskii arkhiv* 7 (1951):

236-53, now available on-line: http://www.vostlit.info/Texts/Dokumenty/Russ/XVI/1500-1520/Maloizv__let__pamjatniki/4.htm (accessed July 15, 2014).

4 Tikhomirov, "Maloizvestnye," 238.

5 For the demographic crisis and still-mysterious vanishing of several aristocratic families in Volynia, see N. M. Iakovenko, *Ukraïns'ka shliakhta z kintsia XIV do seredyny XVII st.: (Volyn' i Tsentral'na Ukraïna)*, 2nd ed. (Kyiv: Krytyka, 2008), 98 ff. Anna-Alojza died childless and her estates passed to the Lubomirski family. Petty nobles lost their lands, as they passed to Polish lords, while magnate families died out (e.g. the Kniazivs'kyis). Some scholars explain the phenomenon with endogamy, but the issue remains open.

6 Tikhomirov, "Maloizvestnye," 248.

7 I use here the Polish spelling (the most frequent one). The text has a curious spelling: "Uniiat vladyka Iasafat."

8 Ibid., 248.

9 Ibid., 249.

10 The language of this entry appears somewhat different from the bulk of the text. Was the compilation made by different authors? Linguistic analysis of the text might clarify this issue.

11 See N. M. Iakovenko, *Paralel'nyĭ svit : doslidzhnnia͡ z istoriï uiavlen' ta ideĭ v Ukraïni XVI-XVII st.* (Kyiv: Krytyka, 2002), 29-30.

12 Ibid., 29-33, 56-63.

13 The full title is: *Zycie ku podziwieniu chwalebne J. O. xiężny Ostrogskiéy Anny Aloyzyi Chodkiewiczowéy, woiewodziny wileńskiéy, hetmanowéy W. X. L.*, od kollegium soc. Iesu iarosławskiego, od niéyże po ostrogskim kollegium w Polu, u Naysw. Panny, fundowanego, na wzór wysokiéy cnoty wydane R. P. 1698 (po Iey świątobliwem zeyściu 44. ex Superiorum Permissu). W Krakowie, w drukarni Mikołaja Schedla 1698.

14 *Życie ku podziiwieniu chwalebne . . . Anny Alojzyi, Xiężny Ostrogskiej* (Kraków, 1698), 41-45. Cf. Zhytets'kyi, "Ostroz'ka trahediia," 2-3.

15 S. Golubev, *Kievskii Mitropolit Petr Mogila i ego spodvizhniki*, 2 vols. (Kyiv: Tip. G. T. Korchak-Novitskogo 1883-89), 2:153, 222-23.

16 Orest Levitskyi, "Anna-Alojza, knjazhna Ostrozhska," *Kievskaia starina* (November 1883), 329-73.

17 The long essay also has practical aims: the author describes the pitiful situation of the Epiphany Church in Ostroh and expresses the wish that the state restore it (ibid., 372-73).

18 See I. Z. Myts'ko, *Ostroz'ka slavo-hreko-latyns'ka akademia XVI-XVII st. Entsyklopediia* (Ostroh, 2010), 319-321.

19 *Die älteste ostslavische Kunstdichtung. 1575-1647*, ed. Hans Rothe , 2 vols. (Giessen: W. Schmitz, 1976-77), 2:377-91. For short literary comments, see Mikhailo Vozniak, *Istoriia Ukraïns'koï literatury* , 3 vols. (Lviv: Prosvita, 1920-24), 2:193-194; *Istoriia Ukraïns'koï literatury u vos'my tomakh*, 8 vols. (Kyiv: Naukova dumka, 1967-71), 1:325-26.

20 Probably Jason of Cyrene and Gaius Licinius Macer, famous in Ancient Rome.

21 Taras Shevchenko, *Povne zibrannia tvoriv u dvanaciaty tomakh*, 12 vols. (Kyiv: Naukova dumka, 1989-), 2:48.

Connecting the Dots: Jewish Mysticism, Ritual Murder, and the Trial of Mendel Beilis

Robert Weinberg
(Swarthmore College)

The prosecution of Mendel Beilis for the murder of thirteen-year-old Andrei Iushchinskii in Kiev a century ago is perhaps the most publicized instance of blood libel since the torture and execution of Jews accused of ritually murdering the infant Simon of Trent in 1475. By the time of the trial in the fall of 1913, the Beilis case had become an international cause célèbre. Like the trials of Alfred Dreyfus in the 1890s and the outcry that accompanied the Damascus Affair in the 1840s, the arrest, incarceration, and trial of Beilis aroused public criticism of Russia's treatment of Jews and inspired opponents of the autocracy at home and abroad to launch a campaign to condemn the trial. The persecution of the innocent Beilis mobilized forces across the political spectrum, from rabid antisemites on the extreme right and revolutionaries on the far left to persons of all persuasions in between.

The killers of Iushchinskii—probably a gang of thieves whose leader was the mother of Iushchinskii's boyhood friend—savagely stabbed the boy some four dozen times in the head and upper torso

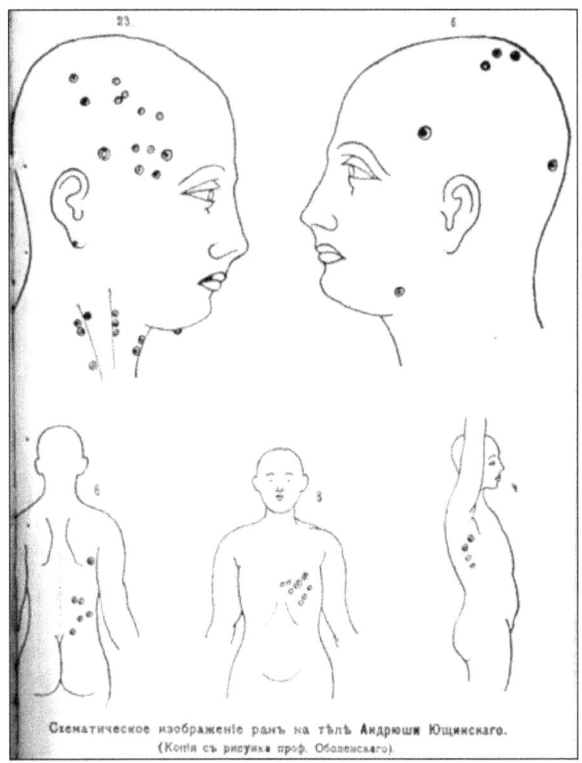

Depiction of Wounds on Body of Andrei Iushchinskii, Based on Drawing by Professor Obolenskii (Andris Grutups, *Beilisada: Delo ob obvinenii Mendelia Beilisa v ritual'nom ubiistve* [Riga: Aetna, 2007]

with what the coroner believed was an awl. Some wounds penetrated bone, and one blow went so deep that the handle of the weapon left an impression on his skin. The corpse was significantly drained of blood, with perhaps only one third of the normal amount of blood remaining in the body. The loss of blood and the placement of wounds prompted members of the Union of Russian People and the Union of the Archangel Michael, two of the empire's most zealous antisemitic and monarchist organizations, to declaim that Iushchinskii was a victim of ritual murder and to call for an investigation that focused on Jews. The government's case was predicated on the belief that the defendant and other unnamed perpetrators had killed the boy as a result of "religious fanaticism for ritual purposes."[1]

This paper seeks to shed light on the nature of antisemitism in the early twentieth century. In many respects, the trial was a struggle between two irreconcilable ways of perceiving and living in the world. As one editorial in the right-wing newspaper *Russkoe znamia* pointed out, defenders of Beilis did not permit themselves to accept that there "could be ritual murders in the century of airplanes and trams."[2] The decision of the prosecution to rely on religious motives to prove its case against Beilis illustrates the extent to which the autocracy believed it was necessary to frame the trial in terms of the Jews' purported religious fanaticism for subverting the Christian foundations of society. The tsarist government relied on the testimony of witnesses who claimed that Judaism obligated Jews to obtain the blood of non-Jews for a variety of ritual purposes, including the baking of matzo. In particular, the prosecution sought to establish a link between the murder and the Kabbalah, or Jewish mystical thought.

And yet the manner by which the prosecution put together its case against Beilis was more than a struggle between two world views. Government lawyers realized that the ritual murder accusation, easily dismissed by defenders of Beilis as a remnant of medieval religious prejudices and hatreds, needed to be supported by evidence that met contemporary scientific and intellectual standards. Even a superstition from the twelfth century had to draw legitimacy from the authority of the written word and modern science. In other words, the ritual murder accusation had to be sustained in a manner befitting late imperial Russia's court system, which jurists in Europe and the United States held in high esteem. Hence, the prosecution turned to Ivan Sikorskii, an expert in the modern science of psychiatry, to develop its case against Beilis. Sikorskii was a prominent psychiatrist and professor emeritus at Saint Vladimir University in Kiev who taught a course about the method used by Jews to murder Christian children. In his evaluation of the autopsy, which comprised his testimony at the trial, Sikorskii asserted that the condition of Iushchinskii's corpse revealed the nationality of the murderers. He claimed that the youth was the victim of ritual murder carried out as the "racial revenge and vendetta of the Sons of Jacob" against gentiles. Sikorskii added that the murder was carried out with the aim of draining Iushchinskii's body of blood, to be used for religious purposes.[3]

Father Justin Pranaitis, a Roman Catholic priest with a checkered past and dubious credentials as an expert on Judaic texts such as the Talmud and Zohar, served as another key government witness.[4] Drawing upon the writings of other supposed specialists who wrote about the roots of Jewish ritual murder, Pranaitis insisted that Judaism dictated the ritual murder of gentiles, though Jews were careful not to spell this out in religious texts. He claimed that the Talmud prohibited putting into words the existence of such a tradition, leaving Jews to pass on knowledge of ritual murder via the spoken word. Even though he lacked legitimate credentials as an expert on the Talmud and other Judaic texts, Pranaitis passed himself off as an authority on Judaism. In *The Christians in the Jewish Talmud, or the Secrets of the Teachings of the Rabbis about Christians*, a pamphlet written in the early 1890s, Pranaitis claimed that Judaism required Jews to kill Christians. Several years before the murder of Iushchinskii, Pranaitis took refuge in Tashkent from the police in Saint Petersburg, pursuing him for attempted extortion. But in 1911 he returned to the capital, where he began to distribute his pamphlet, thereby capturing the attention of other believers in the ritual murder accusation who then steered the police and prosecution toward a Jew as the culprit.

The indictment of Beilis drew upon the ideas of Pranaitis and offered a concise statement of the priest's views:

> All the rabbinical schools . . . are united by their hatred of non-Jews who, according to the Talmud, are not considered human beings but only animals in human form. The hatred and the spite that the Jews, from the point of view of their religious law, feel toward people of a different nationality and religion are especially strong toward Christians. Because of this sentiment, the Talmud allows and even commands the killing of non-Jews. . . . The extermination of non-Jews is commanded as a religious act . . . that hastens the coming of the Messiah.[5]

When Pranaitis testified at the end of the trial, he tried to establish his scholarly credentials by grounding his testimony in a long-established tradition of like-minded thought. He claimed that his ideas on ritual murder had been sparked by a book written in the early nineteenth century by a converted Romanian Jew by the name of Neophyte (a term that refers to recent converts to Christianity). Neophyte, a former rabbi by the name of Noah Belfer who adopted his new moniker when he became a monk, claimed that he had knowledge of the secret practices of Jews. He laid out his views in *Argument against the Jews upon Their Law and Customs,* published in 1803.[6] Pranaitis drew liberally from Neophyte in his testimony, which went on for hours over the course of several days.

Like Neophyte before him, Pranaitis found himself in good company when it came to his belief in this calumny against Jews. Also known as blood libel, the ritual murder accusation against Beilis was one in a long line of similar charges against Jews dating back to the Middle Ages. The canard that Jews engage in the murder of Christians, particularly young boys and girls, emerged in England in the twelfth century and soon spread to the continent, where Christians accused Jews of using Christian blood for religious rites and to mock the killing of Jesus. However, by the fourteenth and fifteenth centuries, it had come to fixate on the Jews' consumption of Christian blood either in sacramental wine or baked into matzo. Not surprisingly, the ritual murder accusation tended to emerge around the time of Passover and Easter. The incidence of such accusations reached a crescendo in German-speaking Europe during the fifteenth century, frequently prompting Christians to attack their Jewish neighbors. By the sixteenth and seventeenth centuries, when ritual murder accusations began to die out in Central Europe, they gained a foothold in the Catholic regions of the Polish-Lithuanian Commonwealth. Nonetheless, accusations of ritual murder reemerged with a vengeance in parts of German-speaking Europe during the final decades of the nineteenth century. Dozens of well-documented incidents occurred, with the 1913 trial of Mendel Beilis as perhaps the best-known incident of blood libel since 1475.[7]

Even though the Orthodox Christian tradition did not share the Western Christian churches' fixation on ritual murder, accusations of blood libel eventually surfaced in the Russian Empire, which had remained immune until the collapse of the Polish-Lithuanian Commonwealth in the late eighteenth century. It was then that large numbers of Jews, Catholics, and Uniates became imperial subjects as a result of the partitions of Poland, and by the early twentieth century the accusation had a secure footing among Russian and Ukrainian Orthodox believers. At the time of the Beilis trial accusations of ritual murder had sunk deep roots in Russian and Ukrainian culture, and strengthened antisemitism on both the popular and official levels.

The testimony offered by Pranaitis reflected the attitudes of the intelligentsia toward Jews and blood libel during Russia's Silver Age, as the literary, intellectual, and artistic revival of the early twentieth century is known. In recent years, scholars have explored the connection between general Russian intellectual and cultural trends and antisemitism on the eve of World War I. In particular, several scholars have focused on the philosopher and writer Vasilii Rozanov's efforts to establish a link between the Jews' purported possession of secret and mystical knowledge, the role of blood in the Jews' experience of the divine, and ritual murder.[8] Rozanov believed that Jewish religious texts were a textual artifice intended to hide the ritual need of Jews to engage in blood sacrifice and the mutilation of the body (for example, circumcision). He insisted that blood, which played a critical role in the sacrifices practiced by Jews in Jerusalem in the centuries before the destruction of the Second Temple, continued to occupy a central position in the practice of Judaism in the twentieth century. In one essay, Rozanov maintained that Hebrew words, which are written without vowels, were designed as a code to disguise the fact that Jews colluded with each other to engage in ritual murder.[9] Jews, claimed Rozanov and others, possessed secret and mystical knowledge hidden in foundational Judaic texts such as the Hebrew Scriptures, Talmud, and Zohar. Other Silver Age writers, not all of whom were antisemites, alluded to blood rituals and the magical qualities of blood in their stories, plays, essays, and poems. For these intellectuals the Beilis case was replete with cultural symbolism and offered an opportunity to elucidate positions on both Jews and Russians.

In recent years Harriet Murav and Judith Deutsch Kornblatt have noted Rozanov's effort to establish a link between Iushchinskii's murder and Judaism. For example, Murav has written that for Rozanov "the wounds reveal a code of letters—each letter standing for a word, and the words taken together forming a magical sentence stating that this was a sacrificial victim to God."[10] Similarly, Kornblatt concurs that Rozanov embraced the view that lines connecting the stab wounds comprised Hebrew words, which have an occult meaning suggesting ritual murder. She also makes explicit references to the role that the Kabbalah purportedly played in this line of reasoning.[11] However, Murav and Kornblatt, do not, in my opinion, pay sufficient attention to the matter—in particular, to the idea that the positioning of the wounds corresponded to letters and words that supposedly revealed, when decoded, the role of the Kabbalah in enjoining Jews to engage in the collective murder of innocent gentile youths. The detailed exegeses of the meaning of the messages embedded in the stab wounds served a

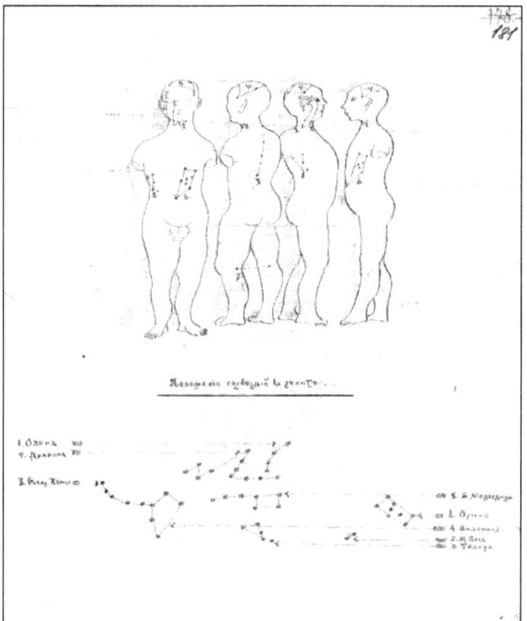

Top: Wounds Connected to Each Other on Body of Andrei Iushchinskii Bottom: Names and Drawings of Constellations Formed by the Wounds (Derzhavnyi arkiv Kyïvs'koï oblasti, f. 183, op. 5, d. 4, l. 180; excerpted from microfilm collection "Beilis Case Papers," copyright East View Information Services, 2005)

purpose far beyond the confines of this particular trial. The scholarly language and claims of learned expertise were deployed in an effort to prove the guilt not only of Mendel Beilis, but of all Jews as participants in this heinous religious rite.

Elsewhere I have discussed how ordinary Russians and Ukrainians, along with tsarist authorities, argued that astrology, the occult, and mysticism could resolve the mystery of Iushchinskii's death.[12] Concerned citizens sent letters to police, prosecutors, and defense attorneys with advice and insight gleaned from séances and hypnosis that purported to reveal who had killed the youth. One letter writer in particular claimed that the wounds on Iushchinskii's right temple, when connected by lines, corresponded to well-known constellations. Figure 24 shows the wounds on the head, neck, and torso of Iushchinskii, while Figure 25 displays the constellations that resulted once the wounds were connected by lines. The star formations are: Aries, Draco, Ploughman, Ursa Major, Orion, Canis Minor, Taurus, and Northern Corona, and the number of wounds correspond to the number of stars in the eight constellations. The author, however, did not offer any explanation and left it up to the police and prosecution to ascertain the astrological meaning.

Another perspective on the significance of the wounds can be found in *The Olfactory and Tactile Relationship of Jews to Blood*, a collection of essays written and published during the Beilis Affair by Rozanov.[13] He looked for confirmation of ritual murder in the writings of other observers of the Beilis trial who were obsessed with demonstrating the veracity of the ritual murder accusation. In particular, Rozanov turned to the essay "'Echad': The Thirteen Wounds of Iushchinskii" by S. D-skii, whose identity is unknown, for corroboration. Rozanov included D-skii's essay in *The Olfactory and Tactile Relationship of Jews to Blood*, arguing that it offered convincing evidence of the Jewish conspiracy to engage in ritual murder.[14]

Judith Deutsch Kornblatt concluded, "D-sky's sources . . . are less than reliable." She referred to his scholarship as "spurious," relying on "unnamed occultists and Christian cabalists" whose know ledge of Hebrew and Aramaic, the languages of the Talmud and

Zohar, was dubious at best.[15] For example, Father Pranaitis claimed that he was an expert on the Talmud and Zohar, but he revealed his ignorance when defense lawyers cross-examined him during Beilis's trial. Likewise, the testimony of theologians, some Jewish and some not, demonstrated that the priest's knowledge of the Talmud was laughable.[16]

D-skii drew upon essays, books, and translations of Jewish texts that supported his view that the positioning of wounds on the right temple of Iushchinskii corresponded to Hebrew letters. D-skii began his cryptographic analysis of Iushchinskii's wounds by asserting that the boy's killers stabbed him according to a "definite system."[17] First, he rotated a drawing of Iushchinskii's head ninety degrees to the right since the boy was found sitting up with his head dangling down and chin toward the chest. D-skii then connected the various wounds with lines and found that they spelled the following Hebrew letters: *alef*, *peh*, *resh*, *tav*, and *shin* (א פ ר ת ש). The positioning of the five wounds also corresponded to the lower half of the ten *Sefirot* (singular *Sefirah*) that represent the creative forces connecting God to the material world. Each *Sefirah* corresponds to a Hebrew letter and, when taken together, symbolize the unity of the spiritual and material worlds.[18] Finally, he also superimposed the lower half of the *Sefirot* on the thirteen stab wounds and concluded that "the puzzling punctures on the right temple

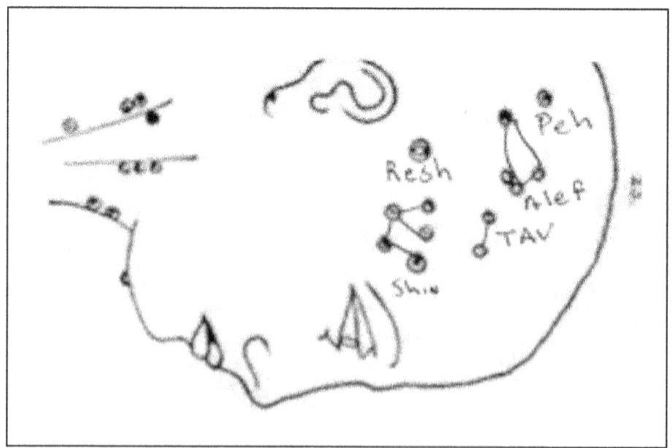

Five Hebrew Letters Formed by Connecting Wounds on Iushchinskii's Head

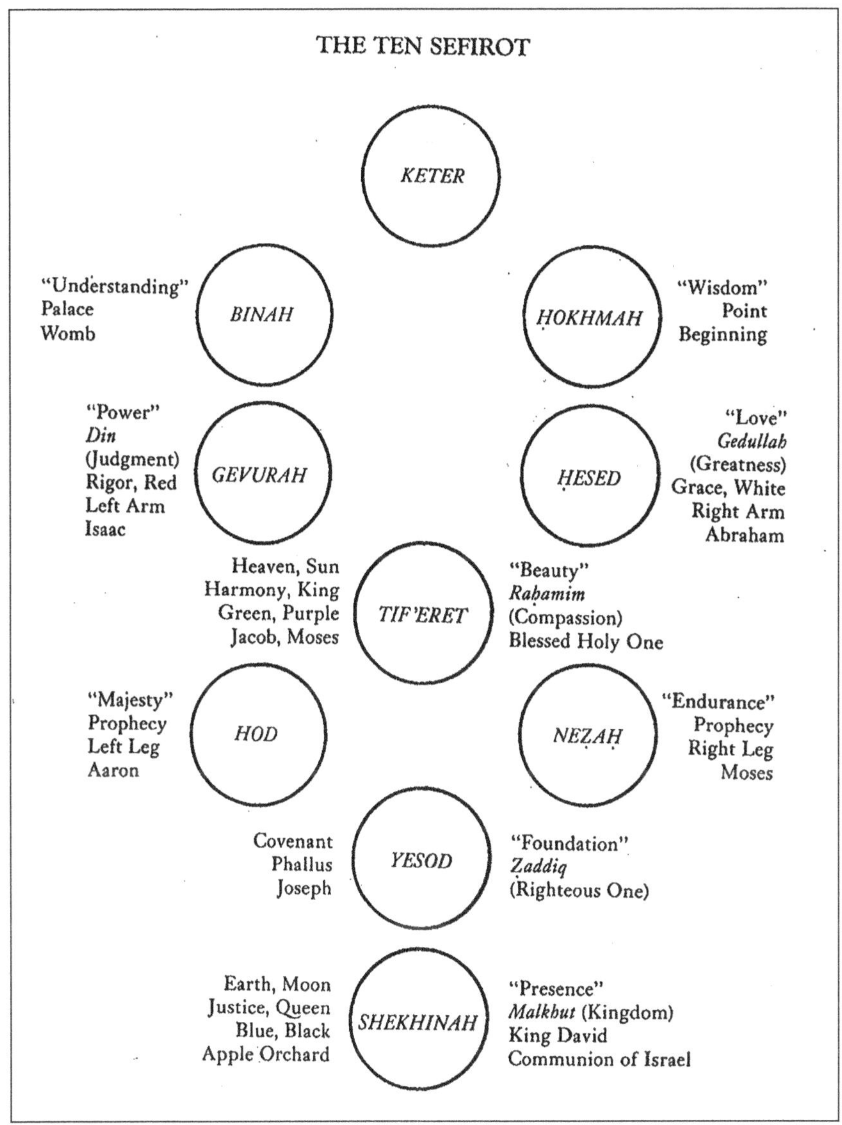

Diagram of Ten Sefirot, *Zohar: The Book of Enlightenment*, trans. Daniel Chanan Matt (New York: Paulist Press, 1983), 35. Courtesy of Paulist Press

of Iushchinskii were by no means accidental." In his words, they represented "a magical alphabetical formula."[19] According to D-skii's reading of the Zohar, the five Hebrew letters signified in Kabbalistic terms: Man (א), Mouth (פ), Head (ר), Chest (ח), and Arrow (ש).

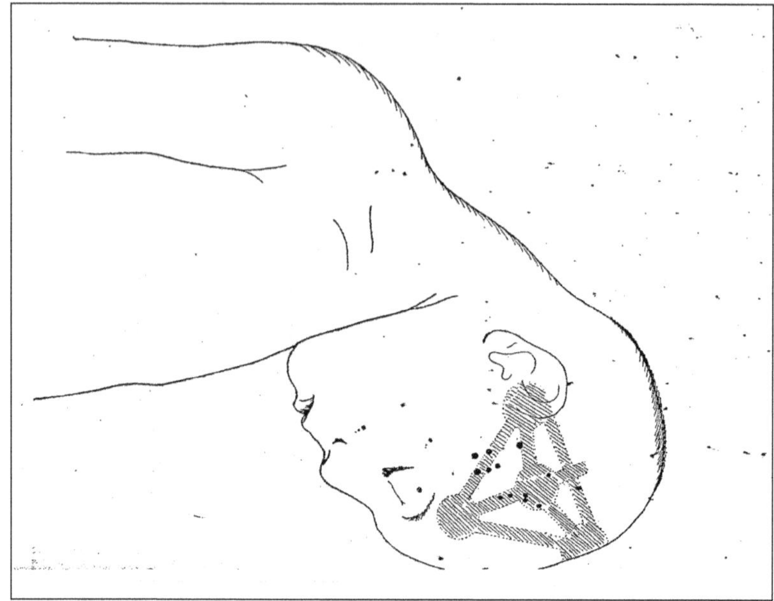

Lower Half of Ten Sefirot Superimposed on Head Wounds (D-skii, "'Ekhad. Trinadstat' ran Iushchinskogo," in Vasilii Rozanov, *Obonitel'noe i oziasatel'noe otnoshenie evreev k krovi* [Saint Petersburg, 1914], 226

D-skii concluded that Iushchinskii, "was killed by strikes to the head and chest like the calf sacrificed to Jehovah."[20] Moreover, he divined that the "secret meaning of *shin* . . . could be understood as weapons or a gun," and associated the letter with Lucifer. In addition, the number of wounds—thirteen—corresponded to a line in the Zohar that refers to thirteen wounds on a sacrificial animal whose mouth was tied shut.[21] Furthermore, D-skii's analysis buttressed the view held by some believers in blood libel that Lubavitcher Hasidim were guilty of killing Iushchinskii since they comprised a "savage sect" of Judaism that engaged in "savage deeds" as outlined in the secret language of the Zohar.[22] Indeed, the case against Beilis was predicated in part on the accusation that he had ties to Lubavitcher Hasidim as a *tsaddik*, a leader of a Hasidic sect, a charge that had no basis in reality.

Finally, D-skii also drew upon his purported facility with astrology when he wrote that the positioning of the wounds, when superimposed on a diagram of the signs of the zodiac, corresponds to the injunction in Exodus that Jews should obtain the blood of non-Jews during the month of Nisan, that is, at the time of Passover.[23] In sum, the positioning of the wounds on Iushchinskii's right temple was a secret code that revealed the sacrificial nature of the killing in light of the Zohar's injunction that Jews kill Christians.

D-skii and Rozanov were not the only ones fascinated by the purported links between the murder and Jewish mystical writings. One author writing under the pseudonym Uranus claimed that the Kabbalah held the secret to Iushchinskii's murder. Like D-skii, Uranus believed that Jewish religious texts and traditions needed to be decoded in order to reveal their covert references to ritual murder. He subjected the wounds on the right temple to an analysis similar to the one performed by D-skii, and concluded that they were not "accidental." Uranus focused on six stab wounds that formed two triangles when connected by lines. When merged with each other, the triangles formed the Star of David, which, along with other letters formed from the wounds, signified blood sacrifice and devotion to the Devil.[24]

Fortunately for Beilis, the jury found him not guilty of participating in the murder of Iushchinskii. But the jury, comprised primarily of peasants, did agree with the prosecution's argument that the killing had the hallmarks of a ritual murder. In other words, the strategy of the prosecution to claim the ritual nature of the killing suceeded. Knowing the case against Beilis as a participant in the murder was based on perjured testimony, imaginary evidence, and innuendo, some police and members of the prosecution anticipated his acquittal. Hence, the government chose to focus on the supposed ritual nature of the murder, hoping to rely on popular belief and values to win its case. The prosecution had a reasonable expectation that the jury and, for that matter, the general public, would not question the veracity of the ritual murder accusation. It pinned its hope on the general ignorance (or, even more dangerously, the little, inaccurate "knowledge") and suspicion of Judaism and Jewish culture among the population at large. Hence, the government did not appeal the acquittal of Beilis for murder, content with the verdict that confirmed the ritual murder accusation. As one member of the prosecutorial team claimed at the end of the trial, "the main task of the trial has been proven, namely the ritual character of the murder."[25] Another lawyer who assisted the prosecution told a newspaper in Kiev that the "verdict satisfies us. It was necessary for us to establish that the murder had a ritual character and we achieved this goal. . . . Had the jury said the prosecution had not proven the ritual aspect of the murder, we would not have been satisfied even if the jurors had found Beilis guilty."[26]

The government's case regarding blood libel, unsurprisingly, did not fall on deaf ears as far as the jury was concerned. The jury accepted the prosecution's assertion that the murder could have been carried out by Jews intent on draining Iushchinskii of his blood for use in religious rituals. By the turn of the twentieth century, many literate and semiliterate, not to mention illiterate, gentiles did not question the preposterous assertion that Jews were not only capable of murdering children for ritual purposes but did so because their religion required it. More than antisemitism and ignorance of Judaism were at work here. Many inhabitants of the Russian Empire, Jew and non-Jew alike, lived in a mental universe where magic potions, amulets, incantations, witchcraft, folk healing, and the occult played prominent roles in daily life. They lived in a world where logic, science, and reason clashed with ignorance, prejudice, and superstition, where the fear of the unknown challenged the science of the modern world. As we have seen, even many highly educated and cultured people subscribed to the canard of the ritual murder accusation.

Government lawyers assumed that testimony about Jewish holy men, cryptic texts, and mystical knowledge would make it more likely for the jury and public to accept their story of ritual murder. But they had to make a case that comported, at least on the surface, to the rules of evidence, drawing from scientific knowledge and textual analysis to establish the veracity of ritual murder. The modern and pre-modern forms of antisemitism coexisted in the early twentieth century. The antisemitism reflected in the Beilis case may have served secular or political objectives (and was cloaked in the vocabulary of contemorary science) and therefore qualifies as a manifestation of what historians refer to as modern antisemitism. But the foundations of this antisemitism remained rooted in long-standing religious prejudices stemming from the late medieval period. In other words, the prosecution adorned a prejudice that stemmed from the medieval period with the trappings of the modern world. State prosecutors used modern, state-of-the-art "science" to prove the existence of a deadly fantasy. As the Beilis trial demonstrates, there was plenty of room for irrational fears to coexist with reason and rational thought.

NOTES

1 *Delo Beilisa: Stenograficheskii otchet*, 3 vols. (Kiev, 1913), 1:37.

2 *Russkoe znamie*, no. 240, October 25, 1913, 2.

3 University of Chicago, Regenstein Library Special Collections, Ludwig Rosenberger Collection 450 D/5, (spelling has been changed for consistency) and *Delo Beilisa* (1913), 2:252–64.

4 The Zohar ("radiance" or "splendor") is a collection of commentaries on the sections of the Torah read during weekly synagogue services, and serves as the foundational work of Jewish mystical thought, Kabbalah. The prosecution was unable to find a Russian Orthodox priest or theologian willing to testify on its behalf.

5 *Delo Beilisa*, 1:32.

6 The book was a best seller: it went through ten printings between 1803 and 1936. Before the Frankist controversy in the mid-eighteenth century, converted Jews did not assert that Jews engaged in ritual murder. However, after Jacob Frank accused Jews of engaging in ritual murder, proponents of the blood libel began to seek out Jews or converted Jews who claimed to have first-hand-knowledge of or experience with ritual murder in order to substantiate their claims. I thank Hillel Kieval for pointing this out to me.

7 A useful overview of the ritual murder accusation can be found in Helmut Walser Smith, *The Butcher's Tale: Murder and Antisemitism in a German Town* (New York: W.W. Norton & Company, 2002), 91-133.

8 Harriet Murav, "The Beilis Ritual Murder Trial and the Culture of Apocalypse," *Cardozo Studies in Law and Literature* 12 (2002): 243; Judith Deutsch Kornblatt, "Russian Religious Thought and the Jewish Kabbala," in *The Occult in Russian and Soviet Culture*, ed. Bernice Glatzer Rosenthal (Ithaca: Cornell University Press, 1997), 75-95; Laura Engelstein, *The Keys to Happiness: Sex and the Search for Modernity in Fin-de-Siecle Russia* (Ithaca: Cornell University Press, 1992), 299-333; Henrietta Mondry, *Exemplary Bodies: Constructing the Jew in Russian Culture Since the 1880s* (Boston: Academic Studies Press, 2009), chapter 3; and Leonid Katsis, *Krovavyi navet i russkaia mysl'* (Moscow: Mosty kul'tury/Jerusalem: Gesharim, 2006), *passim*.

9 See "Iudeiskaia tainopis'," in Vasilii Rozanov, *Obonitatel'noe i osiazatel'noe otnoshenie evreev k krovi* (Saint Petersburg, 1914), 1-11.

10 Murav, 248.

11 Kornblatt, 91.
12 Robert Weinberg, "The Trial of Mendel Beilis: The Sources of 'Blood Libel' in Late Imperial Russia," in *Russia's Century of Revolution: Parties, People, Places. Studies Presented in Honor of Alexander Rabinowitch*, eds. Michael S. Melancon and Donald J. Raleigh (Bloomington: Slavica Publishers, 2012), 17-35.
13 Rozanov, *Oboniatel'noe i osiazatel'noe otnoshenie*. The Beilis Affair stretched from March, 1911, when Iushchinskii was murdered, to October, 1913, when Beilis was acquitted of murder.
14 S. D-skii, "'Ekhad'. Trinadstat' ran Iushchinskogo," in Rozanov, *Obonitatel'noe i osiazatel'noe otnoshenie*, 215-61. *Ekhad* or *echad* is the Hebrew word that signifies the oneness or unity of God.
15 Kornblatt, 91.
16 See *Delo Beilisa*, 2:293-440.
17 D-skii, 217.
18 D-skii, 218-235.
19 D-skii, 227.
20 D-skii, 234.
21 D-skii, 234-235; Evidence indicated that the killers of Iushchinskii had indeed tied something to his mouth, presumably to prevent him from screaming.
22 D-skii, 244.
23 D-skii, 235-238.
24 Uranus, *Ubiistvo Iushchinskago i kabbala* (Saint Petersburg, 1913).
25 *Kievskaia mysl'*, no. 301, October 31, 1913, 4.
26 *Vecherniaia gazeta*, no. 162, October 29, 1913, 1.

Education and the East: The Omsk Asiatic School

Janet M. Hartley
(London School of Economics and Political Science)

Gary Marker has made a significant and original contribution to our understanding of education, censorship, publishing, and the reading public in eighteenth-century Russia.[1] In an article published in 1993, he asked, "Did the Public-School project genuinely reflect the spirit of the Enlightenment and humaneness, or was it merely another agency of the authoritarian rationality and expanding state power?"[2] He concluded that, even if schools did not fulfill all expectations, they nevertheless provided "useful skills" for pupils. The present article contributes to the debate that focuses upon education in Siberia in the late eighteenth and early nineteenth centuries, and discusses the role of the Omsk Asiatic School in imparting "useful skills" in eastern languages.

The first school in Siberia was opened in the home of the bishop of Tobol'sk in 1702-1703 to educate sons of clergy, and by 1791 was educating 285 boys.[3] In the reign of Peter I, garrison schools were set up throughout Russia to teach basic literacy, numeracy, and the catechism to the sons of soldiers and Cossacks; the unfortunate pupils were also required to listen to a reading of the military regulations every Sunday! The schools continued to provide a rudimentary education for future military servitors, albeit often with brutal methods and in Spartan conditions. By 1767, the Omsk garrison school was teaching 150 pupils, who were the sons of Cossacks and soldiers.[4] In 1806, eighty-two sons of Cossacks, aged between six and seventeen, were receiving basic instruction in religion, reading, and writing in the remote fort of Gizhiga.[5] Peter attempted to establish a network of elementary schools, and in 1721 instructed town magistracies to open schools in every town, but since he provided no funding, the decree remained a dead letter. In the mid-eighteenth century, specialist institutions known as navigation schools were set up to teach boys naval skills. In the 1740s and 1750s, navigation schools opened in Irkutsk (because of Lake Baikal), Iakutsk (on the river Lena), and Okhotsk (a port on the Pacific coast). Of the 142 pupils who studied at the navigational school in Irkutsk between 1754 and 1768, 16 became navigators, 36 were employed in the Nerchinsk mines, 15 worked in other mines, and 32 joined the army.[6] Specialist schools were also opened in mines in the Altai region and in Nerchinsk.

Only in the reign of Catherine II was an attempt made to establish state schools in the major towns of the Russian empire. In 1775, the Statute of Provincial Administration instructed that schools should be set up in all provincial (*guberniia*) and district (*uezd*) towns. Catherine established boards of social welfare (*prikazy obshchestvennogo prizreniia*) in each province, with an initial capital of fifteen thousand rubles each to maintain schools and other welfare institutions (hospitals, asylums, foundling homes, and houses of correction).[7] The boards were, in effect, supposed to act like local banks and to increase their capital by charging interest on loans and receiving charitable donations.[8] In 1786, the Statute on National Schools determined that there should be a major national school in the main town of each province, comprising four classes of instruction, and a minor school in each main district town, comprising two classes.[9] In Siberia, major schools were opened in Tobol'sk (in western Siberia), Irkutsk (in eastern Siberia), and Barnaul (in the Altai region), and minor schools were opened in the towns of Tiumen', Turinsk, Tara, Kuznetsk, Krasnoiarsk, Eniseisk, Verkhneudinsk (Ule Udine), Tomsk, and Narym.

By 1789, 108 pupils were being taught in the Irkutsk major school and eighty-eight in the Tobol'sk major school; by 1792, the Krasnoiarsk minor school had ninety-one pupils and the Kuznetsk minor school had thirty-two pupils. Pupils—mostly boys, although in principle the schools were open to both sexes—came from a variety of social backgrounds, including Cossacks, soldiers, officers, minor officials, merchants, and artisans; one Bukharan (that is, the child of a Muslim trader from Central Asia) was a pupil at the Tobol'sk school in 1789 and one "tribute-payer" (that is, from an indigenous background) was a pupil at the Krasnoiarsk school in 1792.[10] Catherine's policy was ambitious, and in practice it was hard for schools in the more remote areas to flourish. Few donors came forward to support the schools and other welfare institutions: in Irkutsk province only five hundred rubles were donated to the boards of general welfare, although donations were higher in the more commercially developed Tobol'sk (4,480 rubles).[11] In reality, most parents were only interested in their sons acquiring basic literacy and numeracy, and were not prepared to let them enter the higher classes. Even in Tobol'sk, the urban institutions claimed they could not support the school (the school did continue to operate, but the number of pupils dropped to seventy-six by 1796).[12] There were also difficulties in finding suitably qualified teachers. Catherine determined that the teachers should be secular, that is, not priests, although most teachers came from a clerical background; a training college for teachers opened only in the reign of Alexander I. The Barnaul major school closed in 1797 and the minor schools in Krasnoiarsk and Kuznetsk had closed by the end of the century.

Catherine's policy was not only ambitious in terms of the number of schools and in her insistence that education should be free and open to both sexes, but also in the syllabus and educational methods, which were to be based on the best European practice of the time (her adviser was the leading Austrian educationalist, F. I. Jankovich de Mirievo). The upper classes of the schools were to teach history, geography, natural history, and physics, and schools were to be supplied with practical items such as maps and globes. Catherine also instructed in 1782 (reiterated in the Statute of 1786) that the languages of the indigenous and neighboring peoples should be taught—Greek in the southern provinces, Tatar and Persian in Irkutsk province, and Chinese in Kolyvan' region.[13]

This was not the first time Asian languages had been taught in schools, but it was the first time that these languages were specified as part of the syllabus of the national school system. There had been attempts to teach Tatar to Cossacks in Tobol'sk (which had, and still has, a large Tatar population) from the late seventeenth century. Earlier in the eighteenth century, schools teaching Asian languages, including Mongolian (Kalmyk) had also been established in Astrakhan' and Stavropol in the south. In the 1760s, a so-called Tatar school opened in Tobol'sk, based on the model of the southern schools, and taught Tatar to a small number of boys from servitor backgrounds (sons of Cossacks and *deti boiarskie*).[14] There was apparently a teacher of Japanese at the Irkutsk garrison school in the 1740s, teaching three Cossack boys,[15] although it is not clear why this language was considered to be useful, considering that there were few Japanese residents or traders in the region at the time.

The new national schools, however, had limited success in teaching Asian languages. The Tobol'sk major school opened a class to teach Tatar in 1793,[16] but we have seen that by this date enrollment in the school was already declining. The Irkutsk major school taught Mongolian, Chinese, and, from 1792, also Japanese. By this date, fifty-two pupils were apparently studying Mongolian, twenty-seven were studying Chinese, and six were studying Japanese. In 1794, however, the former two languages ceased to be taught "because of the difficulty and unintelligibility of these languages and the lack of desire by pupils and parents to continue studying them." Nevertheless, Japanese continued to be taught until 1816 (and was taught at the grammar school after its foundation in 1805). [17] In Simbirsk and Ufa, in the Urals, the governor-general, Count Osip Igel'strom, attempted to find people who could translate Russian school books into Tatar and Kirghiz for the national schools, but with little success.[18]

The real success in teaching Asian languages in this period came at the Omsk Asiatic School, but this institution was not part of the national school structure. The school was quite unlike the national schools in that its educational aims were more limited. The school served an important function in training sons of Cossacks, and, to a lesser extent, non-Russian state officials, to perform service to the state as translators and interpreters.

The Omsk Asiatic School was opened in 1789, three years after the Statute on National Schools was issued. The costs of teacher salaries, of maintaining and supplying the school and its buildings, and of providing food and clothing for pupils were met by the central government (and later by the Ministry of Foreign Affairs). This was an indication that the school was seen to be performing a state service, by training sons of state servitors and officials for state business. Accordingly, the Omsk Asiatic School was differentiated from the national schools established in 1775 and 1786, which were to be funded by urban institutions and through local banks in major towns. The Asiatic School quite clearly was seen as serving a national and not simply a local purpose. Omsk was an important garrison town and a major administrative center. The school was originally housed within the guardhouse and then in 1804 moved to the building of the former military orphanage; in other words, its location was firmly within the military establishment of the town.

In 1789, it was estimated that the school would cost 483 rubles and 94 kopeks a year, a sum that would cover the one-hundred-fifty-ruble annual salary of the teacher of Tatar, as well as the provision of books, food, and clothing for twenty-five pupils.[19] As we shall see below, pupils at the school were sent to the Kazan' grammar school (*gimnaziia*) and Kazan' university (founded in 1804) to further their study in Asian languages. The cost of six hundred rubles a year for pupils sent to Kazan' institutions—and there were two pupils in the early 1820s—was met by the Asiatic Department of the Ministry of Foreign Affairs.[20] The funding for the Omsk school was inadequate, and required a further injection of five thousand rubles in 1822 to keep functioning. In 1828, it was estimated that it was costing 581 rubles and 34 ¾ kopeks a year to maintain twenty pupils (the number of students had risen to twenty-five by 1836).[21] It was not possible, however, to sustain the school on this financial basis; in 1836 the Omsk Asiatic School closed, and the remaining pupils transferred to the local Cossack Cadet Corps school (founded in 1813).[22] By this time Omsk had become the administrative center of Western Siberia, and the Cadet Corps was one of the central administrative buildings in the town. Pupils continued to study Asian languages and the state continued to pay not only for their maintenance at the Cadet Corps school, but also for additional study by the most able pupils.

The number of pupils at the Omsk Asiatic School remained fairly constant—it enrolled somewhere between eighteen and twenty-five pupils each year during its nearly five decades of operation. A list of nineteen pupils in 1824 showed that the youngest were ten years of age, and the oldest were twenty; the majority were fifteen to seventeen years old.[23] Most of the pupils were sons of Cossacks. That was certainly the intention behind the founding of the school: to provide another way in which Cossacks would be trained in order to serve the interests of the state on the frontiers of Russia. The school was also, however, open to sons from another category of state servitors: non-Russians who had, normally, converted from Islam to Christianity and who were in the service of the state. In 1827, Tazhmanet Seifulin was a pupil at the school; he was the son of a Kazan' Tatar who had been in Russian service and reached the rank of collegiate registrar (rank fourteen, that is, the lowest civil rank in the Table of Ranks).[24]

The social origins of the first teachers in the Omsk Asiatic School are unknown. The main language taught in the school was Tatar, and the original salary of the teacher was 150 rubles a year. In 1792, however, the school appointed an additional teacher of Mongolian and Chinese at a salary of only seventy-five rubles a year. He was called Sharin, and was a garrison sergeant and almost certainly a converted Kalmyk.[25] Appointing a sergeant demonstrated that acquiring these languages had a military purpose, and as he only had five pupils, he may well have assumed this role in addition to performing other military duties. Thus teachers' salaries at the Omsk school were in line with the lower level of salaries paid to the teachers working in *minor* national schools, but below those paid at major schools, including to teachers of foreign languages in the major schools. In principle, at least, after 1786, teachers in the major national schools were paid a salary of four hundred rubles a year (and three hundred rubles for teaching foreign languages), and in the minor schools were paid one hundred fifty or two hundred rubles a year. In 1823, Nikolai Pirozhkov, teacher of Tatar at the Omsk Asiatic School, successfully requested that his salary be raised from one hundred fifty rubles to three hundred rubles a year in accordance with these regulations.[26]

Teachers in national schools, however, regularly complained that their salaries were delayed, or not paid in full, or not paid at all. In 1788, the National Commission of Schools sent Osip Kozodavlev to investigate how schools had been established. He found that salaries of many teachers in minor schools were lower than specified in the Statute on National Schools. Some teachers complained that they had not been paid at all. One teacher in Saint Petersburg province claimed that he had no salary and needed "shirts, books and other minor necessities."[27] At least teachers in the Omsk Asiatic School were paid by central and not local funds, and this may have made their salaries a little more reliable.

The role of teacher in the Omsk Asiatic School was regarded as a service post and was recognized by the appropriate rank. Nikolai Pirozhkov held the rank of collegiate registrar, that is, rank fourteen, the lowest civilian rank. In 1831, the teacher of Tatar, Kirotkov, held the rank of a provincial secretary (rank twelve, equivalent to a second lieutenant, or *podporutchik* in the army), and the teacher of Mongolian, Lobanov, held the higher rank of titular councilor (rank nine, the equivalent of a captain in the army).[28] These ranks seem to be a little higher than those of teachers in national schools; a teacher in a minor school had to work for eight years before reaching the lowest rank, fourteen, and teachers in the second class of the major schools could rise to the ninth rank after nine years' service.

The wording of a request in 1823 for a post as teacher of Tatar and Mongolian in the Omsk Asiatic School by Kurban (or Kurman) Kurbatov, a converted Tatar who was currently a pupil at the school, is significant in its understanding of the nature of the post. Of course, it would be absurd to expect a modern-style application highlighting key linguistic and organizational skills and academic qualifications, but it is striking that Kurbatov worded his request in the same language that a Cossack or other servitor would request a military or civilian posting. He made no reference to his knowledge of languages or his record at the school, but stated that his father had been in Russian service as a translator and interpreter in Petropavlovsk Fortress, and pleaded that he needed a post after the death of his father as he "lacked the means to support his family." It is not clear from the documents whether Kurbatov was successful.[29]

The Omsk Asiatic School taught Tatar to all its pupils, and other languages to a smaller group. By 1792, the school was teaching Tatar to twenty pupils and Mongolian (Kalmyk) to five pupils.[30] In 1821, the school recruited a new teacher of Mongolian from the Chinese frontier. The school, as we have seen, closed in 1836 and merged with the Cossack Cadet Corps school in Omsk. At that date both Tatar and Mongolian were still being taught. The following year, one hundred eighteen boys were learning Tatar in the Cadet Corps in four levels of classes; in addition, seven pupils were listed as studying Persian and Arabic. [31] The Asiatic School was not purely a language school, of course. The syllabus, however, was modeled on the pragmatic approach of the garrison schools rather than on the broader syllabus covering the humanities and sciences in the national schools. Boys were taught practical subjects for military service, such as mathematics and topography, although they were also taught French. The pupils were regularly tested and reports made on their progress in all subjects to the Cadet Corps administration. In 1836, a report noted that "the pupils of the Asiatic School achieved tolerable success in all subjects they were taught."[32] Only a few comments revealed what conditions were really like, but one report in 1837, that is, just after the transfer of pupils to the Cadet Corps, noted the lack of space at the school. It stated that the pupils were "almost sitting on each other," and some had to stand as there was nowhere to sit down.[33]

Able pupils were sent to further their studies at the Kazan' grammar school and Kazan' university (the two institutions are listed together and interchangeably in the documents) at state expense. Grigorii

Fromov was learning Arabic, and Iakov Cherovaev Persian, at the Kazan' grammar school in 1821; it was reported that both were making good progress.[34] In 1824, two more pupils—called Bikmaev and Kurbanakov—were sent to the Kazan' grammar school and the university.[35] In that year one boy, Aleksei Zuev, "by the will of God," died in the grammar school (this was a time when plague ravaged the southern provinces of Russia) and the Omsk Asiatic School asked if it could send another boy in his place to the Kazan' school.[36] In 1827, Tazhment Seifulin, son of a Tatar official, was sent to the Kazan' university with two other pupils to learn Tatar, Persian, and Arabic.[37] In 1836, another student—a certain Menytsikov—was sent to study at the Kazan' university.[38]

The education in the Omsk Asiatic School was practical, and further practical training could be conducted on the ground as well in other educational institutions. In 1818, Stepan Lobanov and Maksim Koptev were sent to Irkutsk to practice their Mongolian,[39] followed six years later by two others—Litvinov and Kornilov.[40] In 1836, five boys were sent to the Kirghiz steppe to learn Kirghiz.[41] By the following year there were twenty-one pupils from the Cadet Corps learning Kirghiz on the steppe, under the supervision of the Tatar teacher, Kurbanakov (who had been educated at the Kazan' grammar school/university a few years before).[42] Eight pupils were learning Kirghiz in this way in 1843.[43]

The practical (and military) focus of the Omsk Asiatic School can be seen most clearly in the careers of its pupils. A list of pupils who left the school between 1826 and 1836 shows that thirty had become translators and interpreters and the same number had moved on to the Cossack Cadet school or to other military schools; two had become teachers at the Omsk school and eight were employed in military surveying work.[44] Some pupils requested a post in the army. For example, in 1836, one pupil, aged sixteen, petitioned to be allowed to leave the school and join a regiment.[45]

Cossacks were a service group and could simply be moved to wherever it was thought they could best serve the state, and in this respect pupils at the school were no different from other Cossacks. In the late eighteenth century "mutinous" Cossacks had simply been moved from the Don region to the Caucasus and Siberia.[46] In 1810, it was decreed that "excess" Cossacks in Siberian towns were to be moved to the Chinese frontier.[47] The fate of pupils who could not master foreign languages was particularly harsh, as they had no control over their postings. In 1836, one Pavel Khorkashenin was unable to continue his studies for medical reasons but was sent to a gold mine. In the same year, another pupil, Ivan Putintsov, was sent to a factory.[48] Cossacks in factories and mines were almost certainly used for guard duties (to protect factory owners and to prevent desertions by workers) rather than as workers, but this was not an attractive posting. Factories and mines were often located in remote parts of Siberia where the climate was severe; both convicts who had been dispatched to factories for forced labor and so-called "free" laborers or "possessional" serfs in factories endured harsh conditions so that there were frequent disturbances in which solders as well as workers could be hurt.[49]

The varied careers of individual pupils at the Omsk Asiatic School demonstrate the ways in which its graduates served the state, and reflect at the same time some of the problems and conflicts as the state attempted to assert control over its vast territory. Most were employed as translators and interpreters, with an appropriate civilian rank, and located in the many forts that ran across the southern borders of Siberia and along river routes in a number of "lines." Some fifty to ninety thousand men served in the garrison regiments throughout the Russian empire in the second half of the eighteenth and the early nineteenth centuries. The Orenburg Line, which ran from the town of Orenburg in the Urals across southern Siberia, had been lightly manned before the Pugachev revolt of the mid-1770s, but by 1817 was manned by over twenty thousand men.[50] The forts on lines that ran along the Chinese frontier and up to the north along river routes became smaller as they became more remote: in 1773 there were some 151 Cossacks and 68 soldiers manning the remote fort of Gizhiga on the northern shores of the Sea of Okhotsk, and 56 men in distant Kamchatka in 1812.[51]

Forts were where the Russian state maintained its presence and control over the local population. They acted as centers for the collection of tribute and other dues, for the administration of justice, and for carrying out punishments; they protected the local population from attack by hostile tribes, and they provided some protection in time of shortage or hardship.[52] Oases of "Russianness" in hostile territory, surrounded by non-Russian peoples who were often violently opposed to the Russian presence, the forts desperately needed men who could act as intermediaries between the army commanders and the local people. Consequently, salaries for interpreters and translators were higher than for teachers in the Omsk Asiatic School, and were on a par with those of provincial secretaries. In 1803, the salaries in the Irkutsk and Tobol'sk provincial administrations were set at six hundred rubles per annum for Chinese translators and four hundred rubles for Mongolian (Kalmyk) translators.[53]

Pupils who became translators and interpreters also accompanied missions to the chiefs of non-Russian peoples and tribes in Siberia and diplomatic missions to China. Semen Elgin, the son of a Cossack, became a translator and interpreter, and was posted to the forts of Zhelezinskii and Nikolaevsk. He accompanied missions outside the Russian frontier and was rewarded with the rank of provincial secretary (rank twelve) after playing a role in apparently "persuading" four hundred fifty Kirghiz to become Russian citizens.[54] Savatei Kurtupov, who served in the Omsk and Nikolaevsk fortresses as a translator and interpreter with the rank of collegiate registrar (rank fourteen), also accompanied a mission to the Chinese frontier for talks with the Kirghiz sultan.[55] Stepan Lobanov, who had studied Mongolian in Irkutsk and then become a teacher of Mongolian at the school, was also sent with a mission to Kiakhta, the border town between Russia and China, as a translator (this was after the Russians had ceded the Amur valley to the Chinese at the Treaty of Nerchinsk in 1689 and before the territory became part of the Russian Empire in 1860).[56]

Trading and diplomatic missions went hand in hand. In particular, missions on the Kirghiz steppe were often intended to purchase or requisition horses. Ivan Usov, who attained the rank of collegiate registrar, was a translator and interpreter at a fortress but was also sent on a mission to Asia to acquire horses in 1818.[57] Filipp Nazarov, who served in forts on the River Irtysh Line, was also sent on a mission among the Kirghiz to acquire twenty-five hundred horses.[58] Horses were of crucial importance for the Russian army, and in particular for the Cossacks who acted as auxiliary cavalry, both for warfare and for transporting weapons and goods. In 1812, during the Napoleonic invasion when the state was at its most vulnerable, the inhabitants of several provinces in western Russia and Siberia were asked to provide horses in place of men, as horses were so valuable.[59] A couple of examples from 1812-13 demonstrate the sheer number of horses required by the armed forces. The fort of Dünaburg (in present-day Latvia) required five thousand carts to bring in supplies in 1812 in advance of the invasion.[60] And after the Napoleonic forces left Russia, the countryside in western Russia was strewn not only with the bodies of combatants from either side, but also with their horses. Some 120,000 horse carcasses had to be buried in Smolensk province alone when the spring thaw exposed them, an indication of the vast number of horses involved in early nineteenth-century warfare.[61]

Finally, graduates from the Omsk Asiatic School worked as translators and interpreters in commercial and other disputes. One pupil was sent on a journey of seven hundred *versty* (some 460 miles) in 1804 to reclaim merchant goods stolen by Kirghiz tribesmen. In 1813 he was sent to release a Kirghiz man from slavery (the eradication of slavery was tackled seriously only in the 1820s by Mikhail Speranskii, while governor-general of Siberia,[62] though it continued in practice), and the following year he accompanied a merchant caravan from China.[63] Disputes between Cossacks and non-Russians, in particular with Kirghiz and Kalmyks, were common and inevitably required translators and interpreters. The records of the Cossack judicial administration in Orenburg in the nineteenth century demonstrate that violent clashes with Kirghiz, Bashkirs, and Nogais were not infrequent. The most common cause of conflict was allegations of theft, usually of horses, but also of other livestock and goods. Fights were common and could lead to kidnapping, injury, and death. In 1808, a Kirghiz murdered a Cossack; in 1822 Kirghiz horsemen set upon a party of Cossacks while they were collecting berries in the forest and one Cossack died of his wounds.[64] Traders—both Russian and

Bukharan—were often attacked and their goods seized.[65] Violence was endemic in the Siberian countryside and all ethnic groups could be both victims and perpetrators. In 1824, a Bukharan trader complained about the theft of his goods from a caravan of ten camels by a gang of Kirghiz. His statement was translated from Mongolian by a collegiate registrar, Tazhmanet Seifulin,[66] whom we have already met as a pupil at the Omsk Asiatic School.[67]

The Omsk Asiatic School was entirely pragmatic in training boys for state service. Although Seifulin was from a non-Russian background, the school did not consider that it had a mission to educate the local indigenous population, let alone attempt to understand or appreciate their culture. It was the Decembrists who, while in exile in Siberia, opened new schools specifically to educate local people who were not ethnically Russian, as opposed to teaching Russians the indigenous languages. I. D. Iakushkin, a former teacher in the Cadet Corps, set up a school in Ialutorovsk (Chita) in 1842 for "all social groups," which included children of peasants and local people.[68] The Bestuzhev brothers opened a school in Selinginsk that taught Buriat children.[69] The Omsk Asiatic School was not an example of an enlightened or humane attempt to make pupils aware of and sympathetic to other cultures and civilizations through the acquisition of new languages. Rather, it was an integral part of the way the Russian state trained children of state servitors to enable the state to assert control in multiethnic Siberia in particular and on its frontiers more generally.

NOTES

1 In particular in his *Publishing, Printing, and the Origins of Intellectual Life in Russia, 1700-1800* (Princeton: Princeton University Press, 1985).

2 Gary Marker, "Who Rules the Word? Public School Education and the Fate of Universality in Russia, 1782-1803," *Russian History* 20 (1993): 16.

3 Rossiiskii gosudarstvennyi arkhiv drevnikh aktov (hereafter RGADA), fond (hereafter f.) 1096, opis' (hereafter op.), 1, delo (hereafter d.), list (hereafter l.) 51, Gizhiga fort, various papers 1785-1807.

4 *Iz istoriia Omska (1716-1917 gg.): ocherki, dokumenty, materialy* (Omsk: Zapadno-Sibirskoe knizhnoe izdatel'stvo, 1967), 100.

5 RGADA, f. 1096, op. 1, d. 51, ll. 182-86, Gizhiga fort, various papers, 1785-1807.

6 A. Sgibiev, "Navigatskiia shkoly v Sibiri," *Morskoi sbornik* 87 (1866): 3-44.

7 See J. M. Hartley, "Philanthropy in the Reign of Catherine the Great: Aims and Realities," in R. Bartlett, J. M. Hartley, eds., *Russia in the Age of the Enlightenment: Essays for Isabel de Madariaga* (London: MacMillan, 1990), 167-202.

8 For the way in which the boards functioned see J. M. Hartley, "The Boards of Social Welfare and the Financing of Catherine II's State Schools," *The Slavonic and East European Review* 67 (1989): 211-27.

9 On national schools see I. M. de Madariaga, *Russia in the Age of Catherine the Great* (London: Weidenfeld and Nicolson, 1981), chapter 31; ibid., "The Foundation of the Russian Educational System by Catherine II," *The Slavonic and East European Review* 57 (1979): 369-95; J. L. Black, *Citizens for the Fatherland: Education, Educators and Pedagogical Ideas in Eighteenth-Century Russia* (Boulder: East European Quarterly, 1979); J. M. Hartley, *A Social History of the Russian Empire 1650-1825* (Harlow: Longman, 1999), 135-40; S. V. Rozhdestvenskii, *Ocherki po istorii sistemy narodnago prosveshcheniia v Rossii v XVII-XIX vekakh* (Saint Petersburg: Tip. M. A. Aleksandrova, 1912); S. V. Rozhdestvenskii, "Iz istorii uchebnykh reform Imperatritsy Ekateriny II," *Zhurnal Ministerstva Narodnogo Prosveshcheniia*, new series, 20 (1909): 47-100; S. A. Kniaz'kov, N. N. Serbov, *Ocherk istorii narodnago obrazovaniia Rossii do epokhi reform Aleksandra II* (Moscow: Knigoizdatel'stvo "Pol'za," 1910); M. V. Sychev-Mikhailov, *Iz istorii russkoi shkoly i pedagogiki XVIII veka* (Moscow: Izdatel'stvo Akademii pedagogicheskikh nauk RSFSR, 1960); A. Voronov, *Fedor Ivanovich Iankovich de-Mirievo ili narodnyia uchilishcha v Rossii pri Ekaterine II* (Saint Petersburg: Tip. Eduarda Pratsa, 1858).

10 A. N. Kopylov, *Ocherki kul'turnoi zhizni Sibiri v XVII – XVIII vv.* (Novosibirsk: Nauka, 1974), 88-91.

11 Quoted in Hartley, "The Boards of Social Welfare," 216.

12 *Istoriia Sibiri s drevneishikh vremen do nashikh dnei*, 5 vols. (Leningrad: Nauka, 1968-69), 2:328.

13 *Polnoe sobranie zakonov Rossiiskoi Imperii*, first series, 40 vols. (Saint Petersburg, 1830) (hereafter *PSZ*), 21:685, no. 1, 553 (September 27, 1782).

14 *Istoriia kazachestvo aziatskoi Rossii*, 3 vols. (Ekaterinburg: Institut istorii i arkheologii, RAN, Ural'skoe otdelenie, 1995), 1:238; Kopylov, *Ocherki kul'turnoi zhizni Sibiri*, 66.

15 Kopylov, *Ocherki kul'turnoi zhizni Sibiri*, 72.

16 M. N. Malysheva, "Iz istorii formirovaniia pedagogicheskikh kadrov grazhdanskikh shkol gorodov zapadnoi Sibiri v kontse XVIII—pervoi polovine XIX v.," in *Goroda Sibiri (epokha feodalizma i kapitalizma)* (Novosibirsk: Nauka, 1978), 192.

17 Kopylov, *Ocherki kul'turnoi zhizni Sibiri*, 88-91.

18 D. A. Tolstoi, "Arkhiv Grafa Igel'strom," *Russkii arkhiv* 24, part 3 (1886): 343.

19 Gosudarstvennyi istoricheskii arkhiv Omskoi oblasti (hereafter GAOO), f. 3, op. 1, d. 754, ll. 3-11, Main Administration of Western Siberia, Omsk Asiatic School papers.

20 GAOO, f. 3, op. 1, d. 417, ll. 6, 16, 20, Main Administration of Western Siberia, Omsk Asiatic School papers.

21 GAOO, f. 366, op. 1, d. 124, ll. 101ob-110, Cherkasov papers, papers on the Orenburg Cossack host, 1828.

22 GAOO, f. 19, op. 1, d. 2, l. 10, Siberian Cadet Corps papers.
23 GAOO, f. 3, op. 1, d. 417, l. 31, Main Administration of Western Siberia, Omsk Asiatic School papers.
24 GAOO, f. 3, op. 1, d. 754, l. 25, Main Administration of Western Siberia, on the Omsk Asiatic School.
25 GAOO, f. 3, op. 1, d. 754, ll. 6-9ob, Main Administration of Western Siberia, Omsk Asiatic School papers.
26 GAOO, f. 3, op. 1, d. 200, Main Administration of Western Siberia, confirmation of the salary of a teacher, 1823.
27 Hartley, "The Boards of Social Welfare," 223, from a source in Saint Petersburg, Rossiiskii gosudarstvennyi istoricheskii arkhiv, f. 730, op. 1, d. 31, l. 25, Commission on National Education, material relating to teachers in Saint Petersburg province.
28 GAOO, f. 366, op. 1, d. 124, l. 107, Cherkasov papers, papers on the Orenburg Cossack host, 1828.
29 GAOO, f. 3, op. 1, d. 219, Main Administration of Western Siberia, petition for a post as teacher, 1823.
30 GAOO, f. 3, op. 1, d. 754, ll. 3-11, Main Administration of Western Siberia, Omsk Asiatic School papers.
31 GAOO, f. 19, op. 1, d. 3, ll. 4ob-5, 13ob, 15-15ob, 74ob, Siberian Cadet Corps papers.
32 GAOO, f. 19, op. 1, d. 2, l. 26, Siberian Cadet Corps papers.
33 GAOO, f. 19, op. 1, d. 3, l. 27ob, Siberian Cadet Corps papers.
34 GAOO, f. 3, op. 1, d. 754, ll. 13ob-23, Main Administration of Western Siberia, Omsk Asiatic School papers.
35 GAOO, f. 3, op. 1, d. 417, l. 6, Main Administration of Western Siberia, Omsk Asiatic School papers.
36 Ibid., 417, l. 31.
37 GAOO, f. 3, op. 1, d. 754, ll. 26, 27ob, Main Administration of Western Siberia, Omsk Asiatic School papers.
38 GAOO, f. 19, op. 1, d. 2, ll. 29, 89, Siberian Cadet Corps papers.
39 GAOO, f. 2, op. 1, d. 251, ll. 35-36, 55ob-56, General Governor papers.
40 GAOO, f. 3, op. 1, d. 417, ll. 16, 20, Main Administration of Western Siberia, on the Omsk Asiatic School.
41 GAOO, f. 19, op. 1, d. 2, l. 70v, Siberian Cadet Corps papers.
42 GAOO, f. 19, op. 1, d. 3, ll. 51ob-52, 58, Siberian Cadet Corps papers.
43 GAOO, f. 19, op. 1, d. 4, l. 28, Siberian Cadet Corps papers.
44 GAOO, f. 366, op. 1, d. 124, ll. 101ob-110, Cherkasov papers, papers on the Orenburg Cossack host, 1828.
45 GAOO, f. 19, op. 1, d. 2, l. 19ob, Siberian Cadet Corps papers
46 J. M. Hartley, *Russia, 1762-1825: Military Power, the State and the People* (Westport and London: Praeger, 2008), 19-20; Hartley, *Siberia: A History of the People* (New Haven: Yale University Press, 2014), 43-44, 91-92.
47 *PSZ*, 31:335-36, no. 24331 (August 26, 1810).
48 GAOO, f. 19, op. 1, d. 2, ll. 17ob, 100, Siberian Cadet Corps papers.
49 Madariaga, *Russia in the Age of Catherine the Great*, 123-25; Hartley, *Siberia: A History*, 57-58.

50 V. S. Kobzov, *Voenno-administrativnaia struktura Orenburgskogo kazach'ego voiska v XVI –pervaia polovina XIX v.* (Cheliabinsk: Cheliabinskii gosudarstvennyi universitet, 1996), 44, 75.
51 Gizhiga: Rossiiskii gosudarstvennyi voenno-istoricheskii arkhiv (hereafter RGVIA), f. 14808, op. 1, d. 47, ll. 38-40, Gizhiga Fortress, out-letters and papers 1773. Kamchatka: *PSZ* 43.2:412, *Kniga shtatov*, no. 25081 (April 9, 1812).
52 See for example, my description of the operation of the remote fort of Gizhiga in J. M. Hartley, "Gizhiga: Military Presence and Social Encounters in Russia's Wild East," *The Slavonic and East European Review* 86 (2008): 665-84.
53 *PSZ*, 44.2:755, *Knigi shtatov*, based on a decree of July 5, 1803.
54 GAOO, f. 2, d. 251, ll. 5ob-6, General Governor papers.
55 Ibid., ll. 17ob-18.
56 Ibid., ll. 35-39.
57 Ibid., ll. 31ob-32.
58 Ibid., ll. 40v-41.
59 Hartley, *Russia 1762-1825*, 82.
60 RGVIA, f. 846, op. 16, d. 3553, l. 18ob, Napoleonic Wars papers, supplies for Dünaberg.
61 J. Hartley, "Russia in 1812: Part I: the French Presence in the Gubernii of Smolensk and Mogilev," *Jahrbücher für Geschichte Osteuropas* 28 (1990): 197.
62 See Hartley, *Siberia: A History*, 112. See also Janet M. Hartley, "Slaves and Spouses: Russian Settlers and Non-Russians in Siberia," forthcoming.
63 GAOO, f. 2, d. 251, ll. 61ob-64, General Governor papers.
64 Hartley, *Russia 1762-1825*, 152, with material drawn from "Opis' 1000 dela kazach'iago otdela," in *Trudy Orenburgskoi uchenoi arkhivnoi komissii*, no. 24 (Omsk, 1870).
65 Hartley, *Siberia: A History*, 38-41, 101-102.
66 GAOO, f. 3, op. 1, d. 557, Main administration of Western Siberia, petition from Safiev, a Bukharan trader, 1825.
67 GAOO, f. 3, op. 1, d. 754, l. 25, Main Administration of Western Siberia, on the Omsk Asiatic School.
68 I. N. Nikulina, *Religiia i politicheskie ssyl'nye zapadnoi Sibiri v XIX v.* (Barnaul: Altaiskii gosudarstvennyi tekhnologicheskii universitet, 2004), 72; *Memuary Dekabristov. Severnoe obshchestvo*, ed. V. A. Fedorov (Moscow: Moskovskii gosudarstvennyi universitet, 1981), 116-17; G. P. Shatrova, *Dekabristy i Sibir'* (Tomsk: Tomskii gosudarstvennyi universitet, 1962), 149-51. .
69 M. K. Azadovskii, *Stranitsy istorii Dekabrizma* (Irkutsk: Vostochno-Sibirskoe knizhnoe izdatel'stvo, 1991), 88; V. B. Bakhaev, *Obshchestvenno-prosvetitel'skaia i kraevedcheskaia deiatel'nost' Dekabristov v Buriatii* (Novosibirsk: Nauka, 1980), 71-86; A. N. Kopylov and M. P. Malysheva, "Dekabristy i prosveshchenie Sibiri v pervoi polovine XIX v.," in *Dekabristy i Sibir'* (Novosibirsk: Nauka, 1977), 89-108.

What Should One Teach? A New Approach to Russian Childhood Education as Reflected in Manuscripts from the Second Half of the Seventeenth Century*

Ol'ga Kosheleva
(Institute of General History, Russian Academy of Science)

The earliest Russian textbooks were very different from how we think of such books today. They took the form of manuscript miscellanies, like most early Russian books. Numerous studies, writes I. M. Gritsevskaia, "confirm that medieval miscellanies, always different and yet very similar to one another, constitute the basic element of early Russian books, the principal form of texts from ancient Russia."[1] These miscellanies could include educational texts (grammars, for instance) side by side with books of entirely different purpose and content. Even abecedaries, which when printed appeared as unitary volumes, were prepared according to the old miscellany model, and included a wide array of general education texts that touched on numerous subjects, including, for example, the origin of Russian writing. Only in the second half of the seventeenth century did some manuscript miscellanies, along with abecedaries and similar readers, come to resemble and anticipate today's textbooks aimed at beginning learners.[2]

These seventeenth-century miscellanies are the subject of our study. Retaining all the main features of a medieval miscellany, they also contained innovations. Unlike their predecessors, the composition of which depended only upon the interests of their owners, the new miscellanies were organized strictly for educational purposes (as the compilers conceived them) and were directed to specific audiences, that is, the various participants in the educational process—teachers, parents, and students.

In and of themselves, thematic miscellanies were not rare among early Russian books. For example, the moralistic and disciplinary miscellany called *Starchestvo* shared a great deal with educational miscellanies, depending upon a collection of texts intended as a guide for older monks in instructing their newly-tonsured brethren.[3] A wide range of religious texts was available for inclusion in miscellanies of this type—from penitentials to monastic statutes.[4] But for educational miscellanies the choice was not so broad, since organized schooling was largely absent in Muscovy. Consequently, the authors and compilers of educational miscellanies found themselves in a difficult position. Let us turn to the work of two such authors, and see what drove them to take up this difficult project and how they fared with their task.

The practice of studying with a private teacher (older than the existence of schools, and, for a time after their appearance, more common) was, once the reader (the pupil) mastered the basic skills, limited to reading the Psalter, the Book of Hours, and the *Oktoikh* (a service book containing readings for evensong, compline, morning prayer, and other services) or the Apostle (containing mostly New Testament readings). These books gave the student a familiarity with texts essential for the various forms of church service.

For those who mastered elementary reading, the next task was to master writing skills. Instruction in writing was not fixed by any pedagogical tracts, but it is mentioned in a variety of sources. For example, the Ukrainian preacher Ivan Vishenskii (before 1550-ca. 1621) in "The Dispute between the Wise Latin and Silly Rusian" offers this explanation of Orthodox education:

> Because of the simplicity of our faith and godliness, and fearing the poisoning of your children with Latin cunning and heresy, I recommend to you an Orthodox school, and advise that [your children] study Greek or Slavonic grammar; then, instead of the cunning dialectics that teaches one how to turn white into black and black into white, they should study the Horologion (Book of Hours); instead of artful syllogisms and rhetoric, let them study the Psalter; instead of secular philosophy . . . they should study the *Oktoikh*. . . .[5]

Clearly Vishenskii understood an Orthodox education primarily in contrast to a Latin one.

In the second half of the seventeenth century there were people who shared this opinion (for example, Archpriest Avvakum), but there were also others who were inclined to devise a more substantial and regular Orthodox education. For them the recent schism in the Orthodox Church, known as the Raskol, which had disturbed parish life throughout the entire second half of the seventeenth century, provided good reason for re-thinking broader education. The idea that the schism was the result of "ignorance," as Simeon Polotsky and Paisii Ligarides declared at the Great Moscow Synod in 1666, was widespread. As a result of the church schism, interest in Greek writing and culture rose sharply and Greeks, who were increasingly numerous in Moscow, encouraged this enthusiasm. In 1681 they organized a Greek-Slavonic school in the Moscow *Pechatnyi dvor*.

In Moscow there also appeared strong proponents of Western learning. The first of these, Orthodox in speech and Uniate in spirit, was the monk Simeon Polotsky, a poet and teacher in the tsar's family.[6] Others with a similar orientation were the translators of the Muscovite Foreign Office (for instance, Nikolai Spafarii), who were directly connected with new Western books and with graduates of the Kiev Academy loyal to Latin learning. In Moscow, Simeon Polotsky's apprentice, Sil'vestr Medvedev, managed to open a Slavonic-Latin school in Zaikonospasskii Monastery. By 1682 he had prepared (probably with the participation of the recently-deceased Polotsky) and submitted to the Tsar Feodor Alekseevich a project for an Orthodox institution of higher learning. However, the tsar was mortally ill, and had no time to act on the proposal.

Numerous facts reflected in the sources tell the same story—about expansions in the body of knowledge, about new forms of education that arose with special urgency, and about the realization of these new forms that began in the 1680s. These questions interested not only intellectuals, but also people high in the clerical hierarchy and the tsar's court, because they thought that a correct Orthodox education could somehow prevent dissent in society and schism in the church. Heated discussions were held inside monastery walls and within Muscovite church yards.[7] What ought school lessons to be? What content should they have? These questions remained controversial, and Moscow intellectuals proposed radically different answers.

These conditions were naturally apparent in the creation of school books such as the printed abecedaries, which took Simeon Polotsky's abecedary of 1679 as an example, and also in manuscript educational miscellanies. Their authors were people who worked as teachers, generally priests and monks from the capital who were relatively receptive to baroque culture.

Several manuscripts of this kind (dating from the last quarter of the seventeenth or early eighteenth century) survive in single or multiple copies. Many had their contents described in print editions, had their texts partially published, or were even quoted in other publications. Before the revolution, historians as well as antiquarians wanted to put these miscellanies immediately into print circulation, since they seemed to constitute a kind of trump card, capable of countering the widespread and painful stereotype of the ignorance of pre-Petrine Russia.[8] These often-hasty publications were not without benefit: because of the subsequent cataclysms in Russian life, many of these manuscripts were lost and today are known only through these publications.

In revolutionary Petrograd, 1918, Vladimir V. Bush succeeded in publishing his research. Here, he attempted to distinguish from the mass of manuscript texts of the seventeenth century those works devoted to the problems of childhood education, and to publish all the texts and their various copies he found.[9] This was the first and last attempt of this kind, and was far from perfect. Until quite recently, there were no surveys of the manuscript legacy of seventeenth-century educational texts. It was the Italian researcher, Christina Bragone, who set a new standard for this kind of work. She published a manuscript of the *Alfavitar' radi ucheniia malykh detei* (Abecedary for the education of little children) with commentary on almost every stanza of text. The commentary underlines parallels with other manuscripts and interprets every fragment, thereby converting publication of the text into serious research.[10] More than that, Bragone identified all manuscript copies of miscellanies that contain the composition of Erasmus of Rotterdam, *De civilitate morum puerilium* (Handbook on Good Manners for Children), evidently translated into Russian in 1675 by Epifanii Slavinetskii, a monk in the Chudov Monastery who had been invited to Moscow to translate Greek and Latin texts.[11] *De civilitate* is, in my opinion, an important marker for identifying educational miscellanies.

I. M. Gritsevskaia is right to say that "practically every Muscovite-era miscellany can be studied as the original, individual object, just as the original, individual old Russian texts that entered these miscellanies can be studied separately."[12] Actually, in recent years several substantial monographs have examined particular seventeenth-century manuscript miscellanies on different subjects;[13] they constitute the historiographical context for studying the miscellanies that interest us here.

In contrast to printed abecedaries, copies of seventeenth-century manuscript miscellanies created for teaching purposes are still insufficiently studied. In my opinion we can provisionally isolate three groups of miscellanies intended to aid the educational process (both for schools and for individual instruction) with informative, didactic, methodological, and moral materials: 1) *Shkol'nye azbukovniki* (The school azbukovniks);[14] 2) the *Alfavitar'* ; and 3) "practical" teachers' miscellanies.

The last group of manuscripts differs from the first two, and includes miscellanies written by individual teachers.[15] The authors are anonymous, but sometimes give the pupils' names (for example, the children of the princely Odoevskii and Cherkasskii families). These manuscripts were probably presented by teachers to their pupils upon completion of elementary education. By then pupils could read these texts independently. Miscellanies like these usually exist in a single author's copy. The form and contents vary, and they were intended for pupils to read at home or for parents to use with their children.

The two other types of miscellanies were intended primarily for teachers. Their various contents were compiled in a more or less strict order on the model of a school book. Generally, each survives in several copies, because they were manually duplicated as the compilers chose. The *Azbukovniki* and the *Alfavitar'* do not resemble each other in the organization of material, style, or content, which is perfectly natural, since they were composed under different circumstances by people who differed from each other in many ways. However, both miscellany types reflect the compilers' enthusiasm for the idea of Orthodox education and the desire to distinguish their contents from books of the Latin school. To this end, the author-compilers selected and reworked familiar material that they combined into miscellanies to which they gave no suitable name, but which today we would call educational books.

The *Azbukovniki* and the *Alfavitar'* are large manuscripts that survive in several copies distinguished by their structure and contents. Both deserve their own monographs, and, as mentioned above, one devoted to *Alfavitar'* already exists, and I myself plan to complete soon a study of the *Azbukovniki.* In the present article I can discuss on a comparative basis only one aspect of that study—how the author-compilers of the *Azbukovniki* and the *Alfavitar'* answered the question, "What should one teach?" However, we cannot proceed without a brief history of their creation.

THE *AZBUKOVNIKI* MISCELLANY (*SHKOL'NYE AZBUKOVNIKI*)[16]

The history of the appearance of this miscellany began around 1680 with the "Letter of an Inquirer," written in verse by a certain Diomid Iakovlev Serkov "and friends" for a priest named Prokhor.[17] A teacher himself, Serkov asked Prokhor to write out what he had earlier said aloud about appropriate exercises for those who wanted to study in schools. The contents of Diomid's letter make it possible to assume that the participants of this correspondence communicated often, talking about things connected to school work. Now, having taken leave of the priest, the inquirer (Serkov) wanted to receive the gist of their conversation in written form from Prokhor, who was, judging by the way he is addressed, the most respected authority on these matters. Diomid's letter did not go unanswered: Prokhor wrote him that he had fulfilled his request.[18]

Indeed, he exceeded what was requested; in addition to a verse "School rules," Prokhor added numerous other materials he thought useful for a teacher's work. The composition of the miscellany is complicated and diverse; these brief verse and prose works appear at first sight to have been collected without any system, mixing together manuals for teachers, pupils, leaders, and parents. One scholar of this miscellany wrote in confusion that these are texts "for which we cannot define a particular place."[19]

However, Prokhor had his own logic for composing the text—an alphabetical arrangement. Every new text begins with specially colored letters, and each is arranged according to alphabetical order within a given chapter (which is why these chapters of the miscellany were called *azbukovniki*). This organizational method had long prevailed in abecedaries, for instance, in alphabetic prayers, and was very popular in baroque verse texts of the seventeenth century.

Unfortunately, neither Prokhor nor his *Azbukovniki* were included in the *Slovar' drevnerusskikh knizhnikov i knizhnosti* (i.e. contemporary biographical compendium of old Russian writers), which is why it is especially important to put information about him into scientific circulation. All the biographical particulars derive from remarks he inserted into his miscellanies, sometimes as author's notes, but also as ciphered phrases that require considerable effort to decode.[20] Prokhor's nickname, "Kolomniatin," indicates that he was born in Kolomna, a town in the Moscow region. He started working on the miscellany in the reign of Tsar Feodor Alekseevich in a place called Marchugi (present-day Faustovo),[21] a village situated on the banks of the Moscow River, not far from the capital. Before 1678 the Marchugi hermitage belonged to the

Andreevskii Monastery in Plennitsy, but later it passed to the Solovetskii Monastery. Prokhor was a monk-priest (*chernyi pop*) at the hermitage.

With the tsar's support, in the 1670s and 1680s two luxurious churches and other structures were built in Marchugi. Being there in the early 1680s, Prokhor could not help but witness the construction, and he may even have helped with it. From Marchugi, Prokhor headed for the Volga (whether voluntarily or not is unknown), settling in the Ipat'evskii Monastery, where he finished his work on the miscellany in 1682. The theme of exile appears several times in texts of the miscellany, providing indirect evidence that Prokhor had not come to the Ipat'evskii Monastery freely.

The contents of the miscellany reveal Prokhor's great erudition—he drew on a multitude of different works. [22] Judging by one of his personal remarks, he was acquainted with printed books published in Moscow and Kiev, as well as those published abroad. For example, when discussing punctuation, he mentioned that Moscow publications had finally started using the correct punctuation marks, after their discovery in Greek, Latin, and especially in Kievan books (fol. 146). Prokhor also advised teachers to make use of the printed abecedaries (fol. 139v).

In 1684/85 Prokhor called himself hieromonk (*hieromonakh*)[23] and compiled a new miscellany—to order, just like the first one—for the cellarer of the Pskovopecherskii Monastery, Archdeacon Feodosii.[24] In this work he taught readers how to write letters in verse.[25]

Information about Prokhor's correspondent, Diomid Serkov, survives in archival documents and in manuscripts that belonged to him. His father was a low-ranked icon-painter of the Moscow Armory Chamber—Iakov Prokhorov Serkov—whose home was located in Moscow's icon-painters' settlement.[26] For his part, Diomid became a scribe, and is known as the author-compiler of the moralizing miscellany *Kriny selnye* (Lilies of the Field, 1692),[27] in which can be found some small borrowings from Prokhor's works. Surviving manuscripts, copied in his hand (the earliest, discovered by S. A. Semiachko, dates to the late 1670s), include acrostic verse and pasted-in engravings.[28] Apparently, in his youth he was a teacher, and in the 1690s worked as a music copyist in the patriarch's chancellery. He knew Greek and could copy poems in Greek. He was also married and had children.[29]

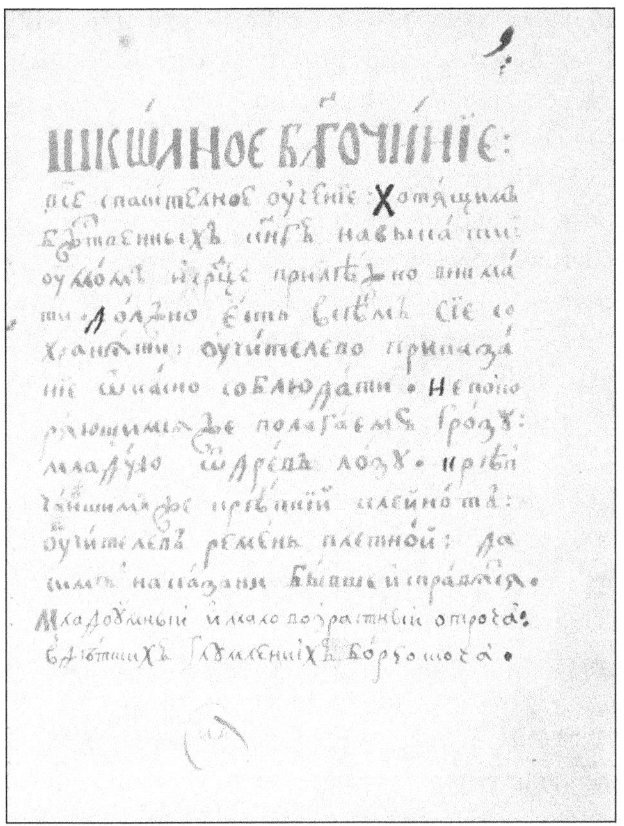

Shkol'noe blagochinie: Sbornik Azbukovnikov, RGADA f. 357, no. 60

The miscellany composed by Prokhor for Diomid is known in nine copies, if one counts both those that have survived and those that are lost but are known from earlier descriptions.[30] The autograph has not survived, but its content can be reconstructed from copies. What content did Prokhor offer to the teacher in this work? The miscellany contains seven works, each called an *azbukovnik* because the texts within are arranged in alphabetic order.[31] All are connected with school and childhood education, but every text has its own specifics and purpose:

1. *Shkol'noe blagochinie* (School rules), a dialog in verse, written by Prokhor himself, that details the rules of proper behavior in school;

2. *Azbukovnik vtoryi* (The second *azbukovnik*) models visits to school by guests and patrons, and provides samples of speeches suitable for the occasion;
3. *Azbukovnik nakazatel'nyi, uchashchimsia pisati* (Instructional *azbukovnik* for those learning how to write) gives students models for studying how to write, simultaneously loading the models with considerable educational baggage;
4. *Azbukovnik, imushchii v sebe mnogiia rechi, godstvennyia glagolati i pisati blizhnim* (*Azbukovnik* that includes many texts suitable for talking and writing to family), a miscellany of models for independent composition of verse;
5. *Azbukovnik [polnyi], ego zhe blagim uchitelem dolzhno chest' v nakazanie uchenikom povsiadnevno prochityvati* (The complete *azbukovnik*, which a good teacher should read to pupils every day) consists of various texts connected mainly to linguistics and grammar. It also includes the work entitled *O semi svobodnykh mudrostiakh* (About the seven liberal arts) along with various recommendations for the teacher;
6. *Azbukovnik o grubouchashchikhsia uchenitsekh* (*Azbukovnik* about poor pupils) is a collection of verse about how to deal with pupils who are not succeeding with their studies;
7. *Azbukovnik otpustitel'nyi, ego zhe uchenikoliubnii o gospode uchitelie dolzhenstvuiut v otpustnoj azbutse pod vsiakoiu literoiu napisovati siia* (Final *azbukovnik*) presents a model of an educational text in alphabetic order, which the teacher should use for the student who has completed his studies.

The sequence of these titles is not accidental: the content proceeds from elementary knowledge for children who have just entered school to the highest level of learning ("About the seven liberal arts"). But within individual *azbukovniki* there is no thematic structure; the author returns to the same theme several times, sometimes repeating himself, sometimes contradicting himself. This is perfectly normal for Muscovite-era miscellanies, often woven together from various texts into a patchwork blanket. But, as mentioned above, the miscellany introduces an innovative structure: every

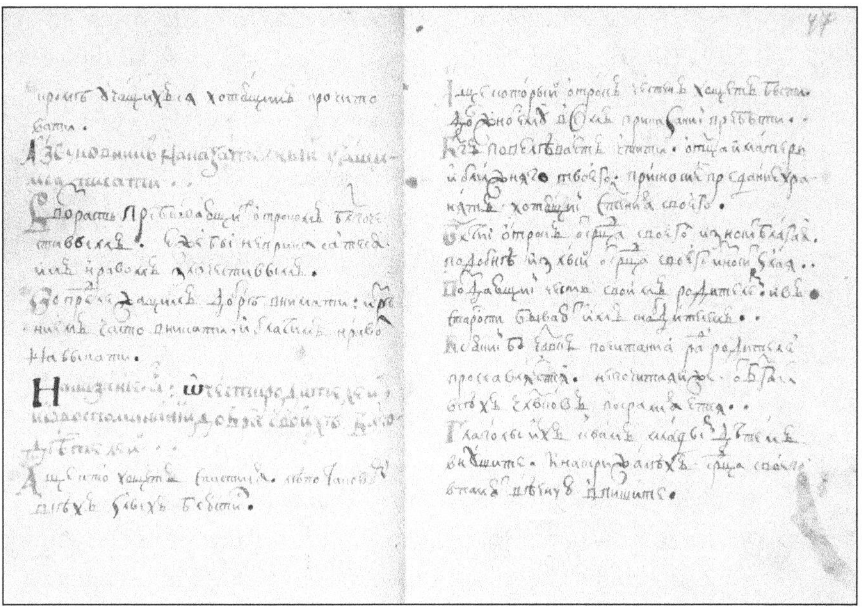

Azbukovnik nakazatel'nyi, uchashchimsia pisati, **Sbornik azbukovnikov, RGADA f. 357, no. 60, fol. 46v.-47**

text took its place according to the order of the Cyrillic alphabet. As a consequence, I shall have to systematize them myself, extracting material on education from the different parts of the miscellany.

According to Prokhor, the main purpose for studying is to learn to recognize the truth by means of reading scripture (Christ is truth). Prokhor proposes that the pupil answer the question about his studies like this: "I study the tiniest part of scripture for the benefit of my soul, for the consolation of my body, for the wonder and salvation of me and all my family," (fols. 147v–148). To see salvation as the main reason for book learning was common among Muscovite-era bookmen.

The pupil needed to know and be able to:

- pray (over and above the usual prayers), to make vows, and to fulfill the rituals connected with studying (fols. 149-150)
- recognize days of the week and Orthodox holidays, and know about the six days of creation and the doctrine of the Trinity

- complete the traditional cycle for learning to read: the abecedary, the Book of Hours, the Psalter, and then a choice among "other Holy books"
- complete the traditional curriculum for learning to write, for which models to be copied were provided
- learn all the elements of grammar as well as all Slavonic letters—their phonetics, syllables, prepositions, cases, and prosody; special attention is paid to prosody because, as the text maintains, a man who reads with the proper voice modulations and appropriate pauses shows himself to be a well-educated person. The text contains numerous marks (for emphasis, pause, etc.) to assist in proper reading, and students should know how to recognize them (fols. 124-27).
- know the history of the invention of writing (from Adam) and especially the history about Kirill the Philosopher's invention of the Slavonic alphabet as well as the translation work of his brother Mefodii (fol. 133)
- know the chronicles' story about the ancient Slavs
- master the manuals of piety (about honoring one's parents, about observing the holy canons and church precepts)
- know the meaning of names and be able to translate into Russian names from various languages (fols. 138v-139)
- know the rules of behavior in society, at school, and in church (fols. 98-99)
- know the rules of conduct and appropriate speeches to welcome guests (benefactors) who visit school
- know about "the complete philosopher," Maksim Grek (Maximus the Greek) and about how he could recognize a genuine poet (fols. 155v-158 v)
- learn the basic information about the seven liberal arts (grammar, dialectics, rhetoric, music, arithmetic, geometry, and astronomy) (fols. 162-197v)
- write poetic letters and orations

Judging by the table of contents, the miscellany included a second part that has not survived. Nevertheless, the contents make clear that the miscellany included several additional texts—about one's soul and body, about the meaning of the sacrament of baptism, several "Indices of human life," which evidently represented a collection of parables and aphorisms "from numerous books," extracts from the Old Testament, explanations of a grammar, and interpolations from the Psalter. The appendices featured works (apparently complete texts, not extracts) on wisdom, on the word of God, about "our life" of pain and joy, and about how Christ made us his heirs.[32]

ALFAVITAR' RADI UCHENIIA MALYKH DETEI (THE *ALFAVITAR'* FOR TEACHING SMALL CHILDREN)

The *Alfavitar'* is known in six copies of varying levels of completeness and preservation, all previously described in scholarly literature.[33] Two complete copies come from the monastic cell of Afanasii (1641-1702), archbishop of Kholmogory and Vaga. By unknown means, one of them surfaced in the late nineteenth century in Zhitomir (Ukraine), and fell into the hands of a man by the name of S. Cheban, who recognized its historical importance. He provided a detailed description in an article, but the manuscript itself was later lost.[34] The manuscript bore a note about its having belonged to Archbishop Afanasii, who on November 16, 1699 sent it as a gift to Ignatii, metropolitan of Tobol'sk.[35]

Afanasii was a passionate bibliophile who did not part readily with the manuscripts that he collected and carefully copied. Therefore, although he dispatched to Siberia a close copy, the original manuscript remained in his library. And it is that manuscript that Christina Bragone published. According to Bragone, the author-compiler of the manuscript was either a certain Evfimii, a monk in the Kremlin Chudov Monastery, or else someone who was related to the Grecophile party.[36] The manuscript contains Evfimii's poetry (1678-1680), the "Epistle" of his teacher, Epifanii Slavinetskii (who lived in the same monastery), and the *De civilitate morum puerilium*, translated by Slavinetskii as well.

Cheban thought that the miscellany was composed by Archbishop Afanasii, who was a passionate Grecophile and one of the best educated people of his time.[37] Both scholars have a point; it seems likely that both Evfimii and Afanasii contributed to the creation of the *Alfavitar'*. They had collaborated for many years, beginning in 1679 when Afanasii was transferred from Siberia by Patriarch Ioakim; then, in March, 1682, Afanasii was elevated to the archbishopric of Kholmogory.

Afanasii was in Moscow when a passionate debate about education swirled around Sil'vestr Medvedev's *Privilei* (Letters patent for the foundation of an academy), which Tsar Feodor had not examined before his death and now passed to the regent, Tsarevna Sophia.[38] The archbishop of Kholmogory maintained friendly contacts with representatives of the intellectual elite who were anxious about the fate of Orthodox enlightenment. Evidence survives about all the guests whom Afanasii received at this time. Among the guests were Evfimii Chudovskii (who translated works from Greek), Sil'vestr Medvedev, and Archimandrite Ignatii (to whom in Tobol'sk decades later Afanasii sent the *Alfavitar'*).[39] Afanasii maintained his friendship and collaboration with Evfimii until his death. Together they put into practice their Grecophile ideas and continued the work, begun with Patriarch Nikon's reform, of correcting Russian manuscripts on the basis of Greek models. Evfimii systematically labored over the translations of Greek Orthodox texts, then sent them for editing and copying to Kholmogory, as is clear from his letters. Several such draft texts were left in Afanasii's library. For his part, Afanasii, using his large diocesan income, financed the translators who worked with Evfimii, who hoped to publish his translations at the *Pechatnyi dvor*. However, because of disagreements with officials at the *Pechatnyi dvor*, Evfimii did not succeed in this ambition.

Afanasii himself collected a library, much of which has survived, revealing the principles he used to collect manuscripts.[40] The archbishop seems to have sought out early copies, uncorrupted by later copyists; this was especially true for translated literature. Afanasii himself carefully read and compared texts, making editorial comments in the margins. In addition, Afanasii prepared strict instructions to guide copyists who worked for him.

The problem of creating schools seems not to have been a crucial issue either for Evfimii or Afanasii. For them, it was not a school but a book (an uncorrupted book of writings of the Church Fathers) that must become the means of acquiring "pure knowledge." Probably they thought that the Slavonic-Greek-Latin Academy of the Likhud brothers settled the question of creating schools.

However, disagreements about the different paths of education were very clearly reflected in Evfimii's polemical epistles. The first epistle, written no later than 1685, is devoted to answering a question that recalls Ivan Vishenskii's remarks about education:

> Is it better for us to study grammar, rhetoric, philosophy, and theology and the art of writing verse and thereby understand scripture? Or is it better in simplicity to please God, and to know him by reading scripture without all these skills? And is it better for Russians to study Greek or Latin?[41]

Afanasii immediately made a copy of this epistle for his own use.[42] A second work, *Dovod vkratse* (The argument in brief), was begun by Evfimii, as scholars now agree, with the participation of other Grecophiles.[43] Both works unambiguously endorsed education, but at the same time introduced numerous arguments on behalf of the superiority of Greek culture. B. L. Fonkich argues that the argument over the better form of education evaporated with the arrival of the Likhud brothers, who proceeded to organize a school according to their own ideas.[44]

Of the fourteen works that entered the manuscript that Afanasii compiled in Moscow in 1685 (including the epistle, "Is it better to study . . . ?"), five later entered the *Alfavitar'*,[45] including Evfimii's verse and the Erasmus *De civilitate morum puerilium*. This coincidence implies that the miscellany of 1685 constituted a preparatory stage for the creation of the *Alfavitar'*: Evfimii's work, "Is it better to study . . .," which was not included in the miscellany, became instead its theoretical basis. Bragone suggested that the *Alfavitar'* was created in the 1680s, but it seems to me that, although work on it began in the 1680s, the final version with Afanasii's corrections (as represented by BAN Arkh. 211 and Cheban's copy) appeared only in the 1690s.

The author-compilers of the *Alfavitar'* defined its content from the very first lines: it is an abecedary that provides an elementary knowledge of Slavonic orthography (with a little bit of Greek), the basics of writing and spelling, and, finally, a familiarity with grammar enabling one to read and understand scripture. The pragmatic aim of the authors is also clearly identified: pupils who learned everything in this work "will be able to distinguish mistakes in any books" (fols. 8-9v). It was exactly to this purpose—to create "correct" manuscripts, free of all errors, unnecessary additions, and inaccurate translations—that Evfimii Chudovskii and Afanasii of Kholmogory bent all their efforts.

Prokhor's miscellany contains a similar statement: "everyone who wishes to copy scripture" must know all the grammatical material (fol. 146).

The *Alfavitar'* has the following contents:[46]

1. A table of contents
2. An introduction that explains the purpose and contents of the miscellany, and includes instructional verse from Evfimii
3. A sermon of Epifanii Slavinetskii about the love of wisdom and learning
4. A grammar (a reworked version of Lavrentii Zizanii's and Meletii Smotrytsky's grammar with parallels from Greek, along with didactic instructions)
5. *Sozrenie khristianskogo ucheniia radi malykh detei* (Review of Christian teaching for children)[47]; The first part is a prayer book that includes prayers said from first awaking in the morning to going to sleep at night—in no way do they differ from the prayers for adults. Joined to these prayers are also chapters from Erasmus *De civilitate morum puerilium*, about how children should frequent church and school, and about seeking permission to play after leaving the school. The second part—"Several questions and answers about Orthodoxy" (a catechism)—introduces several gospel and clerical commandments, articles on sin, good behavior, honoring parents, etc.
6. "About the actions of a Christian"—about the duties of a Christian and about proper relations with various social types

(parents, friends, servants, hired workers, enemies, authorities, aged men, beggars, sinners, etc.); all the texts are taken from books of the Old Testament and accompanied by references

7. About the body—a similar selection of biblical texts about how one should speak, look, sleep, eat, etc.; there are also provisions on death and burial
8. Poem about the rod [i.e., about the rod and punishment]
9. Aesop's fable about theft, discussion of behavior that should be rooted out in childhood, and a grammatical analysis of this text
10. Verses about good habits (which should be reread constantly)
11. *De civilitate morum puerilium*
12. The Questions and the answers of Afanasii from Alexandria, about how to fight against sin (texts from the works of the Church Fathers)
13. "The beginning of the numeric craft," about arithmetic

Here we have the rare and fascinating opportunity of observing how several monastic intellectuals, working independently of one another, answered the same question of what should be included in an educational miscellany. Their work began at the same time—the early 1680s—and continued into the late 1690s; this process was reflected in various copies of both miscellanies. That is why there is a certain difficulty in their comparison: copies of each miscellany differ, one from the other. With this difficulty in mind, I will focus on the most complete and best-preserved copies, since there is not space here for a detailed comparison.[48] Our purpose is to reveal the possibilities discovered by these people who wished to renew Orthodox education and introduce it to the institution of schools.

First, let us examine the physical differences between the manuscripts, for they are quite significant. In Afanasii's copies, the *Alfavitar'* opens with colored illustrations and the entire text is written in the same calligraphic hand. The miscellany bears clear signs of the archbishop's attention to detail: the material is arranged accurately and thoughtfully, chapters and paragraphs are divided and identified by titles, all the stanzas are arranged in columns (*stolbikom*), ample margins contain references to all biblical sources cited, and the editor's notes are carefully inserted in red ink. The texts of the miscellany were checked by the editor against a copy of the original. For example, in one place the pronoun "his" is accompanied by a marginal note reading: "here there is no pronoun 'his,' not in the Greek, Latin, Polish, or Slavonic variants: manuscript of Aleksei the Miracleworker" (fol. 67).

Copies of the *Azbukovniki* have a rather different appearance. These manuscripts are done in quarto, and almost all of them are similar in appearance. Their pages are filled with close handwriting, without the least pretension to elegance; the lines are undivided, making it difficult to recognize verses, and stanzas are divided only by a colon or big red period. All these traits are signs of an economical use of paper. The calligraphic skill of the copyists is not very high. The letters of the alphabet, painted in red (cinnabar), which are an especially important element for abecedaries, are written in a simple way. All this evidence allows us to conclude that Prokhor's miscellany, unlike the *Alfavitar'*, was copied in a rather poor, monastic environment.

The *Alfavitar'*, on the other hand, is so elaborately divided into chapters and paragraphs that it is not easy to recognize it as a miscellany—outwardly it resembles instead a unique, special-purpose book. The *Azbukovniki*, although they have pretensions to a similar form, in fact convey immediately the impression of a miscellany.

Now let us compare the contents of the works. The main similarity is that both are thematic miscellanies. Their creators, widely-read, competent *literati*, did their best to select texts suitable for educational purposes. Thus their miscellanies reflect the general situation of Muscovite educational literature. The texts in the miscellanies appear to be different (except the poem about the rod used for punishment).[49] However, their contents are thematically similar. In the first place, the main section in both types of miscellany is a complete grammar. The grammatical material in the *Azbukovniki* cannot be traced to any grammar known in the seventeenth century.[50] Secondly, the necessity of studying is explained and, in connection with this, the meaning of "wisdom" is revealed. Thirdly, much attention is paid to the norms and rules of pupils' conduct. Fourthly, the texts provide abundant instructions on piety, as well as threats for ignoring these instructions. In addition, catechisms and the texts of prayers are included. Both miscellanies have instructions for teachers, and in the *Azbukovniki* there is also a panegyric on the teacher's work. The miscellanies conclude with a discussion about humankind (about the soul and the body in its several parts).

In these thematic sections one finds both traditional texts borrowed from Muscovite literature as well as new, translated works that only appeared in the seventeenth century. In addition, both compilers included texts of their own composition.

Borrowing grammatical material from the repertoire of Muscovite-era literature was easy, and both authors made full use of this material, each in their own way. Writing about his miscellany, Prokhor noted that he had gathered material "from many books and especially from grammars."[51] The selection of grammatical material was based on printed models of books intended "for the teaching of children." Bragone emphasizes that the *Alfavitar'* "testifies to the stable structure of the traditional abecedary, worked out in the *Azbuka* printed in Lvov in 1574 by Ivan Feodorov."[52] In the *Azbukovniki*, the grammatical material is accompanied by traditional articles about the origin of Slavonic writing, about Kirill and Mefodii, etc., which were also in abecedaries. In the *Alfavitar'*, one of Aesop's fables ("About a mother and her son"), along with a grammatical analysis of it, has been added to the section on grammar.

It was easy to find in the books of the New and Old Testaments instructions about proper Christian behavior, about avoiding sin and living a pious life, about keeping God's precepts, and about genuine faith—in other words, an entire colossal compendium of admonitions to Christian piety. In his time, the author of the Domostroi, the priest Sil'vestr, pointed to the Books of Jesus, son of Sirach, and to the Proverbs of Solomon for the same purpose.[53] Citations from the works of the Church Fathers—especially from John Chrysostom, a favorite in Russia—were also readily used as instructions for children. However, in the *Azbukovniki* and in the *Alfavitar'* these texts are presented differently. Afanasii and Evfimii accurately cited the texts and gave references to sources in the margins. Prokhor, however, very seldom provided references, and he habitually rearranged biblical texts in verse form. This practice was not his invention: rearrangement of instructional texts from scripture into verse was popular in baroque culture. Already in the 1640s, a monk named Savvatii, an editor (*spravshchik*) in the *Pechatnyi dvor*, directly explained the structure of his manual of "Instructions for the student" with these words:

> Although composed in couplets,
> All the same it is taken from Holy Scripture.
>
> (*Ashche i dvoestrochiem slogaetsia,*
> *no obache ot togo zh Bozhestvennogo pisaniia izbiraetsia*).[54]

With these materials our author-compilers exhausted the possibilities of Muscovite book learning, except for some tiny, additional fragments. Therefore, they both addressed new translated works, but again, different ones. The *Alfavitar'* borrowed Erasmus's work, *De civilitate morum puerilium*. For Evfimii, the apprentice of the translator, it was quite natural to use this text. It seems paradoxical that the translation of this work, written by a Western author in a genre unusual for Muscovite literature (secular rules for the behavior of youth), should have been undertaken within monastic walls by adherents of Greek culture. But the Chudov Monastery was no ordinary monastery, and was situated beyond the Kremlin walls. One of the foreigners who visited Moscow in 1675 wrote down these impressions of the Chudov Monastery: "better to call it an aristocratic educational institution than a monastery; for there one rarely sees anyone other than the children of boyars and important officials. They place them there to separate them from ordinary society and to teach them proper behavior."[55] It was evidently for these pupils that the *De civilitate morum puerilium* and the instructional epistles of Epifanii Slavinetskii (about the "bright rays" of Greek learning destroying "the gloomy darkness of ignorance" [fol. 10]) were intended. Certainly the inclusion in the *Alfavitar'* of lessons on arithmetic (even in very abbreviated form) side by side with those on grammar represented a new trend.

Prokhor also addressed the theme of secular behavior, especially in school. He evidently used the charters of Ukrainian and Belorussian schools, somewhat arbitrarily rearranging them into verse. The text "About the seven liberal arts" occupies much of Prokhor's *Azbukovniki*, and Prokhor generated his own prefaces for the speeches delivered by each personified liberal art, or "wisdom."[56] Prefaces like these had been written by Nikolai Spafarii in the 1670s,[57] but it appears that Prokhor did not know about this work and independently produced his own prefaces. His style of thinking emerges here as completely different from that of Spafarii, who provided a definition for each art (for instance, geometry or rhetoric), and then developed the points of the text, referring to antique authorities. For Prokhor the starting point for the discussion of each art is the divinity of the universe: God encourages human understanding of the world He created, but without forgetting human limitations.

The poem about the rod appears in both miscellanies: it is used twice in different variants in the *Azbukovniki*;[58] in the *Alfavitar'* there is a third version, titled "A gift to children who study" (fol. 68). This verse also has a Western origin: one encounters similar verses in German textbooks of the sixteenth century and also in Ukrainian *koliadki* (Christmas carols).[59]

The absence in both the *Alfavitar'* and the *Azbukovniki* of Simeon Polotsky's legacy, familiar to the authors of both miscellanies, is remarkable. That Evfimii Chudovskii was critical of Polotsky is evident in several sources, including his epigram on Polotsky's work, *Obed dushevnyi* (Dinner for the soul, published in 1681):

> This newly-created book, Dinner,
> Is full of food harmful to the soul.[60]

What works of the compilers' own authorship were included in these miscellanies? The *Alfavitar'* contains an extended preface, beginning "dear reader," that explains the purpose of the textbook and its importance. It also contains Evfimii's verses about death ("Death must never be forgotten . . ."), about ascetic rules of sleeping ("Young man, don't sleep on a made bed . . ."), and several others, including some translated from Greek. Evidently Evfimii did not write these verses for a children's textbook, but they were later adapted for that purpose. So, for example, the word "monk," was replaced by the word "youth."[61]

The *Azbukovniki* opened with a work entitled *Shkol'noe blagochinie* (School rules) that Prokhor himself composed; indeed, in the majority of texts Prokhor introduced something of his own. For example, in "the complete *Azbukovnik*" he added an eight-lined verse introduction to each letter.

The *Azbukovniki* paid considerable attention to orations and epistles, both in verse and in prose. Determining what Prokhor himself composed and what he borrowed from other authors is impossible, but several details (for example, the repetition of epistles in his other miscellany composed for the cellarer Feodosii) point to his authorship. He compiled a list of citations with which one could independently compose an epistle in verse (fols. 53-82). This material constituted an important part of one's education, and helped young people learn how to organize communications. Knowing how to write letters also entered into the educational program of the Kiev-Mohilev Academy, whose texts combined knowledge of both rhetoric and poetics. An obligatory part of these texts was their request for protection and patronage.[62] Epistles or letters had to help youths appeal for protection from influential people. They were original, and appeared in "high" verse forms, unlike common prose letters—and this helped a youth attract special attention.

So, the two miscellanies are both very similar and, at the same time, very different. They both bear the spirit of the age and the intellectual inclinations of their authors. Compilers of the *Alfavitar'* used it to advance their Grecophile cultural program. The compiler of the *Azbukovniki*, on the other hand, seemed not to lean toward either Greek or Latin culture; he evidently felt closer to Kievan learning. In general, the content of the *Azbukovniki* is broader and displays more variety than the contents of *Alfavitar'*. Apparently Prokhor was more interested in word-play—composition of verse, acrostics, ciphered writing, etc.—than in pedagogy. For the sake of education, he wanted to cultivate in both pupils and their teachers a love of writing.

So how does our analysis of these educational miscellanies answer the question of our title, "What should one teach?" The answer seems to be, "teach everything that was taught previously"—an ability to read books that are spiritually edifying, and to understand scripture, through which one can travel the true path to salvation. However, Prokhor (and the other authors of educational miscellanies) proposed to teach all this material in a new way—using poetic texts. In general, the proportion devoted to verse in both miscellanies significantly exceeds that of the various abecedaries.

What was radically new in the miscellanies examined here was, first, the inclusion of secular rules of behavior for children at home and in public, and, secondly, instruction in the norms of communication with people of various social ranks. Here was laid out the principle of learning civilized manners, not only moral and customary behavior, but also etiquette. For the first time a teacher's work was devoted not only to saving a pupil's soul, but also to his socialization. Exactly this theme was continued in the eighteenth-century textbook, *Iunosti chestnoe zertsalo* (The fair mirror of youth, 1717) that was especially popular in Petrine times. However, "Mirror" was directed towards Western European etiquette. The *Alfavitar'*, by presenting to readers Erasmus's text on behavior, involuntarily leaned in the same direction, but counterbalanced this inclination by also referencing strict church rules. The *Azbukovniki* was oriented to the pre-Petrine traditions of etiquette, about which very little is known. All the same, it is clear that traditional Russian polite behavior (depending upon hierarchical relations in society) differed significantly from its Western European parallel. Even persons who were equal in social status deployed a certain calculus to determine who was "higher"—using age, rank, the monarch's favor, distinguished ancestors, etc. Consequently, the code of politeness was egocentric—politeness was embodied in self-abnegating forms.[63] Prokhor's epistles and orations reflect exactly this type of social relations.

Overall, learning how to communicate with God through pious behavior, through prayers, and through reading religious material—all of which was accepted in monastic practice—was supplemented with education in the etiquette of communication in society.

In comparison with the literature of the Latin tradition, Orthodox literature could boast but few texts connected with education, which was natural, given the absence of school practices. The last quarter of the seventeenth century saw the creation of books devoted to the education of Orthodox children and a search for the optimal form and contents of these books. This search proceeded along various paths, but its beginning had been established. Already at the century's end there appeared the first educational book that was not a miscellany of various texts. This was Karion Istomin's common letters abecedary, in which every letter in Cyrillic, Latin, and Greek is accompanied by verses and pictures.

NOTES

* I am grateful for support from the Russian Foundation for Humanities while researching and writing this article (grant 13-06-00149a). This article was translated by Maria Ispol'nova and Daniel H. Kaiser.

1 I. M. Gritsevskaia, *Chtenie i chet'i sborniki v drevnerusskikh monastyriakh* (Saint Petersburg: Dmitrii Bulanin, 2012), 150.

2 Gary Marker has taught us a lot about printed abecedaries. See his "Petrine Civil Primers Reconsidered: A New Look at the Publishing History of the 'Grazhdanskaia Azbuka,' 1708-1727," *Solanus*, NS 3 (1989): 25-39; Marker, "Primers and Literacy in Muscovy: A Taxonomic Investigation," *Russian Review* 48 (1989): 1-19; Marker, "Literacy and Literary Texts in Muscovy: A Reconsideration," *Slavic Review* 49 (1990): 74-89. Here I examine the manuscript history of abecedary miscellanies.

3 S. A. Semiachko, "'Starchestvo' i sbornik 'Starchestvo' na Rusi," *Russkaia literatura*, no. 1, 2008, 144-153.

4 S. A. Semiachko, "Sbornik 'Starchestvo': variant Solovetskogo monastyria," *Trudy otdela drevnerusskoi literatury* 55 (2004): 343-357; Semiachko, "Sbornik 'Starchestvo' v Kirillo-Belozerskom monastyre," in *Knizhnye tsentry Drevnei Rusi: Kirillo-belozerskii monastyr'* (Saint Petersburg: Dmitrii Bulanin, 2008), 211-295.

5 Cited from *Antologiia pedagogicheskoi mysli Ukrainskoi SSR* (Moscow: Pedagogika, 1988), 96-97.

6 On the works of Simeon Polotsky from a confessional point of view, see M. A. Korzo, *Nravstvennoe bogoslovie Simeona Polotskogo: osvoenie katolicheskoi traditsii Moskovskimi knizhnikami vtoroi poloviny 17 v.* (Moscow: IFRAN, 2011).

7 B. L. Fonkich, *Greko-slavianskie shkoly v Moskve v 17 veke* (Moscow: Iazyki slavianskikh kul'tur, 2009), 235-37.

8 I. K. Kuprianov, "Materialy dlia istorii russkoi pedagogii. Iz rukopisi proshlogo stoletiia: Nastavlenie malym detiam i ob obychaiakh v uchilishe," *Zhurnal Ministerstva Narodnogo Prosveshcheniia* (January 1856): 32-37 (app. 7); D. L. Mordovtsev, *O russkikh shkol'nykh knigakh 17 veka* (Moscow, 1862); A. N. Petrov, "Ob Afanas'evskom sbornike 17 veka i zakliuchaiushchikhsia v nem azbukovnikakh," *Pamiatniki drevnei pis'mennosti* 120 (1896), app. 4; S. Cheban, "K istorii uchebno-pedagogicheskoi literatury Moskovskoi Rusi 17 veka," *Zhurnal Ministerstva Narodnogo Prosveshcheniia* (October, 1915): 129-64.

9 V. V. Bush, *Pamiatniki starinnogo russkogo vospitaniia (k istorii drevne-russkoi pis'mennosti i kul'tury)* (Petrograd: Tip. Kiugel'gen, Glich i Ko., 1918).

10 M. Ch. Bragone, *Alfavitar radi uchenija malych detej. Un abbecedario nella Russia del Seicento.* Biblioteca di Studi Slavistici (Firenze: Firenze University Press, 2008).

11 M. Ch. Bragone, "*De civilitate morum puerilium* Erazma Rotterdamskogo v Rossii (kon. XVII - perv. pol. XVIII v.)," in *Eighteenth-Century Russia: Society, Culture, Economy*, ed. Roger Bartlett and Gabriela Lehmann-Carli (Berlin: Lit, 2007), 191-206. For more on the historiography of this work, see O. E. Kosheleva, "*Grazhdanstvo obychaev detskikh*: istoriia izucheniia pamiatnika i ego rol' v russkoi kul'ture XVII v.," in *Aktual'nye voprosy istoriografii i istochnikovedeniia istorii shkoly i pedagogiki* (Moscow: APN, 1986), 119-39; Bragone, "*De civilitate morum puerilium*," 191-93.

12 Gritsevskaia, *Chtenie*, 319.

13 Daniel C. Waugh, *Istoriia odnoi knigi: Viatka i "ne-sovremennost'" russkoi kultury v epokhu Petra Velikogo* (Saint Petersburg: Dmitrii Bulanin, 2003); B. N. Morozov and P. S. Stefanovich, *Roman Vilimovich v gostiakh u Petra Ignat'evicha: Pskovskii arkhiv angliiskogo kuptsa 1680-kh godov* (Moscow: Indrik, 2009); O. S. Sapozhnikova, *Russkii knizhnik 17 veka Sergii Shelonin* (Moscow: Al'ians-Arkheo, 2010); Gritsevskaia, *Chtenie;* Semiachko, "'Starchestvo' i sbornik 'Starchestvo,'" and her numerous other works on this subject.

14 The manuscript of this miscellany does not bear a title, and therefore none appears in the historiography either; consequently, I have given it the conditional title *Sbornik shkol'nykh azbukovnikov*.

15 Spravshchik Savvatii, "Nastavleniia ucheniku (kn. M. N. Odoevskomu)," *Pamiatniki literatury Drevnei Rusi,* 10 vols. in 13 books (Moscow: Pamiatniki khudozhestvennoi literatury, 1978-94), vol. 10, bk. 3, 18-20; RNB. Q.I.347; RNB. Q.I. 327; RNB. Ermitazhnoe sobranie, d. 22.

16 Here I cite the text of the *Azbukovniki* from the copy of RGADA, f. 357, no. 60. Folio numbers appear in brackets in the text.

17 See A. S. Demin, "Dialog 'Shkol'noe blagochinie' Prokhora Kolomniatina," in A. S. Demin, *O drevnerusskom literaturnom tvorchestve. Opyt tipologii s 11 po 18 vek. Ot Illariona do Lomonosova* (Moscow: Iazyki slavianskoi kul'tury, 2003), 433-39.

18 Ibid.

19 Bush, *Pamiatniki*, 32.

20 Bush, *Pamiatniki*, 23-29; Petrov, "Ob Afanas'evskom sbornike," 86-101; Demin, "Dialog 'Shkol'noe blagochinie' Prokhora Kolomniatina," 434-38.

21 Petrov, "Ob Afanas'evskom sbornike," 98.

22 See O. E. Kosheleva, "Formation of the 17th century intellectual elite and the works of Prokhor Kolomniatin," *Questio Rossica* 1 (2013): 79-89.

23 Ibid., 85.

24 Ibid.

25 O. E. Kosheleva, "Kak sochiniat' poslania v virshchakh? Uroki Prokhora Kolomniatina (1680-e gg.)," in *Chelovek chitaiushchii: mezhdu real'nost'iu i tekstom istochnika* (Moscow: IVI RAN, 2011), 283-316.

26 M. V. Nikolaeva, *Slovar' ikonopistsev i zhivopistsev Oruzheinoi Palaty 1630-1690-e gody: dvorovladeniia, sobytiia povsednevnoi zhizni, rabota po chastnym zakazam* (Moscow: Drevlekhranilishche, 2012), nos. 179, 197 (pp. 325-27, 377-82).

27 S. A. Semiachko, "Ob avtografe Diomida Serkova v sbornike 'Kriny sel'nye,'" *Trudy otdela drevnerusskoi literatury* 54 (2003): 613-22.

28 A. M. Turilov, "Diomid Serkiv," in *Slovar' knizhnikov i knizhnosti Drevnei Rusi,* 3 vols. in 7 bks. (Leningrad/Saint Petersburg: Nauka/Dmitrii Bulanin, 1987-2012), vol. 3, bk. 3, 351-52.

29 S. A. Semiachko, "Avtograf Diomida Serkova v Biblioteke Akademii Nauk," *Materialy i soobshcheniia po fondam Rukopisnogo otdela BAN* (Saint Petersburg: Biblioteka Rossiskoi Akademii Nauk, 2013), 133-35.

30 1) Afanasievskii copy (late seventeenth century), lost; 2) RGB, F. 96 (lost); 3) Collection of Florishev Monastery (late seventeenth century, lost); 4) RNB Q.III.6 (late seventeenth century); 5) RNB, Mikhailovsky collection, № 521 (late seventeenth – early eighteenth century); 6) BAN, 3315.137 (late seventeenth century); 7) RNB. F. XIV. 73 (early eighteenth century); 8) RGADA. F. 357, no. 60 (late seventeenth century), 9) Kazan' university library, Otdel redkikh knig, no XII/81 1415 (late seventeenth century).

31 "Az" and "buki" are the first letters of the Cyrillic alphabet. The word "azbukovnik" is taken from these letters and refers to an alphabetically organized book or text. This name was given to several types of manuscripts: primarily dictionaries, but also miscellanies containing various text extracts or verses gathered by the compiler into alphabetic order. In our case, the compiler Prokhor named seven different compositions for schoolchildren each as an "azbukovnik . . . [with further description of the text]" and put them together in one miscellany. As Prokhor did not provide any title to the whole document, I conditionally name this miscellany as "The school azbukovniki".

32 For the table of contents, see Petrov, "Ob Afanas'evskom sbornike," 98.

33 RGB, f. 173, no. 108; RGB, f. 299, no. 487; RNB, Sophiskaia collection, no 1208; RNB, Q. I. 237; BAN, Arkhangel'skaia collection, no. 211; manuscript used by S. Cheban (lost). Here I cite from BAN, Arkh. 211, which had been published by Bragone, *Alfavitar radi uchenija malych detej.*

34 Cheban, "K istorii uchebno-pedagogicheskoi literatury," 129-64.

35 Ibid., 137.

36 Bragone, *Alfavitar*, 286.

37 V. Veriuzhskii, *Afanasii, arkhiepiskop Kholmogorskii, ego zhizn' i trudy v sviazi s istoriei Kholmogorskoi eparkhii za pervye 20 let ee sushchestvovaniia i voobshche russkoi tserkvi v kontse 17 v.* (Saint Petersburg, 1908).

38 For more detail, see B. L. Fonkich, "'Privilegiia na akademiu' Simeona Polotskogo—Sil'vestra Medvedeva," *Ocherki feodal'noi Rossii* 4 (2000): 286-91.

39 Veriuzhskii, *Afanasii, arkhiepiskop*, 496.

40 M. V. Kukushkina, *Monastyrskie biblioteki Russkogo Severa* (Leningrad: Nauka. 1977), 185-97.

41 BAN, Arkh. no. 164, fols. 153-185. For the published text, see B. L. Fonkich, *Greko-slavianskie shkoly*, 239-45.

42 Fonkich, *Greko-slavianskie shkoly*, 236.

43 RGB, f. 173. II, no. 35. fols. 153-58; Fonkich, *Greko-slavianskie shkoly*, 241-43.

44 Fonkich, *Greko-slavianskie shkoly*, 237.

45 BAN, Arkh. no. 164.

46 For more detail, see Bragone, *Alfavitar*, 18, 24.

47 V. V. Bush, who didn't know BAN, Arkh. 211, published the text from other copies; see Bush *Pamiatniki*, 58-87.

48 BAN, Arkh. 211; RGADA, f. 357, no. 60.

49 BAN, Arkh. 211, fols. 68-68v.; RGADA, f. 357, no. 60, fols. 1-2.

50 Demin, "Dialog," 435.

51 Mordovtsev, *O russkikh shkol'nykh knigakh*, 38.

52 Bragone, *Alfavitar*, 178-79.

53 Domostroi: RGADA, f. 188, no. 1380, chapters 14-18.

54 Savvatii, "Nastavlenia," 18-20.

55 *Posol'stvo Kunraada-fan-Klenka k tsariam Alekseiu Mikhailovichu i Fedoru Alekseevichu* (Saint Petersburg, 1900), 521.

56 A. I. Sobolevskii, *Perevodnaia literatura Moskovskoi Rusi XIV-XVII vekov* (Saint Petersburg, 1903), 166-68.

57 O. A. Belobrova relates these prefaces to the genre of teaching aids: *Nikolai Spafary. Esteticheskie traktaty*, ed. O. A. Belobrova (Leningrad: Nauka, 1978), 15.

58 For more details, see O. E. Kosheleva, "Ustrasheneie detei rozgami v russkikh tekstakh XVII veka: Literaturnaia traditsiia ili real'nost'?" *Istoriia* 6 (22) (2013) http://www.history.jes.su/issue.2013.4.11.6-22 (accessed June 18, 2012).

59 Gerald Strauss, *Luther's House of Learning: Indoctrination of the Young in the German Reformation* (Baltimore: Johns Hopkins University Press, 1978), 180, 355 (I thank Margarita Korzo for this reference); Bragone, *Alfavitar*, 218-219.

60 Cited from L. I. Sazonova, *Literaturnaia kul'tura Rossii. Rannee Novoe vremia* (Moscow: Iazyki slavianskikh kul'tur, 2006), 98.

61 Bragone, *Alfavitar*, 178-79.

62 A. S. Demin, "Otryvki is neizvestnykh poslanii i pisem XVI - XVII vv.," *Trudy otdela drevnerusskoi literatury* 21 (1965): 66.

63 T. V. Larina, *Kategoriia vezhlivosti i stil' kommunikatsii. Sopostavlenie angliiskikh i russkikh lingvokul'turnykh traditsii* (Moscow: Iazyki slavianskikh kul'tur, 2009), 140.

The Education of Parish Clergy in the Kyiv Eparchy in the 1770s

Maksym Iaremenko
*(National University of Kyiv-Mohyla Academy)**

Over the course of the eighteenth century, the ecclesiastical authorities of the Russian Empire strove to prepare suitable successors for the parish clergy by compelling clerical children to study in Latin schools, the early modern term for the Orthodox Ukrainian Kyiv Academy and other colleges modeled on Catholic practices.[1] In Ukraine, however, efforts aimed at the "educational disciplining" of the clergy date back to the reforms of Petro Mohyla in the 1630s and 1640s. These reforms, which were intended to strengthen the Orthodox Church and codify the faith, placed an emphasis on the preparation of a well-educated clergy; one of the most important steps in implementing these changes was the foundation of the Collegium in 1632. Thus, we can hardly speak of an eighteenth-century "new world" of schooling in the Kyiv Eparchy.[2]

Petro Mohyla's concern for the preparation of well-educated priests was shared by later generations of church hierarchs. The model for a parish priest offered in the 1680s by the Bishop Joseph

Shumlianskyi (of Lviv) was concerned, among other things, with clerical education, which was supposed to include the study of Polish and Latin (thus, Latin schools); the bishop also demanded that priests attend to the education of their sons.[3] A decree of the Kyiv Synod issued in 1691 includes education as a requirement for the acquisition of an ecclesiastical livelihood:

> Priests should send their sons for education to the Kyivan confraternal schools for seven years; priests unwilling to send their children to schools should be compelled by the archpriest to this act, beneficial to the holy church; otherwise, the sons of priests who do not study in the Kyivan schools should not hope to receive ordination to the priesthood, while those who study well will acquire it easily without expenses.[4]

If students progressed well through the mandatory seven years of schooling, they would advance to higher levels and begin the study of philosophy.

Consequently, by the second half of the seventeenth century, the Kyiv Eparchy already had in place the necessary institutional means (i.e., the academy) to educate sons of parish priests before they began clerical service. But did the requirement for schooling and the provision of schools actually result in a better educated Ukrainian clergy? Existing scholarship has yet to evaluate the success of this "educational disciplining" of the parish clergy, in large part because of pessimism about the available evidence. Some, like Sophia Senyk, have asserted the impossibility of statistical analysis, relying instead on impressions gained from study of individual documents.[5]

In fact, at least from the last third of the eighteenth century, sufficient data survive to permit a quantitative evaluation of the success of the educational efforts of the church in several deaneries (*protopopii*) of the Kyiv Eparchy.

In compliance with a decree of August 30, 1771, reports from the deaneries, which included detailed information about the parish clergy (such as their education, age, marital status, and children), had to be sent to the consistory. Evidently, the initiative to record clerical information in this manner came from Metropolitan Gabriel (formerly the archbishop of Saint Petersburg), who had recently been nominated to the Kyivan seat.[6] It seems likely that the decree was motivated by the need to learn the state of affairs in the eparchy, particularly in the aftermath of the plague (which struck Kyiv in 1770 and receded only in January, 1771), since similar reports about monks were also requested from monasteries.[7]

Data recorded in compliance with this decree are perfectly suited for the study of the parish clergy in the Kyiv Eparchy. Inasmuch as the consistory archives contain a variety of reports about the clergy from the 1770s, and since annual rosters of students in the Kyiv-Mohyla Academy survive from the late 1730s on, church authorities could easily have cross-checked parish data against other documents, thereby improving accuracy. Although the outbreak of plague in 1770-71 interfered with the completeness of the data (indeed, there are records of parishes without any priests), the percentage of such incomplete data is very low, justifying confidence in the records. Furthermore, in some ways the outbreak of the epidemic is actually useful for our purposes here—if priests were dying, church authorities had an excellent opportunity to implement their policies by nominating graduates of the Latin schools to the vacant parishes.

On the other hand, it was possible to recover clerical data from only seven denearies of the Kyiv Eparchy; the others either do not survive or have not been identified in archival inventories. All seven registers were compiled roughly at the same time—between 1771 and 1774—and contain information on a total of 304 churches, 405 priests, and 36 deacons.[8] These numbers confirm that, as a rule, deacons were present only in towns and cities, and their number was regulated by statute.[9] The decree of 1768, in particular, dictated that there should be two deacons appointed for every three priests and one deacon for every two priests. A deacon could be appointed to a single parish, but only in "important places" (*znatnye mesta*).[10] For purposes of the present analysis, priests and deacons are combined into a single group: the ordination (or permission to serve in a parish, in instances where the candidate had been ordained prior to entering the eparchy) was, in both cases, supervised by the bishop. Therefore, church authorities could verify the attainment of relevant educational qualifications for both offices.

In 1770, the Kyiv Eparchy was divided into twenty-three deaneries and one vice-deanery (*khrestova namistniia*); these units included a total of 1,249 churches (excluding churches under the administration of monasteries), 1,841 priests, and 169 deacons.[11] In 1772, the number of churches rose to 1,256; in 1776, there were 1,250.[12] In other words, the seven deaneries studied here represent about a quarter (just over 24%) of the churches, 22% of the priests, and 21% of the deacons in the Kyiv Eparchy.

The seven deaneries were not equidistant from the center of the eparchy, where the Kyiv-Mohyla Academy (the institution where the priests of this particular eparchy were educated) was located: five deaneries (Glukhivs'ka, Romens'ka, Sorochyns'ka, Reshetylivs'ka, and Kobeliats'ka) were situated some distance from Kyiv, whereas Pyriatyns'ka and Kyiv-Pechers'ka found themselves in the immediate vicinity. Location had additional consequences: some deaneries were far from international borders (Pyriatyns'ka, Sorochyns'ka), while others lay near those shared with the Polish-Lithuanian Commonwealth (Kyiv-Pechers'ka), Russia (Glukhivs'ka), Slobozhanshchyna (Romens'ka), or with Zaporozhian lands and the steppe (Kobeliats'ka, Reshetylivs'ka). Some of the deaneries were located close to the centers of other dioceses, where one could obtain education in a different Latin school. Pyriatyns'ka, for example, was located closer to the center of the Pereiaslav Eparchy than to Kyiv.

Other differences among the deaneries stand out. While some had predominantly urban parishes, others were mostly rural. In some the Cossack class (the upper social stratum of Little Russia) predominated, whereas in others the lower orders were most numerous. Finally, data allow study of the clergy of the two capitals of the Hetmanate: a part of Kyiv (capital of the eparchy and the administrative district) and Glukhiv (capital of the Hetmanate). Thus, even if at present it is impossible to judge how representative of the entire eparchy these deaneries are, their records offer sufficient detail to permit a thorough analysis of the education levels of the late eighteenth-century parish clergy. The evidence indicates that, despite important differences in educational levels (and, therefore, different levels of success in "educational disciplining"), parish culture generally resisted the efforts of the authorities to obtain a better-educated clergy.

GENERAL DATA

General statistical data for the seven deaneries indicate that the level of clerical education within the Kyivan Eparchy was far from ideal: only 37% of priests and deacons had gone through the Latin education. Only a quarter of these had attended or completed theological studies and about a third had mastered philosophy and rhetoric. There were some who had left school early, without reaching even the intermediate level (poesy or *piïtyka*), but these clergy constituted less than 6% of the former students. Of the clergy mentioned in the records, 60% were literate—that is, had an elementary level of education and had mastered *rus'ka gramota*, a term that seems to have signified proficiency in reading and writing.[13]

After analyzing literacy and education in eighteenth-century Russia, Gary Marker concluded that students educated in the traditional elementary schools, which used the primer, the Book of Hours, and the Psalter, would be unable to read books printed in the civil script. Therefore, the ability to read books printed in the two scripts implied a kind of bilingualism, two separate types of literacy—religious and secular. Apparently the secular clergy was the carrier of the former; according to synodal records that Marker studied, most parish priests in the 1780s could not read books in the civil script.[14] Professor Marker's conclusions match information about the social composition of the reading public gleaned from records of subscriptions to books and periodicals during the second half of the eighteenth century. According to one study, clergy constituted only 6.1% of the 8,500 individual subscribers to secular publications. More than half of these were bishops and abbots, meaning that less than 3% of subscribers came from the lower clergy. In the 1780s, the number of archpriests, presbyters and deacons who subscribed to these publications, and who therefore can be presumed to have read civil script, was only 215 for the whole empire.[15]

The relationship between mastery of *rus'ka gramota* and the ability to read civil script deserves special study. Nevertheless, in my own work I have never encountered any mention of a priest's inability to read the civil script. On the contrary, clergy signatures that appear in church records do not resemble the Church Slavonic script found in primers, the Book of Hours, etc., and therefore suggest that Ukrainian priests could cope with the civil script.

The evidence indicates a wide dispersion of educational experience across the deaneries: the proportion of clergymen who had partaken in Latin learning ranged from a low of 27% to a high of 55%.

CENTER VS. PERIPHERY

Evidently, being located in the metropolitan capital or close to it did not guarantee that the ecclesiastical authorities would comply with the instructions to nominate well-educated pastors: there were fewer educated priests in the Kyiv-Pechers'ka *protopopiia*, located close to the metropolitan and the Kyiv Academy, than in the remote frontier deaneries (Reshetylivs'ka and Kobeliats'ka; see Table 1). On the other hand, both the general data of the seven *protopopii* (51% vs. 37%) and the data from the individual church-administrative centers within the deaneries indicate that clergy serving within deanery centers had higher levels of education than did their parallels in the peripheries.[18] Only in the Kobeliats'ka *protopopiia* was the percentage of those who had gone through Latin courses slightly higher in the entire region than in the town of Kobeliaky itself (47% and 43%, respectively). In my opinion, this feature has to do with the unique nature of Kobeliats'ka, which was the most urban of all the *protopopii*. Only five of its thirty-three parishes were rural, and 85% of its churches were located in small towns. However, in the majority of deaneries (five out of seven), former students constituted no more than half the clergy, even in the places where the administrative authorities were located (see Table 2).

Table 1 Education of the Parish Clergy/Numbers of Individuals Reporting Study of the Following Subjects*

Educational level / Deanery, year	Theology	Philosophy	Rhetoric	Poesy	Syntax	Grammar	Latin learning	Some Latin (*Malo i latyni*)	*Rus'ka gramota*	Some *Rus'ka gramota* proficiency ("*Ruskoj gramoty pochasti umijet*")	Not specified	Total number of persons	Number of parish churches
Romens'ka, 1771	6	10	12	4	–	1	–	–	57[16] (63%)	–	–	90	61
	33 (37%)												
Kobeliats'ka, 1772	6	5	8	2	–	–	–	–	22 (49%)	–	2	45	33
	21 (47%)												
Pyriatyns'ka, 1772	8	16	12	2	3	–	–	–	53 (56%)	–	1	95	64
	41 (43%)												
Sorochyns'ka, 1772	5	6	12	1	–	–	–	1	56 (68%)	1	–	82	58
	25 (30%)												
Reshetylivs'ka, 1773	1	4	4	1	–	–	1	–	9 (45%)	–	–	20	14
	11 (55%)												
Glukhivs'ka, 1774 p.	7	4	5	–	1	–	–	1	45[17] (67%)	–	4	67	43
	18 (27%)												
Kyiv-Pechers'ka, 1774	5	5	5	–	1	–	–	–	24 (57%)	–	2	42	31
	16 (38%)												
Total	**38**	**50**	**58**	**10**	**5**	**1**	**1**	**2**	**266 (60%)**	**1**	**9**	**441**	**304**

* Here we define "Latin learning" as encompassing any of the first 8 columns from the left: from Theology to "Some Latin."

Table 2 Education of the Parish Clergy from the Centers of the Deaneries (*Protopopii*)

Educational level / Center Of Deanery	Theology	Philosophy	Rhetoric	Poesy	Syntax	Latin learning	Some Latin	*Rus'ka gramota*	Not specified	Total number of persons	Number of parish churches
Glukhiv	5[19]	1	–	–	–	–	1	12	–	19	7
	7 (37%)										
Kyiv-Pechers'k	1	3	1	–	–	–	–	4	1	10	5
	5 (50%)										
Kobeliaky	1	1	3	1	–	–	–	8	–	14	9
	6 (43%)										
Pyriatyn	–	1	2	–	1	–	–	4	–	8	4
	4 (50%)										
Reshetylivka	1	3	1	–	–	1	–	1	–	7	6
	6 (86%)										
Romny	3	2	3	–	–	–	–	5	–	13	4
	8 (62%)										
Sorochyntsi	–	1	–	1	–	–	1	3	–	6	3
	3 (50%)										
Total	**11 (14%)**	**12 (16%)**	**10 (13%)**	**2 (3%)**	**1 (1%)**	**1 (1%)**	**2 (3%)**	**37**	**1**	**77**	**38**
	39 (51%)										

CLERICAL ELITES VS. SUBORDINATES

The Kyiv Eparchy was divided into *protopopii*, which, in turn, were managed by archpriests who were assisted by *namisnyky*. As it turns out, all the archpriests in the seven deaneries studied here had attended Latin schools, but not all had mastered theology: only one had completed the full curriculum, and another had studied theology for one year instead of the required four. Two more archpriests had studied philosophy; the other three, rhetoric. Among the ten assistants, on the other hand, there were three who had not attended any school and possessed only basic literacy skills. Of the rest of the *namisnyky*, four had studied theology, and one each of the remaining three had studied philosophy, rhetoric, and syntax. If we combine the two groups, we find that 82% of the "top brass" had received education beyond elementary literacy but only 35% had completed or even begun the study of theology, the level mandated by the authorities. Thus, the program of "educational disciplining" was not fully successful even at the middle level of the administration.

This situation can be explained by the fact that the ecclesiastical authorities were not always free to follow the legal requirements, as they also had to take into account the wishes of powerful patrons and the social status of the candidates. For instance, in order to reward Oleksandr Ladynskyi, a former chaplain who had managed to secure the patronage of Grand Duke Pavel Petrovych, forty-seven churches were removed from the Nizhyns'ka Deanery in 1777 to create a new Ivanogorods'ka *protopopiia*. This provided Oleksandr with a suitable ecclesiastical livelihood at a time when there was no vacant archpriest's post in the eparchy.[20]

Individuals who belonged to the middle managerial sector, such as Oleksandr and other archpriests, occupied relatively powerful positions on the local scene. The archpriest of the Romens'ka *protopopiia*, Pavlo Svit (†1760), who had been the court singer for Peter I, had six children. His family's social success shows how far the informal influence of a patron could extend. Pavlo's eldest son, who had started his career in the Cossack company (*sotnia*) administration in 1747, finished it in 1771 as a flag-bearer (*khorunzhyi*).[21] Svit's eldest daughter married a brigadier and colonel of Gadiach; the second eldest married a lieutenant of the Russian regular army from Okhtyrs'ka province, and the third and the fourth each married a fellow of the standard (*bunchukovyi tovarysh*). Pavlo's grandchildren included a major in the regular service, a Hussar ensign, two wives of *bunchukovi tovaryshi*, one wife of a military comrade (*viiskovyi tovarysh*), one wife of the Georgian prince Major Iegor Osyhmanov, one wife of a *sotnyk* of the Myrgorod Regiment, and a widow of a regimental aide-de-camp (*polkovyi osavul*) of Pryluky. Only Svit's youngest son, Petro, was assigned to an ecclesiastical career. It is likely that his father's parish in the village of Velyki Bubny was intended for him, since it remained empty for eleven years (!), perhaps until Petro could finish his education and reach the age required for ordination. Young Svit, it should be noted, only completed the study of rhetoric and was unlikely to continue his education, as he already had a wife and two children.[22] He did not become a priest, however, choosing a secular career instead, dying as a *viiskovyi tovarysh*. Still, the Svit family held on to the deanery, and from 1790 to 1813 Pavlo Svit's post was occupied by his grandson Iakiv.[23]

Comparison of the educational level of the Kyiv metropolitan clergy with that of their Russian Orthodox, Ukrainian Uniate, and Belorussian Uniate colleagues can only be tentative, due to fragmentary data. According to P. Znamenskii, a scholar of the parish clergy of the Russian Empire, in diocesan schools "almost until the middle of the eighteenth century, the majority of the clergy did not complete more than two or three grades; except for [the study] of Latin grammar, they engaged in the same study of the Psalter as they would have at home."[24]

If Znamenskii's report is accurate, the education of the Ukrainian Orthodox clergy may have been better than many of their Russian counterparts. However, the level of education in the Russian dioceses shows considerable geographical variation over the course of the eighteenth century. In the case of Moscow, for example, there is evidence of significant success in "educational disciplining": between 1734 and 1781, the number of those who attained proficiency in rhetoric increased from 12 to 116 persons. By 1774, 50% of archpriests, 20% of priests, and 10% of deacons had completed the highest levels of Latin school.[25]

If we turn from the Orthodox to examine the situation among the Uniates, we find that the vastness of the territory occupied by the Uniate dioceses makes it difficult to draw comparisons. Moreover, there is insufficient information about the education of the Uniate clergy during the period analyzed here; more complete data come only from later decades, but indicate that 69% of men ordained in Radomyshl' in 1786 had had some experience of Latin learning (the majority of them progressed no higher than rhetoric). Data on the educational level of all Uniate parish priests in the Russian Empire in 1798 offer a different picture—fewer than half the parish priests had attended school. The number of persons "stuffed with" learning decreased as one moved from the west (where it could reach 55%) to the east (where it could be as low as 5% in some places, such as Mstyslav region). The percentage of those who studied at seminaries or attended theological classes was even smaller, and similarly decreased from west to east. Not all parish priests sent their sons to schools, but there was notable progress over the course of the century: at times, more than half of all clerical sons attended classes.[26]

VILLAGES VS. TOWNS

Scholars of the history of literacy are well aware of the general pattern of higher literacy skills among urban residents: this was more or less the case everywhere in early modern Europe (although, as always, with exceptions stemming from confessional identity, regional customs, cultural traditions, etc.). Urban life, it seems, stimulated all social groups to become literate, so that town dwellers generally had higher levels of education than did rural representatives of the same social classes.[27]

The same pattern applies to Ukraine, although relevant studies are still scarce. Nevertheless, anecdotal evidence indicates that in Ukraine, too, urban clergy were more highly educated. For instance, in their orders to the Legislative Commission in 1768, the ecclesiastical authorities of the Kyiv Eparchy boasted about the academic instruction of the urban clergy:

> In Little Russia, especially, so many of the teaching priests came from that [Kyiv] academy that all regimental capitals of the Kyiv

> Eparchy are sufficiently staffed by them, and also most of the other cities and towns, and also some of the greater villages are supplied and will in the future be supplied with the same people, who successfully work to instruct and enlighten the common people.[28]

The same characterization appears in a book about the responsibilities of the parish presbyters. Possibly written by a bishop or by a graduate of the Kyiv Academy, the book, first published in 1776, describes urban priests as people with the "most educated minds, and [who] know books."[29]

The seven deaneries examined here confirm the general judgment. Although only about one-third of the parishes could be called urban, 47% of urban clergy had attended Latin schools, while in rural areas the figure was only 30%. Nevertheless, there is little reason to trust the optimistic statements of church authorities, since more than half (52%) of the urban clergy of the seven *protopopii* had only studied *rus'ka gramota* (see Table 3).

Table 3 Education of Urban and Rural Clergy/Numbers of Individuals Reporting Study of the Following Subjects

<table>
<tr><th></th><th colspan="3">Town/Small town</th><th colspan="2">Village/Small village</th></tr>
<tr><td>Theology</td><td colspan="2">26 (14%)</td><td rowspan="8">88 (47%)</td><td>12 (5%)</td><td rowspan="8">77 (30%)</td></tr>
<tr><td>Philosophy</td><td colspan="2">24 (13%)</td><td>26 (10%)</td></tr>
<tr><td>Rhetoric</td><td colspan="2">29 (15%)</td><td>29 (11%)</td></tr>
<tr><td>Poesy</td><td colspan="2">4 (2%)</td><td>6 (2.4%)</td></tr>
<tr><td>Syntax</td><td>1</td><td rowspan="4">5
(3%)</td><td>4 (1.6%)</td></tr>
<tr><td>Grammar</td><td>1</td><td>-</td></tr>
<tr><td>Latin learning</td><td>1</td><td>-</td></tr>
<tr><td>Some Latin</td><td>2</td><td>-</td></tr>
<tr><td>Rus'ka gramota</td><td colspan="3">97 (52%)</td><td>169</td><td rowspan="2">170 (67%)</td></tr>
<tr><td>Some Rus'ka gramota</td><td colspan="3">-</td><td>1</td></tr>
<tr><td>Not specified</td><td colspan="3">3</td><td colspan="2">6</td></tr>
<tr><td>Total number of persons</td><td colspan="3">188 (100%)</td><td colspan="2">253 (100%)</td></tr>
<tr><td>Total number of churches</td><td colspan="3">102</td><td colspan="2">202</td></tr>
</table>

Data on the educational level in the seven *protopopii* of the Kyiv Eparchy in the first part of the 1770s show that church authorities failed to accomplish the goal of supplying all parishes with priests who had obtained a theological education prior to ordination. Despite all the effort, the deaneries studied here reveal differences that cannot easily be easily explained. The Reshetylivs'ka *protopopiia,* where former students made up 55% of the clergy, followed by the Kobeliats'ka *protopopiia* (47%) were the most successful. The leading position of these deaneries seems to depend upon the prevalence of urban parishes within them: for example, in the Kobeliats'ka *protopopiia,* only 5 out of the 33 parishes were rural, in Reshetylivs'ka, 6 out of 14. In the Sorochyns'ka *protopopiia,* on the other hand, where 41% of parishes were urban, only 30% of priests had completed some level of Latin learning. At the same time, to confound the apparent explanation, Pyriatyns'ka *protopopiia*, in which 84% of parishes were rural, could boast that 43% of its clergy had finished some level of Latin learning (see Table 4).

Perhaps the high percentage of former students among the clergy of the remote Reshetylivs'ka *protopopiia* was the result of a tradition or precedent set by their famous countrymen, whose education had helped them ascend the steps of the ecclesiastical hierarchy. One such example is the Metropolitan Arsenii (Mohylians'kyi, 1757–1770), a native of Reshetylivka. Arsenii's great grandfather, also a member of

Table 4 Correlation between Educational Level and Parish Composition

Deanery (*Protopopiia*)	Latin learning	Percentage of urban parishes
Reshetylivs'ka	55%	57%
Kobeliats'ka	47%	85%
Pyriatyns'ka	43%	16%
Kyiv-Pechers'ka	38%	32%
Romens'ka	37%	21%
Sorochyns'ka	30%	41%
Glukhivs'ka	27%	21%

the clergy, had apparently studied in Kyiv and composed the text *Nauka Khristianskaia* (1670).[30] Mohylians'kyi's brother, Evstafii, who had begun a successful ecclesiastical career before Arsenii himself came to occupy an important ecclesiastical post, was a preacher at the court of Empress Elizabeth and later went on to govern great monasteries in the Kyiv Diocese.[31] Finally, a son of a priest from Reshetylivka became a professor of grammar in the Kyiv Academy in the second half of the 1760s.[32]

Examples like these, however, offer only anecdotal evidence in the absence of a comprehensive explanation.

PATH TO THE PARISH

Another possible explanation for the generally unsuccessful efforts of the church hierarchy to improve the education of its clergy takes us beyond the data of the seven deaneries studied here: perhaps the general failure of raising the clergy's educational level should be sought in the process of becoming a parish priest. One could hardly call the appointment and ordination of priests a blank spot in the historiography, whose main conclusions can be summarized in two points.[33]

The first is that, up to the end of the eighteenth century, Orthodox clergy were elected by parishioners who had less stake in the educational accomplishments of their priests and deacons than did church authorities. Requirements for the candidates put forward by the laity were different (and much simpler) than for the sons of the clergy. For instance, in 1722, 1723, and 1726, the Kyiv Archbishop Varlaam (Vanatovych) reminded archpriests not to send for ordination those candidates elected by parishioners who "had not learned by heart the Decalogue, the beatitudes, the seven sacraments, and other teachings from the Catechism that are necessary to the office of a priest."[34] In 1731, Varlaam's successor Rafail (Zaborovskyi, 1731-1747) admonished:

> He who wants to be a presbyter should be able to read the Psalter and understand everything that he reads—the holy law, the sacred Gospels, the books of the apostles, and all the divine scriptures; otherwise he will not be ordained.[35]

Eight years later, he again enumerated the same requirements: after the approbation of "their good and sinless life and perfect skill in the reading of Holy Scripture and in church singing," the candidates had to be entrusted to the care of

> honorable priests who could teach everything that is proper to the priestly office; more specifically, candidates should know the Lord's commandments, the church sacraments, the tradition of the apostles and Holy Fathers, and other dogmas of the faith.[36]

The situation did not change under Rafail's successor, Tymofii (Scherbatskyi); the majority of the clergy still studied only in the deacons' parish schools. The metropolitan continued his predecessor's policy in the 1740s and 1750s: he repeatedly demanded not to be sent candidates who could barely read or write, and who, even after studying in the cathedral monastery, "were still 'mediocre,' 'limited,' and even 'dull' in reading and writing."[37] Arsenii (Mohylians'kyi, 1757–1770) was also known for strict decrees about the education of clerical children, though he did leave one loophole: those who did not attend one of Kyiv's Latin schools but still asked for ordination could pay a fine (between three and twenty rubles) to the academy. Like his predecessors, he stipulated that candidates put forward by the laity had to be at least literate.[38]

The Kyiv metropolitans were concerned with the same issues even in the late eighteenth and early nineteenth centuries: in 1797, Ierofei (Malyts'kyi) ordered the eparchial examiner to check the candidates' knowledge not only of the Catechism (as before) but also of the rules for the clergy from the Ecclesiastical Regulation (*Dukhovnyi Reglament*).[39] Gavryil (Banulesko-Bodoni, 1799-1803) followed a similar course (although under both metropolitans the situation was complicated by the division of the Polish-Lithuanian Commonwealth, which added the former Uniate parishes [with their newly-converted clergy] to the Kyiv Eparchy). The result was that government organs of the deaneries (*Dukhovni pravlinnia* and *blagochyniia*) continued to put forward candidates "unskilled in reading books, and especially in delivering sermons, [and who were] also untrained in singing and church regulations."[40]

The second distinctive feature of the path to the parish in the eighteenth century is the practice of parish inheritance by family members (although the priest who wanted to pass the parish to a relative also had to secure the support of parishioners and the owner of the settlement).[41] Data from the *protopopii* provide a rough idea of the persistence of the election principle and the practice of inheritance, as well as the openness of the office to other social strata. Although not all report their clergy's familial ties, at least 43% of the parishes in the Reshetylivs'ka *protopopiia* in 1773 had been inherited. In the Kyiv-Pechers'ka *propotopiia* this number was between 51.6% and 61.3%; in Glukhiv it was 48.8% (if we also take into account the inheritance of lower church offices).[42]

It should be emphasized that when parish posts were bequeathed within the family line, they were not always transferred to a son or another relative who had studied in a Latin school. In records from the first part of the 1770s, slightly more than half the active priests and deacons (224 persons) were listed as clerical children. This means that their parents should have seen to their educations before providing them with ecclesiastical posts. However, only 106 people had followed the instructions of the ecclesiastical authorities. Among those who had studied in Latin schools, the greatest number (forty-four persons) had mastered rhetoric. Only eighteen persons had studied theology, thirty had studied philosophy, eight had studied poesy, four had studied syntax, and one had studied grammar; 114 persons had studied *rus'ka gramota*. One young man had studied in "Latin courses" (unspecified), and there is no information on the other four.

In other words, even when the parish was inherited, which, I will stress once more, did not exclude the necessity of securing the parishioners' support, priests' sons did not necessarily have to be graduates of Latin schools. An elementary education was often sufficient. In the eyes of the parishioners, the model of a good priest or deacon (regardless of whether he was an outsider or a relative and heir of his predecessor) did not include such a crucial requirement as the study of theology or other courses.

Thus, "parish culture" successfully resisted the educational initiatives of the authorities. To compel the clergy's children to attend schools, it would have been necessary not only to make education compulsory or introduce reforms within the educational institutions, but also to change the process of parochial nomination. An integrated approach to church reforms in the late eighteenth and early nineteenth centuries helped change the situation, but, before then, the efforts of the authorities often clashed with the inertia of the "good old ways" of parish life.

NOTES

* Translated by Olga Greco with the assistance of Daniel H. Kaiser and Valerie A. Kivelson.

1 Without detailing the content of eighteenth-century synodal decrees on compulsory education for clerical children, I want to mention that, in a passage from 1758, which was copied out in the Synod Chancery especially for the Kyiv Academy, there is mention of legislative incentives from 1708, 1710, 1721, 1722, 1723, 1725, 1728, 1730, 1731, 1737, 1738, and 1758. Not all the incentives applied equally to every diocese; some of them can be considered legal precedents that were also known in Kyiv (see Instytut Rukopysu Natsional'noi Biblioteky Ukraiiny im. V. I. Vernads'koho, f. 312, spr. 438 [438/430c], ark. 91-97).

2 Gregory Freeze, in writing about the radical changes in the education of the Russian clergy in the eighteenth century, quite adequately titled one of his chapters "The New World of the Seminary." Gregory L. Freeze, *The Russian Levites: Parish Clergy in the Eighteenth Century* (Cambridge: Harvard University Press, 1977), 78-106.

3 Piotr Wawrzeniuk, *Confessional Civilising in Ukraine. The Bishop Iosyf Shumliansky and the Introduction of Reforms in the Diocese of Lviv 1668–1708* (Sweden: Södertörns högskola, 2005), 68-76.

4 "Kievskii sobor 1691 goda," *Kievskie eparkhial'nye vedomosti*, 1865, no. 8, otdel II, 319.

5 Sophia Senyk, "Schools for Priests: Orthodox Education in Eighteenth-Century Ukraine," *Orientalia Christiana Periodica* 70 (2007): 312.

6 See, e.g., Tsentral'nyi Derzhavnyi Istorychnyi Arkhiv Ukrainy, m. Kyiv (hereafter CDIAKU), f. 127, op. 1024, spr. 2179, ark. 1.

7 John T. Alexander, *Bubonic Plague in Early Modern Russia: Public Health and Urban Disaster* (Oxford: Oxford University Press, 2002), 111-13.

8 All information for the analysis of clerical education was taken from CDIAKU, f. 127, op. 1009, spr. 3, ark. 1-50 (for Glukhivs'ka *protopopiia*); f. 127, op. 1020, spr. 4201, ark. 5-12 (for Reshetylivs'ka *protopopiia*) and ark. 19-32 (for Kobeliats'ka *protopopiia*); f. 127, op. 1024, spr. 2042, ark. 1-37 zv. (for Romens'ka *protopopiia*); f. 127, op. 1024, spr. 2132, ark. 1-23 (for Pyriatyns'ka *protopopiia*); f. 127, op. 1024, spr. 2133, ark. 1-34 zv. (for Sorochyns'ka *protopopiia*); Derzhavnyi arkhiv mista Kyieva, f. 314, op. 1, spr. 326, ark. 1-10 zv. (for Kyiv-Pechers'ka *protopopiia*).

9 On the appearance of deacons in the deaneries, see Evfimii Kryzhanovskii, "Ocherki byta iuzhnorusskogo sel'skogo dukhovenstva v XVIII veke," in Kryzhanovskii, *Sobranie sochinenii,* 3 vols. (Kiev, 1890), 1:397.

10 P. V. Znamenskii, *Prikhodskoe dukhovenstvo v Rossii so vremen reformy Petra* (Kazan', 1873), 68.

11 CDIAKU, f. 127, op. 1020, spr. 4066, ark. 4 zv., 11 zv.-12, 17 zv.-18, 21 zv.-22, 25 zv., 27 zv.-28, 37, 43, 56 zv., 60 zv., 63 zv.-64, 67 zv., 73 zv., 76 zv., 78 zv.-79, 83, 86 zv., 91 zv., 99 zv., 102, 107 zv., 110 zv., 115 zv., 119 zv.-120, 152 zv.-157, 160.

12 Oksana Prokopiuk, *Kyivs'ka mytropoliia: topografiia posviat. Reconstruktsiia reiestru khramiv za vidomostiamy pro tserkovnosluzhyteliv* (1780–1783) (Kyiv: DP "NVTS͡ 'Priorytety,'" 2012), 34.

13 The one recorded case of partial proficiency in *rus'ka gramota* (see Table 1) must be considered an exception and interpreted to mean only the ability to read. For a more detailed analysis, see Maksym Iaremenko, "Osvitnii riven' parafiial'noho dukhovenstva Kyivs'koi mytropolii 1770-kh rr. (na prykladi Glukhivs'koi protopopii)," *Proseminarii: Mediievistyka, Istoriia Tserkvy, nauky i kul'tury* 7 (2008): 285-86.

14 Gary Marker, "Faith and Secularity in Eighteenth-Century Russian Literacy, 1770-1775," in *Christianity and the Eastern Slavs,* 3 vols. (Berkeley: University of California Press, 1993-95), 2:3–24.

15 A. Iu. Samarin, *Chitatel' v Rossii vo vtoroi polovine XVIII veka (po spiskam podpischikov)* (Moscow: Izdatel'stvo Moskovskogo gosudarstvennogo universiteta, 2000), 133-34. However, it should be noted that the author has studied the subscribers of only 1% of texts printed in the "civil script."

16 One priest was taught icon painting in addition to *rus'ka gramota.*

17 One priest was taught icon painting in addition to *rus'ka gramota.*

18 Periphery here refers to all parishes outside the center of the *protopopii.*

19 Two had studied theology for one year, and one had studied it for two years instead of four.

20 Prokopiuk, *Kyivs'ka mytropoliia,* 25.

21 On Cossack ranks and hierarchy, see George Gajecky, *The Cossack Administration of the Hetmanate,* 2 vols. (Cambridge: Harvard Ukrainian Research Institute, 1978).

22 CDIAKU, f. 127, op. 1024, spr. 2042, ark. 17–18.

23 Vadim L. Modzalevskii, *Malorossiiskii rodoslovnik,* 5 vols. in 6 bks. (Kiev, 1914-2004), 4:568.

24 Znamenskii, *Prikhodskoe dukhovenstvo,* 124.

25 Freeze, *The Russian Levites,* 103, 263.

26 Barbara Skinner, *The Western Front of the Eastern Church: Uniate and Orthodox Conflict in 18th-century Poland, Ukraine, Belarus, and Russia* (Illinois: Northern Illinois University Press, 2009), 71-75.

27 For these conclusions and data on literacy rates in various countries, see Peter Burke, *Popular Culture in Early Modern Europe* (United Kingdom: Ashgate, 2002), 251-52; C. F. Kaestle, "The History of Literacy and the History of Readers," *Review of Research in Education* 12 (1985): 12, 2122, 25; R. A. Houston, *Literacy in Early Modern Europe: Culture and Education 1500-1800* (London:

Longman, 1988), 140, 143; W. Urban, "Sztuka pisania w województwie krakowskim w XVII i XVIII wieku," *Przegląd historyczny* 75 (1984): 77.

28 "Punkty ot Kievskoi eparkhii," *Sbornik imperatorskogo Russkogo istoricheskogo obschestva,* 148 vols. (Saint Petersburg, 1867-1916), 43:529, 533-36.

29 *Kniga o dolzhnostiakh presviterov prikhodskikh* (Kiev, 1779), 36.

30 *Akty i dokumenty, otnosiaschiesia k istorii Kievskoi akademii. Otdelenie* II (1721-1795 rr.), 5 vols. (hereafter, *AiD*) (Kiev, 1904-1908), 2:201-202.

31 V. N. Zhuk, "Mohylians'kyi Ievstafii (Ostap) Vasyl'ovych, cherneche im'ia Iepifanii," in *Kyievo-Mohylians'ka akademiia v imenakh, XVII–XVIII st.: Entsyklopedychne vydannia* (Kyiv: Vydavnychyĭ dim "K M Academia," 2001), 374.

32 *AiD* 3:485.

33 It is obviously unnecessary to list all the works dedicated to the process of parochial nomination. I will just mention two specialized publications: the early (and now classic) work of Kryzhanivskyi, which has been cited by almost all researchers, and one of the more recent publications by Senyk, which is an incomplete summary of the achievements of previous scholarship, and which is, moreover, based on a limited number of the published sources. Although they emerged almost half a century apart, both publications are characterized by a descriptive approach. Still, Kryzhanivs'kyi's work was new in its contemporary historiographical context (see Kryzhanovskii, "Ocherki byta," 391-439, first published in 1861); Sophia Senyk, "Becoming a Priest. The Appointment and Ordination of Priests in the Orthodox Church in Ukraine in the Eighteenth Century," *Orientalia Christiana Periodica* 69 (2003): 125-51.

34 A. P. Rybolovskii, *Varlaam Vanatovich, arkhiepiskop Kievskii, Galitskii i Malyia Rossii* (Kiev: Tip. I. I. Gorbunova, 1908), 55-56.

35 P. I. Orlovskii, *Skazanie o blazhennom Rafaile mitropolite Kievskom* (Kiev: Tip. I. I. Gorbunova, 1908), 8.

36 Ibid., 19.

37 I. S. Graevskii, *Kievskii mitropolit Timofei Scherbatskii* (Kiev: Tip. P. Barskogo, 1912), 129-30, 155, 225-26.

38 Nikolai Shpachinskii, *Kievskii mitropolit Arsenii Mogilianskii i sostoianie Kievskoi mitropolii v ego pravlenie (1757-1770)* (Kiev: Tip. T-va N. A. Girich, 1907), 335, 397.

39 A. V. Belgorodskii, *Kievskii mitropolit Ierofei Malitskii (1796-1799 gg.)* (Kiev: Tip. I. I. Gorbunova, 1901), 99-100.

40 V. Chekhovskii, *Kievskii mitropolit Gavriil Banulesko-Bodoni (1799-1803 gg.)* (Kiev: Tip. I. I. Gorbunova, 1905), 193.

41 As scholars have repeatedly pointed out, parish inheritance became prevalent on Russian territory during the first decades of the eighteenth century. The exceptions were very few and mostly date to the first quarter of the century.

42 Iaremenko, "Osvitnii riven' parafiial'noho dukhovenstva," 296; Iaremenko, "Uspikhy ta nevdachi 'osvitn'oho dyscyplinuvannia' parafiial'noho dukhovenstva Kyievo-Pechers'koi protopopii 1770-kh rr.," *Kraieznavstvo. Naukovyi zhurnal,* 2010, no. 4, 132-34; Iaremenko, "Osvita parafiial'noho dukhovenstva Reshetylivs'koi protopopii 1770-kh rr.: mizh pastyrs'kymy i synodal'nymy nastanovamy ta povsiakdennymy praktykamy," *Visnyk Kharkivs'koho natsional'noho universytetu imeni* V. N. Karazina, Seriia Istoriia, 982 (2011): 77-78.

"The Opinion of One Ukrainian Landowner": V. N. Karazin, Alexander I, and Changing Russia

Patrick O'Meara
(Durham University)

V. N. Karazin (1773-1842) is best known for his key role in the 1805 founding of Khar'kov University, which the Ukrainian government finally named after him in 1999. On Alexander I's accession in 1801, Karazin anonymously sent the emperor a challenging agenda for change. The tsar was so intrigued that he had Karazin traced and invited to a personal audience, the first of many. Despite the initial warmth, however, the relationship lasted less than eighteen months. Karazin rapidly fell victim to court intrigue, and after many vicissitudes was eventually arrested in November, 1820, in connection with the Semenovskii Regiment's mutiny. He was incarcerated in Shlissel'burg Fortress for six months and then exiled to his Ukrainian estates. The article draws on a wide range of contemporary sources to explore the fate of this outspoken advocate of both change and continuity in early nineteenth-century Russia, his uneasy relationship with the tsar, and to assess what his interactions with the emperor tell us about the limits of "public opinion" at that time.[1]

Vasilii Nazarevich Karazin was born in Ukraine's Slobozhanshchina district on February 10, 1773, in the village of Kruchik on the estate that Catherine the Great had awarded his father, Nazar Aleksandrovich, for valor in the Seven Years War. Karazin was educated at home by his mother, Varvara Iakovlevna Kovalevskaia, and then in private boarding schools in Kremenchug and Khar'kov. His education culminated at the Mining Institute in Saint Petersburg where, as an officer of the Semenovskii Regiment, he studied physics, mathematics, botany, chemistry, medicine, Latin, French, and German. Allegedly inspired by his reading of Radishchev's *Journey from St. Petersburg to Moscow*, in the last years of Paul's reign Karazin undertook several tours around Russia's provinces, which led him to abandon military service in favor of natural and social sciences.[2] In 1798, aged twenty-five, he took the highly unusual step for a nobleman of marrying a fourteen-year-old peasant girl in his mother's household, Domna Ivanovna. Sadly, she died in childbirth shortly afterwards. Under Emperor Paul, Karazin held the post of official translator at the state treasury and in the office of Baron Vasiliev, director of the principal medical college.[3] Here he wrote two quite diverse works: "A history of medicine in Russia," and "On the causes of the fall in the ruble's exchange rate and the means of restoring it," both of which attracted some attention. This "Ukrainian Lomonosov" not only founded Khar'kov University but also the first ministry of public education in Europe and Russia's first meteorological station.[4]

In 1801, just ten days after the new tsar's succession, Karazin attracted the attention of the sovereign by anonymously sending him an innovative and extensive agenda for his reign; financial reform, comprehensive education, and the notions of rule of law, public opinion (*obshchestvennoe mnenie*), and human rights (*prava chelovechestva*) for serfs featured prominently. It was effectively the unofficial manifesto of the liberal nobility at the turn of the century. Karazin concluded by affirming that, as tsar, Alexander would surely complete Catherine the Great's vital work of "making *Russians* of us."[5] According to Alexander Herzen, the letter moved the young tsar to tears. Deeply impressed by what he read, Alexander ordered its author to be traced and summoned to an audience.[6] Alexander thanked Karazin for his patriotism and urged him always to speak up truthfully—an entreaty that the tsar would soon have cause to regret. Karazin responded to the tsar's invitation by proposing as priorities the establishment of a ministry of public education and an overhaul of the legal system. So rapidly had Karazin earned the emperor's total confidence that Alexander promptly invited Karazin himself to develop these projects.[7] Russia's first ministry of public education was duly set up in September, 1802, under Count P. V. Zavadovskii, and Karazin was put in charge of the main directorate of secondary and higher education. The ministry's creation remained a source of pride for Karazin for the rest of his life. Just months before his death he remarked in a letter of May 23, 1842, to M. P. Pogodin, "Who now knows that it was someone still alive today . . . who first devised and sketched out the proposal for a dedicated ministry of national education such as then existed nowhere else in Europe?"[8]

Karazin was convinced that education should be made available to all Russians, regardless of class, gender, and age, not only as a means of promoting respect for learning and producing good citizens, but also of breaking down class barriers. For their time, such views were novel and original, as was Karazin's campaign for the foundation of a university for Ukraine in Khar'kov. The "well-known enthusiast," as A. N. Pypin dubbed him, rapidly succeeded in securing Alexander's blessing for the project and, equally impressively, in the summer of 1802 persuaded the local nobility to pledge four hundred thousand rubles to fund it.[9] But when in January, 1803, the Preliminary Regulation confirming the establishment of Khar'kov University nominated Count Seweryn Potocki as curator, Karazin's name figured nowhere. His feeling that he was losing the tsar's confidence is clear from his long letter to Alexander of August 16, 1803, which begins: "Many circumstances compel me to think that with every passing day I am increasingly distanced from your heart." There follows a lengthy litany of complaints detailing the sheer incompetence of the relevant government departments and officials in their dealings with him, both in relation to Khar'kov's new university and to his own department of the ministry. These included the "outright hostility" shown to the establishment of Khar'kov University, reflected in the delay in transferring the funds allocated to pay the professors already recruited and in place.[10] His importunate letter earned him an imperial reprimand, as we learn from Karazin's next letter to the tsar just a week later. In it he thanked Alexander for his "gift," asked him to forgive "a rustic dreamer," and assured the tsar that in the future he would contact him only through the proper channels.[11] However, later that year he again wrote directly to the tsar in even greater desperation. Mystified by the lack of response from his patron, though well aware of his enemies at court, Karazin shared with Alexander his suspicion that N. N. Novosil'tsev, Adam Czartoryski, and M. M. Speranskii had sat on his latest proposals relating to national education, although he had submitted these to them as long ago as the previous December. Karazin could not believe that Alexander had actually had sight of them, since otherwise, "having read there [his] own thoughts set out . . . [the tsar] would surely have commanded their author to be sent at least one kind word from the throne."[12]

Despite these setbacks, Karazin continued with his efforts to drive forward the development of the university, sending its council a stream of memoranda during the second quarter of 1804 containing information, instructions, and advice. But this activity abruptly ceased in June following a formal complaint from Zavadovskii to Alexander, who immediately commanded Karazin to stop "meddling."[13] Finding himself increasingly marginalized and demoralized by the whispering campaign designed to turn his imperial patron against him, on August 11, Karazin submitted his resignation to the tsar. It was immediately accepted and he was removed from his posts.[14] Alexander thus lost a loyal, if personally irritating, collaborator who had already shown himself to be a resourceful official. Accordingly, Karazin was not present at the formal opening of his brain-child in January, 1805, and his singular role in the establishment of Khar'kov University was not officially recognized until 1811 when he was awarded an honorary degree. The council's citation generously acknowledged that "the foundation of a university in Khar'kov is due entirely to his efforts and labor."[15] Moscow University, however, despite Karazin's fall from imperial favor, had been quicker to recognize his "patriotic zeal for the spread of enlightenment throughout the fatherland" with the award of an honorary degree on March 28, 1805, just weeks after Khar'kov University had opened its doors.

Thus, Karazin's initial success and drive met with scant reward: his exactitude and "immoderate zeal," combined with his quickness to criticize the failings of others, were tiresome qualities that earned him many powerful enemies at court.[16] From the outset, members of the Unofficial Committee (Czartoryski, Novosil'tsev, P. A. Stroganov and V. P. Kochubei) resented Karazin's sudden closeness to Alexander, as did several senior courtiers, such as Zavadovskii, D. P. Troshchinskii, and G. R. Derzhavin, who simply regarded Karazin as an upstart and a nuisance. These men evidently took every opportunity to undermine him in Alexander's eyes, ensuring the hapless "rustic dreamer" a fall from grace as rapid as had been his rise. Alexander actually needed little persuasion: apparently intoxicated by the trust the tsar showed him in the first eighteen months of his reign, Karazin wrote the tsar in overly familiar terms, urging him to show resolute leadership. No doubt his letters were well-meaning, but they depicted their author as a hectoring sycophant. According to Herzen, Alexander dropped Karazin in 1804 after angrily confronting him with reports that he had been heard to boast openly about their strictly private correspondence.[17]

At any rate, Karazin's original anonymous letter to Alexander clearly did not remain a secret. In a letter from August, 1809, Joseph de Maistre, a long-term resident of Saint Petersburg as envoy of the Kingdom of Sardinia, referred to the episode and invited his correspondent to agree that "in a country of despotism a letter such as this constitutes a rather curious document."[18] The editor of Karazin's papers and correspondence specifically refers to "the four letters" which Karazin received from Alexander at the start of his reign, "which would have shown more clearly than anything else how much he was valued and respected by the tsar himself." However, they were apparently among the papers seized from Karazin at the time of his Shlissel'burg incarceration in 1820 and so remain unpublished. But it is claimed that Alexander's hand-written, three-page letter of December 12, 1801, contained the tsar's crucial entreaty to Karazin: "always continue to talk frankly, even if you notice that it displeases me. Believe me, sooner or later I will come to value the boldness that drives you."[19] If so, it does much to explain Karazin's subsequent dogged determination to abide by the tsar's injunction.

Even though Karazin clearly did much to bring it upon himself, the sudden and unexpected reversal of Alexander's favor was nevertheless characteristic of the tsar: it was remarkable just how impressionable and inconsistent he could be. For example, after his disastrous negotiations with Napoleon at Tilsit in 1807, his relations with the four members of the Unofficial Committee, perhaps his closest friends to date, shifted drastically in favor of Speranskii who, in turn, would soon find himself suddenly disgraced and exiled. Thus Karazin was no more likely to enjoy a stable and enduring relationship with Alexander than anyone else.

Despite Alexander's refusal to receive him any longer, Karazin chose to assume that he was free to correspond directly as before, without having to go through the proper channels. Thus, in November, 1804, as quixotically as ever, he wrote to the tsar, listing his debts and begging him for funds to alleviate his rural destitution.[20] He also assumed that Alexander would still want to have his candid opinions on matters of national importance, including foreign policy. Again, he wrote to Alexander in 1809, urging him in a memorandum entitled "On non-interference in European affairs" to pursue a policy of strict isolationism rather than give Napoleon an excuse to attack Russia. Infuriated, the tsar responded by ordering Karazin detained in the Khar'kov guardhouse for eight days, "for his absurd views on matters which are not his concern and about which he can know nothing."[21] In desperation Karazin turned for support to his former colleague, Mikhail Speranskii: writing him on April 18, 1810, Karazin contrasted their situations ("You are all-powerful; I stand in urgent need of assistance"), reminding him of their former friendship and appealing for his help, but the letter went unanswered.[22] Speranskii's biographer, Marc Raeff, blames Karazin entirely for the loss of Speranskii's support, remarking that "he was anything but a steady and reliable individual, as even a superficial acquaintance with this biography will show."[23] Given what our sources reveal about Karazin's impetuous character, Raeff's judgement, while harsh, is not unreasonable.

On his enforced return to Ukraine, Karazin married Aleksandra Vasil'evna Blankennagel', continued his scientific work, maintained his interest in Russia's current social and political affairs, and set about amassing an enormous library. In 1805, he fulfilled a long-standing ambition by opening in Kruchik a parish school for his peasants' children, the first of its kind in the province, and for its time a rare initiative indeed. Karazin also continued to make known his original ideas and strongly-held convictions on a broad range of topics through numerous articles and a very active correspondence. Even by the standards of the day, Karazin was an inveterate and prolific letter-writer. Between 1798 and 1842, he wrote to three tsars and many of their ministers, including Troshchinskii, Kochubei, Novosil'tsev, Zavadovskii, Speranskii, Arakcheev, and Benkendorf. [24] Particularly striking is his correspondence with Arakcheev, especially from 1813 to 1816 when he wrote to the "grand vizier" several times a year in quite familiar terms. Thus, in one letter (June 26, 1816) he asked Arakcheev for an invitation and travel expenses for himself and his family (he had six children) to visit Saint Petersburg to discuss with Arakcheev ideas for a "system of finances."[25] Karazin may have seen in Arakcheev's closeness to Alexander a potential conduit for the resumption of his own relationship with the tsar. But perhaps it was Karazin's way of ensuring that he was not forgotten in the remoteness of Kruchik, reminiscent of the bizarre appeal of Bobchinsky and Dobchinsky in Gogol's *Government Inspector*, who were happy just to have Saint Petersburg reminded of their existence.

Karazin certainly had a lot to write about. He was passionately concerned with questions of the environment, forestry, and conservation. In connection with these concerns, in January, 1811, he founded the Khar'kov-based Technophiles' Society for the promotion of science, technology, and industry in Ukraine. By April it numbered forty-eight members, noblemen from eight provinces. In the official announcement of its inception, Karazin urged members "to increase tenfold the society's significance in Russia and to make it the object of respectful attention in all of Europe!"[26] His own contribution amounted to over sixty published papers. These ranged from meteorology (to which he attached enormous importance for accurate forecasting to assist with successful agriculture) to agronomy (fertilizers were his great interest), agricultural engineering, and, remarkably, global warming ("On the probable cause of the general change in temperature").[27]

Karazin ensured that the society's fame spread well beyond Khar'kov. From a letter of thanks Arakcheev sent to Karazin dated May 17, 1813, we learn of the powerful minister's pleasure at being elected to membership of the society.[28] Of particular interest is that Karazin succeeded in securing an audience with Alexander when, in September, 1817, the tsar passed through Khar'kov. In what was presumably their first encounter in fifteen years, Karazin presented the tsar with a report on the Technophiles' Society, drawing attention to his own ideas. Although irritated by Karazin's wonted audacity, Alexander instructed his secretary of state, V. R. Marchenko, to procure further details. This inquiry led to Karazin visiting Moscow in February, 1818, to prepare a memorandum for Alexander's consideration ("On the application of the electrical forces of the upper strata of the atmosphere to meet mankind's requirements"). The tsar passed this on to A. N. Golitsyn for evaluation by the Academy of Sciences, whose report was duly submitted to Alexander on August 4. The academicians did not endorse Karazin's ideas, because, as the article's author concluded, they did not fully understand them; a different outcome would have ensured that Karazin's impressive scientific originality earned him fame even greater than he received for his founding of Khar'kov University. As it was, for Karazin the Academy's rejection was a bitter blow and it effectively killed off the Technophiles' Society that same year.[29]

Karazin's central focus, however, both before and after his Shlissel'burg imprisonment in 1820, was on the serf question and peasant welfare. The fullest statement of his vision for the development of Russia's rural economy is set out in a long letter of January 30, 1810, to I. I. Bakhtin, Governor of Slobodsko-Ukraine.[30] Karazin was convinced of the need to ease the bonds of serfdom, without abolishing the institution altogether, through the active participation of landowners, who were "as essential to the well-being of village life as monarchs are to the welfare of their subjects."[31] For Karazin, serfdom as a system was intrinsically sound, but seriously marred by chronic abuse. He argued that the state should use its powers to regularize the institution and end the peasants' slavery. Ever the idealist, he considered the proper management of the peasants on their estates to be the landlords' absolute duty of service to the state.

As a young landowner himself, Karazin had already drawn up regulations for his peasants, or "settlers," as he called them. Subsequently, he published a plan for the regulation and management of the serfs on his own estates: "Towards the agricultural regulation of landlord estates based on quitrent."[32] Among its most important provisions was the granting to each adult male a plot of seven and a half desiatins (just over eight hectares or almost twenty acres) of arable land to be inherited in perpetuity, but which, after ten years, he was free to sell, thus recognizing the peasant's right to land ownership. The notion was central to his article devoted to the subject: "The opinion of one Ukrainian landowner expressed after a discussion with his peers about the *ukaz* of 23 May [1816] and its Estland provisions." Here Karazin attacked the emancipation—without land—of peasants in the Baltic province on the grounds that "the land is the property of the people and the landowners equally," and that "the landowners have ever been only the managers of the land." This article achieved a wide circulation, and was well known to the Decembrists. Thus, in his memoirs, which were first published three years after his death by Alexander Herzen in 1863, S. P. Trubetskoi scathingly remarked that "the Khar'kov landowner Karazin campaigned with all his considerable eloquence against the emancipation of the peasants and compared the condition of those lucky enough to live under his yoke with those who were freed without property of their own."[33] Nevertheless, as V. I. Semevskii, the great historian of the "peasant question," conceded in the 1880s, while Karazin's outlook generally could hardly be described as progressive, he was one of the very few who realized that serfs could not be freed without land, giving his proposals "one massive advantage" over those of most of his contemporaries.[34]

On December 12, 1819, Karazin wrote to Kochubei, minister of the interior, about serious infractions of the laws relating to peasants. Kochubei requested more details and by January, 1820, received from Karazin three further memoranda describing the widespread and flagrant abuse of serfs and Karazin's suggestions for dealing with the problem. This led to a number of meetings between Karazin and Kochubei the following spring to discuss the issues raised and possible solutions.[35] Thus, despite the earlier sanctions imposed on him, Karazin was not deterred from pursuing his unsolicited and often unwanted correspondence. As an early biographer put it, Karazin, "a voice crying in the wilderness," was by temperament irrepressible, exasperating senior courtiers and the tsar himself with his continual interventions.[36] But at least on the matter of serfdom, Karazin's was not a lone voice. Late in 1819, N. I. Turgenev sent to M. A. Miloradovich, governor-general of Saint Petersburg, for the tsar's attention a memorandum on the condition of serfs in Russia, pointing out that the only agency capable of ending the peasants' slavery in Russia was the throne. Alexander was so impressed by Turgenev's argument that he told Miloradovich he would "definitely do something for the peasants." The tsar's declaration prompted General Prince A. S. Men'shikov, an aide-de-camp of the tsar, to join with M. S. Vorontsov and Karazin to explore ways of promoting the tsar's resolve, canvassing opinion, and forming a society dedicated to improving the peasants' lot. Vorontsov wrote to Karazin on April 14, 1820, agreeing to join the proposed society on the grounds that the Russian nobility needed to rebut the charge that it continued to resist the "sacred and essential achievement" of the serfs' gradual emancipation. N. I. and A. I. Turgenev, as well as P. A. Viazemskii, supported the initiative, and it was in this context that Karazin was received by Kochubei on April 12 and then by Alexander himself on April 21. But there was no meeting of minds, and it is clear that

Karazin's projected Society of Good Landlords (*Obshchestvo dobrykh pomeshchikov*) found no support.[37] On the contrary, it was very far from what the tsar had intended. He checked the unwanted initiative by dismissing Men'shikov, whereupon those who had expressed initial interest in the project immediately withdrew their support, not least, according to Prince I. V. Vasil'chikov, commanding officer of the Guards Corps, because of Karazin's direct involvement.[38]

Although a contemporary of the Decembrists, Karazin was far from sharing the reforming aspirations of the conspirators, and, like the equally garrulous Pushkin, would have been a hopelessly unreliable member of a supposedly secret society. Indeed, in the letter to Kochubei referred to above, Karazin found it necessary to alert him to the spread of the Western "infection" among Russia's nobility: "Young men from our foremost families," he wrote, "are praising French liberty and do not hide their wish to see it introduced to their fatherland."[39] Karazin's attitude to the eastward spread of the "Western infection" is further evident from a diary entry of November 24, 1820, in which he reported with utter dismay that twelve officers had been heard to raise a toast in a Saint Petersburg restaurant to a future Russian constitution: "This monstrous spirit is spreading further day by day," Karazin lamented.[40] In conversation with Kochubei he identified S. G. Volkonskii, V. K. Kiukhel'beker, K. F. Ryleev, F. N. Glinka, and A. S. Pushkin as "suspicious individuals." Deeply troubled by the scurrilous and subversive content of some of the literature being passed from hand to hand in Saint Petersburg, Karazin effectively became Kochubei's self-appointed informer, and kept the minister of the interior abreast of developments in the Free Society of Lovers of Russian Letters and the "learned republic." A diary entry of November 18, 1819, reveals his grave objection to Pushkin's insulting characterization of the tsar in his 1818 poem "Noel" as "a wandering despot."[41] There seems little doubt that it was Karazin's April 2, 1820, report denouncing Pushkin as "a seditious epigrammatist" that helped trigger Pushkin's banishment from Saint Petersburg on May 6, 1820. The poet was dispatched to the southern city of Ekaterinoslav to serve in the chancellery of General I. N. Inzov; his absence from Saint Petersburg lasted seven years.[42] As the Soviet historian S. S. Landa commented, "The democratic content of enlightened ideology" in Karazin's case "degenerated into political subservience and even denunciation."[43]

Meanwhile, in November, 1819, Karazin submitted his peasant project to the Free Society of Lovers of Russian Letters. Its president, Fedor Glinka, responded with an invitation to Karazin to accept honorary membership in the society for his "outstanding erudition and publications in the sciences and Russian literature."[44] With characteristic energy, Karazin threw himself into its life and work, and already on December 29 was appointed vice-president and assistant to Glinka. At the society's meeting of March 1, 1820, Karazin gave a speech on learned societies and the periodical press; he declared that Russian writers and scholars must disseminate useful knowledge and contribute actively to the development of public opinion if they really were to live up to their self-designated status as "champions of enlightenment."[45] Unsurprisingly, Karazin's patronizing thrust and politically conservative tone (including the March 1 speech) rapidly made him unpopular with many Free Society members.

It was clearly a difficult time for Karazin. On April 21, 1820, the day of what proved to be his last audience with Alexander, he wrote the tsar a letter, prophetically declared to be "the swansong of a loyal subject." Expatiating on the "strange direction of minds" in Russia, Karazin urged the tsar to keep a "vigilant eye" on the threat posed by secret societies, and implored him to pay urgent attention to the injustices of life in Russia.[46] This time his letter was not ignored: Alexander immediately commanded Karazin to explain himself more fully to Kochubei, and to furnish details of precisely to what and to whom his letter referred. The very next day, as instructed, Karazin wrote to Kochubei. The otherwise willing informer indignantly declined the tsar's command to provide the names of those with whom he had discussed Russia's problems on the grounds that his conscience would not allow him such a "betrayal of all noble sentiments." Instead, he offered to set up a "department of statistics" to provide the government with all the data it needed "to form in a systematic way a clear picture of the true state of affairs in Russia."[47]

His report or "explanatory memorandum" took the form of a rambling exposition of his views that consumed seven notebooks, which, even so, remained unfinished. Karazin submitted the first of these to Kochubei on May 13 and the last on November 17, 1820.[48] They reveal the direction of Karazin's own mind, especially in relation to the failings of the current regime. He inveighed against the government's heavy-handedness in its dealings with non-Orthodox citizens, particularly Lutherans and Roman Catholics; its lack of respect for the Orthodox Church; its unjust treatment of the Russian people generally; its financial illiteracy, inadequate stewardship of the armed forces, and poor provision of medical services. He criticized the prevailing trend of "secretive" religion and mysticism, singling out the Bible Society with the comment that it was not clear that reading the Bible improved morality, proof of which was "our priesthood, one of the country's most depraved classes."[49] With each successive notebook of his memorandum Karazin became increasingly outspoken in his determination to "tell the truth" to Alexander. He was clearly aware of the risk this involved, commenting in his covering note to Kochubei that "to speak the truth is more dangerous than taking to the battlefield," since flatterers surrounding the throne would consider his observations "an insult to His Majesty." In conversation with Kochubei, Karazin nevertheless insisted that he felt obliged to tell the tsar the truth, regardless of the personal consequences, since no one else would dare. And in any case, he claimed to know better than anyone in government, including Kochubei, what ordinary folk, young people, and soldiers returning from France were actually thinking.[50]

And so it proved: Karazin's outspokenness did indeed render him vulnerable. In a note to Vasil'chikov of November 10, 1820, Alexander expressly associated Karazin "and his ilk" with the Semenovskii mutiny of October 16-18. The immediate cause of Alexander's suspicion was a scurrilous leaflet found on the pavement outside the regiment's barracks. Its authorship was never proved, but it was rumored to be a product of Karazin's subversive spirit. It is true that, as a former officer of the Semenovskii Regiment, Karazin made no secret of his sympathy for the mutineers. The tsar, however, dismissed claims of the provocative behavior of its commanding officer, Colonel Shvarts, convinced that the mutiny had been incited by secret society members. He told Vasil'chikov that he was certain he would find "the real culprits outside the regiment, in such individuals as Grech and Karazin." His readiness to blame Karazin and his apparent determination to make him a scapegoat for the mutiny was reinforced by Vasil'chikov's response on November 26, 1820, in which the latter described Karazin as "a most dangerous individual," who, "under the guise of unbounded personal loyalty to Your Imperial Majesty," could prove to be an "enemy of the very worst sort."[51] Karazin, who had just submitted the seventh notebook of his memorandum to Kochubei, was arrested the same day, November 26, and immediately sent to the grim fortress of Shlissel'burg where he would languish for six months. His papers were seized and ordered destroyed. Some have rightly argued that Karazin was being punished for continuing to adhere to a reformist political credo that, when shared with Alexander in 1801, had earned him the tsar's admiration and attention, but which almost twenty years later was no longer acceptable, since Alexander had moved so far away from his original liberal stance. To quote Tikhii's judicious comment "What could be said in 1801 could no longer be said in 1820."[52]

Among the more serious of Karazin's offences, as listed in his police file, was writing a plea for the legal rights of property to be developed and extended in line with the "general principles of monarchical government" and in the interests of the "genuine welfare of the people"; he also declared an interest in "supporters of the so-called rights of man in England," among the "most perceptive" of whom he cited the "remarkable" John Locke, the Enlightenment father of liberalism and author of the 1690 treatise on government that Karazin had read in French translation.[53] Karazin was no radical, however. He dismissed any idea of constitutional representation as "completely opposed to the spirit of religion which clearly proclaims that 'there is no other power than from God.'" Such sentiments defined him for one nineteenth-century commentator as "a typical representative of the conservative elements of his day," alongside N. M. Karamzin.[54] Yet in point of fact a free press was central to Karazin's conception of Russian political life such that, as he put it, "everyone [must be] free to express their views on matters in respectful [*skromnye*] conversations in print." Indeed, Karazin confidently anticipated a gradual convergence of public opinion and the tsar's intentions without the need for any major constitutional or institutional reform.[55]

According to A. I. Chernyshev, Governor-General Miloradovich, knowing the "undesirable direction of [Karazin's] thoughts, his restlessness, and his passion for intrigue," for some time had intended to arrest Karazin, but had decided to wait for a specific pretext, now provided by the tsar.[56] Kochubei, like Miloradovich, certainly knew that Karazin was not the author of the Semenovskii proclamation and admitted to Alexander in his report on the affair that its author was unlikely to be identified. But he did nothing to save Karazin from arrest.[57] He had, perhaps, been irritated by Karazin long enough, as is clear from the assessment he gave Nicholas I on his accession. In it, Kochubei summarized the official view of the importunate Ukrainian landowner: "It cannot be denied that there is a lot of good in what Karazin has written. However, the sheer audacity of the way he expresses his views . . . wholly outweighs any use he intends such opinions to be."[58]

What was particularly poignant, even ironic, about Karazin's fate is that some months before his arrest he had proclaimed in the pages of Nikolai Grech's *Syn otechestva* his confidence in the long-awaited emergence in Russia of freely expressed public opinion, and credited the tsar for facilitating this development. His article is an account of the annual assembly of the Russian Academy on January 10, 1820, chaired by A. S. Shishkov in the Imperial Public Library, and it concludes:

> I will long remember this extraordinary day. It confirms for me that public opinion is developing in Russia, and the dark ages [*mraki*] of centuries past *cannot* now return. . . . All praise to you, Great Sovereign, before whose face *such* discussions can take place![59]

Karazin's arrest and disappearance from Saint Petersburg prompted some sympathetic responses from liberal members of the emergent "noble intelligentsia," such as P. A. Viazemskii. Evidently, Karazin somehow learned of Viazemskii's sympathy for his plight: on his release from "six months' detention in dreadful [Shlissel'burg]," he wrote to thank him for his "part in alleviating [his] fate," and to beg him to do what he could to obtain the tsar's permission to write him one last letter.[60] N. M. Karamzin wrote Miloradovich on November 28 that he assumed Karazin's arrest was due to "yet another injudicious letter," adding that Karazin "should long have expected this [fate] for his enthusiastic, even fanatical, political declarations."[61] As Kochubei implied in a letter to Nicholas I in the first weeks of his reign, Karazin's besetting sin was "to forget all the respect subjects owe to the throne" and "in audacious language to denigrate the government's every action."[62] Commenting on the Karazin case in 1908, the historian N. K. Kul'man remarked, "The fate of V. N. Karazin in the reign of Alexander I is a total enigma . . . shrouded in some kind of fog that to this day no published documents can disperse."[63] However, Kul'man himself provides an answer with his assertion that "facts are facts and Karazin's lack of caution went beyond tolerable limits."[64] The difficulty for Karazin and other independent-minded nobles in their dealings with the tsar was that such "tolerable limits" remained undefined until they had exceeded them. And by then it was too late.

On his release Karazin was confined to his estate at Kruchik and permitted to correspond only via the provincial governor. Not until the accession of Nicholas I, and then only after the trial and sentencing of the Decembrists, was he allowed in the autumn of 1826 to leave his estate; even so, Saint Petersburg remained off-limits. Karazin protested his innocence, insisting that all he had ever tried to do was to alert Alexander to the imminent danger of revolution. Happily, his relations with the local Ukrainian nobility apparently proved more enduring that those he enjoyed with court circles in Saint Petersburg. In 1833 he faced financial ruin following years of financial mismanagement including his over-zealous support of Khar'kov University far beyond his means. But he was saved from expensive litigation and ultimate insolvency by collections made on his behalf by the provincial nobility and the townspeople of Khar'kov. In 1836 the vast library Karazin had amassed over the years, and which was reputed to have "embraced, as he did himself, all fields of human knowledge," was ravaged by fire: as many as five thousand volumes and numerous manuscripts, including—sadly for historians of Alexander's reign—his memoirs up to 1821, were lost.[65]

On November 16, 1842, Karazin, then seventy years of age, died of a fever while touring the Crimea, and was buried in Nikolaev. [66] Always driven by a vision of a better future for his countrymen, and brimming with ideas about how this might be achieved, Karazin died almost without notice from contemporaries. He did not languish in total obscurity, however, and was recalled from time to time both for his remarkable gifts and his obtuseness. Thus, in his article on Alexander I and Karazin, Alexander Herzen praised Karazin for his "indefatigable activity" and for "bringing to every issue a completely new view."[67] Kiukhel'beker thought Karazin's style could be labored and his views often mistaken, but admitted that he enjoyed reading him because "he has *ideas*, and that's the main thing."[68] The editor of the most complete collection of Karazin's letters and papers, D. I. Bagalei, then rector of Khar'kov University, considered Karazin "one of the most outstanding Russian public figures of the first half of the nineteenth century.[69] But others found him a controversial and ambivalent individual. Writing in 1871 and referring optimistically to the Great Reforms then underway, one commentator expressed his confidence that their continued progress would not be frustrated by the "assorted Magnitskiis and Karazins of our own day."[70] Although the centenary of Khar'kov University was marked in 1905 by the unveiling of a statue of Karazin, only since 1999 has the university borne his name. The inscription on his statue at the main entrance reads: "Abundantly blessed by the opportunity granted me to do some small good for my beloved Ukraine."[71]

Karazin was an indefatigable champion of both continuity and change in Russia under Alexander I, and an intelligent and vigorous advocate of public welfare. But his personal style and unabashed garrulousness were too unconventional for his own good. In his determination to pursue his vision for a Ukrainian university at Khar'kov he was fortunate that this project, at least, coincided with the tsar's own ambitions for the expansion of universities and schools throughout the empire early in his reign, thus ensuring its success. Karazin clearly had an original mind that, remarkably, led him to explore the possibility of clean energy, alternative fuel sources, and electricity as early as 1818, and even to articulate, far ahead of his time, the notion of global warming. However, Karazin's equally elaborate ideas about changing Russian society and political institutions to the advantage of all the tsar's subjects very quickly tested the limits of Alexander's tolerance of such views—indeed, within months of an initially promising personal rapport between the two men, which the tsar himself had initiated. Like many of his forward-thinking and imaginative contemporaries, Karazin simply placed too much confidence in Alexander's openness to individual opinion. Also like them, he failed to realize that, despite the sometimes conflicting signals, Alexander ultimately retained a very definite view about the extent to which he would tolerate expressions of both individual and public opinion. Thus, after such a brilliant start, Karazin was destined to live out the bulk of his career deprived of the imperial favor he craved and languishing in provincial seclusion, far removed from the imperial court at Saint Petersburg with which he nevertheless continued so strongly to identify.

NOTES

1 Karazin's police file is held in the Gosudarstvennyi arkhiv rossiiskoi federatsii (hereafter GARF), f. 109 (Archive of the Third Department), op. 229, d. 11. The fullest published collection of Karazin's correspondence is D. I. Bagalei, *Sochineniia, pis'ma i bumagi V. N. Karazina* (Khar'kov: Khar'kovskii Universitet, 1910). Other important sources for Karazin include V. Sreznevskii, "Karazin, Vasilii Nazar'evich," *Russkii Biograficheskii Slovar'*, 25 vols. (Saint Petersburg, 1896-1918) (hereafter, *RBS*), 8:486-99; Ia. V. Abramov, *V. N. Karazin, Osnovatel' Khar'kovskago Universiteta. Ego zhizn' i obshchestvennaia deiatel'nost'* (Saint Petersburg, 1891); N. Tikhii, *V. N. Karazin, vinovnik uchrezhdeniia universiteta v Khar'kove* (Khar'kov: Parovaia tip. i litografiia M. Zil'berberg i S-via, 1905); A. I. Herzen, "Imperator Aleksandr I i V. N. Karazin," *Poliarnaia zvezda 1862*, no. 7, vyp. 2, 8-56; V. G. Bazanov, *Uchenaia respublika* (Leningrad: Nauka, 1964); A. G. Sliusarskii, *V.N. Karazin: ego nauchnaia i obshchestvennaia deiatel'nost'* (Kharkov: Khar'kovskii gosudarstvennyi universitet, 1955).

2 RBS 8:486.

3 RBS 8:487.

4 Tatiana Khlebnikova, "Ukrainskii Lomonosov," *Rabochaia gazeta*, no. 71 (April 18, 2009). The two articles cited here do not appear to have been published.
5 The letter is quoted extensively in Abramov, *V. N. Karazin*, 16-19. The full text is in Bagalei, *Sochineniia Karazina*, 1-16.
6 Herzen, "Imperator Aleksandr I i V.N. Karazin," 16.
7 Karazin's own account of his first meeting with Alexander is contained in a well-documented, anonymous account of his efforts to fund and establish Khar'kov University: Vospitannik Khar'kovskogo universiteta 1820kh gg., "Vasilii Nazarovich Karazin, osnovatel' Khar'kovskogo universiteta," *Russkaia starina* (hereafter *RS*), 1875, no. 2, 329-38, esp. 330; see also ibid., no. 5, 61-80; ibid., no. 9, 185-200; ibid., no. 10, 268-79; ibid., no. 11, 470-77.
8 Bagalei, *Sochineniia Karazina*, 914.
9 A. N. Pypin, *Obshchestvennoe dvizhenie v Rossii pri Aleksandre I* (Petrograd: Ogni, 1918), 114, 122. See also Tikhii, *V.N. Karazin, vinovnik*, 74-75.
10 Bagalei, *Sochineniia Karazina*, 649-54 (esp. 649).
11 Ibid., 654-55 (letter of August 23, 1803).
12 Ibid., 656-57 (letter dated 1803).
13 On this, see James T. Flynn, *The University Reform of Tsar Alexander I, 1802-1835* (Washington, DC: The Catholic University of America Press, 1988), 48-49.
14 Bagalei, *Sochineniia Karazina*, 676-77 (Karazin's letter of resignation and the imperial *ukaz* confirming it). Thirteen memoranda from Karazin to the Khar'kov University council are found here (ibid., 666-76).
15 *RBS* 8:497; V. N. Karazin, "*Ia smelo mogu stat' pred sudom potomkov . . .*": *Karazinskii sbornik*, ed. I. K. Zhuravleva and E. A. Uzbek (Khar'kov: Maidan, 2004). Despite Karazin's fall from imperial favor, Moscow University had been quicker to recognize his "patriotic zeal for the spread of enlightenment throughout the fatherland" with the award of an honorary degree on March 28, 1805, just weeks after Khar'kov University had opened its doors (B. L. Modzalevskii, "Izbranie V. N. Karazina pochetnym chlenom Moskovskogo universiteta," *RS*, 1900, no. 4, 186).
16 Pypin, *Obshchestvennoe dvizhenie*, 124.
17 Herzen, "Imperator Aleksandr I i V. N. Karazin," 34.
18 Joseph de Maistre, "Pis'ma iz Peterburga v Italiiu," *Russkii arkhiv*, 1871, no. 6, 136.
19 Bagalei, *Sochineniia Karazina*, 897.
20 Ibid., 678-79.
21 *RBS* 8:491.
22 F. V. Karazin, "Pis'mo V. N. Karazina k M. M. Speranskomu," *RS*, 1872, no. 1, 82-83; Bagalei, *Sochineniia Karazina*, 699-700 .
23 Marc Raeff, *Michael Speransky, Statesman of Imperial Russia, 1772-1839* (The Hague: Martinus Nijhoff, 1969), 24.
24 Many of these are published in Bagalei, *Sochineniia Karazina*, esp. 609-871.
25 Ibid., 725-26.
26 Ibid., 186.
27 The articles mentioned here may be found in Bagalei, *Sochineniia Karazina*.
28 Ibid., 890.

29 Iu. B., "V. N. Karazin i gospodstvo nad prirodoiu," *Russkii arkhiv*, 1892, no. 5, 75-90; D. P. Miller, "Arest i ssylka V. N. Karazina," *Istoricheskii vestnik*, 1900, no. 3, 1047-53 (see p. 1048 for the eyewitness account of Karazin and Alexander I in Khar'kov drawn on here).

30 See *RS*, 1871, no. 3, 335-66.

31 *RBS*, 8:492.

32 V. N. Karazin, *Opyt sel'skogo ustava dlia pomeshchich'ego imeniia, sostoiashchevo na obroke* (Saint Petersburg, 1818); *RBS*, 8:493-94.

33 *Memuary dekabristov. Severnoe obshchestvo*, ed. V. A. Fedorov (Moscow: Izdatel'stvo Moskovskogo universiteta, 1981), 30, 321; *Nikolai I: Lichnost' i ephokha. Novye materialy*, ed. T. V. Andreeva (Saint Petersburg: Nestor-Istoriia, 2007), 238.

34 V. I. Semevskii, *Krest'ianskii vopros v Rossii v XVIII i pervoi polovine XIX veka*, 2 vols. (Saint Petersburg, 1888), 1:378.

35 Tikhii, *V.N. Karazin*, 215; Abramov, *V. N. Karazin*, 60-66.

36 Tikhii, *V. N. Karazin*, 212.

37 S. V. Mironenko, *Samoderzhavie i reform: politicheskaia bor'ba v Rossii v nachale XIX v.* (Moscow: Nauka, 1989), 131-32.

38 Tikhii, *V. N. Karazin*. 220-22, 224; T. V. Andreeva, *Tainye obshchestva v Rossii v pervoi treti XIX v.: pravitel'stvennaia politika i obshchestvennoe mnenie* (Saint Petersburg: Liki Rossii, 2009), 214-15. For an evaluation of Andreev's substantial volume, see Patrick O'Meara, "Recent Russian Historiography on the Decembrists: from 'Liberation Movement' to 'Public Opinion,'" *Kritika: Explorations in Russian and Eurasian History*, 14 (2013): 805-22.

39 Quoted in Mironenko, *Samoderzhavie i reform*, 128.

40 Quoted in Bazanov, *Uchenaia respublika*, 54-55.

41 M. V. Nechkina, *Dvizhenie dekabristov*, 2 vols. (Moscow: AN SSSR, 1955) 1:259.

42 Bazanov, *Uchenaia respublika*, 135, 141, 147; Mironenko, *Samoderzhavie i reformy* 145, n. 150; T. J. Binyon, *Pushkin. A Biography* (New York: Alfred A. Knopf, 2003), 97-102; A. S. Pushkin, *Eugene Onegin*. tr. Vladimir Nabokov, 4 vols. (London: Routledge & Keegan Paul, 1975), 2:193.

43 S. S. Landa, *Dukh revoliutsionnykh preobrazovanii . . . Iz istorii formirovaniia ideologii i politicheskoi organizatsii dekabristov 1816-1825* (Moscow: Mysl', 1975), 197.

44 Bagalei, *Sochineniia Karazina*, 894 (letter of November 8, 1819).

45 Ibid., 568-73; S. S. Shashkov, "Dvizhenie russkoi obshchestvennoi mysli v nachale XIX veka," Delo, 1871, no. 6, 157.

46 Bagalei, *Sochineniia Karazina*, 117-20.

47 Quoted in Tikhii, *V. N. Karazin*, 218-20; Abramov, *V. N. Karazin*, 84. The letter to Kochubei was written on April 22, 1820, and is published in Bagalei, *Sochineniia Karazina*, 120-23.

48 See Bagalei, *Sochineniia Karazina*, 123-154.

49 Quoted in Tikhii, *V. N. Karazin*, 226.

50 Kochubei's account of his conversation with Karazin is reproduced in Bazanov, *Uchenaia respublika*, 170-72.

51 Quoted in Tikhii, *V. N. Karazin*, 230; see also N. M. Druzhinin, *Revoliutsionnoe dvizhenie v Rossii v XIX v.* (Moscow: Nauka, 1985), 404.

52 Tikhii, *V. N. Karazin*, 57-58.
53 GARF, f. 109, op. 229, d. 11, ll. 23, 100, 109-10.
54 Shashkov, "Dvizhenie russkoi obshchestvennoi mysli," 156, 159.
55 Abramov, *V. N. Karazin*, 25, 27, 29; V. I. Semevskii, *Politicheskie i obshchestvennye idei dekabristov* (Saint Petersburg, 1909), 61.
56 Bazanov, *Uchenaia respublika*, 184-85, 187-88.
57 Vl. Lapin, *Semenovskaia istoria, 16-18 oktiabria 1820 goda* (Leningrad: Lenizdat, 1991), 166.
58 Bazanov, *Uchenaia respublika*, 166.
59 V. K., "Eshche otryvok iz dnevnoi zapiski ukraintsa," *Syn otechestva* 59, no. 2 (1820), 93-96 (italics are Karazin's). Karazin's fall from grace has interesting parallels with that of another temporary favourite of Alexander's, the Livonian nobleman, Timotheus von Bock. These are discussed in Patrick O'Meara, "Timotheus von Bock: Prisoner of Alexander I," *Slavonic and East European Review* 90 (2012): 98-123 (especially 121ff.).
60 Bagalei, *Sochineniia Karazina*, 908. Although undated, the letter was written in 1821.
61 Quoted in Tikhii, *V. N. Karazin*, 235
62 Bazanov, *Uchenaia respublika*, 165.
63 N. K. Kul'man, "Iz istorii obshchestvennogo dvizheniia v Rossii v tsarstvovanie imperatora Aleksandra I," *Izvestiia otdeleniia russkogo iazyka i slovesnosti imperatorskoi Akademii Nauk*, 1908, kn. 1, 99-147 (esp.122).
64 Ibid., 130.
65 Abramov, *V. N. Karazin*, 94. The comment on Karazin's library was made by an anonymous author in the February 1854 issue of *Sovremennik*, and is quoted in Iu. B., "V. N. Karazin i gospodstvo nad prirodoiu," 78.
66 Abramov, *V. N. Karazin*, 95.
67 See Bazanov, *Uchenaia respublika*, 119-20; Herzen, "Imperator Aleksandr I i V. N. Karazin," 32, 42.
68 V. K. Kiukhel'beker, *Puteshestvie, Dnevnik, Stat'i*, ed. N. V. Koroleva and V. D. Rak (Leningrad: Nauka, 1979), 269 (diary entry of August 25, 1833).
69 Bagalei, *Sochineniia Karazina*, xvii.
70 Shashkov, "Dvizhenie russkoi obshchestvennoi mysli," 22.
71 Abramov, *V. N. Karazin*, 96; *RBS*, 8:486-99.

The Imperial Russian Noble Elite and Westernization: The Family Eizen-fon-Shvartsenberg

Roger Bartlett
(School of Slavonic and East European Studies, University College London)

Among Gary Marker's writings on Russia is a thoughtful essay on "The Westernization of the Elite, 1725-1800."[1] He provides a vivid and wide-ranging picture of Russia's higher social strata, primarily the nobility but also the higher clergy and literati, surveying their social, cultural, and political development and their relationships with rulers and the system. He concludes persuasively that the educated Russian elites "reacted favorably and optimistically to the changes that went on around them" in the eighteenth century: some had discontents, and some felt a disconnection between their "Europeanization" and "that which they considered to be native" that could amount to a crisis of identity. But "all of them, even the doubters, fundamentally embraced almost matter-of-factly the westward-looking orientation" introduced by Peter I, until the shock of the Decembrist revolt called this stance into question.[2]

To this skillfully portrayed "abbreviated synopsis of Russia's eighteenth-century elite"[3] some additional brush-strokes may be added. One feature of the westernization process described so well by Professor Marker that deserves further consideration is the exposure of the elite to direct foreign influences. Successive eighteenth-century governments' cultural policies compelled close attention to imported foreign forms, but equally important was direct contact with things foreign in travel, work, or study abroad. The impact of foreign experiences on Tsar Aleksei Mikhailovich in Poland, and still more on his son Peter I during the Grand Embassy, is very well known. The new education of eighteenth-century nobles, with whom we are primarily concerned here, was also calculated to confront them with the outside world and its ways of thinking and seeing. Many of the iconic figures of Russian eighteenth-century culture received formative education abroad, from Feofan Prokopovich (Krakow and Rome) and V. N. Tatishchev (Berlin and Dresden) to A. N. Radishchev (Leipzig). The protagonists of the first debates on new Russian literary forms brought to their arguments a formative personal exposure to foreign cultures, V. K. Trediakovskii his experience of France (Paris), M. V. Lomonosov his of Germany (Marburg and Freiburg) – not to mention the foreigner and international diplomat A. D. Kantemir. Direct foreign sources of education could also be found inside the Russian Empire: Petr Rychkov, a merchant's son, historian of Orenburg, subsequently ennobled, learned his foreign languages and mental discipline in manufactures owned by foreigners, an education which gave him a good start in state service; while Andrei Bolotov's formative educational experiences came in the house of a Baltic German nobleman and in occupied Koenigsberg.[4] And by the end of the century, more prosperous young nobles who did not attend one of the new educational establishments that Professor Marker discusses[5] received the domestic education celebrated—caricatured—by Pushkin in *Evgenii Onegin*, which also commonly involved face-to-face westernization:

> *Sperva* Madame *za nim khodila,*
> *Potom* Monsieur *ee smenil.*
> *Rebenok byl rezov, no mil.*

Monsieur l'Abbé, *frantsuz ubogii,*
Chtob ne izmuchilos' ditia,
Uchil ego vsemu shutia,
Ne dokuchal moral'iu strogoi,
Slegka za shalosti branil
I v Letnii sad guliat' vodil.

At first *Madame* looked after him,
Then she was replaced by *Monsieur.*
The child was lively but charming.
Monsieur l'Abbé, a decrepit Frenchman,
So as not to exhaust the infant,
Taught him everything with a joke,
Didn't exasperate him with strict morality,
Ticked off his pranks mildly
And took him walking in the Summer Garden.[6]

Onegin's turn-of-the-century education, conducted by foreigners, produced a fashion-conscious "London dandy," full of self-confidence and *savoir vivre*, especially in matters of the heart; able to discourse superficially but widely on topical matters; fluent in French and lightly acquainted with Latin literature. . . . This was an elite education, proper to a member of the *beau monde*: "Society decided that he was clever and very sweet" (*Svet reshil / Chto on umen i ochen' mil*).[7] Fluency in French, a marker of late-eighteenth- and early-nineteenth-century Russian elite culture, itself sharpened the interaction with European culture. Research is only now uncovering the extent to which Russian nobles of the period both spoke and wrote in French.[8] Wealthy young Onegins also increasingly gained immediate experience of the European world through variants of the Grand Tour.

A second facet of direct interaction with things foreign was the rise in immigration. With the growth of the Moscow German Quarter after its relocation in 1652, the physical presence of foreigners had already made itself increasingly felt in the seventeenth century; but with Peter the trickle of immigrants became a flood, and foreigners (including such as Onegin's later tutors) embedded themselves in many aspects of Russian life. In particular, foreigners made up 26 percent of the Petrine officer corps, 40 percent in the infantry.[9] In the early years, many incomers came from Kiev and what is now Ukraine—something which Professor Marker has also investigated. But the greatest impact over time came from other parts of Europe. Erich Amburger provided an approximate analysis of natives and foreigners among the some twenty-nine hundred individual officials named in his monumental study of the imperial state apparatus of administration (ca. 1700-1917).[10] After certain exclusions, his data gave 1758 "natives" (Great, White, Little Russians/Ukrainians) and 1079 "non-Russians," of whom 914 had West European names. Excluding 355 (354?) Baltic Germans, the remaining 560 "West-Europeans" consisted of 122 born Orthodox, suggesting assimilation despite foreign ancestry, 225 officials born abroad, and 213 born in Russia to parents of non-Orthodox confessions. Thus a significant proportion of Imperial Russia's higher officials were immigrants or their offspring. In due course most of these incomers merged into the Russian nobility, which (like many others) was extremely mixed in its ethnic origins and composition.[11] Recent decades have seen great interest among both Russian and European scholars in foreign elements in Imperial—especially eighteenth-century—Russian society: research in this area has become a well-resourced international industry.[12] A particular feature of this work is its determinedly national orientation: Britons have primarily studied Britons, Germans have studied Germans, and French have studied French. The adventures and achievements of the different national groups are all valid in their own right, but this approach isolates and ghettoizes its subjects; a fresh examination of the place of foreign elements as a whole in Imperial Russia is overdue.

A third factor often understated in accounts of the westernization of Russia's elites is the formative significance of state service. Russia had long been a service state, but Peter I greatly increased the service burden on all estates, in particular requiring the nobility to become educated and, ideally, to administer the country in a rational way conforming to foreign models of law.[13] The new Petrine system of senatorial government, and the continually rising level of education demanded of its servitors, increased the "systematization of Russian government," in George Yaney's phrase; it compelled the elite to adopt more systematic ways of thought and standards of knowledge that approximated those of modern society elsewhere in Europe. These in turn led on both to the nineteenth-century bureaucratization of government and to the independence of mind that increasingly characterized significant parts of the elite.[14] This was the case not only in civil service, but also in the military, generally more prestigious and attractive to men of talent—as one recent author puts it, "officers' epaulettes attracted the most capably active and gifted part of the Imperial Russian nobility like a magnet."[15] Military service encouraged both specialist knowledge and systematic behavior. In its structure and social relations the imperial army reflected the existing features of Russian society, but it was also a sphere of technical modernization (and especially in such branches as artillery and engineering). The processes that culminated on December 14, 1825, took place primarily among military men: here the crisis of identity was most acute, and foreign experiences during the Napoleonic period played a significant role in the radicalization of many Decembrists.[16]

Professor Marker ends his investigation in 1800. By then the fundamental processes of change involved in westernization were indeed largely complete. The imperial noble elite (especially the wealthy and high-ranking nobility most exposed to these processes) had by now completely adopted European forms of material and personal culture, standards of knowledge and education, and arts and sciences, to the point where they were becoming contributors as well as consumers. At the same time, Russian national consciousness had been developing rapidly, although still intertwined with western influences: as internalization of western norms grew, so did critical distance from them. Karamzin for example, the well-educated and linguistically competent "Russian Traveler," was able in 1789-90 to hold his own as a Russian on visits to the great and good of Western Europe. On his return he wrote up his experiences in a bestseller whose sentimental mode was influenced by Laurence Sterne,[17] but his later literary performances increasingly stressed the dignity and worth of things Russian. The Napoleonic Wars, and especially 1812, hastened this process. By 1825 it was still more advanced, while the growing sense of difference between

Russia and Europe could express itself in both liberal and conservative terms. The Decembrist conspirators, broadly speaking, were essentially European by upbringing and education, but passionately wished to be able to take pride in their Russian fatherland; their equally westernized contemporary, Sergei Uvarov, formulated a different but conservative pride in Russia in his doctrine of Official Nationality. This expression of Russian exceptionalism, which at the same time represented a Russian form of the conservative national thought widespread across post-Napoleonic Europe, became the philosophy of the elite and the establishment.[18]

The army provided a context for both these extremes. It was also a stabilizing factor, standing guard before the established order; over time it increasingly became associated with the tsar and Russian national values.[19] Consequently it enjoyed majority noble support. One non-Russian ethnic group which shared this orientation and was well-represented in the military was the Baltic Germans, excluded from the calculation of foreign servitors above. This group was relatively highly educated, geographically and politically separate from the rest of the Empire's population, and through its culture uniquely linked to the West; but over the eighteenth century, after integration into the empire following the Great Northern War, most of its members came to see themselves as patriotic sons of the Russian fatherland and supporters of the imperial regime. Livonia (the imperial Baltic German provinces of Lifland and Estland) is sometimes construed as a cultural bridge between Russia and the West;[20] at the same time, the Baltic German contribution to the internal life of the empire, whether in civilian, military, or cultural affairs, is often underestimated, as Amburger's figures suggest.[21]

Many Baltic Germans served in the army. Figures for the officer corps at Borodino show that in 1812 a relatively large proportion of serving Baltic German officers held senior or staff positions.[22] They were particularly prominent in the Imperial Suite (*Svita E. I. V.*) and especially in its elite Quartermaster Department, equivalent to the modern general staff.[23] Baltic Germans made up 4.3 percent of all officers at Borodino, but 9.7 percent in the Quartermaster's Department.

The suite was also notable for the prominence not only of Baltic Germans, but of foreigners generally, especially Germans. The number of Germans overall in Russian government service rose steadily during the eighteenth century, falling away after the mid-nineteenth.[24] The imperial officer corps, even under Peter, was always primarily Russian, but Germans tended to be over-represented compared to their numbers in the population, especially in higher ranks.[25] Their favorable treatment, whether in the 1730s or the Napoleonic period, became a source of grievance for Russians. Aleksei Ermolov's response to Alexander I's offer of a reward for outstanding service—"Sire, promote me German!"—is well known. In 1806 Alexander had felt compelled personally to justify his award of a high army command to the Hanoverian L. L. Bennigsen, on the alleged grounds of foreign officers' superior education and qualifications.[26]

The army was also a linking factor between social classes, and the most straightforward ladder of social advancement.[27] Consequently, for foreigners in Russia, military service could also be an attractive means to stabilize and improve their social position. It is not surprising that the descendants of Catherine's outstandingly successful "Scottish Admiral," Samuel Greig (1736-88), continued in their ancestor's footsteps. His son became an admiral, but did not serve during the Russo-British stand-off 1807-12; he took Russian subjectship (*poddanstvo*) in the 1820s. Samuel's grandson had no compunction about fighting the British in the Crimean War, achieved general officer rank in the army, and also served as the imperial finance minister.[28] Perhaps less to be expected were the military careers of the descendants of Leonhard Euler (1707-83), the great Swiss mathematician, who divided his adult life between the academies of Berlin and Saint Petersburg. Euler's three sons were a physicist, a court physician and a lieutenant-general. The military line continued in succeeding generations, producing numerous general officers. A grandson, artillery general and member of the Military Council, took Russian subjectship in 1844 and the family's diploma of imperial Russian nobility was signed by the emperor in 1846.[29] A similar pattern marked the history of the Eizen-fon-Shvartsenbergs, another less well-known immigrant family, of German origin, which rose into the imperial Russian nobility through military service and achieved high service and social rank, with their history spanning most of the imperial period.

In 1831, Emperor Nicholas I stood godfather to the son of one of his senior officers, Colonel Karl Fedorovich Eizen-fon-Shvartsenberg, offspring of a "new" noble line:[30] it had taken only two generations of military service to bring them to the heights where they might hope for personal imperial patronage for their child.

The founder of the family in Russia, the colonel's grandfather, Johann Georg Eisen (1717-1779), was a civilian, an immigrant from Franconia, in southern Germany, to Estland. Here he found a post in 1741 as a domestic tutor and then served for nearly thirty years, from 1745 to 1775, as the Lutheran pastor of the parish of Torma, near Lake Peipus.[31] Johann Georg Eisen was the son of Pastor Gottfried Eisen (1683-1764), for fifty-five years Lutheran minister of the village of Polsingen in Franconia. Johann Georg was the fourth of sixteen children (several of whom died young) born from two marriages.[32] The only sibling about whom information is available is Johann Gottfried Eisen (1725-95), for a time in the 1750s chaplain ("field preacher") to the Ansbach Dragoon Regiment and from 1774 Pastor and Deacon of the Franconian town of Langenzenn, who in his turn left behind him a son and one or two daughters.[33] On the death of father Pastor Gottfried Eisen in Polsingen in 1764, his widow petitioned to be allowed to remain in the pastor's house for one year (a quite common practice), citing among other burdens "the many persons left behind by the deceased with very limited means, viz. a widow, many children who are either poorly or not at all provided for, and needy half-orphaned grandchildren."[34] This impoverished tribe is possibly significant for our story because (as will be seen) Johann Georg's direct descendants were apparently not the only Eisen von Schwarzenbergs in Imperial Russian service.

Johann Georg Eisen brought with him to Russia in 1741 the ideas and values of the German popular Enlightenment,[35] which he had absorbed in youth and as a student. He was highly educated, a theology graduate and student of cameral sciences and medicine at Jena University, which allowed him to find work in Livonia. He became an outspoken critic of serfdom, the first person in the Russian Empire to write and speak persistently and publicly against the institution, and for a short period in the 1760s he had a significant role in the peasant question in Russia.[36] He also became known as an advocate of smallpox inoculation, and found favor in military circles with an apparently revolutionary means of provisioning armies in the field. He succeeded in engaging influential and highly-placed figures in Saint Petersburg and at court with his ideas and his projects—G. F. Mueller, Peter III, I. I. Betskoi, the Counts Chernyshev, Grigorii Orlov, and Catherine II herself; however, he ended his life, a disappointed man, as a steward on the Chernyshev estate of Iaropolets, north-west of Moscow.

The coat of arms of the Nuremberg Eisens, also to be found on Pastor Gottfried Eisen's gravestone outside the parish church at Polsingen.

As minister of an Estland country parish, with Baltic-German landowners and Estonian peasants as parishioners, J. G. Eisen had nothing directly to do with the military; but he chose to enroll his two surviving sons, Gottfried (1749-1809) and Karl Christoph (1753-94), from birth in the imperial Russian army. Technically speaking, this was a step open at this time only to noble boys, who could be inscribed in a regiment, then released for education, so that by the time they were recalled to the colors they had served long enough to reach junior officer rank—a practice shortly (1782) to be outlawed by Catherine II.[37] Hence, it was important for the young Eisens to demonstrate noble status. Pastor J. G. Eisen had a complex relationship with noble status. The family in Franconia, although bourgeois, had a coat of arms, something not entirely uncommon in Germany at the time.[38] They also claimed connection to a distant noble line associated with the name Schwarzenberg, and in Livonia Eisen was evidently not indifferent to the temptation of reviving the noble patent for his own family. His position as a parish minister in the Baltic Lutheran church gave him status in some respects on a par with the nobility (he was allowed to own serfs, for instance), but not membership in the Baltic nobility itself. He had himself named Eisen von Schwarzenberg in public prints, and employed this name to secure the standing of his sons in their military career. But he only ever signed himself—whether in his extensive correspondence or his various publications—simply as Eisen.

Contemporaries commented on this anomaly, and Eisen explained it, somewhat hesitantly, to his friend and biographer, the chronicler F. C. Gadebusch:

> Following the example of various of my ancestors I let my sons style themselves so. This was done on account of an estate in Bohemia lost in the Thirty Years' War, and I wish I had not followed those people's example. But as my sons are now registered with this name, nothing can be altered in their case. So I think you should say: "A branch of the family habitually writes itself as Eisen von Schwarzenberg."[39]

Thus Eisen's sons Gottfried and Karl Christoph, as he intended, were the beneficiaries of his genealogical claims, not only adding the noble "von" to their names but probably benefiting also from sharing (without any actual connection) the name of the distinguished Austrian princely house of Schwarzenberg.

Gottfried and Karl Christoph, the first soldiers of the new imperial Russian family, had their initial brush with warfare on the outbreak of the Russo-Turkish war of 1768-74. On December 4, 1768, their father wrote to a correspondent:

> My sons have been called to their regiment, and as I hope reached it yesterday, to fight against Turks and [Polish] confederates. But as the younger one who is not yet 15 would play a partly troubled, partly laughable role, unless he could go as an orderly, I went after them in haste today.[40]

Father was able to retrieve younger son, who remained at home at his lessons until his service began in earnest: in 1771 Eisen reported, "My younger son was examined, passed with flying colors, became a sergeant, and was assured that at the next promotion he would be made an officer."[41] Both sons later fought against Pugachev.[42]

J. G. Eisen died in 1779. Six years later, in 1785, Gottfried Eisen von Schwarzenberg, with the rank of Captain of Artillery, appeared in the baptismal register of the Church of St Gertrude in Riga as father of a new-born son. By now Gottfried (in Russian Fedor Ivanovich) was well integrated into the Baltic noble milieu. His wife was the noble Charlotte Monica née von Scheltinga, and for witnesses at the baptism he could call upon representatives of the elite, including a major-general, a lieutenant-general, the wife of a *Landrat* (elected executive officer of the Baltic nobility) and the Countess l'Estoque.[43] The baby, baptized Carl Johann Gottfried, would subsequently make a notable military career as Karl Fedorovich Eizen-fon-Shvartsenberg (1785-1846 or 48).[44] Two years later came another son, Johann Leonhard (1787-1812), subsequently killed as a *shtabs-kapitan* of the Eighteenth Artillery Brigade at Borodino.[45] Further evidence of integration was membership in Freemasonry. The 1793 membership list of the Riga lodge Zur Kleinen Welt (Small World) includes at no. 16 'Eisen von Schwarzenberg, russisch-kayserlicher Capitain der Artillerie'.[46] Gottfried died in 1809 with the rank of Colonel of Artillery; his younger brother Karl

Christoph had predeceased him, apparently childless, in 1794, also in the rank of Colonel.[47]

Saint Gertrude's was a Lutheran church, indicating that Gottfried Eisen remained in the faith of his father. The available records give little further information on the religious affiliation of Johann Georg's descendants. The first two generations married into the (predominantly Lutheran) Baltic German nobility, but in the third generation Russian marriages became common. The interest of Gottfried's grandson Carl Gottfried, also known as Ioann, in the Orthodox church of Odessa University may suggest an inclination towards the majority imperial confession, though his painting style is neither particularly Lutheran nor Orthodox. The will of Carl Gottfried's sister-in-law, widow of his younger brother Nikolai, was processed in 1917 by the Lutheran Consistory. It was not uncommon for foreigners who took Russian subjectship also to accept Orthodoxy, assimilating to the dominant confession of their new environment. But since Peter I's reign this was by no means obligatory, especially in the imperial armed forces, and the Protestant churches were strong among the empire's German population (in Riga over the same period the prominent British immigrant family of Armitstead, repeatedly marrying into the Baltic German nobility, moved from Anglicanism to Lutheranism).[48]

Some documents of the Eisen von Schwarzenberg family are held at the Latvian State Historical Archive (LVVA) in Riga. One file of 1910 contains the registers of a large collection of family papers, which, however, seem not to have survived the vicissitudes of the twentieth century.[49] Another LVVA file documents a search for family information made by Carl Johann Gottfried/Karl Fedorovich in 1838, when he was about to obtain his patent of imperial Russian nobility from Saint Petersburg province and was anxious to acquire reliable information about his family name and origins:

> As I observe from some papers which have been found here that only my father and grandfather have borne this double family name. . . . It is really essential for me to obtain information about the matter at this time when my diploma of nobility is being drawn up, as well as for the status of my children and for all my descendants in general.[50]

Carl Johann Gottfried's subsequent correspondence with the Bavarian Chargé d'Affaires Baron de Tannenberg and the Windesheim Royal Land Court brought him contact with Eisen relatives still resident in Franconia, and also further information. He learned that the estate near Heidelberg held by the Nuremberg Eisen family, to whom his grandfather was related, was in fact called Schwarzenbrunn rather than Schwarzenberg; acquired in 1609 as a feudal grant, after allodification it had been sold twenty years previously. The claim to nobility had some substance but had always been controversial; the family coat of arms he had inherited was identical with that of the Nuremberg Eisens.[51]

By this time Carl Johann Gottfried/Karl Fedorovich had received his diploma of imperial nobility and was inscribed in the genealogical register of the nobility of Saint Petersburg province, the final step in the embedding of the family in imperial Russian noble society.[52] A later report of the Saint Petersburg Noble Deputy Assembly shows confirmation of nobility for eight (unspecified) members of the family.[53] This formal recognition of noble status crowned a distinguished career, in which the tsar's readiness to stand godfather to his son was but one step along the way.[54] After education in the Cadet Corps, Karl Fedorovich had entered service in the artillery about the turn of the century,[55] and was made a junior ensign (*podporuchik*) in 1801. He fought in the wars of the Napoleonic period, winning promotion, awards, and decorations: a gold cross and three years' seniority for skill and bravery as an ensign at Preussisch-Eylau (1807), a gold sword inscribed "For Bravery" for accurate fire against the Turks as staff captain at the siege of Silistria (1810), and the Order of Saint Vladimir, Fourth Class with ribbon for bravery at the siege of Napoleon's Free City of Danzig (1814). At the end of these campaigns he was assigned to the Kiev Arsenal, being promoted to lieutenant-colonel in 1816. In 1822, as "Lieutenant-Colonel and Commander of no. 3 Pontoon Artillery Battalion," he received the Saint George, Fourth Class, for twenty-five years' faultless service. The same year he became a Freemason, joining the Kiev Lodge of the United Slavs. In 1825 he was appointed to the Kiev Arsenal staff (*shtab-ofitserom po iskusstvennoi chasti pri Kievskom arsenale*). The following year he fell under suspicion of involvement in the Decembrist conspiracy and was placed under investigation, but acquitted. A full colonel from 1827, he was honored again the following year with the Saint Anne, Second Class, "in recompense for his excellently zealous service." It was in 1831 that the emperor stood godfather to his son; in that year he also helped crush the Polish revolt. His excellent service was later repeatedly recognized—again with the Saint Anne, Second Class, now "adorned with Our Imperial Crown," in 1831, and the Saint Vladimir, Third Class, in 1832. In 1834, now commander of the Kiev Arsenal, he received the "emblem of distinction" (*znak otlichiia*) for thirty years' blameless service, "to be worn according to the regulation on the St George ribbon," and the following year came promotion to major-general, with seniority from April 7, 1836 (OS). 1843 brought the Saint Stanislas, First Class, 1844 the forty-year service medal, and 1846 the Saint Anne, First Class. Karl Fedorovich died on August 22, 1848 (OS).[56]

At some point in his career Karl Fedorovich acquired landed property in the village of Borka in Cherepovskii District of Novgorod province, with twenty souls and 860 desiatinas of land. The peasants paid him an annual *obrok* totaling 137 silver rubles and sixteen kopecks.[57] Karl Fedorovich's acquisition of peasants was atypical: most officers of his generation were *bezpomestnye*, living from their service salary.[58]

Karl Fedorovich married Johanna von Pichlau,[59] of an established Baltic family, and they had four daughters and two sons. Of the daughters, Ekaterina was married to Colonel of Engineers Rodde; and Anna's husband, Ianovskii (Janowski), also reached the rank of colonel. Konstantsiia became the wife of Actual State Counsellor Dolgov and Mary of Councellor of State Kalinskii.[60] The elder son, Carl Gottfried, appears as Ioann Karlovich in official records, but was apparently known as Karl in the family. Born February 20, 1824 (OS), he died as a retired major-general in Sevastopol in 1906.[61] He served in the Caucasus,[62] and it seems that he was the Eizen-fon-Shvartsenberg who wrote brief memoirs of M. S. Vorontsov's Caucasian campaign against Shamil and the bloody Dargo expedition of 1845. At the time he was a junior ensign in the Second Reserve Sapper Battalion. By the 1860s he was a colonel of the Semenov Guards Regiment.[63] The memoirs were published in Odessa many years after the event, in 1892, in *A Southern Miscellany*, sold in aid of famine relief.[64] In that same year Ioann Karlovich Eizen-fon-Shvartsenberg donated to the Alexander Nevskii Church of the Novorossiiskii University in Odessa a picture of the Transfiguration of Christ.[65] He appears to have been an amateur painter himself—a picture of Virgin and Child with his name on it as the artist appeared recently on the internet.[66]

It was Ioann, named in the relevant documents as Karl, who after 1861 became responsible for the Borka estate and dealt with the emancipation of its peasants. The Borka inheritance had until then been owned jointly by the six children. The now twenty-one "temporarily obligated" former serfs had previously had use of all their master's land. At emancipation the local statute fixed their allotment at a considerably lesser amount (although their new *obrok* was to be exactly the same as the old), with 484 desiatinas and 1200 sazhens of forest reverting to the landowner: the siblings entrusted Karl Karlovich with its sale.[67]

Ioann/Karl's younger brother, the tsar's godson Nicolai Fabian or Nikolai Karlovich Eizen-fon-Shvartsenberg (b.1831, d. 1910 in Tsarskoe Selo), made an equally if not even more successful military career. Educated at the First Cadet Corps, he graduated in 1849 and became an officer in the Semenov Guards regiment. He was evidently a crack shot, winning two prizes for shooting. Guards captain from 1862, he

Virgin and Child, with saints at each side. On the reverse, in Cyrillic: *Ris[oval] Ioann Eizen f. Shvartsenberg*

was made colonel in 1864, major-general in 1870, and lieutenant-general in 1880; his papers included six patents for service awards, four patents for the receipt of orders of chivalry, including the Polish White Eagle, and four patents for promotion in the presence of the emperor. He fought in the 1849 Hungarian campaign and the Crimean War, 1853-56. From 1864 he was senior adjutant on the Staff of Guards Forces (*starshii ad'iutant shtaba voisk gvardii*) and of the Saint Petersburg Military District, from 1867 military commander of Saint Petersburg province, and from 1876 also commander of local troops in the Saint Petersburg Military District. From 1882 as general of infantry he commanded the Thirty-Fourth, and from 1884, the Thirteenth Infantry Division, and from 1886 to May, 1891, the First Grenadier Division.[68]

During his colonelcy (1864-70), Nikolai Karlovich was for a time head of a Saint Petersburg military hospital.[69] The hospital had been founded by Nicholas I in 1835 as the Saint Petersburg First Military Land Forces Hospital (*Pervyi voenno-sukhoputnyi st-peterburgskii gospital'*) and renamed in 1869 by Alexander II as the Petersburg Nicholas Military Hospital. The list of directors of the hospital is another reminder of the significant numbers of senior officers of German extraction in the imperial Russian army. In succession they were Lieutenant-General fon Vendrikh, Colonel fon Talberg, Colonel N. K. Eizen-fon-Shvartsenberg, Colonel I. S. Biriukov, Major-General Medler, Major-General K. K. Strandmann (the latter occupying the post from 1874 to 1883). Thus, with one exception, until the late nineteenth century all *nachal'niki* of this hospital were of Germanic descent.[70] Nikolai Karlovich was evidently able to combine this post with his other commands in or near the capital.

How far the generations kept in touch with their roots in Franconia and in Torma is hard to judge: evidence is sparse and episodic. Johann Georg corresponded from Torma with his brother in Germany. Karl Fedorovich, as we have seen, made contact with relatives in Nuremberg. At the end of his life, in 1909, Nikolai Karlovich instituted a charitable fund or foundation (*Eisen-Stiftung*) in Torma in memory of his great-grandfather: it provided an annual sum of sixty rubles to the Torma parish school for the education of ten 'disadvantaged but industrious' children.[71] He also donated to the church a small silver chalice, into the bottom of which is set a silver medal awarded to Johann Georg Eisen by the count of Schaumburg-Lippe:[72] this is still preserved among Torma's church treasures.

With this generation the direct male Eizen-fon-Shvartsenberg line, and so the name, died out. No wife or children of Ioann Karlovich are reported. Nikolai Karlovich was survived by his widow, Elena Aleksandrovna (d. 1917), daughter of Major-General A. N. Karlin. They had two daughters, Varvara who died young, and Elena, living in 1917.[73] The women of the family are often difficult to trace: the 1898 published record in the *Sankt-Petersburger Zeitung* of the death of Anna Janowski (Ianovskaia) née Eisen von Schwarzenberg[74] is a rare exception. At the same time, however, the currently available records provide fragmentary indications that other members of the extended Eisen family may also have found their way to Russia and into Russian service. Among the extant family papers is a passport for a Johann Philip Eisen, candidate in theology ("*Candidatus Theologiae*"), who worked as a domestic tutor with the Bistram family in Livland in the 1760s.[75] And the records of the soldiers who survived and were decorated at Borodino in 1812 include another Eizen-fon-Shvartsenberg, twenty-four-year-old Ensign Iogan Leonardovich of the Twenty-Sixth Artillery Brigade, closely similar in age and profile to Staff Captain Johann Leonhard of the Eighteenth Artillery Brigade, who died there. The available service record of Iogan Leonardovich lists him as a noble and a graduate of the First Cadet Corps, also as a foreigner; he is shown as a bachelor.[76]

J. G. Eisen's presence within the empire, his ideas, and his activities all exemplify aspects of the westernization process discussed by Professor Marker. While Leonhard Euler and Samuel Greig were summoned to Russia by rulers intent on promoting change—new and western skills and knowledge—Eisen came unbidden, as a private person. But his compulsive desire to make new discoveries that would serve the public good made him, like them, an advocate of innovation on western lines. The descendants of all three used imperial service both to rise socially and to serve tsar and state, with Eisen's children appearing in the artillery, one of the technologically more modern branches of the army. Available evidence is insufficient to draw detailed conclusions about their intellectual and philosophical worldview. Eisen's sons, Gottfried and Karl Christoph, received their education at home and in Baltic German institutions; later generations passed through the Cadet Corps. Karl Fedorovich was close enough in time and space to the southern Decembrist uprising to be placed under investigation, but was exonerated; doubtless his Masonic affiliation played a part here, though Masonic membership is not itself very indicative. There is no information on subjectship, but (as far as judgment can be made) successful integration into the nobility seems to have brought with it quite rapidly an acceptance of the dominant conservative values of the imperial elite. Karl Fedorovich's acquisition of Borka made him a *pomeshchik*, absentee owner of some of the servile peasants whom his grandfather had wanted to free; Karl Fedorovich's heirs were in no hurry to liberate them. Ioann Karlovich's artistic efforts were not in the Orthodox tradition, but his philanthropic and religious interests, fragmentary as the evidence for them is, were entirely congruent with the values of a late imperial general officer. While Johann Georg Eisen, a foreign immigrant and civilian intellectual, sought to bring about change within imperial Russian society, the succeeding military generations of the Eizen-fon-Shvartsenberg family, like those of Greig and Euler, appear to have accommodated themselves fully to the prevailing status quo and the establishment lifestyle and values and conventions of their new milieu.

NOTES

1 Gary Marker, "The Westernization of the Elite, 1725-1800," *A Companion to Russian History*, ed. Abbott Gleason (Chichester: Wiley-Blackwell, 2009), 180-95.

2 Ibid., 192-93.

3 Ibid., 181.

4 *Russkii Biograficheskii Slovar'*, s.v. Rychkov, Petr Ivanovich, and email from Prof. Colum Leckey; *A. T. Bolotov v Kenigsberge*, ed. B. Antonov et al. (Kaliningrad:

Kn. Izd-vo, 1990); A. Rexheuser, "Andrei Bolotov. Königsberg als Bildungserlebnis eines Aufklärers," in *Zentren der Aufklärung, II: Königsberg und Riga*, ed. H. Ischreyt (Tübingen: Niemeyer, 1995 = Wolfenbütteler Studien zur Aufklärung, Bd. 16), 87-121.

5 Marker, "Westernization," 183.

6 *Evgenii Onegin*, I, iii-viii. This hopelessly plodding literal translation—a poor thing, but mine own—serves only to indicate the basic meaning. For a respectable version by C. Johnston, and discussion, see http://lib.ru/LITRA/PUSHKIN/ENGLISH/onegin_j.txt (accessed July 29, 2014).

7 Ibid.

8 See, for example, E. P. Grechanaia, *Kogda Rossiia govorila po-frantsuzski* (Moscow: IMLI RAN, 2010), and the large-scale project "The History of the French Language in Russia," University of Bristol, UK, 2011-2014, of which first fruits are published in *Vivliofika* 1 (2013) and *European Francophonie. The Social, Political and Cultural History of an International Prestige Language*, ed. V. Rjeoutski et al. (Oxford: Peter Lang, 2014). Of officers serving in 1812 at Borodino, over 90 percent of Guards but only 30 percent in total knew French, 25 percent German. Some 51 per cent had only basic literacy. D. G. Tselorungo, *Ofitsery russkoi armii—uchastniki borodinskogo srazheniia: istoriko-sotsiologicheskoe issledovanie* (Moscow: IIK "Kalita," 2002), 128.

9 Tselorungo, *Ofitsery*, 97.

10 Erik Amburger, *Geschichte der Behördenorganisation Russlands von Peter dem Grossen bis 1917* (Leiden: E. J. Brill, 1966), 517-18.

11 For ethnic origins—and claims—of Russian noble families, see, e.g., A. B. Lobanov-Rostovskii, *Russkaia rodoslovnaia kniga*, 2nd ed., 2 vols. (Saint Petersburg: A. S. Suvorin, 1895). The corporation's title, *rossiiskoe dvorianstvo*, possibly also reflected this multiethnicity, since in nineteenth- and twentieth-century usage "*[r]ossiiskii* refers to the state and its citizens (hence usually irrespective of ethnicity), while *[r]usskii* refers to the Russian language and the ethnolinguistically defined Russian nation that constitutes a subset of Russia's citizenry" (T. Kamusella, "The Change of the Name of the Russian Language in Russian from Rossiiskii to Russkii: Did Politics Have Anything to Do with It?" *Acta Slavica Iaponica* 32 [2012]: 73-96 [80]). The lack of any differentiation in English between *rossiiskii* and *russkii* obscures a significant divide. However, this usage had serious historical ambiguities, duly laid bare by Kamusella and his commentator O. Ostapchuk (ibid., 97-104).

12 The literature produced is much too extensive to list here. Principal scholarly authors, leaders, and facilitators include Vladimir Berelowitch, Anthony Cross, Dittmar Dahlmann, Gianluigi Goggi, Sergei Karp, and Francine-Dominique Liechtenhahn.

13 Marc Raeff, *The Well-Ordered Police State: Social and Institutional Change through Law in the Germanies and Russia, 1600-1800* (New Haven: Yale University Press, 1983); see also a pugnacious counter-view—Andre Wakefield, *The Disordered Police State: German Cameralism as Science and Practice* (Chicago: University of Chicago Press, 2009).

14 George L. Yaney, *The Systematization of Russian Government: Social Evolution in the Domestic Administration of Imperial Russia, 1711-1905* (Urbana: University of Illinois Press, 1973).

15 Tselorungo, *Ofitsery*, 3. On the attractiveness of service, particularly military, see Janet M. Hartley, *Russia 1762-1825: Military Power, the State and the People* (Westport Conn.-London: Praeger, 2008), 49-52.

16 Hartley, *Russia 1762-1825*, 65-67.

17 Andrew Kahn, *Nikolai Karamzin,* Letters of a Russian traveller. *A translation, with an essay on Karamzin's discourses of Enlightenment* (Oxford: Voltaire Foundation, 2003). Kahn's essay discusses Karamzin's literary strategies. His notes to the text should be treated with caution.

18 On the Decembrists and Uvarov, see recently Nicholas Riasanovsky, *Russian Identities: A Historical Survey* (Oxford: Oxford University Press, 2005), 126-29, 132.

19 Hartley, *Russia 1762-1825*, 189.

20 Most recently by M. Schippan, who excludes Baltic Germans from his study of the Enlightenment in Russia: Michael Schippan, *Die Aufklärung in Russland im 18. Jahrhundert* (Wiesbaden: Harrassowitz, 2012), esp. 43.

21 M. Iu. Katin-Iartsev, "Baltiisko-nemetskoe dvorianstvo na rossiiskoi sluzhbe, XVII-konets XVIII v.," *Vestnik moskovskogo universiteta,* Seriia 8. Istoriia, 2000 no. 2: 25-49. A case study: Roger Bartlett, "Culture and Enlightenment: Julius von Canitz and the Kazan' *gimnazii* in the Eighteenth Century," *Canadian-American Slavic Studies* 14 (1980): 339-60.

22 Tselorungo, *Ofitsery*, passim, esp. 97-98.

23 Ibid., 28, 97-98. Service requirements for officers of the Suite were very high: ibid., 132.

24 Amburger, *Geschichte*, 518.

25 See Hartley, *Russia 1762-1825*, 57-58 (somewhat self-contradictory); Walter Pintner, "The Nobility and the Officer Corps in the Nineteenth Century," in *The Military and Society in Russia 1450-1917*, ed. Eric Lohr and Marshall Poe (Leiden-Boston-Köln: Brill, 2002), 250, referring to the later nineteenth century.

26 Tselorungo, *Ofitsery*, 97-98.

27 Ibid., 72

28 See the relevant articles in *Russkii Biograficheskii Slovar'*.

29 S. V. Volkov, *Generalitet Rossiiskoi Imperii. Entsiklopedicheskii slovar' generalov i admiralov ot Petra I do Nikolaia II*, 2 vols. (Moscow: ZAO Tsentropoligraf, 2009), 1:789-90; *Sankt-Peterburgskaia dvorianskaia rodoslovnaia kniga*, *Litera Ė.*, comp. I. A. Anisimova et al. (Saint Petersburg: Izd. VIRD, 2003), 8-9.

30 Latvian State Historical Archive, Riga (hereafter LVVA), fonds [f. (archive number)]1100, apraksts [a. (archive register)]14, lietas [l. (file number)]199, lapuse [lp. (folio, page)]2. The name occurs both with and without hyphens.

31 On J. G. Eisen, see Roger Bartlett, "Russia's First Abolitionist: The Political Philosophy of J. G. Eisen," *Jahrbücher für Geschichte Osteuropas* 39 (1991): 161-76; Roger Bartlett and Erich Donnert, eds., *Johann Georg Eisen. Ausgewählte Schriften. Volksaufklärung und Leibeigenschaft im Russischen Reich* (Marburg: Vg Herder-Institut, 1998).

32 Sophie Maria Elisabeth, 1711-12; Juliana Margaretha, b.1714; Christian Friedrich, 1715-17; Johann Georg, 1717-79; Christian Friedrich, b. 1718; Magdalena Margaretha, 1720-29; Juliana Elisabeth, b. 1721; Johann Gottfried, 1723-25; Johann Gottfried, 1725-95; Johanna Christiana, b. & d. 1726; Johanna Christiana, b. 1727; Johann Wilhelm, b. 1727; Johann Sigmund, b. 1731; Georg Heinrich, b. 1732; Johanna Magdalena, b. 1734; from the second marriage, Anna Catharina,

b. 1743. Polsingen, Kirchenarchiv, Trauungs- und Tauf-Register 1701-1760 (K2), passim.

33 Johann Gottfried, b.1777; Johanna Euphrosinia, b.1780. A first son, Georg Albrecht (1765-88), succumbed to scarlet fever: Archiv des evangelisch-lutherischen Pfarramts Langenzenn, K6, Taufregister 1753-92, ff. 177, 209; Totenregister 1753-96, 1788 no. 29. On Pastor Gottfried Eisen and his son Johann Gottfried, see also Matthias Simon, *Ansbachisches Pfarrerbuch. Die Evangelisch-Lutherische Geistlichkeit des Fürstentums Brandenburg-Ansbach 1528-1806* (Nürnberg: Verein für bayerische Kirchengeschichte, 1957), 99-100, nos. 594-97. Johann Gottfried senior apparently shared his elder brother Johann Georg's temperamental nature: he left violent comments on the papers of legal cases in which he was involved: Landeskirchliches Archiv Nürnberg (hereafter LKAN), Markgräfliches Dekanat Langenzenn, B154, N[4]; B237, Pfarramt Langenzenn 163. The brothers evidently maintained contact after Johann Georg settled in Estland: *Ausgewählte Schriften*, 673.

34 LKAN, Markgräfliches Konsistorium, Ansbach, C687 (Polsingen 1710-72), ff.114-15.

35 See Roger Bartlett, "German Popular Enlightenment in the Russian Empire: Peter Ernst Wilde and Catherine II," *Slavonic and East European Review* 84 (2006): 256-78; on J. G. Eisen, note 31 above.

36 Roger Bartlett, "30 October 1763: The Beginning of Abolitionism in Russia," in *Days from the Reigns of Eighteenth-Century Russian Rulers, Proceedings of a Workshop, dedicated to the memory of Prof. Lindsey Hughes. . . . Ravenna, Italy, 12-13 September 2007,* 2 parts, ed. A. G. Cross (Cambridge: Study Group on Eighteenth Century Russia, 2007), 2:135-48.

37 Hartley, *Russia 1762-1825*, 56.

38 *Grosses Wappen-Bilder-Lexikon der bürgerlichen Geschlechter Deutschlands, Österreichs und der Schweiz*, ed. O. Neubecker (München: Battenberg, 1985), Bd. V, Tafel 4, entry "Eisen." Reproduced by kind permission of H. Gietl Verlag, Regenstauf.

39 *Ausgewählte Schriften*, 3-4 and note 8.

40 Ibid., 592.

41 Ibid., 603.

42 Ibid., 633, 673.

43 LVVA, f. 1100, a. 14, l.197, lp. 1, 1785 baptismal register, no. 68: Carl Johann Gottfried Eisen von Schwarzenberg, born May 14, baptized May 21 (copy dated 1836).

44 http://ru.wikipedia.org/wiki/, "Eizen-fon-Shvartsenberg, Karl Fedorovich" (accessed September 9, 2012), which gives date of death as 1846; for 1848 see note 55 below.

45 LVVA, f. 1100, a.14, l.197, lp. 7; Tselorungo, *Ofitsery*, 345; http://www.kulichki.com/gusary/istoriya/vojny/bitvy/borodino/hram__spasitelya.html#ubity (accessed August 10, 2012).

46 Probably Gottfried. The date of birth given, 1743, is incorrect for either brother.

47 LVVA, f. 1100, a.14, l.197, lp.7, family tree.

48 See Roger Bartlett, "The British Community in Riga in the Eighteenth and Nineteenth Centuries: A Preliminary View," in: *Riga im Prozess der Modernisierung. Studien zum Wandel einer Ostseemetropole im 19. und frühen 20. Jahrhundert,* ed. E. Muehle and N. Angermann (Marburg: Verlag Herder-Institut, 2004), 52-70.

49 LVVA, f. 1100, a.14, l.199, lp. 1 o. p. [*otra puse*, verso]
50 LVVA, f. 1100, a.14, l. 197, lp. 3.
51 LVVA, f. 1100, a.14, l. 197, lp. 5, letter from Windesheim Royal Land Court, September 4, 1838; Angelika Gailit-Miķelsone, "Jānis Georgs Eisens un 18. gadsimteņa latvju zemnieka raksturojums," *Izglītības Ministrijas Menēsrakts* (Riga), 1926, no. 2 [February], 136-49; ibid., no. 3 [March], 217-30 (2:138-41).
52 LVVA, f. 1100, a. 14, l.199, lp. 2 o. p.
53 Rossiiskii gosudarstvennyi istoricheskii arkhiv, Sankt-Peterburg (hereafter RGIA), f. 1343, op. 51, d. 658, l. 157; also cited in *Sankt-Peterburgskaia dvorianskaia rodoslovnaia kniga, Litera Ė*, 8. The RGIA file gives no individuals' names: most probably they were Karl Fedorovich, his wife, and six children. I am greatly indebted to Polina Evgen'evna Poddelkova for help with materials from RGIA.
54 The following is based upon LVVA, f. 100, a. 14, l. 198 and http://ru.wikipedia.org/wiki/ "Eizen-fon-Shvartsenberg, Karl Fedorovich." Where the indications of these sources differ, I have preferred LVVA.
55 The exact date is not recorded in LVVA, and subsequent long-service medals point to either 1796 or 1804; Wikipedia gives 1801.
56 RGIA f. 577, op. 22, d. 3904 (1865), l. 14 ob.
57 Ibid., l.1ob. Papers on the case refer to the family's holding variously as part or all of Borka.
58 Tselorungo, *Ofitsery*, 100; Pintner, "The Nobility and the Officer Corps," 244-45.
59 LVVA, f. 1100, a. 14, l.199, lp. 1-1o.p.
60 RGIA f. 577, op. 22, d. 3904, l. 20. Anna Janowski's death, aged 70, recorded in *St. Petersburger Zeitung*, vol. 172, no. 304 (October 31, 1898):7; see also the Amburger Archiv Datenbank (Munich), no. 64537.
61 LVVA, f. 1100, a.14, l.197, lp. 7 (gives date of birth as 1822); f. 1100, a.14, l.199. lp. 2 o.p. (specifies name as "Ioann (on-zhe Karl) Karlovich Eizen-fon-Shvartsenberg")
62 Ibid.
63 RGIA f. 577, op. 22, d. 3904, l. 8ob. (1864).
64 Eizen-fon-Shvartsenberg, "O voennykh deistviiakh na Kavkaze v 1844-1845 gg.," in *Iuzhnyi sbornik v pol'zu postradavshikh ot neurozhaia* (Odessa, 1892), 101-10; also cited at http://www.vostlit.info/Texts/Dokumenty/Kavkaz/XIX/1840-1860/Delvig/pred1.htm (accessed September 9, 2012)
65 V. V. & G. S. Levchenko, "Iz istorii Imperatorskogo Novorossiiskogo Universiteta," in *Vorontsovskii Sbornik*, Issue 4 (Odessa: Studiia "Negotsiant," 2011), 40–46 (p. 41), at http://memory.od.ua/books/levchenko11.pdf (accessed September 9, 2012).
66 http://sammler.ru/index.php?showtopic=68330 (accessed March 3, 2013). Repeated efforts to contact the copyright-holder have failed.
67 RGIA f. 577, op. 22, d. 3904, ll.10, 17.
68 http://regiment.ru/bio/EE/27.htm (accessed September 9, 2012); LVVA, f. 1100, a.14, l.199, lp. 2.
69 442-й окружной военный клинический госпиталь, http://www.mil.ru/848/1045/1272/1365/1363/23356/1924/29835/index.shtml (accessed January 19, 2010).
70 http://www.mil.ru/848/1045/1272/1365/1363/23356/1924/index.shtm (accessed January 19, 2010).

71 "10 unbemittelte aber fleissige Kinder": "Nachrichten für folgende Generationen", 4, information deposited in the Torma church spire-ball in 1911 by the then Pastor A. Laas. The ball was taken down and opened during renovation work in 2014. My thanks to Ylo Pärnik (Lilastvere) for this and other material.

72 See *Ausgewählte Schriften*, p. 69; Anton Jürgenstein, *Huwitaw peatükk Eesti minevikust. Johann Georg Eisen von Schwartzenberg (Torma-Lohusoo õpetaja 1746-1775.)* Tartu 1921 (Eesti Kirjastuse-Ühisuse "Postimehe" kirjastus), 32.

73 RGIA f. 1480, Acta des Petrograder Evangelisch-Lutherischen Konsistoriums, op. 1, d. 2116 (1917), concerning the will of E. A. Eizen-fon-Shvartsenberg, l.51 ob.

74 See note 60.

75 LVVA, f. 4011, a.1, l.1205 (Personalien in Riga und Baltikum: Eisen von Schwarzenberg), lp. 1, August 30, 1765. The only evidence for a family connection, however, is the presence of the document in this file.

76 Tselorungo, *Ofitsery*, 345; http://karpets.livejournal.com/872468.html (accessed October 30, 2012); http://adjudant.ru/cadet/065.htm, http://www.adjudant.ru/cadet/067.htm (accessed October 8, 2012): *Lieutenant (from January 7, 1810), Staff Captain (from August 26, 1812) Eizen fon Shvartsenberg Iogan Leonardovich* 26th battery battalion of the 26th artillery brigade (from 26.01.1811). 1.3: At 1.01.1812 – 24 years old. 2.6: Foreigner, of noble descent. 4.1: Graduated from the 1st Cadet Corps in 1806 5.6: Preisisch-Eilau, 26-27.01.1807. 6.4: Smolensk, 4.08.1812. 6.6: Borodino, 24, 26.08.1812. 7.2: Wounded in the head, Borodino, 1812. 8.8: Gold sword "For bravery," Borodino, 1812. 8.10: Staff Captain, Borodino, 1812. 9.2 Has not been a prisoner of war. 10.2: Single. No other information on this person has come to light; extant records show him serving in a different battery from Johann Leonhard, but suspicion arises—could the two in fact have been one and the same person?

"Only the principle of public life and the full rights of citizenship": The Russian Technical Society, the Public Sphere, and the Revolution of 1905

Joseph Bradley
(University of Tulsa)

Founded in 1866, the Russian Technical Society (RTO) was the most prominent of a generation of societies created to promote industrial development and technical education. During the last fifty years of the imperial regime, RTO facilitated the development of industry, communications, and transport; it also disseminated scientific and technical knowledge and undertook scientific research. It provided the tsarist government with memoranda and reports that evaluated technical projects and their benefit to the state. RTO's meetings were not only a source of scientific and technical information but also an arena for the discussion of policy questions, thereby making RTO an inter-departmental and public forum where the technical intelligentsia, industrialists, and government officials could discuss important problems of industry, labor, and technology. Like its counterparts in France and Britain, RTO furthered technical education; it ran a variety of enterprises including vocational schools and classes, Sunday and evening schools, schools for children of factory workers, and public lectures. It became a resource center for vocational curriculum development and pedagogy and, eventually, an advocate of universal compulsory education. RTO organized congresses on vocational education and technical training, congresses that became a forum for a variety of public issues. Through its myriad projects, RTO provided an example of what private initiative could do to study problems, facilitate solutions, and mobilize talent.

As it had nurtured public science since the eighteenth century, officialdom recognized that the state needed the technical expertise generated in civil society. Because private initiative helped the government to achieve its goals of bringing prosperity and prestige to the empire, the government encouraged private initiative. The very fact that the recommendations of RTO were taken seriously and discussed by officialdom demonstrates the organization's importance. At the same time, the bearers of this expertise were becoming more and more independent of the state. They regarded themselves less as servants of the monarch or of the state; nor were they servants primarily of an abstract science. Instead, more and more they were servants of the nation, of the people.

Such civic activism challenged the tutelage of the authorities, and the efforts of RTO to promote industry and industrial education received mixed signals from the government. The tension between private initiative and officialdom, whose intellectual origins Gary Marker examined in his first book on eighteenth-century publishing, came to a head on the eve of the Revolution of 1905. The present article will trace the contribution of RTO to Russian public life at the beginning of the twentieth century as well as its involvement in the Revolution of 1905. Although the revolution radicalized the society, especially its Moscow branch, well before this fateful year in Russian politics, RTO, and in particular its education commission, had asserted a role in the formulation and assessment of government policy.

On the eve of the 1905 Revolution RTO had nine divisions: Chemical, Mechanical, Construction, Military, Photography, Electricity, Aviation, Railroad, and Technical and Vocational Education. There were thirty-two branches of RTO all across the empire, from Vilna to Vladivostok. The branches addressed problems of local industry, transport, and municipal services, and also organized public lectures. On January 1, 1905, RTO had 685 members, not counting the members of the branches.[1] The society published *Zapiski Imperatorskogo Russkogo tekhnicheskogo obshchestva* beginning in 1867, and several of the branches published their own *zapiski*. In addition, RTO published three more specialized journals: *Zheleznodorozhnoe delo*, *Elektrichestvo*, and *Tekhnicheskoe obrazovanie*. The society ran a museum, a library, and a laboratory in Saint Petersburg.

RTO was incorporated in 1866 by a government-approved charter that authorized considerable opportunity for public examination of many problems of Russian technology and industry. The highest decision-making body was the General Members' Meeting, five meetings of which convened in 1905 in the Museum of Applied Knowledge in Saint Petersburg. The chief executive organ was the board, which met nineteen times during 1905. Although the charter was commonly regarded as a document that indicated the limits of a Russian society's activities, Evgenii Nikolaevich Andreev, one of RTO's founders, encouraged a different interpretation. The organizational structure and administration outlined in the charter, Andreev argued, were "not the limits of the society but its rights, approved by a legal act, rights that [would] be the key to the society's success."[2] Because government ministers tolerated voluntary associations in the framework of duties and privileges, it is significant that RTO's guiding spirit framed his interpretation of the charter in the language of rights, not yet as widespread in Russian discourse as it was in Western Europe. Indeed, the charter outlined the most far-reaching approval yet by the government of a private association's public activity, a fact that underscores the government's support of private initiative when it was channeled in certain directions.

Even before the Revolution of 1905, RTO became a critic of government policy in the field of education. For decades RTO had organized extensive programs of technical education, an area in which Russia had been a latecomer. Prior to the founding of RTO, neither the state nor the industrialists made a concerted effort to support technical education. Russia's few technical schools catered to the ministries that ran or supervised them. Yet by the early 1860s, recalled Peter Kropotkin, "all Russia wanted technical education." Still, the many schemes for technical education in and out of government, including the short-lived Sunday school movement, lacked an institutional focus, direction, and guidance.[3]

The division of RTO charged with the study and improvement of technical education was the Standing Commission of Technical and Vocational Education. The commission's bylaws conferred certain rights and responsibilities. The members themselves elected the officers, subject to approval by the curator of the school district, an official of the Ministry of Education. At the same time, according to the commission's bylaws, membership on the education commission was neither limited in number nor subject to approval by the authorities. To support its projects, the commission received an annual budget from RTO and annual subsidies from the Ministry of Finance; in addition, it had the right to solicit donations from private sources, largely from industrialists.[4] The education commission regarded the Ministry of Finance's interests as an expression of confidence and a validation of its authority to manage the schools.

Similarly, RTO had broad powers to found and administer technical schools and vocational classes at factories and in worker districts.[5] Thus in 1882, when the government issued charters to the schools run by RTO, "the government, in return for a certain amount of desired public initiative, offered private persons a wide range of independent activity."[6] RTO ran a variety of educational establishments: specialized vocational schools, classes for adult workers and minors, courses on special subjects, and primary schools for children of factory workers. At the beginning of the twentieth century RTO ran fifty-five schools and classes. In 1905, RTO schools enrolled 7,272 pupils and employed 563 teachers, many of whom worked pro bono.[7] Despite Russia's long tradition of central control of education, an in-house history of RTO observed, "[The society's schools] represent something unprecedented anywhere in Russia, even at the present time."[8]

One of the most important missions of RTO was the creation and dissemination of useful knowledge in order to publicize certain issues within its competence. This mission involved more than just information gathering and dissemination; it also involved advocacy.[9] The education commission became a resource center for technical and vocational education in myriad ways. Publications, of course, were often the most widely used method of such outreach, and the education commission published its own *Proceedings* (*Trudy*), "in order to offer its affairs to public discussion [*glasnost'*]."[10] It drafted model rules and regulations for vocational schools and classes. In addition to overseeing the teaching at vocational schools, it surveyed textbooks and teaching manuals and drew up curricula and lesson plans. It ran weekly colloquia on pedagogy and methodology, modeled after the technical colloquia that were run by the engineering divisions of RTO, and open to teachers at all of RTO's schools. RTO appointed commissions to study specific problems (such as workers' education, women's technical education, the teaching of drawing classes, apprenticeship, and many others) and to petition the government on questions of technical education. In 1892, the education commission launched the Mobile Museum of Teaching Aids, which quickly became well known throughout Russia for its innovative collection. The education commission organized excursions, founded and maintained homes in the countryside for sickly children, ran pensions to house teachers, and raised money for insurance, burial funds, and financial aid to students. It also provided legal aid and mediation to individuals desiring to open societies and mutual aid funds at schools. In all activities, the education commission solicited the opinion of outside (non-member) experts on educational issues, thereby promoting horizontal linkages in Russian civil society.[11]

Well before 1905, the Standing Commission on Technical and Vocational Education came under the watch of the authorities. The commission attracted the attention of the Ministry of Education for allegedly "instilling in its worker-pupils anti-government and anti-religious ideas" and for distributing "harmful underground publications."[12] In the eyes of the police, the education commission had too much autonomy and too little supervision over its members and meetings; the membership was allegedly filled with politically "unreliable" public activists (*obshchestvennye deiateli*) and few government officials. It had taken "an extremely undesirable direction in the area of worker education." As a result

> The education commission is a nursery of anti-government ideas, the favorite stage for the illegal activities of unreliable persons with ill-intentioned and hostile thoughts who, having penetrated the teaching and administrative staff of the vocational schools, have freely and legally begun to educate workers in anti-government and anti-religious principles.[13]

In the view of the authorities, meetings of the education commission not only contained anti-government content, but were also too open. According to Article Twenty-Seven of RTO's bylaws, guests could attend meetings by invitation from a member; Article Fifty allowed students to receive free passes to meetings. Students and guests were supposed to sign a register, but the society's officers had not been vigilant about enforcing even these rather liberal regulations. The political police complained that workers and students freely attended "undesirable" lectures and received anti-government propaganda under the guise of the education commission's "lawful meetings." The commission went so far, according to one report, as to "use public meetings to proclaim the urgent need of a constitutional form of government in Russia."[14]

More troubling to the authorities than the membership and meetings of RTO's education commission were the vocational education teachers; they, after all, had direct, repeated, and government-sanctioned contact with workers. The political police claimed that technical and vocational schools, in Europe as well as in Russia, had been "targeted" by revolutionary groups because of their concentration of factory workers. Such projects allegedly had "nothing to do with technical education and everything to do with spreading liberalism and socialism among the populace."[15] Insofar as the commission was granted the right to hire teachers, the Ministry of Education thought that it had only a minimal supervisory role. Consequently, according to the authorities, the commission hired "unreliable" teachers. Using legal means, "they [had] freely begun to educate workers in anti-government and anti-religious principles." The government, the authorities insisted, must ensure that institutions created to educate the population be "protected from the fashions of the time (*ograzhdeny ot prekhodiashchikh veianii vremeni)*" and that technical and vocational education be conducted in a "spirit favorable to the government."[16]

The friction between RTO and the authorities emerged in the open at three congresses on technical education organized by the education commission. In the last half-century of imperial rule, more than one thousand congresses debated all manner of intellectual and policy matters. In Europe congresses were quintessential components of the public sphere: venues for people to come together to deliberate matters of common concern. Procedures schooled participants in the language and practices of representative institutions, and the participants represented themselves, or their "constituents," before an assembly of their peers. Congresses also represented certain causes or projects before the larger arena of public opinion and before governments.

Not surprisingly, in Russia such public assemblies came under government scrutiny. Although there are studies of the censorship of the printed word in tsarist Russia, with the exception of the theater, censorship of the spoken word has been less well documented.[17] Congresses, including topics of sessions and even of individual papers, required the approval of the authorities and were subject to a variety of rules and regulations, eventually codified in 1906. The organizers were responsible for maintaining order but, as an extra precaution, the local governor or chief of police sent representatives to attend the meetings. The police could close the meeting—that is, censor speech—if the discussion deviated from approved topics, if unauthorized persons were present, or if demonstrations incited insubordination to the authorities. Congresses organized by Russia's most prestigious societies, such as RTO, were routinely granted permission, and most were pacific in character until the eve of the Revolution of 1905. Nevertheless, the authorities took no chances, creating a cat-and-mouse situation between the authorities and an increasing number of activists, especially among Russian physicians, engineers, economists, and teachers. The resulting paper trail in the archives of various government ministries, the Department of Police, and local police provides the historian with a peephole into the deliberations at meetings, often not recorded in the official congress publications.[18]

Dissemination of useful knowledge and publicity were the stated goals of Russia's many congresses, and the congresses of technical education were no exception. They were convened to collect data, to study "the conditions for the proper organization" of technical education, and to acquaint the public with the state of Russian technical education. Of course, commissions in the ministries of Education and Finance had been discussing technical education for years, but now information gathering was set up in such a way as to authorize a rather open-ended discussion of Russian social and economic life, and to solicit and shape public opinion. Gathering data from educators as well as from representatives of the zemstvos and city councils "to elucidate the degree of preparation of the population for technical and vocational education" justified the discussion of general as well as technical education.[19] At the Second Congress on Technical and Vocational Education in 1896, several speakers stated that general education was a prerequisite to successful technical training. "The vocational school," claimed I. A. Anopov in his study prepared for the congress,

> must wherever possible develop and prepare the student to face all the unforeseen circumstances of life by making learning easier. One can specialize later . . . the system is better that does not create an educational dead end prematurely (*ne pritypliaet cheloveka prezhdevremenno*).[20]

Indeed, one might say that advocacy of an education "platform" consisting of issues framed not only by RTO, but also by other technical and education societies and even by government officials, was an unstated goal of the technical congresses. Not surprisingly, the results of this form of public interactivity—the soliciting and shaping of public opinion—indicated that further progress in industry and in technical education would depend on literacy and the level of general education of the working population.

The section on general questions was a congress within a congress, and fired off some fifty petitions on a wide variety of issues. Several resolutions aimed to revitalize the Sunday schools for workers—to open more Sunday schools and to broaden their curriculum, to allow more books at their libraries, and to make more space available in regular schools for Sunday schools. According to Ia. V. Abramov, the chronicler of the Sunday school movement, the ninth section, attended predominantly by "Sunday people" (*voskresniki*), became a de facto congress on Sunday schools and "clarified many matters to the participants, as well as united and energized them."[21] The section also drew up plans for model schools based on data collected from 147 officials of elementary schools; the data were published in the *Proceedings* (Trudy) of the congress. A quarter of a century after RTO established its first vocational school, the congress aired criticisms of the existing framework of technical schools, thereby pushing the boundaries of public criticism of government policy. The section passed resolutions critical of government education policy: in particular, the absence of local control of the schools and the absence of universal primary education. Other resolutions aimed to expand opportunities for extramural learning—to remove restrictions faced by local educators in organizing public lectures, to allow public lectures in the native languages on the borderlands, and to do away with the restrictions placed on the books that public libraries could acquire.[22] Although N. M. Pirumova, a Russian authority on the zemstvo liberal movement, claims that there were no significant political discussions at the first two technical congresses, in fact the ninth section of the second congress drafted petitions for a greater public role in worker education, for a limitation of child labor, and for greater regulation of artisanal enterprise and the relations between master artisans and apprentices.[23]

The Third Congress on Technical and Vocational Education in December 1903-January 1904 was closed by the Saint Petersburg city governor (*gradonachal'nik*) for allowing anti-government speeches, thereby becoming, according to one Soviet historian, the first volley of the intelligentsia in 1905.[24] The opening address by V. I. Kovalevskii, former assistant minister of finance and future president of RTO, stated outright that "further progress in vocational education depended on a change in the existing political system."[25]

Controversial topics came up in various sections. Reflecting the advocacy of local control, an issue that animated many of the delegates, the first section passed a resolution stating that secondary schools needed more autonomy and the freedom to select their own personnel; the third section passed a resolution calling for the government to eliminate the obstacles to Jews in all educational institutions. But most stormy was the section on workers' education. At the session of December 29, the chair, Karl K. Mazing, announced that all sessions would be open to the public and that everyone had the right to participate in discussions, a decision that allegedly opened the door to "all the agitators" of the congress.[26] Delivered in front of education administrators, papers criticized the Ministry of Education for thwarting the outreach efforts of RTO and other technical societies. Despite the efforts of the congress officers to keep the discussion on topic, the section discussed all manner of subjects—public school teachers, the expansion of the powers of the zemstvos and city councils, universal education, zemstvo taxes, government insurance, workers' hours, adult education, Sunday schools, temperance, leisure time—all of which would work better, the argument ran, with the granting of civil liberties.[27]

On the eve of the Revolution of 1905, several Russian congresses had become more turbulent, the best example being the Pirogov congresses of Russian physicians.[28] One incident at the Technical Education Congress was especially provocative and suggests that while the authorities might tolerate dispassionate criticism of government policy, they could not countenance incendiary language or disorder in the meeting hall. A delegate from the Social-Democratic Party, German Nikolaevich Vasil'ev, criticized the "servile language" of the congress officers who discussed "minor questions of technical education at a time when all of Russia wants to overthrow autocracy." Vasil'ev continued: "You boast that you work hard and have organized some 130 panels—well, the Committee of Ministers has a mass of meetings, but nothing ever comes of them." Laughter from the audience momentarily stopped Vasil'ev before he continued: "Enough of these conciliatory speeches, let's speak plainly what we all want, let's boldly cry 'Down with autocracy, long live the constituent assembly!'" The memorandum of the Department of Police noted that this speech prompted the "furious applause of the participants."[29]

The report of the Department of Police assessed the shortcomings of the third congress and implicitly, it might be added, the laxity in their own censorship procedures. First, the absence of any qualification requirement to attend the congress allowed too many "outsiders," allegedly without competence in the areas of vocational and technical education, to take part in the proceedings. Second, the rules of the congress were violated frequently, papers were not carefully examined in advance, and too many chairs of sessions were unprepared or incapable of conducting a meeting. Finally, the programs of the individual sections were too broadly defined, providing an opportunity to discuss extraneous matters. Because there were insufficient measures to guarantee "a peaceful and orderly conduct of business," any "objective discussion" was impossible. One commentator noted, "You can't discuss complex and serious matters before a crowd. . . . Those speakers who didn't talk about serious matters but spoke in loud, empty phrases . . . were rewarded by noisy applause." The officers of the congress found it impossible to keep order. At the same time, they feared that closing the section on workers' education would merely result in the agitators flocking to other sessions; indeed, the police noted that work at other sections was occasionally interrupted by "invasions of flying detachments" from the workers' education section. As a result, "from the very first meeting, the most well-attended section turned into a noisy mob that interfered with the business of other sections and provoked the most extreme measure—shutting down the congress," which the Saint Petersburg city governor did one day ahead of schedule.[30] Even Tsar Nicholas II weighed in, penning on the police report, "This is appalling! They don't know how to behave at a serious meeting."[31]

Osvobozhdenie, the liberal oppositionist paper published abroad, gloated, "Now in Russia not one meeting of educated people can go by without a discussion of the need to change the existing, unbearable order." Like more and more meetings of this period, the congress demonstrated to its participants that they were not alone: "All over Russia there is the same pulse of public dissatisfaction. . . . Everywhere the dismantling of the political order has proceeded quite far such that activists scattered all over the country are not isolated but are soldiers in a single army in the struggle against autocracy."[32]

After Bloody Sunday politics was no longer confined to the education commission and its congresses but entered the general meetings of RTO and meetings of its board. At the meeting of January 29, 1905, members unanimously passed a resolution critical of the government:

> Whereas the convulsions in Russian industry owing both to the general disruptions of Russian life and also to the lawless position of our workers that have damaged the development of technology and industry, the General Meeting deems that the Imperial Russian Technical Society is morally obligated to give top priority to the labor question and to immediately convene an all-Russian congress on the labor question. . . . Recognizing that under current conditions (the ban on public discussion and the restrictions on the freedom of the press and assembly) a productive and many-sided study of the labor question is impossible, the General Meeting finds imperative the immediate realization of complete freedom of discussion in the press and in meetings as well as other guarantees that public meetings and organizations have repeatedly insisted on, including the meeting of Russian engineers of 5 December 1904.[33]

From the beginning of March there were large meetings every week at RTO's headquarters in Saint Petersburg, attended by students, workers, and other guests. Hats bearing the words "For arms," "For the Socialist-Revolutionary Party," "For the victims of Bloody Sunday," "For workers exiled from Petersburg," "For striking workers," etc. were passed around for donations.[34] Large stormy meetings took place at the same time in the schools at which workers and agitators sharply criticized the actions of the government and called for an armed insurrection. Despite this, RTO and its branches were not subjected to the tsar's decree of May 21, 1905, according to which the minister of internal affairs could shut down congresses whose activity was deemed harmful to public security and order; the decree also authorized the ministry to close for a year any type of society, assembly, or union.[35]

RTO left its greatest mark on the events of 1905 through its involvement in the union movement and its study of the labor question. The All-Russian Union of Engineers and Technical Specialists had its beginning at a banquet on December 5, 1904. The driving force of the Union of Engineers was RTO member L. I. Lutugin, a geologist and mining engineer, one of the organizers of the Third Congress on Technical and Vocational Education, and member of the Executive Committee of the Union of Liberation; many members of RTO joined the union.[36] The engineers called for the immediate convocation of a national assembly to determine a new basis of statehood. In order for such a union to work effectively, the engineers also called for the removal of emergency measures, freedom of the press, and amnesty for all political prisoners.[37]

On January 28, 1905, the Sixth Division of RTO (Electricity) decided to organize symposia on the labor question and to invite members of other associations and of the Union of Engineers. On January 31, the RTO executive board offered its auditorium to the Union of Engineers, and from this moment began joint meetings of the union and RTO, organized by a special commission to study the labor question, consisting of members of RTO and the Union of Engineers, as well as economists, physicians, and jurists. The special commission organized five symposia between February 4 and March 19, 1905. The symposia were crowded and lively; at the symposium of February 10 there were over one thousand participants, including many students and three hundred workers.[38]

The symposia also discussed the government commission to investigate the reasons for worker dissatisfaction, better known as the Shidlovskii Commission, which was announced on January 31. The engineers mistrusted the government and regarded the Shidlovskii

Commission as too "*anketnaia*," that is, created solely to gather information. On the other hand, the engineers regarded their own special commission as a better forum for a full discussion of the labor question. The engineers reasoned that, as the bearers of technical knowledge, they were in the best position to be intermediaries between all sides—government, industrialists, and workers. At the same time the members of RTO guarded the privileges of RTO as a government-approved association. Consequently, at a symposium organized by the special commission on February 11, RTO members voted against a resolution put forward by representatives of the Russian Social-Democratic Party that supported worker demands for revolutionary action. At the symposium, one worker proclaimed that liberals wanted to manage the labor movement in their own interests. Another worker shouted that workers did not need tutelage, neither from the tsarist government, nor from the engineers. Thus, in a situation of political polarization the moderate members of RTO were caught between an untrustworthy government and a radicalized labor movement.[39]

Meetings at the branches of RTO also discussed the labor question. The annual meeting of the Libava branch on March 25 appointed a special commission to study measures to improve workers' lives. Meetings of the new Novocherkassk branch on March 12 and 19 expressed support for freedom of the press, speech, and assembly; inviolability of person and domicile; removal of the state of strengthened security; release of political prisoners and prisoners of conscience; and the convocation of a constitutional assembly. The Tula branch investigated workers' hours, wages, medical aid, sanitary conditions, and educational opportunities. The study of working conditions asserted that searches, conducted of workers to guarantee the integrity of factory property, were inappropriate and that workers needed to have the right of association and assembly without permission in order to discuss their needs. Although the Ministry of Internal Affairs authorized the Odessa branch to open a mobile museum of teaching aids, the Odessa city governor (*gradonachal'nik*) imposed a series of restrictions pertaining to assemblies, public lectures, concerts, plays, and donations.[40]

But Moscow had the most active and politicized organization. On January 1, 1905, the Moscow branch had 357 members; its long-time head (serving from 1904 to 1921) was K. K. Mazing. At a meeting of the Moscow education commission on November 10, 1904, N. I. Kuliabko-Koretskii delivered a report on "Education in Bulgaria," examining the Bulgarian constitution, Bulgaria's political freedoms, and the need to introduce such a political system into Russia, as well as about the important role of teachers and the teachers' union in preparing the population for a constitution. The memorandum of the Department of Police, always sensitive to disorder, noted that "Kuliabko-Koretskii's report prompted noisy ovations from the large audience of workers."[41]

More than one thousand people attended a meeting of December 29, 1904. Mazing announced at the opening that it was arranged as a public meeting in which all participants had the right to comment on the reports. N. V. Kasatkin, an instructor of drawing and secretary of the Moscow branch, opined that the work of RTO would be more productive were it not for the current government, and he appealed to the intelligentsia "to wrest [from the Ministry of Education] the right to educate the ignorant masses." Another speaker, P. I. Korzhenevskii, reported on the restrictions the government placed on public education and on the necessity of guaranteeing the free and unrestricted work of educational institutions. "The time is ripe," Korzhenevskii claimed, "to settle accounts with the government and destroy the bureaucratic wall that separates the people from the intelligentsia. . . . Only the principle of public life and the full rights of citizenship can lead the Russian people to happiness."[42] Mazing's request that the remaining speakers avoid matters unrelated to the purposes of the commission was met with catcalls and whistles. Finally, a paper on public libraries ended by stating that a library system could be properly organized "only under a constitutional order, when the government would be made up of representatives freely elected by the people."[43] As a result of such manifestations, the Moscow police chief refused to permit the next scheduled meetings of the commission on December 30-31.

A members' meeting of January 25, 1905, voted for a resolution that stated that normal operation of the Moscow branch was impossible without fundamental changes in the state structure; the resolution called for popular representation and the convocation of a constituent assembly.[44] At a meeting of March 7 of the Moscow branch's Sanitary Division, one speaker ended his report with the words, "Down with the bureaucracy; in order to cast off this yoke we must be armed."[45] Finally, at a March 26 meeting of the Commission's Museum of Assistance to Labor there were anti-government speeches, three choruses of the "Marseillaise," shouts of "Down with autocracy!" and leaflets titled "To arms!"[46]

For such outbursts, on March 30 the Moscow city governor forbade further meetings of the Moscow branch. A May 5 memorandum of the Department of Police to the Ministry of Internal Affairs gave an extremely negative assessment of the Moscow branch. Thus, at meetings "politically unreliable persons" gave "confrontational speeches," and tried to arouse in the audience "revolutionary ideas about the necessity of introducing a constitutional government in Russia." In addition, the educational institutions of the Commission on Technical Education were "a fertile field for the illegal activities of unreliable persons who, moreover, utilizing a legal base, started to instill anti-government principles in the workers."[47] For the remainder of 1905, many layers of the bureaucracy exchanged correspondence in which they proposed shutting down the Moscow branch completely, but that desire was never actualized, and in the fall of 1905 the divisions of the Moscow branch reopened.

Not all RTO activity was incendiary. Especially active in 1904-1905 was the Fourth Division (Army and Navy), chaired by N. N. Beklemyshev, chief of the Office of Merchant Marine Ports of the Naval Ministry. The most important work of the Fourth Division revolved around three issues: support of domestic industry, the workers' question, and the creation of a League for the Renovation of the Navy. On December 18, 1904, Beklemyshev proposed a special committee to study the capacity of Russia's shipbuilding and machine plants. At a meeting of the Fourth Division on March 1, 1905, and at a general members' meeting of RTO on March 12, 1905, Beklemyshev reported on the need to strengthen the navy by developing native industry; the members' meeting followed suit, and resolved to petition the government to give shipbuilding orders to Russian factories.[48] At a meeting of December 13, N. I. Dmitriev reported on the technical and administrative organization of European shipbuilding factories, arguing that, unlike in Russia, in Germany, where "entrepreneurship is encouraged and well paid," there were bonuses for building ships with German materials, which led to a high level of shipbuilding.[49]

The workers' question emerged in these same discussions. For instance, at a meeting on November 8, 1905, the Fourth Division discussed measures for profit-sharing that would include workers as a way to raise labor productivity at shipbuilding plants. Many participants at the meeting viewed such profit-sharing as premature, though dividing the wealth among all was deemed desirable. N. I. Dmitriev noted that more was required of workers in the West than in Russia, where the demand for factory workers exceeded the supply. Moreover, Dmitriev added, since the current "agitation" of workers was "part of a big campaign against Russian industry," in order to prevent future hardship "we must find other means to improve the condition of workers such as insurance and housing." One participant proposed inviting workers' representatives to discuss this matter, but another demurred, noting that "the reason for all our difficulties is the animosity of workers against capitalists."[50]

RTO ended its work in 1905 with a very important initiative, founding the League for the Renovation of the Navy. An examination of naval issues against the backdrop of Russia's naval defeats at the hands of Japan convinced members of the Army and Navy Division that naval affairs needed to attract a broader public; to be successful this matter must be "democratized" and receive the support of the "entire Russian nation."[51] At a meeting of November 8, Beklemyshev proposed the creation of a League for the Renewal of the Navy, initially as part of the Army and Navy Division of RTO. At meetings on November 22 and 29 and December 13 and 18, members drafted a plan for the league and a charter; on December 20 officers were elected and the League commenced its work. The model for the league was a similar league in Germany (*Deutscher Flottenverein*), founded in 1898 in order to stimulate interest and support for naval affairs among the public. According to its charter the purpose of the Russian league was to "cooperate in every possible way with the development of the Russian Navy in order to meet the requirements of national security, usefulness to the fatherland, and peaceful progress." One point of the league's program stated that the construction of new ships "must be offered primarily to native industry with as much support as possible of private enterprise." Beklemyshev proposed a competition to organize public lectures and compositions on topics corresponding to the purposes of the league in order to "disseminate knowledge about naval affairs"; he also proposed popularizing the league by means of letters depicting its logo and detailing its goals. By October, 1906, the league had one thousand members, and had opened branches in Moscow, Odessa, Batumi, Archangel'sk, Sevastopol, Berdiansk, Khabarovsk, Nikolaevsk, Tuapse, and Murmansk.[52]

In the years preceding the Revolution of 1905, the work of RTO began to change. After decades devoted primarily to Russia's industrial development, the society began to take an interest in more general questions and in politics. RTO's activism increased greatly as the technical intelligentsia faced the challenges of revolution. In 1905, RTO studied the labor question, actively assisted in the organization of trade unions, offered its meeting space to individual unions and to the Union of Unions, represented and mediated interests in a new public sphere, and created a League for the Renovation of the Navy—in short, pushed the boundaries of civic engagement. By the beginning of 1906, RTO took on a new responsibility, "to make its technical expertise available to the State Duma" and "to become the chief economic and technical arbiter for the entire country."[53] At a members' meeting at the end of 1905, President V. I. Kovalevskii closed his brief address with the words: "If by our efforts we can accomplish something, then to our mathematical slogan 'Measure, Weight and Number' we will have the right to add a moral slogan 'Truth, Peace and Love.'"[54] The tsarist government understood this new public role of RTO but evaluated it differently. Especially in the sphere of the labor question, the authorities regarded RTO with suspicion. Characterizing the work of education societies, the Department of Police concluded that "in a word, the

Imperial Russian Technical Society has been very helpful to the revolutionary movement."[55]

At the beginning of the twentieth century RTO facilitated communication and networking among a wide spectrum of government officials, engineers, and industrialists dedicated to Russian industrial development, and also created an extensive unofficial infrastructure of technical and vocational education. Although the government claimed the right to authorize and supervise the activities of private associations, by and large the authorities left associations free to carry out their various projects. In a system greased by personal patronage, RTO and its projects had protectors in high places, and patronage helps to explain the survival—even the flourishing—of RTO's education projects as well as those of other technical societies. Well-patronized private efforts in behalf of technical education and vocational training were evidence of a state-society partnership in the mutual pursuit of national betterment. Members of RTO believed that private efforts could complement the work of the government.

The great service of RTO was to facilitate and coordinate education programs and to become a font of information about public education. Thus RTO was a vehicle by which a private organization could enter the public arena and claim a role in public policy, much as the private publishers documented by Gary Marker had asserted their public voice more than a century earlier. But beginning in the 1890s, the partnership between government and one of Russia's most prestigious and privileged associations was strained, as RTO broadened the scope of its activities; more and more it claimed a voice in public policy and in popular education. RTO and other technical and education societies challenged the state's monopoly in public life, asserted their expertise in policy-making and implementation, and eroded autocratic authority.

NOTES

1 "Otchet o deiatel'nosti Imperatorskogo Russkogo tekhnicheskogo obshchestva v 1905 godu," in *Zapiski Imperatorskogo Russkogo tekhnicheskogo obshchestva* (hereafter *Zapiski RTO*) 1906, no. 7-8, 1.

2 *Pamiati E. N. Andreeva: Torzhestvennoe zasedanie Russkogo tekhnicheskogo obshchestva 21 noiabria 1890 g.* (Saint Petersburg: Brat. Panteleevy, 1890), 30.

3 Peter Kropotkin, *Memoirs of a Revolutionist* (Boston: Houghton-Mifflin, 1930), 247; I. M. Maksin, *Ocherk razvitiia promyshlennogo obrazovaniia v Rossii* (Saint Petersburg: Tip. S-Pb. Odinochnoi tiur'my, 1909), 6-9; A. G. Nebolsin, *Istoriko-statisticheskii ocherk obshchego i spetsial'nogo obrazovaniia v Rossii* (Saint Petersburg: V. Kirshbaum, 1883), 131; I. A. Anopov, *Opyt sistematicheskogo obozreniia materialov k izucheniiu sovremennogo sostoianiia srednego i nizshego tekhnicheskogo i remeslennogo obrazovaniia v Rossii* (Saint Petersburg: Ministerstvo putei soobshcheniia, 1889), i-ii. On the Sunday school in general, see Thomas W. Laqueur, *Religion and Respectability: Sunday Schools and Working Class Culture, 1780-1850* (New Haven: Yale University Press, 1976). The standard history of the Sunday school in Russia is Ia. V. Abramov, *Nashi voskresnye shkoly, ikh proshloe i nastoiashchee* (Saint Petersburg: Tip. M. Merkusheva, 1900), especially 6, 24-41,73-74. Abramov compares the Russian movement in the 1850s and 1860s with the French League of Education. See also Reginald Zelnik, *Labor and Society in Tsarist Russia: The Factory Workers of St. Petersburg, 1855-1870* (Stanford: Stanford University Press, 1971), 174-99.

4 B. N. Tits, *Ocherk istorii Postoiannoi komissii po tekhnicheskomu obrazovaniiu pri Imperatorskom Russkom tekhnicheskom obshchestve, 1868-1889* (Saint Petersburg: E. A. Evdokimov, 1889), 1-3, 21-22; N. M. Korol'kov, *Kratkii obzor deiatel'nosti Postoiannoi komissii po tekhnicheskomu obrazovaniiu* (Saint Petersburg: M. A. Aleksandrov, 1912), 59. The education commission became an autonomous division of the society in 1883 but retained the name "commission."

5 Gosudarstvennyi Arkhiv Rossiiskoi Federatsii (hereafter GARF), f. 63 (1897), d. 616, l. 1 ["Ob uchilishchakh RTO"]; GARF f. 102, 4 d/p (1914), d. 124, pt. 20, l. 22 ob. ["Dokladnaia zapiska o s"ezdakh russkikh deiatelei po tekhnicheskomu obrazovaniiu"]; "Ob uchilishchakh, uchrezhdennykh Imperatorskim Russkim tekhnicheskim obshchestvom," *Polnoe sobranie zakonov rossiiskoi imperii,* 3d ser., 33 vols. (Saint Petersburg, 1885-1916), 11 (1882), no. 915; Korol'kov, *Kratkii obzor,* 11; Nebolsin, *Istoriko-statisticheskii ocherk*, 250-51; Anopov, *Opyt,* 417-18; Tits, *Ocherk istorii Postoiannoi komissii,* 53-54; A. G. Nebolsin, "Ob ustroistve periodicheskikh vystavok i s"ezdov po tekhnicheskomu i professional'nomu obrazovaniiu," in *Trudy s"ezda russkikh deiatelei po tekhnicheskomu i professional'nomu obrazovaniiu v Rossii: Doklady na obshchikh sobraniiakh otdelenii* (Saint Petersburg, 1890), 3-15, especially, 9; S. V. Rozhdestvenskii, *Istoricheskii obzor deiatel'nosti Ministerstva narodnogo prosveshcheniia, 1802-1902* (Saint Petersburg: Gos. tip., 1902), 664.

6 GARF f. 63 (1897), d. 616, ll. 73-74 ["Zapiska Moskovskogo okhrannogo otdeleniia, MOO"]. A list of the schools founded by RTO and placed under government supervision may be found in *Uchilishcha Imperatorskogo Russkogo tekhnicheskogo obshchestva: Spravochnaia kniga Postoiannoi komissii po tekhnicheskomu obrazovaniiu za 1888/89 uchebnyi god* (Saint Petersburg, 1889), 15-35.

7 "Otchet o deiatel'nosti RTO v 1905 godu," 60.

8 Korol'kov, *Kratkii obzor,* 4, 9-10. See also V. I. Sreznevskii, "O khode dela po ustroistvu Russkim tekhnicheskim obshchestvom s"ezda russkikh deiatelei po tekhnicheskomu i promyshlennomu obrazovaniiu," *Zapiski RTO* 8 (1888): 26;

Tits, *Ocherk istorii Postoiannoi komissii*, 25; Nebolsin, *Istoriko-statisticheskii ocherk,* 249-54. Coverage of the opening of the Prechistenka evening and Sunday classes for workers and of the Giubner vocational school in Moscow, for example, may be found in *Russkie vedomosti,* nos. 255 and 283 (September 15 and October 13, 1897), 2. See also Kevin Donald Haukness, "Educating the Russian Worker: The School System of the Russian Technical Society in St. Petersburg, 1869-1917," unpublished Ph.D. dissertation (University of Minnesota, 1994), 414-17, 442.

9 Nebolsin, "Ob ustroistve," quotation, 3; *S"ezd russkikh deiatelei po tekhnicheskomu i professional'nomu obrazovaniiu v Rossii, 1889-1890: Obshchaia chast'*, ed. V. I. Sreznevskii (Saint Petersburg: L. Mordukhovskaia, 1891), 3.

10 Tits, *Ocherk istorii Postoiannoi komissii*, 38.

11 E. N. Andreev, *Shkol'noe delo v Rossii: Nashi obshchie i spetsial'nye shkoly* (Saint Petersburg: Dobrodeev, 1882): 57, 62, 69, 81; N. G. Filippov, *Nauchno-tekhnicheskie obshchestva Rossii, 1866-1917* (Moscow: Moskovskii gosudarstvennyi istoriko-arkhivnyi institut, 1976), 169; Korol'kov, Kratkii obzor, 15; Tits, *Ocherk istorii Postoiannoi komissii*, 38, 110.

12 GARF f. 102, 3 d/p (1905), d. 513, l. 18.

13 GARF f. 63 (1897), d. 616, l. 11 ob. ["Dokladnaia zapiska popechitelia Moskovskogo uchebnogo okruga"]

14 GARF f. 102 3 d/p (1905), d. 513 [Moskovskoe otdelenie RTO], l. 2; RGIA f. 1284 [Ministry of Internal Affairs], op. 188, d. 90 ["O zakrytii Moskovskogo otdeleniia RTO"], l. 1 ["DP to DOD MVD 5 May 1905"].

15 GARF f. 63 (1897), d. 616, l. 68 ob. ["Zapiska MOO"]

16 GARF f. 63 (1897), d. 616, l. 13-13 ob. ["Dokladnaia zapiska popechitelia Moskovskogo uchebnogo okruga"], 67, 71-71 ob. ["Zapiska MOO"], 116.

17 On censorship, in addition to Gary Marker's *Publishing, Printing, and the Origins of Intellectual Life in Russia,* see Charles A. Ruud, *Fighting Words: Imperial Censorship and the Russian Press, 1804-1906* (Toronto: University of Toronto Press, 1982); Marianna Tax Choldin, *A Fence around the Empire: Russian Censorship of Western Ideas under the Tsars* (Durham: Duke University Press, 1985); Jeffrey Brooks, *When Russia Learned to Read: Literacy and Popular Literature, 1861-1917* (Princeton: Princeton University Press, 1985); and Louise McReynolds, *The News under Russia's Old Regime: The Development of a Mass-Circulation Press* (Princeton: Princeton University Press, 1991). On the theaters see Murray Frame, *School for Citizens: Theater and Society in Imperial Russia* (New Haven: Yale University Press, 2006); and E. Anthony Swift, *Popular Theater and Society in Tsarist Russia* (Berkeley: University of California Press, 2002). Public lectures were subject to censorship according to regulations codified in 1876 ("Pravila dlia ustroistva narodnykh chtenii v gubernskikh gorodakh," *Polnoe sobranie zakonov Rossiiskoi imperii,* 2d ser., 51, no. 56762).

18 See Joseph Bradley, "Russia's Parliament of Public Opinion: Association, Assembly, and the Autocracy, 1906-1914," in *Reform in Modern Russian History: Progress or Cycle?*, ed. Theodore Taranovski (Cambridge: Woodrow Wilson Center Press and Cambridge University Press, 1995), 212-36.

19 GARF f. 102, 4 d/p (1914), d. 124, pt. 20, l. 27 ["Dokladnaia zapiska"]; "S"ezd russkikh deiatelei po tekhnicheskomu i professional'nomu obrazovaniiu," *Trudy*

IX sektsii S"ezda (Moscow, 1896), 5. Following the directives of the congress, Anopov wrote his study of technical education (Anopov, *Opyt*). See also Nebolsin, "Ob ustroistve," 3; *S"ezd russkikh deiatelei,* 3; Sreznevskii, "O khode dela," 1-4.

20 Anopov, *Opyt*, 229.

21 Abramov, *Nashi voskresnye shkoly*, 300-301, 303-305, 312-13.

22 GARF f. 102, 4 d/p (1914), d. 124, pt. 20, l. 28 ["Dokladnaia zapiska"]; "Vtoroi S"ezd russkikh deiatelei po tekhnicheskomu i professional'nomu obrazovaniiu, byvshii v Moskve v 1895-96 godu," *Zapiski RTO* 1897, no. 5, quotation 1. The congress expressed the hope that there soon would be a national congress on primary education. See also Christine Ruane, *Gender, Class, and the Professionalization of Russian City Teachers, 1860-1914* (Pittsburgh: University of Pittsburgh Press, 1994), 105.

23 "Vtoroi s"ezd," 1-58. See also N. M. Pirumova, *Zemskaia intelligentsia i ee rol' v obshchestvennoi bor'be do nachala XX v.* (Moscow: Nauka, 1986), 186; Ruane, *Gender, Class, and Professionalization*, 105; Ruane, *The Empire's New Clothes: A History of the Russian Fashion Industry, 1700-1917* (New Haven: Yale University Press, 2009), 81-85; Ben Eklof, *Russian Peasant Schools: Officialdom, Village Culture and Popular Pedagogy, 1861-1914* (Berkeley: University of California Press), 110-14.

24 V. R. Leikina-Svirskaia, *Intelligentsiia v Rossii vo vtoroi polovine XIX v.* (Moscow: Mysl', 1971), 42.

25 "Itogi III-go s"ezda deiatelei po tekhnicheskomu obrazovaniiu," *Osvobozhdenie*, 17 [41] (1904): 310; "S"ezd deiatelei po tekhnicheskomu obrazovaniiu," *Osvobozhdenie,* 15-16 [39-40] (1904): 289. On Kovalevskii, see V. Fedorchenko, *Imperatorskii dom: Vydaiushchiesia sanovniki,* 2 vols. (Krasnoiarsk: Bonus, 2001), 1:552-53.

26 "Tretii tekhnicheskii i professional'nyi s"ezd," *Novosti i birzhevaia gazeta*, no. 357 (December 29, 1903): 2. K. K. Mazing, long-time head (1904 to 1921) of the Moscow branch of RTO, was one of the organizers of the technical education congresses, and from 1895 chaired the Commission on Technical and Vocational Education of the Moscow branch. He was one of the founders of the well-known Prechistenka courses for workers, which the Moscow branch opened in 1895. In 1901 the Moscow Museum of Assistance to Labor was founded on his initiative. See John M. Davies, "The Russian Technical Society and the Reconstruction of Entrepreneurial Culture in Late Imperial Russia," unpublished Ph.D. dissertation (Brown University), 219-22.

27 *Rezoliutsii Tret'ego s"ezda russkikh deiatelei po tekhnicheskomu i professional'nomu obrazovaniiu* (Saint Petersburg, 1903).

28 See Joseph Bradley, *Voluntary Associations in Tsarist Russia: Science, Patriotism and Civil Society* (Cambridge: Harvard University Press, 2009), 233-36, 242-53.

29 RGIA f. 1284, op. 188, d. 90, l. 2.

30 GARF f. 102, 4 d/p (1914), d. 124 pt. 20, l. 34 ob. ["Dokladnaia zapiska"]; "III S"ezd russkikh deiatelei po tekhnicheskomu i professional'nomu obrazovaniiu 26 dekabria 1903—6 ianvaria 1904 g.," *Dnevnik* (Saint Petersburg, 1903-1904), various issues.

31 GARF f. 102, 4 d/p (1914), d. 124 pt. 20, ll. 33-34, 36 ["Dokladnaia zapiska"]; GARF f. 124, op. 43 (1905), d. 1571, l. 4 ["Delo o proiznoshenii"]. See also "Dva s"ezda," *Mir Bozhii* (February 1904): 22-23.

32 "S"ezd deiatelei po tekhnicheskomu obrazovaniiu," *Osvobozhdenie,* 15-16 [39-40] (1904): 289; "Itogi s"ezda deiatelei po tekhnicheskomu obrazovaniiu," *Osvobozhdenie,* 17 [41] (1904): 310.
33 "Zhurnal Obshchikh sobranii Imperatorskogo Russkogo tekhnicheskogo obshchestva 29 ianvaria 1905 g." *Zapiski RTO* 1905, no. 5, 149-50.
34 GARF f. 102, Osobyi Otdel (1906), d. 194, pt. 2, l. 284 ob.
35 N. N. Gritsenko, *Nauchno-tekhnicheskie obshchestva v SSSR: Istoricheskie ocherki* (Moscow: Profizdat, 1968), 26.
36 Jonathan Sanders, "The Union of Unions: Political, Economic, Civil, and Human Rights Organizations in the 1905 Russian Revolution," unpublished Ph.D. dissertation (Columbia University, 1985), 218-19.
37 GARF f. 102, Osobyi Otdel (1906), d. 194 pt. 2, l. 282 ob.
38 Sanders, "Union of Unions," 439-47.
39 Ibid., 451-58.
40 "Otchet o deiatel'nosti RTO v 1905 godu," 86, 93-94, 101-102.
41 RGIA f. 1284, op. 188, d. 90, l. 1 ob.
42 GARF f. 124 [Ministry of Justice], op. 43 (1905), d. 1571, l. 4 ["Delo o proiznoshenii protivopravitel'stvennykh rechei na zasedanii Moskovskogo otdeleniia RTO 29 December 1904"].
43 GARF f. 124, op. 43 (1905), d. 1571, l. 4 ob. See also Davies, "Russian Technical Society," 215-16.
44 Davies, "Russian Technical Society," 215-16.
45 RGIA f. 1284, op. 188, d. 90, l. 3.
46 GARF f. 102, 3 d/p (1905), d. 513, l. 14.
47 RGIA d. 1284, op. 188, d. 90, l. 1.
48 "Otchet o deiatel'nosti RTO v 1905 godu," 43, 46.
49 "Zhurnaly zasedanii IV-go Otdela (Voennogo i Morskogo)," *Zapiski RTO* 1906, no. 3, 80.
50 "Zhurnaly IV-go (Voennogo i Morskogo) otdela Imperatorskogo Russkogo tekhnicheskogo obshchestva. Zasedanie neprimennykh chlenov 8 noiabria 1905 g." in *Zapiski RTO* 1906, no. 1, 22-27.
51 "Otchet o deiatel'nosti RTO v 1905 godu," 49.
52 Ibid., 49-50; "Zasedanie neprimennykh chlenov 8 noiabria 1905 g.," 22; Davies, "Russian Technical Society," 304-305.
53 "Otchet o deiatel'nosti RTO v 1906 godu," *Zapiski RTO* 1907, no. 7-8, 42-43.
54 "Otchet o deiatel'nosti RTO v 1906 godu," 3.
55 GARF f. 102 Osobyi otdel (1906), d. 194, pt. 2, l. 284 ob.

Publications of Gary Marker

Daniel H. Kaiser

1977

"Publishing and the Formation of a Reading Public in Eighteenth Century Russia." PhD diss., University of California, Berkeley.

1981

Review of *Leon Trotsky: A Biography*, by Ronald Segal, *Historian* 43 (1981): 277-78.

Review of *Citizen for the Fatherland: Education, Educators, and Pedagogical Ideals in Eighteenth Century Russia*, by Joseph L. Black, *Slavic Review* 40 (1981): 110.

1982

"Russia and the 'Printing Revolution': Notes and Observations," *Slavic Review* 41 (1982): 266-83.

"Novikov's Readers," *Modern Language Review* 77 (1982): 894-905.

"Merchandising Culture: The Market for Books in Eighteenth-Century Russia," *Eighteenth-Century Life* 8, no. 1 (1982): 46-71.

1984

"Printing, Publishing and Journalism in Eighteenth-Century Russia: A Comment," in *Russia and the West in the Eighteenth Century*, ed. A. G. Cross (Newtonville: Oriental Research Partners, 1984), 118-22.

1985

Publishing, Printing, and the Origins of Intellectual Life in Russia: 1700-1800 (Princeton: Princeton University Press, 1985).

Reviewed in *American Historical Review* 91 (1986): 435-36; *American Journal of Sociology* 92 (1987): 1534-36; *Archiv für Sozialgeschichte* 28 (1988): 349-54; *Canadian Journal of History* 22 (1987): 120-21; *Comparative Studies in Society and History* 31 (1989): 784-90; *English Historical Review* 103 (1988): 510-11; *The History Teacher* 21 (1988): 257-58; *Jahrbücher für Geschichte Osteuropas* 35 (1987): 468-69; *Journal of Interdisciplinary History* 18 (1987): 167-69; *Journal of Library History* 22 (1987): 99-100; *Journal of Modern History* 62 (1990): 208-209; *Library Quarterly* 56 (1986): 325; *Minerva* 26 (1988): 436-45; *Russian Review* 45 (1986): 225-26; *Slavic and East European Journal* 30 (1986): 567-68; *Slavic Review* 45 (1986): 320-21; *Slavonic and East European Review* 64 (1986): 609-10; *Society* 23 (1986): 87-88; *Solanus* 1 (1987): 98-99; *Times Literary Supplement* Mar 7, 1986, p. 239.

1986

"Russian Journals and Their Readers in the Late Eighteenth Century," *Oxford Slavonic Papers*, New Series 19 (1986): 88-101.

Review of *Gosudarstvennaia deiatel'nost' V. N. Tatishcheva v 20-kh—nachale 30-kh godov XVIII v.*, by A. I. Iukht, *American Historical Review* 91 (1986): 961-62.

1987

Review of *Russkaia istoricheskaia mysl' i zapadnaia Evropa (XVIII-pervaia polovina XI v.)*, by M. A. Alpatov, *American Historical Review* 92 (1987): 1005-6.

1989

"Primers and Literacy in Muscovy: A Taxonomic Investigation," *Russian Review* 48 (1989): 1-19.

"Petrine Civil Primers Reconsidered: A New Look at the 'Grazhdanskaia Azbuka,'" *Solanus* 3 (1989): 25-39.

Review of *Imperatorskaia biblioteka Ermitazha, 1726-1917*, by Zhermena Pavlova, *Slavic Review* 48 (1989): 301-302.

1990

"Literacy and Literacy Texts in Muscovy: A Reconsideration," *Slavic Review* 49 (1990): 74-89.

"Istoriia gramotnosti v Rossii, 1649-1801 gg.: knigovedcheskie metody i vyvody," in *Kniga v rossii: Vek prosveshcheniia*, ed. V. P. Leonov (Leningrad: Biblioteka Akademii nauk SSSR, 1990), 6-8.

1991

Review of *Catherine the Great: A Short History*, by Isabel De Madariaga, *Canadian Slavonic Papers* 33 (1991): 366-67.

1993

Ideas, Ideology, and Intellectuals in Russian History. A Festschrift in Honor of Nicholas Riasanovsky, ed. Gary Marker, *Russian History/Histoire russe* 20 (1993): ix-380.

"Editor's Introduction," ibid., 1-2.

"Who Rules the Word? Public School Education and the Fate of Universality in Russia, 1782-1803," *Russian History/Histoire russe* 20 (1993): 15-34.

Review of *The News Under Russia's Old Regime: The Development of a Mass-Circulation Press,* by Louise McReynolds, *Russian Review* 52 (1993): 110-12.

Review of *Russkii risovannyi lubok kontsa XVIII-nachala XX veka: Iz sobraniia Gosudarstvennogo istoricheskogo muzeia*, ed. E. I. Itkina, *Slavic Review* 52 (1993): 868-69.

1994

Reinterpreting Russian History, 860s to 1860s, ed. Daniel H. Kaiser and Gary Marker (New York: Oxford University Press, 1994). Reviewed in *Historische Zeitschrift* 262 (1996): 523-24; *The History Teacher* 30 (1997): 374-75; *Jahrbücher für Geschichte Osteuropas* 44 (1996): 309-10; *Slavic Review* 54 (1995): 470-71.

"Faith and Secularity in Russian Literacy, 1708-1775: The Consequences of Diglossia," *California Slavic Studies, Christianity and the Eastern Slavs* (Berkeley: University of California Press, 1994), 3-24.

1995

"Nikolai Novikov," in *Early Modern Russian Writers, Late Seventeenth and Eighteenth Centuries*, ed. Marcus Levitt (Detroit: Gale, 1995), 249-60.

Catherine the Great and the Search for a Usable Past, ed. Gary Marker, *Russian Studies in History* 33, no. 4 (Winter 1994-95): 3-96.

"Introduction," ibid., 3-6.

Review of *Istoriia Rossii. Dialog rossiiskikh i amerikanskikh istorikov: Materialy rossiisko-amerikanskoi konferentsii (g. Saratov, 18-22 maia 1992)*, ed. A. A. Kreder, in *Russian Review* (1995): 623-24.

1996

Review of *Out of the Red Shadows: Anti-Semitism in Stalin's Russia*, by Gennadi V. Kostyrchenko, *Europe-Asia Studies* 48 (1996): 1053-54.

Review of *Magnetic Mountain: Stalinism as Civilization*, by Stephen Kotkin, *Slavic and East European Journal* 40 (1996): 774-75.

Review of *Reform and Regicide: The Reign of Peter III of Russia*, by Carol S. Leonard, *Slavic Review* 55 (1996): 184-85.

1997

"The Creation of Journals and the Profession of Letters in the Eighteenth Century," in *Literary Journals in Imperial Russia*, ed. Deborah A. Martinsen (Cambridge: Cambridge University Press, 1997), 11-37.

"Russia in the Age of Enlightenment, 1740-1801," in *Oxford History of Russia*, ed. Gregory Freeze (Oxford: Oxford University Press, 1997), 114-42.

Review of *V. O. Kliuchevskii, Historian of Russia*, ed. N. A. Umov, *Slavic and East European Journal* 41 (1997): 355-56.

Review of *Russian Overseas Commerce with Great Britain During the Reign of Catherine II*, by Herbert H. Kaplan, *Slavic and East European Journal* 41 (1997): 349-50.

1998

"Books and Print in the Reign of Peter the Great," in *Russia in the Reign of Peter the Great: Old and New Perspectives*, ed. Anthony Cross (Cambridge: Study Group of Eighteenth-Century Russia, 1998), 119-32.

Review of *The Russian Empire in the Eighteenth Century: Searching for a Place in the World*, by Aleksandr B. Kamenskii, *Slavic Review* 57 (1998): 447-48.

Review of *Peasant Rebels under Stalin*, by Lynne Viola, *Slavic and East European Journal* 42 (1998): 163-64.

1999

Review of *Reading Russian Fortunes: Print Culture, Gender and Divination in Russia from 1765*, by Faith Wigzell, *Social History* 24 (1999): 338-39.

2000

"The Enlightenment of Anna Labzina: Gender, Faith, and Public Life in Catherinian and Alexandrian Russia," *Slavic Review* 59 (2000): 369-90.

"Zhurnalistika i istoricheskaia nauka," *Kritika: Explorations in Russian and Eurasian History* 1 (2000): 789-93.

Review of *Russia in the Age of Peter the Great*, by Lindsey Hughes, *Slavic and East European Journal* 44 (2000): 495-96.

Review of *By Honor Bound: State and Society in Early Modern Russia*, by Nancy Shields Kollmann, *Slavic and East European Journal* 44 (2000): 688-90.

2001

S. M. Solov'ev, *A History of Russia from Ancient Times*, vol. 32: *The Last Years of Peter the Great*, trans., ed., with an introduction by Gary M. Marker (Gulf Breeze: Academic International Press, 2001).

Days of a Russian Noblewoman: The Memories of Anna Labzina, trans., ed. Gary Marker and Rachel May (DeKalb: Northern Illinois University Press, 2001).
Reviewed in *Canadian Slavonic Papers* 43 (2001): 590-91; *Historian* 65 (2003): 762; *Jahrbücher für Geschichte Osteuropas* 52 (2004): 284-85.

"Solov'ev's Peter: Otets Otechestva, Otsovstva i Muzhestva," in *Reflections on Russia in the Eighteenth Century*, ed. Joachim Klein, Simon Dixon, and Maarten Fraanje (Köln: Böhlau Verlag, 2001), 73-83.

"The Ambiguities of the Eighteenth Century," *Kritika: Explorations in Russian and Eurasian History* 2 (2001): 241-52.

Review of *A Social History of the Russian Empire, 1650-1825*, by Janet M. Hartley, and *The Russian Peasantry, 1600-1930: The World the Peasants Made*, by David Moon, *Social History* 26 (2001): 251-53.

2002

"The Russian Veneration of St. Catherine of Alexandria," *Newsletter of the Study Group on Eighteenth-Century Russia* 30 (2002): 7-11.

Review of *A Prodigal Saint: Father John of Kronstadt and the Russian People*, by Nadieszda Kizenko, *Slavic and East European Journal* 46 (2002): 415-16.

Review of *The Rise of the Public in Enlightenment Europe*, by James Van Horn Melton, *Journal of European Studies* 32 (2002): 69-70.

Review of *Peter the Great: The Struggle for Power*, by Paul Bushkovitch, *European History Quarterly* 32 (2002): 434-36.

2003

Japanese translation of *Publishing, Printing and the Origins of Intellectual Life in Russia* (Nihon Scholarly Press, 2003).

"God of Our Mothers: Popular Orthodoxy and Spirituality in Russian Women's Autobiographical Writings in the Late Eighteenth and Early Nineteenth Centuries," in *Orthodox Russia: Beliefs and Practice Under the Tsars*, ed. Valerie Kivelson and Robert H. Greene (University Park: Penn State University Press, 2003), 193-211.

"Academies in Russia," in *The Encyclopedia of the Enlightenment*, ed. Alan Charles Kors, 4 vols. (Oxford University Press, 2003), 1:13-16.

"N. I. Novikov," ibid., 3:203-204.

Review of *Russia Reads Rousseau, 1762-1825*, by Thomas Barran, *Slavic Review* 62 (2003): 625-26.

Review of *Le mirage russe au XVIIIe siècle*, ed. Serguei Karp and Larry Wolff, *Russian Review* 62 (2003): 314-15.

2004

"Ladies of Ransom: Peter the Great's Knightly Order of St. Catherine," in *Russian Society and Culture in the Long Eighteenth Century: Essays in Honour of Anthony G. Cross*, ed. Roger Bartlett and Lindsey Hughes (Münster: Lit Verlag, 2004), 35-48.

"A Cautious Embrace: Empire, Print, and the Russian Enlightenment," *Solanus* 18 (2004): 51-71.

"Catherine the Great," in *Europe 1450-1789: The Encyclopedia of the Early Modern World*, ed. Jonathan Dewald, 6 vols. (New York: Charles Scribner's Sons, 2004), 1:411-15.

"Ekaterina Dashkova," ibid., 2:108.

"Empress Anna," ibid., 2:68-69.

"Empress Elizabeth," ibid., 2:250-51.

"Nikolai Novikov," ibid., 4:301-302.

"Paul I," ibid., 4:423-24.

"Peter the Great," ibid., 4:443-47.

"Feofan Prokopovich," ibid., 5:77.

"Pugachev Revolt (1773-75)," ibid., 5:109-10.

"Russian Literature and Language," ibid., 5:388-91.

Review of *The Play of Ideas in Russian Enlightenment Theater*, by Elise Kimerling Wirtschafter, *American Historical Review* 109 (2004): 646-47.

2005

"Plach smirennogo knigoveda," *Solanus* 19 (2005): 41-47.

Review of *The Transfigured Kingdom: Sacred Parody and Charismatic Authority at the Court of Peter the Great*, by Ernest A. Zitser, *Social History* 30 (2005): 527-29.

Review of *The Revolution of Peter the Great*, by James Cracraft, *Historian: A Journal of History* 67 (2005): 348-49.

2006

St. Petersburg and the Ceremonials of Power, ed. Gary Marker. Special issue of *Russian Studies in History* 45, no. 3 (Winter 2006-7): 3-85.

"Guest Editor's Introduction," ibid., 3-8.

Review of *Serfdom, Society, and the Arts in Imperial Russia: The Pleasure and the Power,* by Richard Stites, *Slavic Review* 65 (2006): 822-23.

2007

An Imperial Saint: The Cult of St. Catherine and the Dawn of Female Rule in Russia (DeKalb: Northern Illinois University Press, 2007). Reviewed in *American Historical Review* 113 (2008): 1265; *Cahiers du monde russe* 48 (2007): 679-82; *Canadian Slavonic Papers* 51 (2009): 374-75; *Catholic Historical Review* 95 (2009): 400-402; *Choice* 45-49 (July 2008); *Church History* 77 (2008): 1071-73; *Eighteenth-Century Studies* 43 (2010): 276-77; *Historian* 71 (2009): 422-23; *Jahrbücher für Geschichte Osteuropas* 56 (2008): 427-30; *Journal of Ecclesiastical History* 60 (2009): 144-45; *Journal of Modern History* 81 (2009):

746-48; *Russian Review* 67 (2008): 698-99; *Slavic and East European Journal* 52 (2008): 484-85; *Slavic Review* 67 (2008): 1022-23.

"Pagan and Godly Women in the Coronation Sermon of 1724," in *Eighteenth-Century Russia: Society, Culture, and Economy*, ed. Roger Bartlett and Gabriela Lehmann-Carli (Berlin: Lit Verlag, 2007), 207-21.

"Anointed in the Image of Saints: Empresses and Clerical Discourse, 1725-1761," in *Women in Russian Culture and Society, 1700-1825*, ed. Wendy Rosslyn and Alessandra Tosi (New York: Palgrave Macmillan, 2007), 171-91.

"October 30, 1708: A Very Bad Day for Peter the Great," in *Days from the Reigns of Eighteenth-Century Russian Rulers: Proceedings of a Workshop, dedicated to the Memory of Professor Lindsey Hughes . . . 12-13 September* 2007, ed. Anthony Cross, 2 pts. (Cambridge: Study Group on Eighteenth-Century Russia, 2007), 1:49-61.

"Love One's Enemies: Ioasaf Krokovs'kyi's Advice to Peter in 1702," *Harvard Ukrainian Studies* 29 (2007): 193-223.

Review of *Cartographies of Tsardom: The Land and Its Meaning in Seventeenth-Century Russia*, by Valerie Kivelson, *Slavic Review* 66 (2007): 548-49.

Review of *The Cambridge History of Russia, Volume 1: From Early Rus' to 1689*, ed. Maureen Perrie, *Social History* 32 (2007): 336-38.

Review of *Voluntary Brotherhood: Confraternities of Laymen in Early Modern Ukraine*, by Iaroslav Isaievych, *Russian Review* 66 (2007): 138-39.

2008

"Iconography and the Power of Women: The Alexander Nevskii Icon of St. Catherine of 1721," in *Picturing Russia: Explorations in Visual*

Culture, ed. Valerie Kivelson and Joan Neuberger (New Haven: Yale University Press, 2008), 63-67.

"Scriptural Pieces: A Publishing History of Books of the Slavonic Bible, 1650-1762," *Russian History/Histoire russe* 35 (2008): 335-56.

Review of *Foreign Churches in St. Petersburg and Their Archives, 1703-1917*, ed. Pieter Holtrop and Henk Slechte, in *Church History* 77 (2008): 734-36.

2009

"Standing in St. Petersburg Facing West, or, Is Backwardness All There Is?" in *Republic of Letters: A Journal for the Study of Knowledge, Politics, and the Arts* 1, no. 1 (2009). http://rofl.stanford.edu/node/35

"The Westernization of the Russian Elite, 1700-1800," in *The Blackwell Companion to Russian History*, ed. Abbott Gleason (Malden: Blackwell, 2009), 180-95.

"Iskhod iz terema: Izobrazheniia tsaritsy v pechati i publichnykh tseremonii pri Petre I-om, 1712-1724 gg.," *Vek prosveshcheniia* 2 (2009): 2-22.

Review of *The Pearl: A True Tale of Forbidden Love in Catherine the Great's Russia*, by Douglas Smith, *Russian Review* 68 (2009): 149-50.

Review of *The Most Intentional City: St. Petersburg in the Reign of Catherine the Great*, by George E. Munro, http://www.h-net.org/reviews/showrev.php?id=23507

Review of *The Emancipation of the Serfs in Russia: Peace Arbitrators and the Development of Civil Society*, by Roxanne Easley, *Slavonica* 15 (2009): 176-77.

2010

Everyday Life in Russian History: Quotidian Studies in Honor of Daniel Kaiser, ed. Gary Marker, Marshall Poe, Susan Rupp, and Joan Neuberger (Columbus: Slavica, 2010).

"A Saint's Intimate Life: The *Diariusz* of Dimitrii Rostovskii," ibid., 127-44.

"Crafting Mazepa's Legacy: Feofan Prokopovich and Pylyp Orlyk," *Slavonic and East European Review* 88 (2010): 110-33; reprinted in *Personality and Place in Russian Culture: Essays in Memory of Lindsey Hughes,* ed. Simon Dixon (London: Modern Humanities Research Association, 2010).

"Staffing Peter's Church: The Transmigration of Kyivan Clergy in the Early Eighteenth Century," *Kyivs'ka Akademiya* 8 (2010): 79-91.

Review of *Languages and Culture in Eighteenth-Century Russia*, by Viktor Zhivov, *Russian Review* 69 (2010): 689-90.

Review of *A Russian Merchant's Tale: The Life and Adventures of Ivan Alekseevich Tolchenov, Based on His Diary*, by David L. Ransel, *Slavic Review* 69 (2010): 189-91.

2011

"Constitution Medievalis: The Language of Politics and the Politics of Language in Pylyp Orlyk's Constitution of 1710," in *Pylyp Orlyk: Zhittya, politika, teksty*, ed. Maksym Yaremenko et al. (Kyiv: Mohylyans'ka Akademiya, 2011), 248-66.

"Nicholas V. Riasanovsky, 1923-2011," *Slavic Review* 70 (2011): 981-82.

Review of *A Voltaire for Russia: A. P. Sumarokov's Journey from Poet-Critic to Russian Philosophe*, by Amanda Ewington, *Slavic Review* 70 (2011): 707-708.

2012

"Imperial Retrospect: Peter the Great's Ideologists Look Back on Kyiv," *Universals and Contrasts* 1 (2012): 113-26.

2013

"Viktor Markovich Zhivov (1945-2013)," *Kritika: Explorations in Russian and Eurasian History* 14 (20123): 691-96.

Review of *Terror and Greatness: Ivan and Peter as Russian Myths*, by Kevin M. F. Platt, *Journal of Modern History* 85 (2013): 232-33.

Review of *Religion and Enlightenment in Catherinian Russia: The Teachings of Metropolitan Platon*, by Elise Kimerling Wirtschafter, *Russian Review* 72 (2013): 692-93.

2014

"Catechizing in the Provinces: The Place of Mary in Dimitrij Rostovskij's *Questions and Answers*," *Russian Literature* 75 (2014): 391-413.

Forthcoming

"Ikonografiia zhenskogo pravleniia v Rossii s tsarstvovaniia Alekseia Mikhailovicha po Ekaterininskaia epokha," in *Vizual'naia antropologiia v russkoi istorii*, ed. Irina Kulakova (Moscow: Moskovskii universitet).

"Marian Miracle Tales and the Geopolitics of Bogomater Between Warsaw and Moscow in the Late Seventeenth Century" (article).

"Mazepa and the Preachers: Ukrainian Clergy and the Discourse of "Russia" in the Early Eighteenth Century" (book).

"The Boundaries of Language: The Practices of Literacy in Russia, 1649-1801" (book).